The Educational Systems in the European Community: A Guide

Edited by Lionel Elvin

The NFER-Nelson Publishing Company

This Guide was edited in cooperation with the Commission of the European Communities, Directorate-General for Research, Science and Education, Brussels

8085

Published by The NFER-Nelson Publishing Company Ltd.,
Darville House, 2 Oxford Road East,
Windsor, Berks, SL4 1DF
for
The Commission of the European Communities,
Directorate-General for Scientific and Technical
Information and Information Management, Luxembourg
© ECSC, EEC, EAEC, Brussels and Luxembourg, 1981

ISBN 0-85633-223-2
Code 8123 02 1

Typeset by Unicus Graphics Ltd., Horsham, West Sussex
Printed in Great Britain
Distributed in the USA by Humanities Press Inc.,
Atlantic Highlands, New Jersey 07716 USA.

CONTENTS

CONTENTS

PREFACE

I have particular pleasure in introducing this publication, which will become an important tool in the process of educational cooperation, essential to the development of the European Community.

This Guide describes the educational system of member countries in the European Community, covering the whole field from pre-primary education up to university education and teacher training. It does not describe the Greek educational system.

It arrives at exactly the right time, when EURYDICE – the Information Network for Education in the European Community – has completed its initial phase of operation. EURYDICE can now help to make the Guide widely known and the Guide can serve as a basic reference document for EURYDICE users.

The Commission decided to publish the Guide in one language only in the first instance; editions in the other official languages of the Community will follow as soon as possible. Equally it is our intention to 'up-date' the Guide at regular intervals.

On behalf of the Commission, I wish to express thanks to all those who have engaged in this work. I should like especially to mention Professor de Kayser of the Catholic University of Leuven who prepared the preliminary study; the experts in the national Ministries who provided the definitive information on each country; the National Foundation for Educational Research for undertaking – with such excellent results – all the stages of publication; and Professor Lionel Elvin on whose intellectual contribution as general editor the completion of the work has chiefly depended. Finally, I would like to express appreciation to the Council of Europe for introducing the idea of such a guide years ago, and thus inspiring the Commission to produce a new version at the beginning of the 1980s.

Ivor Richard
Member of the Commission
of the European Communities

February 1981

INTRODUCTION

The drawing together of the countries of Western Europe into the European Community has led them to take an increased interest in each other's educational arrangements. In education, as in intellectual and cultural life generally, there has in the broadest sense always been a European Community, but since the Middle Ages its institutional forms have resulted from national decisions, or at least national movements. The result in the nineteenth century was that common needs, such as the necessity for general literacy, were met in differing contexts (the relations of the State with religious bodies is one outstanding example). The common educational problems of Europe in the present century — for example, the need to make secondary education general, the need for a more developed vocational and technical education, the need in turn to facilitate mobility between the various systems — have resulted in a variety of structures in the different countries that, bafflingly, sometimes look more alike than they are and sometimes are more alike than they look.

The stream of inquiries received by the Commission, whether from students of education or from those, firms or families, who increasingly move about the countries of the Community, shows that there is a practical need to set down clearly, if only in outline·form, what the structure of the educational system is in each of the member countries. It is the purpose of this Guide to do just that.

This sounds quite straightforward, but it is not quite as simple as it sounds and a brief editorial word may be in order to indicate what this Guide is, and what it is not.

First, it is an official publication. Each of the country chapters has been drafted in the Ministry of Education concerned. The reader should therefore be able to rely on the facts, figures and explanations of the functions of institutions. The only necessary warning is that educational arrangements are now changing so quickly in all our countries that what is correct in 1981 may be in need of modification even in two or three years' time, and therefore, if this work does prove to have met a need, new editions will be called for.

Secondly, the Guide is descriptive, not evaluative. It describes the structure of our educational systems. It does not explicitly indicate the things in which one country is distinctively good and the things in which it would seem to lag behind its partners. Such evaluative questions, even though they are the most anxious ones that may be in the minds of families moving from one country to another or of students and Ministries seeking to learn from one another's failures and successes, are not attempted in a publication of this nature. In any case there might be no agreement as to the answers that should be given. Such evaluations can only come from studies that are designed for this purpose and are made by specialized individuals or interested groups of persons.

Nevertheless, for them as for others, the first thing is to get the structure of the education systems right. How long is the period of compulsory education? What age-range does a given kind of school cater for? What is the length of professional courses for this or that purpose? What do the names of institutions really mean, especially where they look deceptively alike? Is a *liceo* in Italy the same thing as a *lycée* in France, and is the French *lycée* now what it was twenty years ago? What is a comprehensive school in the United Kingdom? Is what might be translated (wrongly) a technical high school in Germany what an English reader might suppose a technical high school to be? Which educational institutions charge fees, and which do not? What is the ratio of staff to students in the schools and universities? Where does specialization of studies begin as a young person moves through the system? What provision is made for adult education, technical or more general? And so on. These are the questions to which reasonably clear answers can be found in the following pages.

Thirdly, as has been said, these chapters give only an outline picture. It was originally the intention to have all the chapters of about the same length, some allowance being made for the different degrees of complexity and size in governmental and in educational structures from one country to another. But it seemed unreasonable to ask for rigid observance of such guidelines. When contributors settled down to their task it was not always possible to follow exactly the same route. Some felt they must go into more detail than others, and it seemed wiser, in spite of some agreed cutting, to leave things like that. The plan of the chapters is, however, broadly common, and that should facilitate comparison when it is desired. On the whole, probably more readers will find the chapters insufficiently detailed rather than too much so. But this was inevitable if an account of all the Community's education systems were to be contained within a single volume. And there are great advantages in doing this, for although the Guide is not itself a study in comparative education it does offer the first data for undertaking such comparisons and will therefore, it is hoped, be a basic book for those making such studies or interested in them.

Fourthly, every effort has been made to guide the user of the book through what really is a linguistic jungle. This pilot volume is in only one of the Community languages, English (it is hoped that versions in other languages may follow), and the editor, valiantly assisted by the translators, has tried to make sure that treacherous terms and modes of expression leave as little room for misunderstanding as possible in that language.

Lastly, I would like to express my thanks to those in the various Education Services who have helped me, and in particular to the appropriate members of the Directorate General for Research, Science and Education of the Commission with whom I have had the pleasure of working.

Lionel Elvin

BELGIUM

General principles
Basic legislation on education
Language structure

Article 17 of the Belgian Constitution lays down that: 'there shall be freedom of education; any measure hindering such freedom shall be prohibited; penalization of infringement shall be governed by law.'

In Belgium, therefore, the organizing power lies with various bodies, and education is thus provided by the State, the provinces, the communes and the free institutions of which Catholic educational institutions are by far the largest group. The other organizing bodies, both private and official, may be subsidized under the terms laid down by law.

Belgium comprises four linguistic areas: the French language area; the Dutch language area; the German language area; and the bilingual, French-Dutch area of Brussels, the capital.

As for education, based on a monolingual principle, there are three cultural communities: French, Flemish and German.

The school population is divided as follows:

French language education system	41.00%
Dutch language education system	58.50%
German language education system	0.50%
National education system	100.00%

The education system of the German community is administered by the French community.

Apart from compulsory schooling, the structure of the education system, the diplomas, the subsidies, the wages and salaries, and the norms of the school population, the general organization of education is governed by decrees of the Cultural Councils, conforming to article 59bis of the constitution.

Organizing powers

The division of the school population in the various school networks is as follows:

Official schools:	– State	19%	
	– Province	2%	
	– Communes	23%	44%
'free' education			56%
			100%

Administration of the education system

The education system is administered by:

the legislative
the executive
decentralized public institutions
private institutions

The legislative is in the hands of:

> the national parliament
> The Cultural Council of the French Cultural Community
> The Cultural Council of the Flemish Cultural Community

In matters of education, the national parliament:

- determines the fundamental dispositions common to all linguistic areas and concerning school obligations, the structure of the education system, diplomas, subsidies, wages and salaries, and the norms of the school population
- determines all other fundamental dispositions concerning the German cultural community, because for the German language area, the Parliament has the power to legislate on all matters which, for their own communities, pertain to the French and Flemish Cultural Councils.

As to the education system in the Dutch and French community, the Cultural Councils determine the fundamental dispositions which are not the responsibility of the national parliament and order decrees which have power of law.

The executive is in the hands of:

> The King, acting as Head of State
> The Ministers of National Education and Culture
> The Cultural Councils of the German Cultural Community

On the advice of the competent ministers, the King passes Royal Decrees which regulate the principal executive measures of laws and decrees.

The Ministers pass:

- Royal Decrees concerning matters pertaining to their competence, by virtue of the dispositions contained in laws, decrees or Royal Decrees
- the ministerial or administrative circular letters which regulate, in detail, the organization modalities of the education system.

The German Cultural Council does not have legislative power, but only consultative power, grafted on that of the King or the Ministers.

The decentralized public institutions are:

- the provincial authorities
- the communal authorities
- the French and Dutch culture commissions, created, especially in the Brussels area, to ensure the peaceful coexistence of the two language communities.

As to private institutions, there are:

- institutions which initiate their own education system
- co-ordinating bodies which do not have the properties of organizing bodies but which represent the latter in discussions or negotiations with the central authorities.

There are two ministerial departments:

- the Ministry for National Education and French Culture (which is also responsible for administrating educational affairs for the German area)
- the Ministry for National Education and Flemish Culture.

In each Ministry, there are two Ministers responsible for policy — one for national education and one for culture. Every Minister of Culture is assisted by a Secretary of State for Cultural Affairs.

Each of the two departments contains a certain number of administrative sections (or Directorates-General) dealing either with national education or with culture.

There are administrative services common to both national education and culture. All these administrative services are co-ordinated by one joint General Secretary.

The national policy on education is thus based on fundamental legislation which is valid for the country as a whole. Its adaptation at the level of the language area and cultural communities and the application of the decrees of the Cultural Councils demand that the structures of the two departments differ.

Figure 1 shows the present structures of the Ministries for National Education and for Culture.

General principles defining the nature of the education system
Freedom of education is provided by the constitution; the law also provides that aid is to be given at the same level to all authorized forms of education within set limits and conditions; this aid system includes the guarantee of a choice between religious or non-religious education; state education must remain neutral.

With this possibility of choice open to them, the nursery, primary, secondary schools and higher education facilities organized or subsidized by the State are open to the children of school age of all persons residing in Belgium, including all persons originating from neighbouring or faraway countries, without distinction and according to their choice.

There are no school fees for nursery, primary and secondary education in Belgium for Belgian children and for foreign children whose parents are resident in Belgium. For children whose parents are not resident in Belgium, school fees have been payable since 1976.

Moreover, the State participates in the purchase of basic material for nursery and primary schools.

Adaptation courses to the current teaching languages (French and Dutch) are organized in primary schools for children of immigrants who have arrived in Belgium within the last three years. After classes, Italian, Spanish, Greek, Turkish and Arab language courses are organized on behalf of the embassies for their nationals. They take place in school rooms.

Pre-school education ($2\frac{1}{2}$ to 6 year old) and primary education (6 to 12 year old) are free of charge. Primary school is compulsory, the attendance rate is 100 per cent. For pre-school education, the attendance rate is 93 per cent in the first year, 99 per cent in the second year and 100 per cent in the third year (5 to 6 year old).

Secondary education is free of charge. Education is compulsory until 14 years of age. After this, the school attendance rate is more or less as follows:

14 to 15 year old: 95%
15 to 16 year old: 87%
16 to 17 year old: 77%
17 to 18 year old: 63%
18 to 19 year old: 50%

Psycho–medico–social centres are another part of the education system. They were established to give psycho-educational aid to children and adolescents attending pre-school, primary or secondary school.

Figure 1: *Structures of the Ministries for National Education and Culture*

MINISTRY OF NATIONAL EDUCATION AND FRENCH CULTURE

GENERAL SECRETARIAT

Joint Services

- **Legal department**
- **Personnel, statutes and administration**
  - Statutory, general and social affairs
  - Recruitment, selection and promotion of State employees
  - Management of administrative and similar State employees
  - Management of State teaching staff and similar matters
- **Budgetary and financial affairs**
  - Budget, finance, accounts
  - Tabulation, data processing and payment of expenditure
  - Study grants and loans

National Education

- **Pre-school and primary education**
  - Organization
  - State establishments
  - Subsidized establishments
- **Secondary education**
  - Organization
  - State establishments
  - Subsidized establishments
- **Higher education and scientific research**
  - Organization
  - State establishments
  - Subsidized establishments
  - Scientific research
- **Special education, correspondence courses and part-time courses**
  - Special education
  - Correspondence courses
  - Part-time education
- **Organization of studies**
  - Structures, syllabuses, method and education documentation
  - Psychological, medical and social guidance
  - Extra-curricular and extra-mural activities, refresher courses for teachers
  - Educational auxiliaries
  - Central library, statistics and programming

Culture

- **Cultural affairs**
- **Arts**
  - Artistic education
  - Protection of cultural heritage
  - Promotion and diffusion of the arts
- **Youth and leisure**
  - Youth
    - Libraries and reading rooms
    - Managerial training
    - Organization and diffusion of culture
  - Continuous education
  - Inspection
- **Physical education, sports, open air and cultural infrastructure**
  - Sports facilities and cultural infrastructure
    - General affairs
    - Subsidies and documentation cultural infrastructure
  - General inspection of sports facilities
- **International cultural relations**

MINISTRY OF NATIONAL EDUCATION AND FLEMISH CULTURE

Group	Directorate	Functions
Joint Services	Directorate for general services	— Statutes, union affairs, administrative documentation — Personnel, social affairs, general affairs and administrative statistics — Organization and accounts, buildings, security and hygiene
National Education	Directorate for primary education	— Legislation and regulations, structures, educational organization — State education, programming and planning, including reception activities — Subsidized education, including reception activities — Special education
	Directorate for secondary education	— Legislation and regulations, structures, educational organization — State education, programming and planning — Subsidized education
	Directorate for higher education and scientific research	— University education — Non-university higher education — Scientific research
	Directorate for National Education, joint services	— Correspondence courses — Teaching films and AV aids — Educational documentation, information, publications, library service and statistics — Vocational guidance and psycho-medico-social guidance — Extra-curricular activities — Study loans and grants
	Directorate for personnel	— Recruitment and promotion — Management of administrative files — Wages and salaries — Allowances added to wages and salaries
	Directorate for material and financial organization	— Equipment for day and boarding schools — School transport and supervision — Tabulation — Running — and equipment — grants
Culture	General affairs and administration	— General administration — General affairs
	Directorate for International Culture Relations	

	Directorate for the Arts and Artistic education	— Artistic education and general affairs
		  — Organization and statutes
		  — Personnel — wages — salaries — allowances
		— Promotion of the arts, culture-based scientific establishments
		  — Promotion of the arts
		  — Scientific establishments and museums, historical monuments

	Directorate for Youth and Leisure	— Youth organizations and training of leaders — Training for youth outside organizations — Secretariat of National Youth Council
	Directorate for Popular education the library service	— Socio-cultural training, continuous education and cultural training
	Directorate for physical education, sports and open air	— General affairs — Management and provision of sports facilities — Recreational sports — Competitive sports, study and information — Sports infrastructure and inspectorate

Their role is defined as:

— the development of human potential
— the prevention of educational handicaps and the realization of potential
— the overcoming of handicaps

Provisions for co-education
In Belgium, schools tend to be co-educational. As a rule, co-education is applied in schools organized by the State or another public authority. In schools subsidized by the State, especially in religious education, many schools are still divided according to sex. Most non-mixed schools, in religious education, are found, on the one hand, in primary education, and on the other hand, in technical and vocational education. During a recent debate in Parliament about equal access to vocational schools for men and women, a proposition imposing co-education in all schools was rejected.

However, the network of schools is so tight that the situation does not entail any discrimination in the choice of study. The degrees required from the members of the teaching staff, the opportunities for education, the syllabuses, the equipment and the school premises are the same in all schools, whether co-educational or reserved only for boys or only for girls.

According to the Royal Decree of 15 September 1978, a commission for equal opportunities for girls and boys in education was created in the Ministry of National Education and French Culture.

Aims and priorities of education and objectives of specific policies
The general aims of education can be defined as follows:

— to assure the broadening of the individual
— to provide a basic education
— to apply to each and every one
— to increase educational opportunities
— to allow the acquisition of a professional training.

Assure the broadening of the individual
Education aims to help the individual to acquire a number of behaviour patterns which can contribute to the broadening of his/her personality.

For example, the physical aspect does not relate solely to physical education or sports. It also applies to everything concerning the human body. Consequently, the education system has to take into account 'motivity', audio-visual potentials, endurance, hygiene, first aid, etc.

As to the psycho-somatic point of view, the system also has to attach importance to manual or gestural adjustment towards precise aims.

As it seems that there is a relation between food and certain behaviour qualities, a nutritional education must also be provided, based on the main dietetic data.

The social-affective, aesthetic, ethical, and possibly religious aspects are also emphasized.

The system must tend to form balanced individuals who are among other things capable of:

— constituting a balanced person;
— solving human problems in life in general and in family life in particular;
— mastering timidity, anxiety, nervousness or an excessive desire to dominate;
— showing moral insight, altruism and a spirit of collaboration;
— adapting to change;
— overcoming handicaps caused by problems of sight, being a foreigner, an orphan or the child of divorced parents;

- persevering in their efforts;
- acting autonomously;
- showing tolerance and respecting the philosophical or religious opinions of others;
- bearing the consequences of an error.

As regards intellectual development, it is important to take into account not only cognitive behaviour, but also all other mental processes centred on action, and notably judgement, invention, spontaneity, creativity, curiosity, imagination and research.

In terms of cognitive behaviour, it is not enough to emphasize the memorization of knowledge; mental operations such as comprehension, analysis, transposition, interpretation, extrapolation, synthesis, induction, observation, experimentation, deduction and argumentation are also requirements which must be insisted upon.

A complete tuition also implies the acquisition of a general culture centred not only around literature and pure sciences, but also around components which, until now, have not been part of a basic education.

This means that the content of education must include a common base including:

- subjects like psychology, sociology, economy, politics, law, technology and fine arts;
- themes such as the environment, sexual education, road safety, the education of the consumer and documentary techniques;
- a non-compartmentalized approach which permits a general idea to be gained of important and complex problems in our contemporary world.

A 'complete' tuition also means an education which associates in the most appropriate proportions:

- concrete and abstract;
- knowledge of the past, aptitude for understanding and comprehending the present and capacity to take the future into account.

All this should be done while bearing in mind that all education must always take into account the fact that it applies to a person who remains constant throughout every action.

The human being is an indivisible entity, and, in everyday life, the various ways of behaving, arbitrarily divided for analysis, are combined into a complicated context of interactions, leading to a unity of action.

We can say that total tuition is that which, as far as possible, makes the pupil acquire a maximum of behaviour patterns in the context of activities adapted to his or her own needs, and not that which handles a maximum of knowledge while ensuring the acquisition of very few behaviour patterns.

Provide a basic education

Vocational training was instituted for the type of pupil interested in a trade (normally a manual one) which would be practised in specific jobs, and it has until now been based on training oriented to a number of industries which are important employers of trained workers. Under the present reform this level of education will provide courses for those who cannot find a suitable place in general or in lower secondary education.

Three essential aims are consequently to be distinguished in vocational education:

- to give to all adolescents the means of facing personal problems in a balanced and dynamic way and to be full-value citizens;
- to prepare the adolescent to enter professional life. This supposes:

(a) training in professional circles (instruction periods can be very useful here);

(b) a disposition suitable to take up a place in active life, have a job, exercise certain functions;

— to give the necessary education (knowledge, abilities, know-how) for the practice of a profession;

For the teacher this implies the aim of preparing each young person to have a command of skills and a pattern of behaviour enabling him or her to enter on a vocational career. This can be done at the level either of a group of trades or of wider aptitudes.

Apply to all

The aim to train all individuals shows that education must answer the needs of the masses and necessarily concern:

— children, adolescents and adults;
— persons of both sexes;
— privileged and disadvantaged people, whether genetically or socio-culturally;
— workers and those having more leisure;
— autochthons and immigrants.

In order to apply efficiently to all these various categories, the school system must be flexible as to structure, curricula, methods, organization of the educational space, timetable, media, etc.

Increase educational opportunities

Either by enabling the acquisition of a vocational training, or the completion of a general education.

The State thus organizes postal tuition and many workers attend evening classes (social promotion), with the benefit of the law on day-release. Let us also mention the fact that the university is open to workers who wish to obtain a complementary education.

Allow to acquire a professional training

In principle, the very general objectives explained above apply to all individuals, from babies to adults. But this does not mean that all objectives are pursued simultaneously. On the contrary, they are more or less intensively taken into consideration at the appropriate moment, in relation to the respective ages of pre-school, primary, secondary and higher education.

However, there are no specific general objectives for each of the four levels, because, except for a few slight nuances, the same considerations would constantly be repeated.

All divisions simply have as an aim to adapt progressively, in a coherent way, all the general objectives of the total system to the age of the person taught.

On every level, the notion of particular objectives applies to types of schooling, specialization, disciplines, behaviour patterns or simply the hours of the courses.

These particular objectives are generally considered to be those necessary for anyone to acquire an education. The curricula assume that those entering on the course will be capable of following it.

Conclusion

Within the humanities, a definition is always controversial, but, as a first approximation, the objectives outlined here can be used as 'leads' to help both teachers and public.

This tentative synthesis also repeats:

— rather old ideas which have not always been translated in reality;
— rather recent considerations expressed in other terms.

For example, the objectives described above implicitly include notions such as:

— a sound mind in a sound body;
— learning to know, to know-how, to know what to be and what to become;
— a mind well ordered is better than a head full of useless knowledge;
— learning to learn;
— the adaptation of the education to the individual, and not the adaptation of the pupil to the school.

These objectives have not been put into concrete form in a synthetic way in any legal text; they appear as threads in the educational directives and especially in many curricula.

Pre-school education

Early education is provided in the nursery schools (*kleuterscholen* in the Dutch-speaking areas), where attendance is optional.

These schools, which are free, are open to children aged at least two and a half.

The attendance rate is 93 per cent in the first year, 99 per cent in the second year and 100 per cent in the third year (5–6 year olds).

The State provides pre-school education throughout the country and it also, on certain conditions, subsidizes nursery schools run by local and provincial authorities and private individuals.

Early childhood conditions the whole future of the individual. Failure and backwardness, in particular, can start as soon as the child gets to school.

A brochure on the reception and education of children from 18 months to seven years has been distributed, informing people of the aims of pre-school teaching and showing how it fits in with the education system as a whole.

The emphasis in nursery schools is on an introduction to life in society, co-ordination, language, mathematical activity and music.

The same regulations cover both primary and nursery education.

Primary education

Traditional primary education

Schooling is compulsory for children between the ages of six and fourteen. The old primary school consisted of eight years of compulsory schooling split into four two-year units, but this has now been cut to three units.

Children who would have been in unit four of primary education before it was discontinued are now in unit one of the secondary school.

At the end of the three units of primary education, a primary school completion certificate is usually awarded, entitling holders to go up to the secondary school.

Primary teaching is dispensed in separate primary schools and in classes and departments attached to middle, technical and ordinary schools.

The 1958 plan of studies provided for a weekly timetable of 25 hours, as follows — 5–6 hours of mother tongue, 3–4 hours of arithmetic and geometry and 2 hours of religion or ethics, the rest being divided between history, geography, natural science, physical education and so on.

This plan was devised in the light of the Decroly philosophy: 'The three aims – vital knowledge, the acquisition of reflexes and the shaping of the personality – sum up our educational ideal . . . The child and its interests must be both the starting point and the constant centre of the educator's concern'.

Children may not go up to the next class unless they have successfully completed a programme of the three Rs. Remedial teaching is provided for children with problems and those who fail have to do their year again.

Both primary teachers and parents, however, were concerned about too much repetition of this kind and so a variety of measures are now being applied to prevent it:

i   anticipation of the difficulties the child is likely to meet in learning the first skills, so that the teacher can take the relevant steps to remedy them;

ii   support for children who find it difficult to master basic skills and to keep up in later years of study through the introduction of a special post – in remedial teaching;

iii better educational backing in classes where there are migrant children with a poor grasp of the language used in the classroom;

iv   the fixing of specific knowledge and skills to be acquired by the end of the second year only, to take better account of the rate at which each child matures.

Modern primary education

The reform, the result of trends in educational psychology, began in a few schools in September 1971 and was gradually spread to all years of study in all primary schools.

A brochure on education for tomorrow explained the general aims of this reform.

The following subjects are taught:

i   mother tongue;

ii   second language;

iii mathematics;

iv   exploration and conquest of the environment; introduction to history, geography, sociology and science;

v   social education;

vi   physical education;

vii music;

viii highway code;

ix   craft;

x   religious instruction and moral codes (Catholic, Protestant, Jewish or Islamic), or ethics.

Co-education is becoming general and there are no longer any differences between time-tables for boys and timetables for girls.

Special education

Education for children and adolescents who are educable, but not in ordinary schools, is covered by the Law of 6 July 1970.

The Royal Decree of 28 June 1978 outlined eight types of special education, for children who:

i   are slightly retarded;

ii   are moderately or severely retarded;

iii are socially disturbed;

iv   are physically handicapped;

v   are sick;

vi   have problems with their eyesight;

vii   have problems with their hearing;

viii   have co-ordination problems.

In principle, the law on special education applies to 3-21 year olds. Before they register with a special school, a report, specifying what sort of special education they need, is drawn up by a psycho-medical-social centre, a recognized educational/vocational guidance office or a doctor appointed by Royal Decree. An advisory committee on special education is set up to give the head of the family a reasoned opinion, to tell him what kind of education his child needs and to provide a full list of establishments in the various sectors offering the relevant teaching.

Special classes are organized at nursery and primary level and special secondary schools and courses are set up with sections corresponding to the various branches of education.

Special schools can award the same certificates and diplomas as ordinary schools of the same level.

The State pays for the books and other standard equipment issued free of charge to pupils at special schools. It also covers, by royal agreement, school transport costs and any expenses involved in teaching at home.

State grants for pupils in special schools are larger than those awarded for pupils at ordinary schools.

Secondary education

French-speaking state schools now only have the traditional system in the first and second years, and the modern system is being phased in there too.

Most of the education organized by the provinces is modern.

Most of the education organized by the big communes is still traditional.

The modern system is gradually being introduced in 90 per cent of private (Catholic) educational establishments.

There are two branches of secondary education:

First, transition, which both prepares for further study in higher education and paves the way for working life.

Second, qualification, which provides practical preparation for a job after the secondary school and enables the student to continue studying to a higher educational level.

General education is always transitional. Technical and art courses split into transition and qualification as from the third year. Vocational education, which begins in the second year, is always of the second type.

Traditional secondary education – General Courses (Type II)

In the traditional system, a distinction is made between general courses (the humanities, or *humaniora* as they are called in Dutch-speaking areas) and vocational and technical courses right from the first year of the secondary school.

Secondary education is divided into two three-year units – a lower secondary school unit, with pupils of an average age of 12-15, and upper secondary school, with pupils of an average age of 15-18. Pupils are normally expected to have completed their primary education successfully to be admitted to the secondary school and to have a certificate of lower secondary education to be admitted to the upper school.

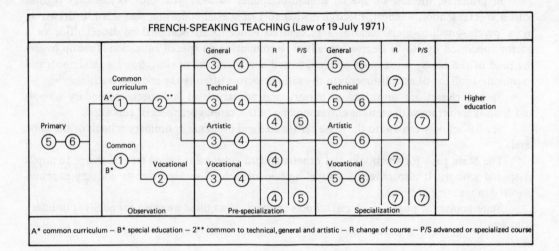

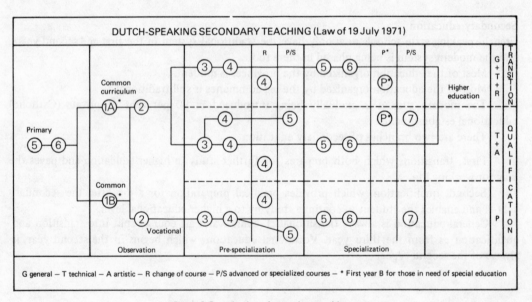

Figure 2 Organization of secondary teaching

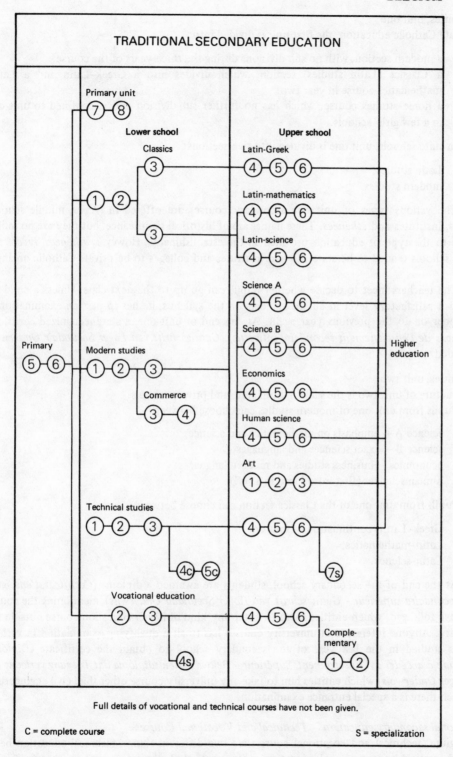

Figure 3 Organization of traditional secondary education

Humanities, unit one
In private Catholic education, the first unit is divided into:

i   a modern section, with no sub-divisions during the three years of the course;
ii   a Classics (Latin studies) section, which divides into a Greek–Latin and a Latin-mathematics course in year two;
iii a home studies course, which has no further sub-division and is confined to unit one, in a few girls' schools.

In state schools, unit one is divided into two sections:

i   Latin studies;
ii   modern studies.

The various types of unit one secondary courses are offered in *lycées*, middle schools, colleges, institutes and *athénées*. These names are of historical significance, but they are no indication as to the type of education provided in the establishments. However, *athénées*, *lycées* and middle schools tended to be state run and institutes and colleges to be private Catholic organizations.

The teachers meet to decide whether pupils can go up to the next class. Unless a child has reached a satisfactory level in all the subjects on the syllabus, he has to pass an examination in September or do the previous year again. At the end of unit one, a state-recognized certificate (*Certificat de l'enseignement secondaire inférieur – Getuigschrift van Lager Secundair Onderwijs*) is awarded.

Humanities, unit two
The structure of unit two is the same in both state and private schools.

Pupils from unit one of modern studies can choose between:

i   science A – emphasis on mathematics and science;
ii   science B – exact sciences and languages;
iii economics – business studies and modern languages;
iv   human sciences (first introduced in 1968).

Pupils from unit one of the Classics section can choose between:

i   Greek–Latin (continuation of unit one);
ii   Latin-mathematics;
iii Latin-science.

At the end of the secondary school, students are awarded a diploma (*Certificat d'enseignement secondaire supérieur – Getuigschrift van Hoger Secundair Onderwijs*), mentioning the course they have followed, which entitles them to enter any kind of higher education course outside the university. Anyone interested in university courses has to sit a qualifying examination in various subjects studied in the last year of the secondary school to obtain the certificate (*Diplôme d'aptitude à accéder à l'Enseignment Supérieur – Bekwaan heidsdiploma dat Toegang verleent tot het Hoger Onderweis*) which entitles him to take any university course other than civil engineering, for which there is a special entrance examination.

Traditional secondary education – Technical and Vocational Courses
In Belgium, technical and vocational courses are two different things, technical education being more theoretical and vocational education more practical. Technical courses are therefore more demanding than vocational ones.

There are two different formulae, involving different amounts of classroom time, in both these types of education – full-time teaching (school) and part-time teaching (courses), or adult education.

There are also various levels:

i   lower secondary;
ii   upper secondary;
iii complementary secondary;
iv   higher.

Vocational and technical education can also be divided according to the various groups of professions for which they prepare:

– agriculture: forestry and fisheries;
– industry: mining, quarrying, metallurgy, mechanics, electrics and textiles;
– building, woodwork and painting;
– chemistry and nutrition;
– clothing and leather;
– applied art – plastic art, architecture, decoration, craft, photography and film, printing and book production and industrial drawing;
– communications;
– commerce, administration and organization;
– services: home economics, community studies, tourism, ancillary medical work, beauty care and social services;
– general and preparatory studies.

Technical and vocational education, unit one

TECHNICAL EDUCATION

Any pupil who has successfully completed his primary education course is eligible for technical studies. A reduced timetable is run parallel to the full-time one. Unit one lasts three years and vocational and technical courses have a common first year.

Pupils who successfully complete the third year of this unit can either move on to unit two of technical education or take a fourth year (qualification) leading to the certificate of lower secondary technical education. There is also a fifth year of specialization, after which an extra certificate is awarded, in some subjects.

Pupils who successfully complete unit one also receive the lower secondary school certificate enabling them, in principle, to move into general secondary courses.

The law has, in fact, assimilated unit one of technical education to unit one of general education to make any changes of course easier.

VOCATIONAL EDUCATION

Vocational courses are practical ones geared more directly to employment. The organization and specializations are very similar to those of technical education and the same sort of certificates are awarded – although they do not entitle holders to enter general education. Four years of vocational schooling lead to a certificate of lower secondary vocational education and pupils may do extra years of specialization and advanced training after this.

Those who successfully complete year three can also go on to upper secondary schools of vocational training.

Technical and vocational education, unit two

TECHNICAL EDUCATION

This complements the training already provided in unit one. A pupil who wishes to change sections must have the agreement of the teaching staff. The course is a three-year one plus a possible fourth year of advanced training or specialization.

Unit two of secondary technical education leads to an upper secondary certificate and a vocational proficiency certificate.

The upper secondary certificate entitles the holder to embark upon courses of higher education outside the university. Those who also take and pass the university qualifying examination are admitted to the university in the same way as pupils from general education. Pupils who successfully complete unit two of technical education can follow first stage courses of higher education.

VOCATIONAL EDUCATION

These courses are open to pupils from year three of unit one — who must stick to the same section unless the teaching staff agrees to a change.

The courses last three years and it is always possible to do a fourth year of advanced training or specialization leading to a special certificate. At the end of year three, pupils are awarded an upper secondary vocational proficiency certificate and extra years of study lead to certificates in advanced training or specialization. Pupils can then go on to a job or to take complementary courses of secondary vocational training in certain subjects. They cannot move on to higher education.

COMPLEMENTARY COURSES OF VOCATIONAL EDUCATION

There are three such courses — in nursing assistant studies, dressmaking and decorative arts.

Candidates for the nursing assistant course must have completed unit two of the technical, vocational or general course. The entrance requirements for dressmaking and decorative arts are successful completion of unit two of the relevant section of technical or vocational training.

This is a two-year course, with the possibility of an extra year of advanced training or specialization, leading to a proficiency certificate.

Apprenticeships
There is a whole parallel system of training here, which does not come under the Ministry for Education.

Training in various branches is provided by industrial, commercial and social associations. In administration, for example, there is the *Landelijke Bedienden Centrale* and there are retailers' associations providing the relevant courses in their field.

In 1959, delegates from the associations representing small firms and traders set up a national vocational and advanced training committee which has since organized vocational training for small and medium-sized businesses in various sectors of the economy (food, clothing, metalwork, building, graphic arts, individual care, plants and flowers, distribution, mechanics, painting and decoration, electrics and woodwork).

The training provided, under the direction of the Ministry for Small Firms and Traders, is in two stages.

The first one lasts four years and is intended for young people who have completed their compulsory schooling. They have a contract of employment and get in-service training and complementary courses of general education (72 hours in year one and 132 hours p.a. thereafter) and technology (72 hours in year one and 124 hours p.a. thereafter) in the classroom. Apprentices who get through their examinations are awarded a proficiency certificate for their chosen profession.

The second stage, training to run a business, is open to apprentices of 18 plus who have their proficiency certificate or have successfully completed unit one in a technical, vocational or middle school. They work full time in the firm during the day and go to evening classes at night (128 hours in all, spread over three years). Candidates who get through the final examination get an advanced certificate in their particular profession, recognized by the Ministry for Small Firms and Traders.

The aim of adult training in this field is to enable individuals to obtain the knowledge they need to carry on one of the independent professions represented on the board of small firms and traders (e.g. professions in the craft, commercial and intellectual sectors).

Adult education involves:

i basic training:

    (a) an apprenticeship under contract, providing basic general and technical education as a preparation for training to run a business. In 1978, 23,000 young people were doing apprenticeships and following courses in 160 centres;

    (b) training to run a business, a course on general, technical, commercial, financial and administrative management of small and medium-sized concerns. In 1978, 11,000 young people were enrolled on courses of this kind.

ii extended training:

    (a) an advanced course aimed at providing a proper introduction to the new problems that crop up in a business;

    (b) retraining – in particular aimed at providing a thorough grounding in new and complex techniques or updating the knowledge of people who have not had the opportunity to gradually get to grips with the problems dealt with in the advanced course;

    (c) individual assistance – aimed at providing people running businesses with any information they require on technology and management.

iii reconversion, which uses appropriate methods of providing heads of businesses with the skills they need to embark upon a different profession.

Traditional secondary education – courses in artistic subjects
Artistic education includes the teaching of music (musical theory and the playing of various instruments), drama and plastic arts (introduction to architecture, painting, sculpture, decorative arts, etc.).

The length of the courses varies with the type of teaching and the ability of the students. Some courses are recognized as full-time secondary education and lead to lower and upper secondary school certificates.

Music is taught in conservatories and the institutes of sacred music in Louvain and Namur. The plastic arts are taught in academies.

Modern secondary education (Type I)

Since 1969-70, the traditional system has been gradually replaced by the modern system. For some years now, schools have been changing, first and foremost from the point of view of numbers of pupils. Secondary schools were originally intended for a privileged minority but they now cater for a wide and heterogeneous public. So the structures, obviously, had to be changed. And a change in the syllabus was also called for because of the incessant advance of science. Lastly, since schools have lost their monopoly in education because of the considerable development of the mass media, they now have an extra job — that of teaching people how to sift, classify, discuss and assess the information they receive.

This was the guiding principle when the modern system of secondary education was designed.

General structures

There are six years of secondary education in the modern system, divided into three two-year units:

    i   observation;
    ii   pre-specialization;
    iii specialization.

In unit two, a distinction is made between transitional courses, which are a preparation for further study, and complete (qualification) courses, which are direct preparation for a job.

All general education courses are transitional. Technical courses may be either transitional or complete and vocational teaching consists entirely of complete courses.

The syllabus is divided into major fields — the study of the natural, human and technical environment, for example, covers an introduction to family, economic, social and political life, to physical and natural science and to geography and history. Natural and physical science covers physics, chemistry and biology, including human biology and physical geography, and human science consists of history, human geography, economics and social science.

    There are eight types of activity:
    i   the common curriculum, followed by all pupils and varied only gradually;
    ii   basic options, the subject of special study;
    iii complementary options, aimed at providing a properly balanced general grounding and helping pupils to discover their interests;
    iv   extra options;
    v   introductory crash courses;
    vi   course change classes;
    vii non-compulsory activities to prepare the pupil for worthwhile leisure-time activities;
    viii remedial activities to breach gaps in one or more of the subjects on the timetable.

The minimum weekly timetable is 32 hours and the maximum 36.

The observation unit

All four types of school (general, technical, art and vocational) have a common first year, although there is an A course for standard pupils and a B course for those who need special teaching.

General, technical and art education have a common second year and the vocational second year course is different.

FIRST YEAR 'A' COURSE
The timetable is as follows:

I. *Common curriculum*

1.	Religious instruction or ethics	2
2.	Mother tongue	5 (4 + 1)
3.	Second language	4
4.	Mathematics	4 (3 + 1)
5.	Study of the environment:	
	(a) natural and human	3
	(history – 1, geography – 1, family life and social education – 1)	
	(b) scientific and technological	3
	(science – 2, technology – 1)	
6.	Physical education	3
		24

II. *Other activities*

1.	Latin studies	2
2.	Technical subjects	2
3.	Artistic activity	2
		30

III. *Complementary activities* — 2

32

IV. *Remedial classes (where appropriate)* — 2

34

FIRST YEAR 'B' COURSE
The timetable is as follows:

I. *Common curriculum*

1.	Religious instruction or ethics	2
2.	Mother tongue	5
3.	Mathematics	4
4.	Study of the environment:	
	(a) natural and human	3
	(b) scientific and technological	3
5.	Technological and artistic activities	6
6.	Physical education	3
		26

II. *Complementary classes* — 6

1. Physical education – 2
2. Other activities chosen by the school – 4

32

III. *Remedial classes (where appropriate)* — 2
(I. 2, 3, and 5)

34

COMMON SECOND YEAR
The timetable is as follows:

        I. *Common curriculum*

1. Religious instruction or ethics	2
2. Mother tongue	5 (4 + 1)
3. Mathematics	5 (4 + 1)
4. Study of the environment:	
(a) natural and human	3
(history $-1\frac{1}{2}$, geography $-1\frac{1}{2}$)	
(b) scientific and technological	3
(science -2, technology -1)	
5. Artistic education	1
6. Physical education	3
	22

     II. *Second language*   4 or 2

         Complementary option $-$ 2

                                       26

    III. *Basic options*

1. Latin studies	
2. Science	
3. Sociology and economics	4
4. Plastic art	
5. Music	
6. Technology	6
	30 32

    IV. *Complementary activities*   2   2

                                      32   34

     V. *Remedial classes (where appropriate)*   2   2

                                      34   36

SECOND YEAR, VOCATIONAL EDUCATION
The timetable is as follows:

        I. *Common curriculum*

1. Religious instruction or ethics	2
2. Mother tongue	4
3. Mathematics	3
4. Study of the environment:	
(a) natural and human	2
(b) scientific and technological	2
5. Physical education	3

     II. *Basic option*   12

                                    28

III. *Complementary classes*

    1. Physical education – 1
    2. Other activities chosen by the school – 5

                          34

IV. *Remedial classes (where appropriate)*   2

                          36

The pre-specialization unit

There are three different courses here:

  i   general and technical transitional courses;
  ii complete (qualification) technical courses;
  iii complete (qualification) vocational courses.

The common curriculum is reduced to make way for options.

The lower secondary certificate is awarded to steady pupils who successfully complete the third year of general, technical or artistic education. A school leaving certificate is awarded to pupils who have completed a fourth year technical or vocational course (successfully or otherwise) and have got through the relevant examination.

GENERAL AND TECHNICAL TRANSITIONAL COURSES
The timetable is as follows:

	Third year	*Fourth year*
I. *Common curriculum*		
1. Religious instruction or ethics	2	2
2. Mother tongue	4	4
3. Second language	4	4
4. Human science	3	3
5. Physical education	3	3
Total	16	16
II. *Basic options*		
A. *Simple options*		
1. Mathematics	6	6
2. Physical and natural science	6	6
3. Economics	4	4
4. Social science	4	4
5. Third language	4	4
6. Fourth language	–	4
7. Latin language and civilization	4	4
8. Greek language and civilization	4	4
9. Industrial chemistry	–	4

B. *Combined options*

10. Agronomy	9	9
11. Electro-mechanics	9	9
12. Woodwork and construction	9	9
13. Clothing industry	9	12
14. Hotels and catering	6	9
15. Social and home economics	9	12
16. Applied art	9	12
17. Personal care	–	12
18. Science and technology	–	9
19. Other technical options warranted by regional circumstances	9	12
Minimum total (A + B)	8	8

III. *Complementary options*

1. Mathematics	3	3
2. Physical and natural science	3	3
3. Economics	2	2
4. Social science	2	2
5. Human science	2	2
6. Third language	2	2
7. Introduction to Latin language and culture	2	2
8. Technology	1	1
9. Technical activities	4	4 (max.)
10. Extra mother tongue	1	1
11. Scientific drawing	2	2
12. Technical drawing	2	2
13. Typing	2	2
14. Office work, book-keeping and secretarial work	2	2
15. Laboratory work	2 or 4	2 or 4

IV. *Complementary activities*	2	2 (max.)
V. *Extra options*	2	2 (max.)
Grand total	32–36	32–36
VI. *Remedial classes or course changes*	2	2

COMPLETE TECHNICAL COURSE
The timetable is as follows:

	Third year	Fourth year	Weekly max.
I. *Common curriculum*			
1. Religious instruction or ethics	2	2	
2. Mother tongue	4	4	
3. Human science	1	1	
4. Physical education	2	2	
Total	9	9	

II. *Basic options*

  A. *Simple option*

    1. Mathematics   4   4

  B. *Combined options*

2. Agriculture	21	21	
3. Horticulture	21	21	
4. Mechanics	21	21	
5. Small-scale mechanics	–	21	
6. Car mechanics	–	21	
7. Electricity	21	21	
8. Woodwork	21	21	
9. Building – roofs and walls	21	21	36
10. Building – finishings	21	21	
11. Sheet metalwork and bodywork	21	21	
12. Hotels and catering	21	21	
13. Applied art	21	21	
14. Hairdressing	21	21	
15. Clothing	21	21	
16. Personal services	21	21	
17. Shorthand and typing	21	21	
18. Office work	21	21	34
19. Sales	21	21	
20. Other options warranted by regional circumstances	21	21	32, 34 or 36, according to option

III. *Complementary options*

1. Mathematics	2	2
2. Second language	2	2
3. Physical and natural science	2	2
4. Consumer education	1	1
5. Technical activities	4	4 (max.)

IV. *Complementary activities*   4   4 (max.)

V. *Extra options*   4   4 (max.)

            Grand total   32–36   32–36

VI. *Remedial classes or course changes*

     Pupils have to follow a mathematics course chosen from either the basic or the complementary options.

VOCATIONAL EDUCATION

The timetable is as follows:

I. *Common curriculum*

1. Religious instruction or ethics	2
2. Mother tongue	2
3. Mathematics	2
4. Current events	1
5. Physical education	2
Total	9

II. *Basic options*

1. Agriculture	25
2. Horticulture	25
3. Mechanics	25
4. Electrics	25
5. Woodwork	25
6. Building — roofs and walls	25
7. Building — finishings	25
8. Sheet metalwork and bodywork	25
9. Hairdressing	25
10. Clothing	25
11. Personal services	25
12. Services	25
13. Other options warranted by regional circumstances	25
Total	34

III. *Complementary options*

1. Second language	2
2. Physical and natural science	2
3. Consumer education	1

IV. *Complementary activites*

	2 (max.)
V. *Extra options*	2 (max.)
Grand total	34–36

VI. *Remedial classes or course changes*   2

The specialization unit
The common curriculum is further reduced here and more time devoted to options. At the end of year six, successful pupils get an upper secondary school certificate which allows them to go on to short courses of higher education.

In addition to this, pupils following complete courses of technical education get a leaving certificate which opens the way to employment. Vocational course students only get the leaving certificate.

Pupils interested in going on to university or other long courses of higher education have to get through the higher educational qualifying examination.

Unit three is also divided into three sections:

i   transitional courses, which prepare for higher education;
ii   complete (qualification) courses, which prepare pupils to start a job;
iii vocational courses, preparing both for jobs and for complementary secondary vocational courses.

GENERAL AND TECHNICAL TRANSITIONAL COURSES
The timetable is as follows:

I. *Common curriculum*

1. Religious instruction or ethics	2
2. Human science	3
3. Physical education	3
	8

II. *Basic options*

A. *Simple options*

1. Mother tongue	7
2. Second language	4
3. Mathematics:	
level A	8
level B	5
4. Physics	3
5. Chemistry	3
6. Biology	3
7. History	3
8. Geography	3
9. Social science	5
10. Economics	5
11. Latin	4
12. Greek	4
13. Third language	4
14. Fourth language	4

B. *Combined options*

These options are those of transitional technical courses, Ministerial Decree of 15 May 1977, p. 75.

15. Applied natural science	9
16. Electro-mechanics	9
17. Public works and construction	9
18. Technology, clothing	9

19.	Applied art	9
20.	Applied economics	9
21.	Applied social science	9
22.	Industrial chemistry	6
23.	Physical education	6
24.	Architectural drawing	6
25.	Other options warranted by regional circumstances	6–9
	Minimum total A and/or B	9

III. *Complementary options*

1.	Mother tongue	4
2.	Second language	2
3.	Mathematics, level C	3
4.	Physics	1
5.	Chemistry	1
6.	Biology	1
7.	Third language	2
8.	Fourth language	2
9.	Psychology	2
10.	Plastic arts	2
11.	Music	2
12.	Philosophy of science and history of technology	2
13.	Physics in the laboratory	1
14.	Chemistry in the laboratory	1
15.	Biology in the laboratory	1
16.	Technology	2
17.	Data processing	2
18.	Scientific drawing	2
19.	Shorthand and typing	2
20.	Typing	2
21.	History of art	2
22.	Introduction to classical culture	2
23.	Social and family education	2
24.	Techniques of expression	2
24a.	Consumer education (circ. 7/4569–73/ GEN/24 of 28 September 1977)	1
25.	Technical activities	2 (max.)
26.	Complementary activities	3 (max.)

IV. *Extra options*   2

V. *Introductory crash courses*

Organization and guidance, 2–4 hours per week.

COMPLETE TECHNICAL COURSES
The timetable is as follows:

Basic training

1. Religious instruction or ethics	2
2. Mother tongue	4
3. Human science	2
4. Physical education	2
	10

Basic options

1. Biology	24
2. Industry	24
3. Chemistry	24
4. Individual and collective services	24
5. Applied art	24
6. Management	24

Complementary options

1. Chemistry	1
2. Biology	1
3. Physics	1
4. Second language	2
5. Current events	2
6. Physical education	2
7. Technical activities	3
Extra options	4 (max.)
Introductory crash courses	4 (max.)

VOCATIONAL EDUCATION
The timetable is as follows:

I. Common curriculum

1. Religious instruction or ethics	2
2. Mother tongue	2
3. Current events	2
4. Physical education	2
	8

II. Basic options
(circ. 7/4343 – 1/24 of 9 May 1975)

1. Agriculture	25
2. Horticulture	25
3. Mechanics	25
4. Electrics	25
5. Woodwork	25
6. Building – roofs and walls	25
7. Building – finishings	25
8. Sheet metalwork and bodywork	25
9. Hairdressing	25

10.	Clothing, needlework	25
11.	Personal services	25
12.	Sales	25
13.	Office work	25
14.	Other options warranted by regional circumstances (hotels and catering, welding, blacksmithery, etc.)	25

III. *Complementary options*

1.	Mathematics	2
2.	Second language	2
3.	Complementary activities	3 (max.)

IV. *Extra options*   3 (max.)

V. *Introductory crash courses*

Organization and guidance for 2–4 hours per week.

Pupils must take mathematics as a complementary option if this subject is not included in their time-table as a basic option.

Features of the modern system

(1) The important thing is no longer for the pupil to assimilate a large number of facts, but to learn how to acquire knowledge on the basis of information received from various sources – i.e. learning how to learn.
(2) The multi-subject approach leads the teachers to work in teams and helps make different subjects more coherent.
(3) The emphasis is on working in groups.
(4) A resource centre containing essential written and audio-visual documents is being set up in each school.
(5) Traditional examinations are being replaced by continuous assessment in which the individual is evaluated in relation to the rest of the group and in relation to his own progress. A report commenting on the child's work and behaviour is sent to the parents four times a year.
(6) In principle, pupils change courses rather than repeat years of study and they are channelled into particular branches in the light of the subjects in which they are most likely to succeed.

Higher education – non-university courses
The Law of 7 July 1970 deals with the general structure of higher education and divides higher non-university courses as follows:

i	technical subjects;
ii	economics;
iii	agriculture;
iv	ancillary medical subjects;
v	social studies;
vi	art;
vii	education.

All these courses, except agriculture (which is only available in official establishments), are offered in both state and private (Catholic) establishments.

Certain categories of higher non-university education operate both long and short courses — short ones comprising a single unit of at least two years and long courses, equivalent to university diplomas, comprising at least two two-year units.

Students wishing to take short courses of higher education must hold an upper secondary school certificate. Those who wish to take long courses have to hold the higher educational qualifying examination.

Higher courses of technical education

Short courses — industrial studies.

Long courses — industrial (mechanical, electrical, chemical, textile, etc.) engineering.

Higher courses in economics

Short courses — commercial studies and computer science.

Long courses — business, finance, diplomatic studies, commercial engineering, translating and interpreting.

Higher courses in agriculture

Short courses — agricultural techniques and landscale gardening.

Long courses — industrial (agricultural branch) engineering.

	FULL-TIME		ADULT EDUCATION†	
	Short (2-3 yrs)	*Long (approx. 4 yrs)*	*Short*	*Long (at least 4 yrs)*
AGRICULTURE				
Tropical and subtropical	☐	☐		
Landscape gardening	☐			
Horticulture		☐		
Agricultural industries	☐			
ARTISTIC SUBJECTS				
Architecture		☐		
Interior design	☐			
Textile arts	☐			
Graphic art	☐			
Plastic art	☐			
Architectural drawing	☐			
Industrial aesthetics	☐			
Design	☐			
Photography and film	☐			
Advertising and window dressing	☐			
Broadcasting techniques	☐	☐		
Town planning			☐	

Table 1: *Continued*

	FULL-TIME		ADULT EDUCATION†	
	Short (2–3 yrs)	*Long (approx. 4 yrs)*	*Short*	*Long (at least 4 yrs)*
ECONOMICS				
Reception	☐			
Administration		☐	☐	
Insurance	☐		☐	
Banking and finance			☐	
Commerce	☐			☐
Accounting	☐		☐	
Distribution	☐		☐	
Ergology			☐	
Tourist guide			☐	
Hotel trade			☐	
Data processing and programming	☐		☐	
Languages	☐	☐		
Secretarial studies	☐		☐	
Tourism	☐			
SOCIAL STUDIES				
Psychology assistant	☐			
Broadcasting and performing		☐		
Librarianship	☐		☐	
Social counselling	☐			
Socio-cultural education			☐	
Welfare work			☐	
ANCILLARY MEDICAL				
Midwifery	☐			
Clinical chemistry	☐			
Dietetics	☐			
Physical education	☐			
Occupational therapy	☐			
Physiotherapy	☐			
Speech therapy	☐			
Hospital nursing	☐			
Pediatric nursing	☐			
Psychiatric nursing	☐			
Social nursing	☐(4 years)			
Home nursing			☐	

	FULL TIME		ADULT EDUCATION	
	Short (2–3 yrs)	*Long (Approx. 4 yrs)*	*Short*	*Long (at least 4 yrs)*
EDUCATION				
Plastic art	□			
Commerce	□	□		
Technical courses	□		□	
Home economics	□			
Education for special classes	□			
Primary teacher training	□			
Secondary teacher training	□			
Design	□			
Religious instruction	□		□	
TECHNICAL				
Assistant engineer	□			
Automation and regulation	□		□	
Chemistry and biochemistry	□		□	
Construction	□	□	□	
Industrial drawing				
Electricity		□	□	□
Electromechanics	□	□	□	
Electronics	□		□	
Electrotechnology				
Smithery			□	
Clothing	□		□	
Industry		□		
Mechanics		□	□	□
Metallurgy and mining				
Engines and attendant skills	□		□	
Photography and film	□			
Textiles		□	□	
Public works		□	□	

† Part-time courses

Table 1: Organization of non-university courses of higher education

Higher courses in ancillary medical subjects
    Short courses – nursing, physiotherapy, occupational therapy, speech therapy and laboratory work. These are three-year courses.
    Long courses – none.

Higher studies in social science
> Short courses – welfare, social counselling and psychological assistance. These are three-year courses.
> Long courses – none.

Higher studies in art
> Short courses – interior design, photography, architectural drawing, industrial aesthetics. These courses last three or four years.
> Long courses – architecture, a five-year course.

Higher studies in broadcasting and social communications techniques
> This is a four-year course.

Higher courses in education
> This is a short course. It includes teacher training for nursery, primary, middle and technical education.

General entrance requirements
Students wishing to embark upon higher courses in education have to have one of the following:

i   a recognized upper secondary school certificate awarded by a state establishment or board;

ii   the entrance examination to mathematics, physics or agronomy degree courses from a university or similar establishment empowered to award such diplomas;

iii the entrance examination to civil engineering degree courses awarded by the state board for secondary education, a university or similar establishment empowered to award such diplomas.

Pre-school teacher training
Since 1974–75 training for nursery teachers, who take children of $2\frac{1}{2}$ to 6, has been part of higher education.
> The course, which lasts two years, leads to a pre-school teaching diploma.
> The syllabus is a general one comprising artistic disciplines (art and music), educational theory, psychology, craft and practical teaching.

Primary teacher training
This is for people who will be teaching 6–12 year olds in the primary school.
> The course, a two-year one, leads to a certificate of primary teaching.
> The syllabus is a general one, comprising artistic disciplines (art and music), educational theory, psychology, craft and practical teaching.

Middle school teacher training
This is a course of training for future teachers of general education and certain special courses in the lower secondary school classes (12–14 year olds).
> This is a two-year course leading to a diploma (of *agrégé* or *régent*) in lower secondary school teaching.
> Organization and content are as follows:

There are six different sections:

i   Mother tongue — history
ii   Modern languages
iii Mathematics
iv   Science–geography
v   Physical education — biology
vi   Art

In each section there are:

1. compulsory classes (general subjects, educational theory and practice);
2. options;
3. a non-compulsory activity from the following list:

   music
   craft
   art
   physical education
   audio-visual aids
   drama
   social education.

Technical teacher training

This is for future teachers of technical subjects at secondary level. There are two types of training — for teachers of middle school technical courses and for teachers of technical courses in upper secondary and higher education.

The former comprises full training in both technical subjects and education.

It is a two-year course leading to a diploma (of *agrégé* or *régent*) in lower secondary technical education.

There are various sections:

1. Dressmaking and cutting
2. Design
3. Art
4. Home economics
5. Agricultural economy
6. Commerce
7. Industrial studies (mechanics — electrics).

The syllabus for each section comprises general courses, education and practicals.

Technical teacher training to provide people in upper secondary school classes and higher education with the notions of educational theory and practice they need to teach their special subjects.

This is a two- to three-year course of adult education.

Organization and content are as follows.

These classes cover general subjects, education and teaching practice.

The certificate of educational proficiency (CAP) is awarded to candidates who pass an examination set by a Ministry for Education board.

Musical education

Teacher training for future teachers in academies of art and schools of music (secondary and adult education) is provided in the Royal Conservatories of Music, comprising educational psychology classes over a two-year period and one year of method geared to the subject to be taught by the individual. The syllabus includes a large number of practical exercises. Entrance requirements for these training courses vary with the subject. Successful candidates are awarded a proficiency certificate in the teaching of their particular subject.

Higher education – the university

In Belgium, any establishment running courses in philosophy, arts, law, science, medicine and applied science leading to academic qualifications is called a university.

There are currently eight universities and ten similar establishments offering such courses. There are three levels of study – *candidature, licence* and *doctorat*.

Most of the similar establishments, the faculties and the university centres only prepare for the first (sometimes the first two) of these.

The administrative situation

There are state universities and free universities. There are four state ones in all, in Ghent, Antwerp, Liège and Mons, and four free ones – the French-speaking Catholic university of Louvain (UCL), the Dutch-speaking Catholic university of Louvain (KUL), the Free French-speaking university of Brussels (ULB) and the Dutch-speaking university of Brussels (VUB). Since 1970, the existence of two linguistic communities has led the old universities of Louvain and Brussels to split.

The state universities are run by three main bodies: the rector (who is appointed for four years); the academic board (consisting of the rector, his deputy and the whole of the teaching staff); and the administrative board (representatives of the teaching, administrative and technical staff, the student body, social and administrative circles and the authorities). Under the Law of March 1971, the free universities are covered by the same rules of financing and administrative control as the state universities – there are a government commissioner and an inspector of finances with identical functions.

The higher educational qualifying examination entitles the holder to embark upon a university course. There is also an entrance examination for the civil and agricultural engineering courses.

The various recognized levels of university studies are:

Candidature, the first two-year unit, leading to the *diplôme de candidat.* This course is intended to provide a general foundation for more advanced specialization.
Licence, the second two-year unit. This is advanced work leading to an end-of-study diploma.
Doctorat, the third unit, which involves writing a doctoral thesis and lasts for an undefined period, is only usually envisaged by students planning on university teaching as a career. Most doctoral students obtain assistant lectureships and teach students on *candidat* and *licence* courses.

There are examinations at the end of each year of study in units one and two and students have to pass these before going on to the next year.

Some faculties deviate slightly from this two two-year unit structure. In theology, for example, there are three years of *candidature* and two of *licence* and in law, two years of *candidature* and three of *licence.* In the faculty of medicine, future dentists and pharmacists have three years of *candidature* and two of *licence* while medical students proper get three years of *candidature* and four years of *doctorat*. Civil engineers have two years of *candidature* and three extra years of specialization.

Teacher training for upper secondary schools and higher education
People intending to teach in the unit two classes of the secondary school have to take courses in education and psychology and give a number of practical classes while studying for their *licence*. The studies for the *agrégation*, the upper secondary teaching certificate, are parallel to *licence* classes. In Belgium, therefore, this examination is not a post-graduate diploma and both *agrégation* and *licence* can be passed at the same time.

The *agrégation* for higher education involves submitting a printed dissertation and three additional theses, defending these before a board and giving an oral lesson on a subject set by the board. It is for people intending to make a career in university teaching (ordinary or extraordinary professor, lecturer, associate professor or associate lecturer). All these staff are appointed by Royal Decree in the state universities and by the administrative board in the free ones.

AGRONOMY (5 years)

Agronomical engineer

General agronomy
Tropical and subtropical agronomy
Stockbreeding
Waterways and forests
Plant protection
Rural engineering
Rural economy and sociology
Rural economy and sociology in developing countries
Soil science
Nutrition and dietetics

Chemical and industrial agricultural engineer

Theoretical chemistry and practical chemistry
Organic and biological chemistry
Agricultural physics and chemistry
Technology and management of food and agricultural industries

LAW

Law (5 years) and notarial studies
Criminology (4 years)

MEDICINE

General medicine (7 years) + a specialization (1–6 years)
Dentistry (5 years)
Pharmacy (5 years)
Veterinary science (6 years)
Physical education and physiotherapy + occupational therapy (4 years + 1 year)

Table 2: *Continued*

    Hospital sciences (at least 2 years after higher study)
    Hospital management (any *candidature* etc. + 2 years)
    Family case work and sociology (any *candidature* + 2 years)

ARTS AND PHILOSOPHY

History	Archaeology and history of art
	Oriental studies
Classical philology	Philosophy and arts
	Linguistics
	Journalism and social communication
Philology	Human science
	African languages
	Verbal techniques
	Spanish and Portuguese studies, Italian studies,
	Brazilian studies
Philosophy	Slavonic philosophy
	History of science

EDUCATION AND EDUCATIONAL PSYCHOLOGY (5 YEARS)

    Psychology
    Educational science
    Educational method
    Speech therapy (after *candidature* − 2 years)

SCIENCE

Mathematics	
Biology	
Botany	
Chemistry	Biology and bacteriology
Geology and mineralogy	Natural science (applied)
Geography	Nuclear science
Physics	
Zoology	

APPLIED SCIENCE

Civil engineering courses in:

Architecture	Aeronautics
Chemistry	Automation
Construction	Hydraulic construction
Electricity	Shipbuilding
Applied mathematics	Nuclear engineering
Mathematics	Geology
Mining	Industrial management
Metallurgy	Data processing
Physics	Petrochemicals
Civil engineering	Telecommunications
operation techniques	Town planning

Table 2: *Continued*

ECONOMICS, POLITICS AND SOCIAL STUDIES (4 OR 5 YEARS)

Business administration
Social communication
Econometrics
Public economics
Commercial engineering   Data processing
Administrative science   Administrative science
Economics
Applied economics   Labour science
Commerce and finance
Political and social science
Sociology
Political theory
Politics and administration
Actuarial studies

THEOLOGY AND CANONICAL LAW

Theology (4 years)
Canonical law (university diploma + 2 or 3 years)
Religious knowledge (4 years)

Table 2: University education

Other forms of education

Adult (part-time) education
These are classes run in the evening, at weekends or during specific periods of the year. They are primarily for people who are at work during the daytime and interested in specializing or obtaining advanced vocational training. Language courses are a common component.

Adult education is provided at three levels – lower secondary, upper secondary and higher (short courses only). In technical and vocational education, there are 6–12 hours of classes per week for 40 weeks per year. There is greater variation in arts subjects.

Parliament has passed a special law (of 10 April 1973) with a view to making it easier for working people to follow these courses of advanced and specialized study.

This enables worker-students to attend post-school training courses during working hours without loss of pay.

The types of course originally covered by the law were state-run or state-subsidized technical and vocational adult education classes at lower secondary, upper secondary and higher (short courses) levels.

Since this basic law was brought out, various decrees have extended its application to:

i   training to run a business (Royal Decree of 24 April 1973);
ii   artistic, agricultural, horticultural, economics and rural economics courses (Royal Decree of 28 December 1973);
iii first year of studies (Royal Decree of 16 September 1974);
iv   university training (Royal Decree of 7 October 1974);
v   general training courses (Royal Decree of 7 October 1974 and 29 April 1975).

The Law of 10 April 1973 should constitute a major step forward in the establishment of a system of continuous education and adult training, as it confirms the fact that the worker is entitled to continue with his general and vocational training:

- by taking time off work;
- for a certain number of hours;
- without loss of pay.

This law applies to Belgian and foreign workers who:

- are no more than 40 years of age;
- are in full-time employment;
- are bound by a contract of employment.

The following people are not covered:

- civil servants;
- frontier workers;
- teachers;
- apprentices on contracts of apprenticeship;
- sick or unemployed workers.

The classes are arranged on the assumption that the worker can take time off without loss of pay:

- for one quarter of the course in the first year;
- for half the course in the second year, if the first year has been successful;
- for the whole of the course in the third (and subsequent) year.

A student who fails to complete a year of study successfully does not lose the benefit of the law provided he does the year again. Two successive failures, however, mean that he has to drop out.

The monthly allowance may not exceed Bfrs 28,000.

The system is financed as follows:

- half by the State;
- half by all the employers who pay special contributions to the national social security office from the amounts paid to all the workers.

More than 200,000 workers are following adult education courses in Belgium at the moment and, in spite of the fact that the law prohibits the sacking of workers who have taken time off for this purpose, far too few people (only about 15 per cent of the labour force) apply to have the provisions of the Law of 10 April apply to them.

Home study courses
These were set up by the State in 1959 and are intended to do three things, namely to:

i   enable candidates who were unable to take the relevant school courses to sit state board examinations with a view to obtaining lower secondary certificates, upper secondary certificates, the higher education qualifying examination and various other higher technical diplomas;

ii   prepare candidates for various civil service competitive examinations;

iii   provide retraining courses for teachers — modern mathematics, science and technology courses are run in liaison with Belgian radio and television and data processing courses are run in liaison with university data processing centres.

These courses are free and it is up to the student to decide how fast he should work as new lessons are not sent off until the previous piece of work has been received. Teachers in this kind of education have to have exactly the same sort of qualifications as those in other branches. An attempt is made to organize monthly meetings between students and the people who teach them.

Adult education activities run by the National Employment Office
Since 1960–61, the National Employment Office (ONEM), a public body under the supervision of the Ministry for Employment and Labour, has been running training schemes in its centres to enable the unemployed to change fields and to provide people with jobs with qualifications that will help them get promotion in the firm.

In the secondary sector, the ONEM offers four kinds of activity:

i   general training – workers who have not had the opportunity to follow initial vocational training can now take a six months' course in metalwork, construction, fashion, etc.;
ii   'tailor-made' courses – run for workers interested in advanced training. They last for one to two months;
iii courses run in the firm, partly in the production cycle;
iv   individual training contracts – for the unemployed and the handicapped. These candidates do a course of training in a firm and are usually taken on permanently afterwards.

In the tertiary sector, the ONEM has set up a number of multi-purpose training centres with two main functions:

i   adapting to all the demands of the national and regional employment market (tertiary sector);
ii   finding the quickest way of providing the sort of vocational training that will enable the candidate to obtain the best-paid and most interesting job, bearing in mind his own talent and aspirations and the local economic situation.

It was to meet this particular aim that the 'tailor-made' courses were devised. Applicants are taken on and, in the space of a few months, put through a syllabus combining both basic and highly specialized training.

The ONEM is financed from a percentage of the social security contributions from wages and salaries, plus an additional amount from the State.

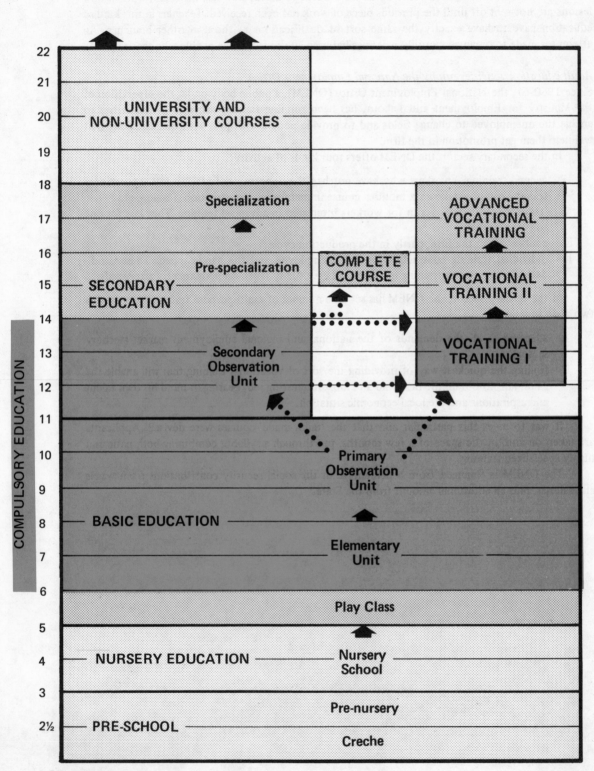

COMPULSORY EDUCATION

22
21
20   UNIVERSITY AND
19   NON-UNIVERSITY COURSES
18
17   Specialization   ADVANCED
16   VOCATIONAL
                                                       TRAINING
15   Pre-specialization   COMPLETE
          SECONDARY   COURSE   VOCATIONAL
14   EDUCATION   TRAINING II
13   Secondary   VOCATIONAL
12   Observation   TRAINING I
11   Unit
10   Primary
9   Observation
8   Unit
          BASIC EDUCATION
7   Elementary
6   Unit
          Play Class
5
4   NURSERY EDUCATION   Nursery
                                     School
3
          PRE-SCHOOL   Pre-nursery
2½
          Creche

AGE GROUP

DENMARK

Levels
Stages
Units

PRE-SCHOOL

1 2 3

PRIMARY

1 2 3 4 5 6

1 2 3

SECONDARY (Law of 1971)

LOWER   UPPER

Observation   Pre-specialization   Specialization

(Coordinated laws of 1957)

1 2 3 4 5 6

1 2 3 4 5 6

1 2 3

HIGHER

NON-UNIVERSITY

1 2

1 2 3 4

UNIVERSITY

1 2 3 4 5 6 7

1 2 3

COMPULSORY SCHOOLING

AGE GROUP

2½ 4 5 6 7 8 9 10 11 12 13 14 15 16 17 18 19 20 21 22 23 24

DENMARK

Population and area

Denmark proper: 5,1 mill., 43,100 sq. km., 16,640 sq. m.
Greenland: 50,000, 3,175,600 sq. km., 840,000 sq. m.
The Faroe Isles: 42,000, 1,400 sq. km., 540 sq. m.

Denmark proper consists of 14 counties which are sub-divided into 275 municipalities. The two metropolitan municipalities, Copenhagen and Frederiksberg, do not form part of any county but have functions like the counties.

GNP 1978: 308,222 milliard D.kr.

Educational expenditure as a percentage of public expenditure 1978: 13.5 per cent.

The Faroe Isles have been a self-governing society within the Kingdom of Denmark since 1948. Greenland achieved the same status in 1979. These are therefore not included in the present survey.

Introduction

The present Danish educational system may roughly be divided into the following main fields:

(1) Pre-primary education.
(2) The *folkeskole* (primary and lower secondary education).
(3) General upper secondary education (*gymnasia* and courses leading to *højere forberedelseseksamen*).
(4) Vocational education and training (apprenticeship training, basic vocational education and courses leading to a basic technical or commercial examination).
(5) Further and higher education.
(6) Youth and adult education.

Education is compulsory for children of 7 to 16 years of age. Children can be admitted to a *børnehaveklasse* (pre-school class), which is voluntary, at the age of 5 or 6.

Public education at the primary level, as well as at secondary and tertiary level, is free of charge, as are text books, teaching aids and teaching materials at the primary and secondary level.

The general aims of education for most courses of education and training are set by the ministry concerned — normally the Ministry of Education — including the regulations for curricula at primary and secondary level.

As far as the primary and lower secondary school are concerned, these regulations (guidelines to the curriculum and teaching guides) are to be considered merely as suggestions, the municipal authorities having the power to issue curriculum regulations on the recommendation of the local educational authorities.

Radical changes have been made in the Danish educational system during the late sixties and seventies. Some of the reasons for change have been: first, the new demands on the educational sector by industrial development; and, secondly, wide agreement that education at all levels should help to remove social barriers.

At the primary and lower secondary level a new education act came into force in 1976 introducing a comprehensive nine year primary and lower secondary school combined with a voluntary pre-school class and a voluntary tenth year.

As the main reforms at the upper secondary level, the introduction of the Higher Preparatory Examination (HF) in 1967, and the basic vocational education (efg) courses in 1972 should be mentioned.

Another important development at this level is the remarkable growth in the number of students who want a general upper secondary education.

In 1950 about 6 per cent of each cohort was admitted to the *gymnasium*. In 1979 the number had risen to 34.5 per cent. The large increase in the number of students who pass a general upper secondary education has made it necessary to intensify the overall planning and the development of the courses of further and higher education.

During the sixties and the seventies the capacity at this level of education was greatly increased and three new universities/university centres (Odense, Roskilde and Aalborg) were founded.

However, in 1976, admission to the courses of further and higher education was restricted by 'numerus clausus'.

At the same time intensive planning has been carried out in order to find new models for the whole range of further and higher education, allowing for more flexible combinations of courses, more opportunities to leave these courses and qualifying exams at various stages. Furthermore, a rearrangement and broadening of the ways of gaining access to higher education has been started.

The most characteristic feature within the development of adult education is the trend towards broadening the possibilities of recurrent education.

In 1977 it was made obligatory for the counties and the municipalities of Copenhagen and Frederiksberg to establish courses for adults wanting to sit for one or more of the leaving examinations of the *folkeskole* or the HF-exams, and the courses have already proved to be of great importance for the continuing education of the adult population in Denmark.

Educational reforms are still under way, as the educational sector is not an isolated area but is under the constant influence of the general social and economic development of society.

A report on Danish educational planning and policy within the next 15 years has recently been worked out by an advisory council of education. The proposals in the report will form the basis for some of the future reforms.[1]

The diagram on p. 86 gives an overall summary of the system of educational opportunities in the so-called *educational pyramid*. The period over which the various educational opportunities extend is shown vertically and the total number of places being offered at each educational stage is shown horizontally.

The total number of places at the bottom, i.e. in the primary and lower secondary school, thus corresponds to the number of children in any particular year.

In 1977 the basic education for everybody consisted of nine years of primary and lower secondary education, but approximately 85 per cent of the students of any particular year received more education than that. Most attended a primary and lower secondary school for ten years, and the majority embarked on a course of study with a vocational bias.

Approximately 30 per cent entered the upper secondary school or the higher preparatory examination courses, and a total of 25 per cent continued their studies by following a short or long course of further or higher education.

However, more than 25 per cent of the young people leaving the ninth or the tenth form still entered the labour market without any further education. Some of them will return to the educational system at a later stage, especially in the 18–22 age group, to get a training qualifying for a trade, but there is still a residual group of approximately 20 per cent who can only make do with their school education and the knowledge they may gradually acquire by attending a course of adult education.

Historical overview

The early historical development of the Danish educational system has by and large run parallel to that of most other Western European countries. The oldest schools in Denmark were the grammar schools, which were run by the Roman Catholic Church until 1536, when the State took over these responsibilities. In 1809 the first Act on the grammar schools came into force.

The children of peasants and artisans received their training in practical work, and from approximately 1400 the training of artisans was controlled by the guilds.

The guilds' control was abolished by an Act of 1857. In their place associations of trades within handicraft and commerce initiated the establishment of technical and commercial schools. 1889 was the year of the first apprenticeship Act.

According to this Act a contract of apprenticeship should be concluded between the apprentice and an independent employer. The training included both education at a technical or commercial school and practical training by the employer.

In the 1700s several rural schools and (in the towns) municipal primary schools were established. In 1791 the first teacher training college was founded. In 1814 seven years of compulsory education was enacted.

It is worth noting that what was introduced in 1814 was seven years of compulsory education, not compulsory schooling. This meant that you were free to give education to your children in whatever way you wanted as long as they got an education in the main subjects which was of a standard comparable to the education given in the official schools.

This freedom to choose the education one considers best for one's children has always been a leading principle in Danish education, and this has especially been stressed by the 'free school movement', which was one of the consequences of the thinking of N. F. S. Grundtvig — a famous Danish poet, clergyman and philosopher — who, in around the 1830s, began to criticize contemporary educational practice in the public schools, which he found too scholastic, especially in the Danish grammar schools.

He felt that children and young people should be educated by listening to 'the spoken word' and that much more stress should be laid upon instruction in religion, Danish history and the Danish language — these being important elements for the understanding of one's own life situation as a member of a nation.

Against the concept of an *academic culture* he advanced the idea of a *folkelig* culture, a culture rooted in the people themselves, and he generated the idea of a Danish people's high school where young people and adults of all classes should receive a general education with an emphasis on 'our native country's natural and historical qualities'.

The first folk high school was founded in 1844, and since then many more have been established, and they have proved to be a vital force in the education of the Danish people.[2]

Grundtvig's pedagogical thoughts in relation to elementary education were not so much taken up by himself as by one of his contemporaries, Kristen Kold, who founded the first 'free school' in 1852.

Today there are different kinds of 'free' or independent schools and all of them can receive subsidies amounting to 85 per cent of their running costs as well as loans on favourable terms for the establishment of the schools if certain requirements are fulfilled.

The main principle behind these large subsidies is that even if Denmark has an efficient educational system with educational opportunities for all children and young people, there should always be a *realistic* possibility of choosing another kind of schooling for one's own children, be it for religious, ideological, political or educational reasons.

In 1978 about 13 per cent of all primary and lower secondary schools were private, independent schools. However, being rather small schools, they were only attended by about 6 per cent of the children in the age group.

Overview of the administration of the educational system

Distribution of responsibility

Responsibility for the educational sector in Denmark rests with the State, the counties, the municipalities,[3] and private individuals and institutions. The primary and lower secondary schools are run by the local authorities with the exception of a few which are run by private bodies. Upper secondary schools and courses leading to the Higher Preparatory Examination are under the counties. A few are under the State or private institutions.

Training colleges for child welfare personnel, nursery school and youth centre teacher training colleges, engineering colleges, schools of social work and most teacher training colleges are mainly private independent institutions.

The State subsidizes county schools, municipal schools and private schools, and in addition it covers the operating costs of state-recognized engineering colleges and colleges of education. The State likewise covers most of the operational expenditure of technical and commercial schools.

The universities and other institutes of further and higher education are for the main part state institutions. Folk high schools, agricultural schools, continuation schools, and some home economics schools are private institutions, but are subsidized by the State.

Main features of the administration of education

The *Folketing* (Parliament)

Today there is legislation on all the more important fields of education in Denmark. Generally the *Folketing* is responsible for that very important part of the control process which consists of formulating aims for the various types of education; apart from that, there is considerable variation in the degree to which the legislature regulates individual types of education. The *Folketing* has in addition another important instrument of control in that it determines how the appropriations are distributed between the various types of education (the Appropriation Act).

The Ministry of Education

Within the limits laid down by legislation, the main responsibility for education in Denmark rests with the Ministry of Education (a diagram showing the organization of the Ministry will be found on p. 45.

The Ministry consists of a Department with three main sections and five directorates:

(1) The Directorate for Primary and Lower Secondary Education, Youth and Adult Education, Teacher Training Colleges, etc.;
(2) The Directorate for Upper Secondary Education;
(3) The Directorate for Vocational Education;
(4) The Directorate for Further and Higher Education;
(5) The Directorate for Building.

Directorates number 1–4 are responsible for definite fields of education. Directorate number 5 is responsible for the planning of the construction of buildings for educational institutions. Matters relating to salaries and conditions of employment in the educational institutions are the responsibilities of a section of the Department. The other sections and divisions of the Department execute specific functions of a more general nature.

The Ministry of Education controls the educational system by the following means: the fixing of regulations in the form of ministerial orders and departmental circulars to inferior instances; the annual allocation of funds to individual types of education and institutions, insofar as the size of the grant is not determined by the relevant legislation; decisions concerning

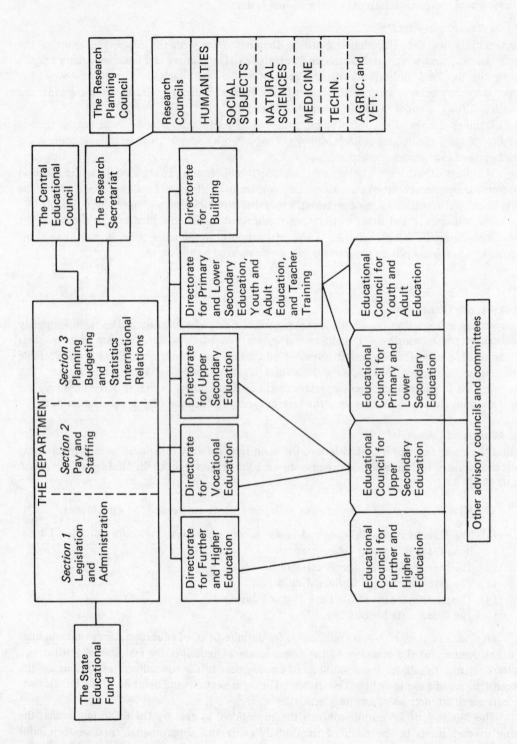

individual cases, which, insofar as the decision is one that involves a matter of principle, can be equivalent to a regulation within that given field; the issue of guidelines; the issue of concrete directions; recommendations (which do not necessarily have to be complied with); supervision and other means of control (the approval of curricula and the appointment of external examiners, for example); and the appointment or the approval of appointment of permanent staff. From an organizational point of view, the Ministry of Education is divided up into one Department with three sections and five directorates, as shown in the figure on p. 45.

The county council

Within each of the 14 counties a council elected by popular vote is responsible for all the educational activities which belong under its jurisdiction, mainly the upper secondary schools and higher preparatory courses and the single subject courses for adults; but at the same time the county council has a number of functions with regard to supervision and approval in its relation to the municipal school system – both the primary and lower secondary schools and the various educational activities relating to the Leisure-time Education Act.

The municipal council

The control and administration of municipal schools rests with the municipal councils, which are also popularly elected.

The supervision of the municipal schools rests with the education committee and the school boards, the latter of which are established at all schools.

The other forms of education, particularly certain types of upper secondary and tertiary education, come directly under the various directorates of the Ministry of Education.

The individual educational institutions

Each educational institution (*folkeskoler, gymnasia,* teacher training colleges and universities etc.) has some sort of management. This can be either a single person, who is usually a public servant, or a governing body. As far as most private educational institutions are concerned, there is usually a board of governors which attends to the administrative and economic leadership of the institution, while daily leadership and responsibility for the educational standards of the institution are generally assigned to a person appointed by the governing body.

A larger or smaller number of collegiate bodies are established at most institutions and take part in the leadership of these institutions in various degrees.

Pre-school education[1]

In Denmark the following types of institutions for children in the age group 0–7 years are being operated: *Vuggestuer* – day nurseries for children between 0 and 3 years; *børnehaver* – kindergartens for children between 3 and 7 years; *integrerede institutioner* – institutions with integrated age groups between 0–14 years of age; and *børnehaveklasser* – pre-school classes for children between 5 and 7 years of age (cf. below).

In 1978 about 10 per cent of all children under 3 years and about 35.5 per cent between 3 and 7 years frequented day-nurseries, kindergartens or integrated institutions.

In addition to the above mentioned institutions, your child can also be looked after in publicly supervised day-care in private homes.

The aim of these institutions is to supplement and support the children's homes through offering care and participation in educational activities for small children in development-oriented surroundings organized according to the age and individual needs of the child.

The pre-school class

Parents are given the option of admitting their child to a pre-school class in the year of his or her sixth birthday. Until 1980, the establishment of these classes was voluntary for the municipalities, but as of the beginning of the school year 1980–81, municipal authorities will be required to establish such classes. In 1978, about 60 per cent of all children in this age group attended such classes.

The pre-school year aims to prepare the child for normal school routine.

There is no actual teaching in the pre-school but the child becomes accustomed to playing and co-operating with other children and is thus gradually acclimatized to the school three hours a day, five days a week.[4]

Administration

The administration of these institutions (except the pre-school classes) comes under the authority of the Ministry of Social Affairs. They are either municipal, self-owning or private institutions. Subsidies from the State and the municipal authorities are granted, but parents pay part of the expenses (35 per cent).

The administration of the pre-school classes comes under the Ministry of Education (cf. below).

The folkeskole

The latest reform of the *folkeskole* was put through in 1975. Behind this reform was the aim of creating equal educational opportunities for all pupils.

As a consequence of this a comprehensive nine year primary and lower secondary school was introduced, combined with a voluntary pre-school class (*børnehaveklasse*) and a voluntary one-year tenth form.

The general aims of the folkeskole education

The aim of the *folkeskole* (as stated in the Education Act of 1975) is — in co-operation with parents — to give pupils the opportunity to acquire knowledge, skills, working methods and ways of expressing themselves which will contribute to their all-round individual development.

In all of its work, the *folkeskole* must try to create opportunities for experience and self-expression which allow pupils to increase their desire to learn, expand their imagination, develop their ability to make independent assessments and evaluations and to form opinions.

The *folkeskole* is expected to prepare pupils to take an active interest in their environment, to participate in decision-making in a democratic society, and to share responsibility for the solution of common problems. Thus, the teaching and the entire daily life of the school must be based on intellectual liberty and democracy.[5]

The organization of the teaching in the folkeskole

Education is compulsory for everyone between the ages of 7 and 16 (9 years). This education may take place in municipal schools, in private schools or through tuition at home. Education at municipal schools is free, and these schools are attended by 94 per cent of all Danish children.

Fees are charged at private schools. However, most of them receive state subsidies of as much as 85 per cent of the approved running costs.

In 1977–78 there were 2,234 primary and lower secondary schools. They were attended by 798,877 pupils. They are in principle comprehensive, as the pupils remain together in their original classes throughout their school attendance.

However, the teaching of arithmetic/mathematics, English and German in the eighth–tenth forms and physics/chemistry in the ninth–tenth forms is primarily offered in two courses, with different content but with the same number of weekly lessons (the basic and the advanced course). The final decision on which of the two courses in each individual subject the pupil is to follow rests with the parents after joint consultation with the pupil and the school.

The Ministry of Education can approve that this division into two courses may be omitted in the eighth and ninth forms for one or more subjects, a procedure which is becoming more and more common.

About 400 of the roughly 1,400 Danish *folkeskoler* make use of the opportunity to make this division in one or more subjects.

The spectrum of teaching subjects is very broad and there is a wide range of optional subjects especially in the three last forms. The curriculum includes a number of practical subjects to enable pupils with a practical bent to develop their abilities.

One of the new subjects which has been introduced is *arbejdskendskab* – vocational studies – which the pupils may choose in the eighth–tenth forms. The actual title of this subject is 'a knowledge of education and training and of conditions prevailing in working life, including visits to and periods of trainee service in firms and institutions'. One of the main aims of this subject is to permit pupils to acquire knowledge and experience of working life and society in general.[6]

Another new subject is *samtidsorientering* – contemporary studies – the aim of which is to give the pupils insight into some central local, national and global problems of our time.

This subject is compulsory in the eighth to tenth forms.[7]

It is also possible to arrange interdisciplinary teaching in some subjects in certain forms.

In addition to the subjects mentioned on pp. 49–50, instruction must be given in the following:

Road safety
Sexual instruction
Norwegian and Swedish
Other religions and philosophies of life
Health information on the most prevalent stimulants and intoxicants
Educational and vocational guidance.

Instruction in these subjects is normally undertaken in connection with the other subjects on the timetable and in *klassens time*.

Furthermore, teaching in a class may temporarily be discontinued for a number of lessons, corresponding to a maximum of ten school days annually in the first to seventh forms, 20 school days in the eighth form and 30 school days in the ninth and tenth forms, in order to make possible pupil participation in school camps, school journeys or practical training periods, etc.

Religious instruction is part of the instruction in the *folkeskole*. Pupils can under certain conditions be exempted from participation in religious instruction.

Administratively the school year begins on 1 August. However, education in schools does not start until the second week of August. The school year normally comprises 200 school days, Saturdays and Sundays being free. The weekly number of lessons for the youngest children must never exceed 20 and for the oldest pupils 34. The number of children in a normal class must never exceed 28; the average number is 19.

Curriculum planning and methods of teaching
While it is the Parliament which sets the general aims of the *folkeskole* and the Minister of Education who sets the objectives for the individual subjects[8] it is up to the local educational authorities and the individual schools to decide how these aims and objectives are to be fulfilled.

THE SUBJECTS	FIRST FORM	SECOND FORM	THIRD FORM	FOURTH FORM
Distributed according to the form levels where they either *must* or *may* be offered at the individual school	Danish Arithmetic/maths Phys. ed. and sport Christian studies Creative art Music	Danish Arithmetic/maths Phys. ed. and sport Christian studies Creative art Music	Danish Arithmetic/maths Phys. ed. and sport Christian studies Creative art Music History Geography Biology	Danish Arithmetic/maths Phys. ed. and sport Christian studies Creative art Music History Geography Biology
	Needlework Woodwork Home economics	Needlework Woodwork Home economics	Needlework Woodwork Home economics	Needlework Woodwork Home economics

Compulsory subjects
Which *must* be offered

Which *may* be offered

Non-compulsory subjects
Which *must* be offered

Which *may* be offered

Table 1

Table 1: *Continued*

	FIFTH FORM	SIXTH FORM	SEVENTH FORM	EIGHTH FORM	NINTH FORM	TENTH FORM
Danish	Danish	Danish	Danish	Danish	Danish	Danish
Arithmetic/maths	Arithmetic/maths	Arithmetic/maths	Arithmetic/maths	Arithmetic/maths	Arithmetic/maths	Arithmetic/maths
Phys. ed. and sport	Phys. ed. and sport	Phys. ed. and sport	Phys. ed. and sport	Phys. ed. and sport	Phys. ed. and sport	Phys. ed. and sport
Christian studies	Christian studies	Christian studies	Christian studies	Christian studies	Christian studies	Christian studies
						Religious studies
Creative art	Creative art	Creative art	Creative art	Creative art	Creative art	Creative art
Music	Music	Music	Music	Music	Music	Music
History	History	History	History	History	History	History
Geography	Geography	Geography	Geography	Geography	Geography	Geography
Biology	Biology	Biology	Biology	Biology	Biology	Biology
Needlework	Needlework	Needlework	Needlework	Needlework	Needlework	Needlework
Woodwork	Woodwork	Woodwork	Woodwork	Woodwork	Woodwork	Woodwork
Home economics	Home economics	Home economics	Home economics	Home economics	Home economics	Home economics
English	English	English	English	English	English	English
			Physics/chemistry	Physics/chemistry	Physics/chemistry	Physics/chemistry
				Contemporary studs	Contemporary studs	Contemporary studs
			German	German	German	German
						Latin
						French
				Typing	Typing	Typing
				Photography	Photography	Photography
				Drama	Drama	Drama
				Film	Film	Film
				Motor knowledge	Motor knowledge	Motor knowledge
				Vocational studies	Vocational studies	Vocational studies
				Electronics	Electronics	Electronics
				Child care	Child care	Child care

Each school is obliged to work out an educational plan which, within the framework set by the Act, states among other things the number of lessons given in each subject, their distribution on the timetable, and the content of the curriculum.

The educational plan has to be approved by the municipal council.

In order to help the local educational authorities as well as individual teachers, the Ministry of Education issues guidelines to the curriculum and teaching guides for individual subjects.

However, they are only meant as guidelines and teaching may be done in other ways and with a different content if this is desired, as long as it is in accordance with the regulations set by the law.

The Ministry of Education can, however, give permission for innovative experiments to be carried out.

Teachers in Denmark are free to choose whatever teaching methods they consider best and consequently many different methods are used, depending on the age of the teacher, where the school is situated and the traditions attached to the particular school. Apart from the freedom to choose teaching methods – a practice much appreciated by teachers in Denmark – the *folkeskole* also employs another system which is both traditionally and uniquely Danish. This is the so-called 'class teacher system'. The class teacher, who is usually the Danish teacher, has social responsibility for the class as a whole and acts as a link between the home and the school. The class teacher deals with any educational and social problems arising in the class and is also responsible for the administrative affairs of the class. For the purpose, a special weekly lesson *klassens time* – free class discussion (period) – is included in the timetable, during which problems can be discussed, parties planned and outings arranged. This lesson may also be used for instruction in such compulsory topics as safety, sex education, health education, educational and vocational guidance, etc.

The latest *Folkeskole* Act opens up possibilities for less authoritative, class-orientated teaching and for more group and project work, and aims at a closer association with society outside the school. As soon as it is deemed right and proper, it is suggested that pupils co-operate in the planning and organization of class instruction. This applies not only to the topics to be studied, but also to the teaching methods and techniques used.

Examinations

As a consequence of the Act on the *folkeskole,* 1975, a new examination system was introduced, which is characterized by the following:

(1) there is no overall examination; there are leaving examinations in each individual subject;
(2) there are only two examination levels.[9] In the large majority of the examination subjects there is in fact only one examination level;
(3) it is the pupils themselves who decide whether they want to present themselves for an examination in the individual subject; and
(4) there is no pass criterion, either with regard to all subjects or in connection with individual subjects.

Pursuant to the Act, the Leaving Examination of the *folkeskole* (LE) may be taken in 11 subjects, and the Minister is empowered to increase the group of examination subjects to include 'other subjects of a practical nature'. In certain subjects the examination may be taken several times, cf. the survey below; this will enable a pupil to improve his examination results a year later.

The Advanced Leaving Examination of the *folkeskole* (ALE) may only be taken in five subjects, and only at the end of the tenth form. In the subjects divided into courses, it is condition that the pupil has followed the advanced course in the tenth form.

Subject/Year of Form	Eighth	Ninth	Tenth	
Danish		LE	LE/ALE	
Arithmetic/Mathematics		LE	LE/ALE	
English		LE	LE/ALE	
Physics/Chemistry		LE	LE/ALE	Advanced course
German		LE	LE/ALE	
Latin			LE	
French			LE	
Handicrafts	LE	LE	LE	
Woodwork	LE	LE	LE	
Domestic science	LE	LE	LE	
Typing	LE	LE	LE	

Table 2: The leaving examinations

Informing the parents about their child's progress

Under current law, marks are not given in the first to seventh forms, but schools are throughout the course of the *folkeskole* obliged to inform pupils and parents regularly — and at least twice a year — of their progress.

Furthermore, marks are given in those subjects in which a leaving examination can be taken in the eighth–tenth forms.

Upon leaving school, the pupils receive a leaving certificate indicating the subjects taken, the level, latest marks for the year's work and the results of examinations passed.

Leaving school

The period of compulsory education is over after a pupil has received nine years of instruction, i.e. normally after the ninth form of the *folkeskole,* but at the latest on 31 July in the year of the pupil's seventeenth birthday.

In special cases the school can permit the partial or total fulfilment of this requirement by the pupil's participation in trainee service or work.

The parents must request this, and there must be special circumstances making this the best solution for the pupil involved. But such an arrangement can be made only after at least seven years of instruction. When a pupil leaves the school in this way, the school is required to offer support and guidance concerning the possibilities of further instruction. If the occasion should arise, it might be a matter of the pupil returning to school. Every pupil who leaves the *folkeskole* after the seventh form has the right to a Leaving Certificate.

It is also possible to complete compulsory education after the seventh year of education by participating in full-time education in the municipal youth school or a continuation school.

Having completed compulsory education different types of continuing education are, on certain conditions, open to the pupils within:

(1) General upper secondary education, e.g.

    a. The *gymnasium.*
    b. The Higher Preparatory Examination courses.

(2) Vocational education and training, e.g.

    a. Apprenticeship training.
    b. Basic vocational education.
    c. Basic technical or commercial examination courses.
    d. Agricultural education and training.
    e. Courses of social and health education.
    f. Courses of pedagogical education.
    g. Other types of vocational education.

Even if there are many different opportunities for continuing education after compulsory education is completed, a considerable number — about 25–30 per cent of each cohort — leaves the educational system without any further education or training, and this is now considered to be a great problem in Danish education.

Health and social arrangements

Municipal authorities arrange for medical and dental examinations at regular intervals for all children of school age. There is a district nurse affiliated to each school and on hand at large schools every day.

Psychological and psychiatric treatment is available for children, and there are special arrangements for remedial teaching to help children with learning difficulties.[10]

The services are carried out by the health, social and educational authorities respectively, though in close co-operation with each other.

As of 1 January, 1980, the care of handicapped persons, including educational facilities for mentally as well as physically handicapped children, will be transferred from the sphere of responsibility of the State to that of the counties and municipalities.

At the same time the jurisdiction of the whole sector of special education comes under the responsibility of the Ministry of Education.

The main consideration behind the whole reform leading to this decentralization is that the life of the handicapped should be normalized as far as possible, that they should be equal to other citizens and have the same opportunities: e.g. the education of the handicapped should wherever possible be integrated in ordinary schools and therefore administered by the same local education authorities, assisted by special advisors.

In addition to the ordinary classrooms, all schools have laboratories, a library, a gym and playing fields.

Many municipalities have established recreation centres near or in connection with the schools, where the children can be occupied until their parents get home from work.

Children of resident foreigners, refugees and immigrants who are resident in Denmark for periods of six months or more are subject to the same regulations concerning compulsory education as Danish children are, and are offered admission to Danish classes in which introductory teaching in Danish and other subjects is given. They are also offered tuition in their mother tongue and native culture for 3–5 lessons a week. This teaching will usually be given outside normal school hours, and very often on Saturdays,[11] as the number of pupils is often limited and normally the pupils are scattered over a wide area.

Administration of the folkeskole

At central and regional level the *Folketing* (Parliament), the Ministry of Education and the county councils are all involved in the administration of education. At local level the relevant bodies are the municipal council, the education committee and the joint teachers' council. At the school level they are the school board, the teachers' council, the principal, the parents and (except in individual matters) the pupils. Parliament lays down general aims for education in the *folkeskole,* and the Ministry sets minimum standards, e.g. for teaching in individual subjects. The county councils see that regulations are observed. The municipal council deals with the organization of the schools within a general framework. The education committee is the supervisory authority for the entire municipal system, acting through the school boards, which can make recommendations and comment on the educational plan. Normally there are 13 members of an education committee, seven nominated by the municipal council, five elected by the school boards from their members, and one from the youth school board. Two pupils can be on the education committee, except when it deals with matters concerning individuals, and without the right to vote. Pupils have a similar position on the school boards, which consist of parents and representatives. Besides the pupils, a representative from the municipal council, two teachers and the principal can participate in the meetings of the school boards – also, however, without the right to vote. Pupils have the right, but not the duty, to set up a pupils' council in each school, and they participate in planning the teaching.

Private schools
As stated earlier 13 per cent of all Danish schools are private schools and approximately 6 per cent of all Danish pupils attend these schools.

Private schools may be established by groups of parents who have special educational ideas or interests or who belong to any one of numerous groups, such as religious denominations or sects, political or philosophical movements, different nationalities, etc.

All private schools are entitled to receive state subsidies covering up to 85 per cent of their operational expenditures directly connected with instruction, as well as loans on favourable terms for the establishment of the schools when certain requirements are fulfilled.[12] For example, instruction must be on a level comparable to that of the *folkeskole* and there must be a certain minimum number of pupils, depending on the size of the schools, e.g. schools having forms 1-7 must have at least 28 pupils.

A supervisor for each school is either elected by the parents, subject to approval by the Ministry of Education, or appointed by local authorities, and is responsible for ensuring that the level of instruction is comparable to that of the *folkeskole.*

Education at upper secondary level
Education at this level is divided into two main streams: general upper secondary education, traditionally preparing students for higher education, and a system of vocational education and training which qualifies students for work in trade and industry.[13]

The *gymnasium* and apprenticeship training which up until now have been the two most common types of education at this level have developed independently of each other, the *gymnasium* as a general type of education, and apprenticeship training as a practical training, but with more and more theoretical instruction included.

Proposals for a full-scale co-ordination of the above-mentioned courses of education, as well as of the other types of education at this level, have been put forward several times and experiments have been carried out, e.g. practical subjects have been introduced at some upper secondary schools and more general subjects have been integrated in the different types of vocational education.

An overall plan for a restructuring of the whole range of courses of education and training for the 16-19 year olds was scheduled to be presented to Parliament during the session 1979-80.

One of the main reasons for the wish for reforms at this level is the fact that at the moment the two types of education do not seem to be equally attractive to students, e.g. it is far easier to be admitted to a general upper secondary education than to an efg-course. Admission to the *gymnasium* is free if the student in question has been declared qualified by his former school and if he has followed certain subjects in the *folkeskole* and passed the required leaving exams, whereas admission to the efg-courses depends on the number of study-places available.

Furthermore, the geographical distribution of the *gymnasia* is more widespread than that of the vocational schools.

Finally, the structure and contents of general and vocational upper secondary education are so different that it is very difficult to change from one type of education to another.

One of the consequences of this has been that the number of young people who decide to continue their education in the *gymnasium* has increased so drastically during the seventies that it can be expected that there will not be enough study-places for these students at the courses of further and higher education (cf. Table 3).

Another indication of the need for reforms at this level is the fact that about 25 per cent of young people never start any further education after the *folkeskole.*

General upper secondary education
The two most common types of general upper secondary education are the three-year courses at *gymnasia* – upper secondary schools – leading to *studentereksamen* – upper secondary school leaving examination – and the two-year courses leading to *højere forberedelseseksamen* (HF) – higher preparatory examination.

Furthermore, a *højere handelseksamen* (Higher Commercial Leaving Examination) can be taken, which is a leaving examination comparable to the *studentereksamen,* but more vocationally slanted.

Besides these three types of general upper secondary education it is possible to attend two-year day or evening courses leading to the *studentereksamen* or to take a whole or part of a *højere forberedelseseksamen* subject by subject in the so-called single-subject courses under the Act on Leisure-time Instruction.

		1960	1970	1977	1979
Vocational education and training:	efg		200	13,000	31,000
	apprentices	33,100	28,000	20,300	16,000
	basic technical examination courses	900	3,000	3,100	3.500†
Vocational education and training in total:		34,000	31,000	36,400	50,300†
General education:	*gymnasium*	7,000	12,300	16,700	23,800
	courses leading to USSLE‡	900	2,900	1,600	1,400†
	HF		3,000	6,400	6,300†
General education in total:		7,900	18,200	24,700	31,500†

† Figures partly based on estimates
‡ Upper Secondary School Leaving Examination

Table 3: Intake to apprenticeship training, basic vocational training, basic technical examination courses, the *gymnasium,* courses leading to the Upper Secondary Leaving Examination, HF

The *gymnasium*

The Danish *gymnasium* gives an education which is a qualification in itself, as well as a preparation for higher education.[14]

Students who have completed the ninth or tenth forms of the *folkeskole* can be admitted to the *gymnasium* on the basis of a statement issued by their earlier school, that they are 'qualified' or 'perhaps qualified' for studies at the *gymnasium*. Depending on their choice of branch, a further requirement is that the pupils have passed the leaving examination of the *folkeskole* in certain subjects with a satisfactory result and have studied at least the basic course in certain other subjects.

The *gymnasium* is divided into two main lines: languages and mathematics. There is no further division of pupils in the first form, while students in the second and third forms are divided into as many as seven different branches of study.

THE ORGANIZATION OF THE TEACHING

The standard timetable for the different lines and branches of the *gymnasium* can be seen on p. 56–7.

In addition to the subjects mentioned in the timetable, educational and vocational guidance must be given and special teaching must be provided for handicapped children.

Furthermore, the Ministry of Education is empowered to accept experimental and innovative teaching, e.g. the introduction of new subjects and interdisciplinary teaching, as long as this does not damage the students' chances of using their education for further studies or diminish their rights in other connections.

In comparison with the *folkeskole* education, the instruction at *gymnasia* is more centrally administered, e.g. the Ministry of Education sets the aims for the individual subjects and issues detailed regulations on the content of the subjects, their scope and inclusion in the various branches.[15]

The specific planning and organization of the individual subjects is, however, done cooperatively between the teacher and students as far as possible.

EXAMINATIONS AND MARKS

In order to complete the *gymnasium* successfully the students have to sit for the *studentereksamen*, which is a state-controlled written and oral examination.

To students who have passed the exams a leaving certificate is issued showing their marks for the year's work and their examination marks.

The *studentereksamen* gives access to universities and other forms of higher education, although admission to certain faculties is granted only to students with a *studentereksamen* from certain of the branches of the *gymnasium*. All other students may be required to pass supplementary examinations in subjects relevant to their chosen field of study.

Højere Forberedelseseksamen (HF)

The HF – higher preparatory examination – was established in 1967. As indicated by the title, HF is an examination, not a kind of schooling like the *folkeskole* and the *gymnasium*. This means that anybody over the age of 18 has the right to sit for the examination, and if they pass they get rights of entrance to most types of tertiary education.

Since most people are not able to pass an examination of that kind without teaching, two year courses have been set up. Courses are given at *gymnasia*, at teacher training colleges and elsewhere. The examination is a single-subject examination so that it is possible to build up a whole examination by passing one subject or even part of a subject at a time.

	Languages Line					Mathematics Line			
	Common Core	Special Subjects				Common Core	Special Subjects		
SUBJECTS	1.2.3	A 2.3.	B 2.3.	C 2.3.	D 2.3.	1.2.3.	E 2.3.	F 2.3.	G 2.3.
Religion	0-1-2					0-1-2			
Danish	3-3-4					3-3-4			
English	4-	4-6	3-5	3-5		5-0-0			
German	3-	3-5				5-0-0			
French (Russian)	5-3-3					5-3-3			
Latin		4-0	4-0		5-5				
Greek and Classical Civilization					8-6				
Classical Civilization	1-	2-0	2-0	2-0		1-2-0			
History and Civics	2-3-3	0-1	0-1		0-1	2-3-3	0-1		0-1
Social Studies				5-5				5-5	
Geography	2			3-2	3-0		3-0	3-2	3-2

(The Mathematics Line Common Core value 5-0-0 is bracketed jointly for English and German.)

Subject	A	B	C	D	E	F	G
Biology	0-0-3				0-3	0-3	3-7
Biochemistry					3-0	1-0	3-0
Chemistry	2-3-0				3-5	2-2	2-2
Physics					5-6	2-2	3-3
Mathematics					5-	3-	3-3
Music as a special subject	4-6						
Physical education	2-2-2						2-2-2
Music (max.)	2-2-1						2-2-1
Music (min.)	2-0-0						2-0-0
Art	0-2-1						0-2-1
	26-17-18	13-12	13-12	13-12	13-12	13-12	26-12-12
	30-17-18	13-12	13-12	13-12	13-12	13-12	30-16-15
					14-15	14-15	14-15

A = Modern languages branch
B = Music-languages
C = Social studies-languages
D = Classical languages
E = Mathematics-physics
F = Social studies-mathematics
G = Natural sciences-mathematics

Table 4: Standard timetable for the *gymnasium* (lessons per week in each year)

Therefore, there are not only two-year courses, which are full-time courses, but also evening school courses which enable a whole examination to be passed in three or four years.

The system has met with great success. In 1967 500 students started at a HF course. In 1979 7,000 full-time and 24,000 part-time students were enrolled. There are about 90 full-time two-year courses in Denmark and around 85 day or evening schools preparing for single subject examinations, but apart from this the HF is being offered, in connection with, for instance, efg, at the folk high schools and in other places as one theoretical part of other kinds of training. There is no doubt that this system is a growing alternative to the traditional *gymnasia,* which are still felt to be the natural preparation leading to tertiary education for 16 year olds, whereas the HF often caters for people who are a bit older and who have worked in trade, in commerce or in industry for some years. HF has therefore become a very important example of recurrent education in Denmark.

HF courses are open to anyone judged to have sufficient ability to participate in work done at this level, ability which may be gained through vocational experience as well as through various forms of education. Most of the students have passed the leaving examination of the *folkeskole* or its equivalent.

THE ORGANIZATION OF THE TEACHING

The curriculum includes the following compulsory and optional subjects:

It is the Ministry of Education which sets the aims of the individual subjects, issues detailed curriculum regulations and approves the examination syllabuses.

The specific planning and organization of the teaching of individual subjects is done by the teacher and the students in close co-operation. At each course, guidance-counsellors are appointed, who give guidance to each individual student on problems concerned with social, economic and personal matters, as well as problems connected with their study-programme. Such guidance also includes careers guidance which is done collectively as well as individually.

EXAMINATIONS AND MARKS

As already mentioned the students have to sit for examinations in all the common core subjects as well as in all the optional subjects they have chosen to follow.

The intention of the HF examination is to prove that the students have attained the knowledge described in the official aims of the HF and can use the knowledge and the working methods they have been taught.

The examination is both written and oral and, as is the case for the *studentereksamen,* the Ministry of Education prepares the examination papers for the written examinations and the individual teacher sets the oral examination questions, which, however, must be approved by the external examiners.

For students who have passed the HF, a leaving certificate is issued, showing their examination marks.

No marks are given during the study period but the teacher is obliged to inform the students about their performance if they wish.

Administration of general upper secondary education

General upper secondary education is now as a rule the responsibility of the counties, with a few exceptions, which are municipal, private or state schools.

As already mentioned, central administration of these types of education is more extensive and detailed than of the *folkeskole* education.

	First Semester	Second	Third	Fourth	
COMMON CORE					
Danish	3	3	4	4	
Religion	0	0	3	3	
History	3	3	3	3	
Biology	3	2	0	0	
Geography	3	2	0	0	
Mathematics	5	5	0	0	
English	4	3	4	4	
German	3	3	0	0	
Social Studies	2	2	0	0	
Music or Art	2	2	0	0	
Physical Education	2	2	0	0	
OPTIONS					*Points*
Biology	0	0	4	4	8
Mathematics	0	0	6	6	12
English	0	1	3	3	7
German	0	0	5	5	10
Social Studies	0	0	3	3	6
Music	0	0	4	4	8
Art	0	0	4	4	8
Physical Education	0	0	4	4	8
Third foreign language†	0	3	4	4	11
Physics	0	3	6	5	12
Chemistry	0	0	5	5	10
Psychology	0	0	3	3	6

† Third foreign language is either French, Russian or Spanish

Table 5: To obtain a full HF examination, a pupil must have passed all subjects in the common core and options giving at least 20 points

The Directorate for Upper Secondary Education in the Ministry of Education is responsible for educational supervision, including the issue of curriculum regulations and the approval of examination syllabuses.

The daily administration of the individual county upper secondary schools, including the schools with which HF courses are affiliated, is in the hands of a headmaster, who is, however, assisted by different governing bodies.

At each school a school council must be established, consisting of the headmaster and one or more representatives from the county council, the teachers, the parents, the students and representatives from the other groups employed at the school.

Among other things, the school council, in co-operation with the teachers' council, acts as a co-ordinator between the school and the home. It approves the weekly timetable and it has a say on the distribution of the budget for the school.

In addition to this body, a teachers' council, a teachers' assembly and a joint consultation committee are established, and furthermore, at HF courses a students' council must be formed.

A students' council can also be established at upper secondary schools, if the students so wish.

The private upper secondary schools with which HF courses may be affiliated are supervised by the Directorate for Upper Secondary Education and, insofar as a number of conditions are fulfilled, they receive a state subsidy covering 85 per cent of the operating expenses.

The private upper secondary schools are all self-governing institutions run by a Board of Governors, who are responsible for the financial administration of the institution in question.

Furthermore, the Governors appoint the headmaster and make appointments to the staff.

Vocational education and training

Radical changes in the structures of vocational education and training schemes have been carried out in the late fifties, the sixties and the seventies.

Before that time almost the only vocational education available was apprenticeship training, which took three to four years and was based on apprenticeship contracts between employer and apprentice. The apprentice learned his trade by participation in day-to-day work supplemented by evening classes in a number of subjects like Danish, arithmetic and draughtsmanship.

A commission on apprenticeships considered the whole set of regulations of apprenticeship and its reports formed the basis for a revised Act of Apprenticeship in 1956.

According to this Act more influence was granted to national trade committees composed of equal numbers of representatives of employers and trade unions. Furthermore, it was stated that instruction at evening courses should be replaced by day school instruction arranged so that it corresponded to the individual trades. The teaching was extended to include also practical subjects; basic courses were set up to give apprentices an introduction to the fundamental methods of their trade.

The re-structuring of apprenticeship training and education was welcomed by the public, and the number of apprentices increased (cf. Table 6).

In the latter half of the 1960s the number of young people entering apprenticeship training, however, began to drop. This drop was not due only to criticism of the apprenticeship system, but also to the decrease in the annual number of births, to the wider range of educational and training alternatives, and to more favourable employment conditions. It was decided to let a committee evaluate the apprenticeship system again.

The introduction of basic vocational education

In June 1967 the Ministry of Education asked a committee to evaluate the apprenticeship system. The committee submitted its evaluation report in February 1971 with the following main observations:

- The choice of trade is made too early in the life of the adolescent. The apprentice and the parent sign the contract before the young person has had sufficient realistic background to make the choice.
- During the apprenticeship no opportunities exist for changes to other forms of education or training. Apprenticeship therefore may seem to be a blind-alley.
- The availability of practice for apprentices depends on the individual employer. This does not give sufficient security for later employment.
- Apprenticeships require co-ordination between the practical training in employment and the education and training at trade colleges. This co-ordination is not always good enough and the practical training in companies is not always sufficiently supervised.
- With increasing specialization in industry and business it may often be difficult to satisfy the requirements of an all-round training. In some fields of industry and commerce the

requirements of an all-round training may appear to be too large and in others too narrow.
- The education and training received at the vocational schools does not include enough general subject content. When a comparison is made with the education received by young people in general upper secondary education, this appears as a handicap.

The committee submitted a proposal for a new type of vocational education and training. It should start with a full year of day-school, with an introduction to a whole family of trades. The students should be guided in the final choice of trade. There should be a larger amount of general education.

This new type of vocational education and training was started as an experiment in a few schools.

In 1977 an Act was passed which confirmed that this new type of education should continue and that it should be expanded to a larger capacity in the schools. Parliament did not decide that apprenticeships should stop. The present situation is therefore that there are two parallel systems: apprenticeship and the so-called efg-courses.

Table 6 illustrates the volume of the two streams.

Apprenticeship training

The training of apprentices takes place pursuant to the Apprenticeship Act of 2 October 1956.

The Act prescribes that a contract of apprenticeship is set up between an independent employer and the trainee.

A condition for entering into an apprenticeship is the completion of the nine years of compulsory education. Some trades may, however, require further qualifications. The period of training is separately fixed for each trade and ranges from two to four years. The training includes both theoretical and practical education at a technical or a commercial school and practical training by an employer. The theoretical part consists of from 700 to 1,800 lessons.

YEAR	INTAKE OF BASIC VOCATIONAL EDUCATION STUDENTS	INTAKE OF APPRENTICES		
		Commerce and office	Crafts and industry	Apprentices total
1939	–	3,700	7,200	10,900
1945	–	4,300	8,400	12,700
1950	–	6,400	12,500	18,900
1955	–	8,000	13,000	21,000
1960	–	12,900	20,200	33,100
1965	–	16,200	21,700	37,400
1970	200	11,200	16,800	28,000
1975	6,400	5,500	9,500	15,000
1976	9,000	8,200	12,800	21,000
1977	13,000	7,800	12,500	20,300
1978	27,000	6,700	12,000	18,700
1979	31,000	5,000	11,000	16,000

Table 6

In the fields of trade and industry, apprentices must at the end of their period of apprenticeship sit for a *svendeprøve* – a journeyman's test, or, if this has not been established, another test approved by the trade concerned.

When the apprentices have passed their journeyman's test, they receive a *svendebrev* – a journeyman's certificate.

No rules for journeyman's tests have been established for apprentices in the clerical and commercial fields. At the end of the period of apprenticeship in these trades the employer must provide the apprentice with a certificate of completed apprenticeship, stating the period of apprenticeship and whether the apprentice has become competent in his or her trade.

However, the certificate of completed apprenticeship may not be given to the apprentices until they have passed the theoretical part of the training, the *handelsmedhjaelpereksamen* (the commercial assistant examination), its equivalent or a more comprehensive examination, *handelseksamen* (commercial examination).

Basic vocational education (*Erhvervsfaglige grunduddannelser* – efg)

Efg-courses normally take three years. They start with a basic one year course which is at present available in eight principal vocational fields: commerce and public administration; the iron and metal industries; construction industry; food trades and occupations; graphic industry and occupations; service trades; agriculture, horticulture and forestry; transport.

The basic course is an introduction to the general vocational field chosen by the student. Approximately 40 per cent of the lessons of this course are devoted to general educational disciplines aiming at giving the student an understanding of society and economic life.[17]

Students are also offered a number of optional subjects.

In some of these subjects it is possible to sit for the leaving examination of the *folkeskole* or the HF examinations or the commercial schools' state-controlled examinations.

After having completed the basic education, the pupil can choose among approximately 75 trade training courses. A successive specialization takes place with each course, and the courses are built up in such a way that the pupil may leave them at a suitable stage with a certain amount of trade qualification, and may later continue his studies from the stage he reached.

It is felt that the structure of training during the second part, i.e. the alternation between the work as a trainee and the education at school is suitable, and the arrangement has been carried out with due regard to the special structure and the needs of the individual main occupational fields.

Admission to efg is given on the basis of the completion of the *folkeskole* ninth form.

In order to apply for admission to the second part of efg the student must have obtained a certificate from basic training as well as an agreement with an employer who is willing to take the student in question for a period of practical training.

During the second part of efg, the student is to be continually evaluated in connection with daily instruction, and only on rare occasions by means of special tests. Upon completion of the second part of efg, the student is given a certificate documenting that his or her qualifications are satisfactory.

Other types of vocational education and training

In addition to the apprenticeship training and the efg the Ministry of Education has established other types of vocational education and training courses at upper secondary level, which are open to pupils who have completed primary and lower secondary education.

Technical schools provide training courses for technical designers, technical assistants, laboratory workers, etc. (*de grundlaeggende tekniske eksamens-uddannelser*). The duration of these courses is 2–4 years of full-time studies, dependent on previous education and practical experience.

The aim of these courses is to provide the students with a theoretical as well as a practical training, qualifying them to become assistants in firms or institutions connected with the technical trades, and to work with planning architects and engineers, as well as with chartered surveyors. The training courses are arranged in such a way that the students normally start with 20 weeks of day school; after that there follows a 12 month period of trainee service in a firm. The training finally ends with 20 weeks of school attendance.

At commercial schools it is possible to take a one-year *handelseksamen* (commercial examination) and a *højere handelseksamen* (two-year diploma course), equivalent to the *studentereksamen,* but more vocationally slanted.

The one-year commercial examination is now equivalent to the one-year basic education in the clerical and commercial field of efg.

There are also other types of vocational upper secondary education *aiming* at either the private or the public sector. Among the courses aiming at jobs in the private sector are courses in navigation, shipping, agriculture and forestry, etc. There is also a large number of courses aiming almost exclusively at jobs within the public sector, e.g. courses within the health, the social and the welfare fields, courses relating to education and courses relating to administration.

Administration of vocational education and training

As a result of their different historical origin and development, different rules and conditions apply to the various types of vocational education. This can be seen in the differences in the administration of the courses, finance, organization of the schools, teacher training and working conditions of teachers and in the fact that the responsibility for vocational education is placed under different ministries (primarily the Ministry of Education, Labour, the Interior and Social Affairs) and many different official and private bodies.

The two main fields, apprenticeship training and basic vocational training education come under the jurisdiction of the Ministry of Education.

However, labour and management have always had, and still have, great influence on the content and scope of vocational training and education.

Different boards and committees of representatives of employers and employees decide on what practical skills and theoretical knowledge the apprentices and the efg-students should learn.

Co-operation goes beyond just the content of the training courses. The technical and commercial schools which take care of the theoretical part of the training are private, self-governing but state-subsidized institutions administered by a board, the majority of the members of which are also appointed by local employers' and employees' organizations.

Further and higher education

Planning and development

With their close connections with research, further and higher education are always bound to change in content and impact. In Denmark as in many other countries there has, however, been a growing public concern for further and higher education. Students completing upper secondary education and pressing to get a higher education have been growing in number. The costs of higher education have increased, but funds available for new appropriations are limited. Planning has become necessary.

During the last 25 years a number of committees have analysed the problems of further and higher education and made recommendations. Since 1974 a more permanent administrative arrangement for planning and development has been established with a directorate for further and higher education with a national council and six national planning committees. To advise on research activities a planning council for research with six research committees assisted by a permanent secretariat has been established.

The aim of the Danish Conference of Rectors (*Rektorkollegiet*) is to encourage co-operation between universities and other institutions of higher education.

By legislation in the years 1970–76 the administration of universities and specialized institutions for higher education has been reorganized. The students and the administrative-technical personnel have been given influence in the administration of each institution through their representation on boards and committees together with professors and other teaching and research staff.

By legislation in 1976 a co-ordinated national regulation of access to further and higher education was introduced.

Admission to institutions of further and higher education
Admission to institutions of higher education has for some years, in principle, been open to all holders of:

(a) the upper secondary school leaving examination.
(b) the higher preparatory examination.
(c) the higher commercial examination.

	1960	1965	1970	1975	1977	Index 1977 (1960 = 100)
University studies						
Natural sciences	350	720	1,010	1,890	1,750	500
Social sciences	380	1,240	1,470	2,430	2,120	560
Humanities and theology	570	1,930	3,020	4,070	2,960	520
Medicine	470	1,030	1,100	1,470	870	180
Specialized studies at various colleges/ universities						
Technical University and Academy of Engineers	560	800	1,080	1,070	1,020	180
Schools of architecture	70	170	550	450	520	740
Pharmacy, dentistry, veterinary medicine, agriculture, dairy, horticulture, forestry, food science	600	710	610	750	730	120
Business administration	160	320	580	860	940	590
Modern languages, correspondence and interpretation	300	480	450	1,480	1,530	510
Other studies						
Engineering colleges (*Teknika*)	1,620	870	1,100	780	690	40
Teachers' colleges	2,470	3,220	3,480	3,600	3,060	120
Other types of education	370	470	830	1,260	1,310	350
TOTAL	7,920	11,960	15,280	20,110	17,500	220

Table 7: **Admission to further and higher education 1960–77**

Applicants without formal examinations can be admitted after a concrete assessment of their qualifications.

As stated earlier there has been a great increase in the number of young persons attending such examinations, cf. Table 3.

Admission to further and higher education was open until 1977, with some exceptions, and as a result entry into further and higher education increased very much in that period (see Figure 7).

Regulation of admission

Admission to many different educational programmes has been regulated for a number of years because of limited capacity. Other types of education have had open admission, provided that applicants were able to meet the basic admission requirements. For example, admission to the schools of dentistry and midwifery has been restricted for decades while admission to the study of medicine was open. On the whole, admission to university studies has until recently been open.

By an Act of 10 June 1976 the Minister of Education was authorized to regulate entry to further and higher education under the ministry. For study programmes under two other ministries similar arrangements were authorized. The new authorization was applied the same year to regulate entry to the study of medicine. The following year (1977) a general system of regulation of entry was introduced, applying to studies of long duration under the authority of the Ministry of Education, the Ministry of Cultural Affairs (architecture and librarianship) and the Ministry of the Interior (physical and occupational therapists). Criteria were defined for the selection among qualified applicants if there were more applicants than study places. Maximum numbers of entrants — quotas — were fixed for each area of admission.

By fixing the quotas consideration is given to forecasts or estimates of the future needs for candidates, and also to the capacity at the institutions and to the geographical distribution of applicants and study places at institutions.

A co-ordinated procedure permits applicants to apply for admission to more than one institution or study programme and thereby increase their chance of being admitted.

The applications are screened to check whether the applicants fulfil the admission requirements. Admittance is granted to the institution/programme of study of higher priority on the individual's application if a place is available. No applicant is by the final allocation given more than one study place.

Study programmes of short duration are not included in this regulation system.

The institutions

Universities

For centuries Copenhagen University was the only university in the country. It was established in 1479.

In 1928 Aarhus University was established.

In 1964 Odense University was established.

Roskilde University Centre was established by an Act in 1970 and started functioning in the autumn of 1972.

Aalborg University Centre started to function in the autumn of 1974.

The universities and the university centres all come under the authority of the Ministry of Education.

Specialized institutions

Under the authority of the *Ministry of Education* the following specialized institutions are found:

— Denmark's Technical University, Lyngby (founded 1829)
— Denmark's Engineering Academy*, Lyngby (founded 1957)

- The Dental College, Copenhagen (founded 1888)
- The Dental College, Aarhus (founded 1958)
- The Royal Veterinary and Agricultural University, Copenhagen (founded 1856)
- Royal Danish School of Pharmacy, Copenhagen (founded 1892)
- The Copenhagen School of Economics and Business Administration (founded 1917)
- The Aarhus School of Economics, Business Administration and Modern Languages (founded 1939)
- Branches of Schools of Economics and Business Administration in Esbjerg, Herning, Kolding, Sønderborg, Varde and Aalborg*
- The Royal Danish School of Educational Studies, Copenhagen (founded 1856) and its branches* in Esbjerg, Haderslev, Odense, Skive, Vordingborg, Aalborg and Aarhus
- 59 Colleges of Education* (education of teachers for primary and lower secondary education, for kindergarten teachers, leisure-time youth leaders and home economics teachers)
- Eight Colleges of Engineering, Teknika, in Copenhagen, Aarhus, Odense, Helsingør, Haslev, Horsens, Esbjerg and Sønderborg.*

Under the authority of the *Ministry of Cultural Affairs* the following specialized institutions are found:

- The Royal Academy of Fine Arts, Copenhagen (founded 1754) with its three independent school departments:

  - The School for Architecture
  - The School for Visual Arts and Sculpture
  - The School for Curators

- The School of Architecture, Aarhus (founded 1965)
- The Royal Danish Academy of Music, Copenhagen (founded 1867)
- The Jutland Academy of Music, Aarhus (founded 1927)
- The West Jutland Academy of Music, Esbjerg (founded 1946)
- The Funen Academy of Music, Odense (founded 1929)
- The Northern Jutland Academy of Music, Aalborg (founded 1929).

Under the authority of the *Ministry of the Interior*:

- Schools for physical therapy and occupational therapy.

The Administration of the institutions for further and higher education
In June 1970 an Act on the administration of the universities was passed. By an Act of 30 May 1973 it was amended to cover both the universities and the specialized institutions. It is not applicable to the institutions under the Ministry for Cultural Affairs or the Ministry of the Interior. The Act was revised in 1976.

In the Act on Administration of Institutions for Further and Higher Education it is stated that these institutions shall aim at research as well as education up to the higher level within the main functional areas, which is entrusted to each institution by the Minister of Education.

The Minister of Education makes the regulations for:

- access to studies
- the study programme
- the obtaining of the degrees of licentiate and doctor

* These institutions do not carry out research, but utilize research results from institutions of higher education.

- the employment of teachers and research staff
- relegation of students.

Every institution is administered by a Rector in connection with a certain number of collegial boards and committees. The precise rules are fixed in statutes, which must be authorized by the Minister of Education.

The Rector represents the institution externally and is responsible for the daily supervision of its administration. It is his responsibility to see that matters are put before the relevant collegial board or committee when decisions are to be made.

The Vice-Rector deputizes for the Rector and assists the Rector in his tasks.

Assisting the Rector is an activity which is placed under a chief administrator, who must have had an education and training in the field of administration.

The konsistorium is the supreme governing body of the university. In addition to the *konsistorium* there is a council for research and studies for each of the various main functional areas within the institution. A main functional area may be sub-divided in two or more subject groups, each governed by a council, which takes over parts of the functions, which normally are within the jurisdiction of the council for research and studies.

The research activity within each functional area normally takes place within institutes. For each institute there will be a committee, which decides on the distribution of the tasks of the institute.

For every main functional area a central staff–student study committee is established. Such committees may also be set up for groups of disciplines, individual disciplines, lines or parts of a subject.

In the collegial boards or committees there are representatives of the teaching staff, the students and the technical-administrative personnel.

Study programmes

In most cases the study programmes resemble common Continental European study programmes. The periods of study are generally rather long. Most of them are of 5–6 years. An arrangement similar to the bachelor's degree is not found at the universities, but only at various colleges.

Output of candidates

University studies are calculated to last between 4 and 7 years.

The course of study at the various other institutions of higher education will in most cases take 3–5 years (cf. Table 9).

Employment

Candidates with further and higher education find employment in many jobs and professions. They also move from one sector to another. There is great variation according to the type of education. An estimate of the distribution in the public sector and the private sector is made in Table 8. Persons in liberal professions, such as lawyers and architects, are included in the column for the private sector.

Education and training of teachers

It is a characteristic feature of the education and training of teachers in Denmark that most of them are trained in separate institutions according to the level or type of institution in which they will become engaged, viz. pre-primary, primary or upper secondary.

TYPE OF CANDIDATE	PUBLIC SECTOR *per cent*	PRIVATE SECTOR *per cent*
Legal professions	60	40
Economic professions	75	25
Humanities	99	1
Natural science professions	97	3
Psychologists	93	7
Medical professions	65	35
Engineers	38	62
Architects	31	69
Business administration professions	20	80

Table 8

Teacher training at pre-primary, primary and lower secondary level
In 1980 there were 26 colleges of education aiming at the pre-primary level, 31 teacher training colleges for the primary and lower secondary level and some different, more specialized colleges, e.g. two colleges of education for home economics teachers. These courses are widely different with regard to content, scope and depth of the specialized subject matter, admission requirements, length and structure.

However, they have the following features in common: they are administered by the same Directorate; they combine the specialized aspects of the course and education theory and practice; and they give vocational qualifications immediately.

Kindergarten and recreation centre teachers
Admission to colleges of education for pre-primary level (kindergarten and recreation centre teachers) is conditional on the applicants being at least 18 years of age and having completed the ninth form of the *folkeskole,* supplemented with a higher preparatory examination in Danish and one other subject plus at least two years' vocational experience, or having an educational background which can be compared with these requirements. The educational programme lasts three years, including 28 weeks practical training, and comprises psychological, educational and social subjects as well as general, creative and workshop subjects.

Folkeskole teachers
The education of *folkeskole* teachers lasts $3\frac{1}{2}$-4 years according to the student's own choice. The practical training lasts 12 weeks. Admission is given on the basis of an upper secondary school leaving examination, Higher Preparatory Examination or a corresponding education.

The educational programme comprises common core subjects such as education, psychology, theory of teaching, social subjects, teaching routine, Danish, arithmetic and Christian studies and three of the following subjects: creative art, singing/music, physical education or needlework.

In addition, two general school subjects at an advanced level and a special study concerning either (a) the teaching of younger children, (b) the teaching of adolescents or (c) special education have to be studied.

Teachers at gymnasia *and at HF courses*
Teachers in upper secondary schools including those responsible for Higher Preparatory Examination Courses are normally university graduates who have undergone a short ($\frac{1}{2}$ year) professional

	FACTUAL	FORECASTS†	
	1976	*1985*	*1990*
Candidates from universities			
Legal professions	9,500	13,200	14,200
Economic professions	2,500	4,000	4,900
Other social science professions	500	3,000	5,500
Humanities	5,700	14,800	20,000
Theologians	2,000	2,200	2,400
Natural scientists	4,000	8,000	11,300
Psychologists	1,100	1,800	3,000
Medical professions	11,500	17,200	19,200
Candidates from specialized colleges/universities			
Engineers	37,400	49,200	56,600
Architects	3,000	5,000	5,800
Veterinary medicine, agriculture, dairy, horticulture, food science candidates	7,000	8,100	9,100
Dentists	4,700	6,100	6,800
Pharmacists	2,900	3,300	3,500
Business administrators	4,400	9,400	12,800
Correspondents, interpreters	5,600	16,800	24,000
Candidates from other institutions			
Teachers for primary and lower secondary schools	60,500	80,700	89,100
Teachers for home economics	3,200	3,300	3,200
Social workers	3,600	7,100	9,000
Librarians	3,100	5,500	6,800
Journalists	3,000	3,400	4,200
Therapists	5,700	7,400	8,200
Midwives	1,000	1,100	1,400
TOTAL	181,900	270,600	321,000

† The forecasts for 1985 and 1990 are based upon the number of students already admitted in the institutions and upon the planned numbers admitted in 1977. These numbers are in the calculations repeated in the following years.

Table 9: Total accumulated number of candidates with further and higher education

post-graduate course in educational theory and a period of practical teaching experience. At the university centres of Roskilde and Aalborg training in education theory and practice are integrated into the educational programme.

Teachers at vocational schools
In principle teacher training under vocational training has the same structure as the training of upper secondary school teachers, i.e. a relevant specialized training period and some occupational

experience form the basis of a practical and theoretical course in educational theory and practice which is offered by the School for Vocational Educational Studies (*Statens Erhvervspaedagogiske Laereruddannelse (SEL)*).

There are a number of different courses for teachers at the different types of vocational schools, e.g. a course for teachers at technical schools which has a duration of about 400 lessons in educational theory and a practical teaching period of about 80 lessons, and a course for teachers at commercial schools which includes about 225 educational theory lessons and 80 lessons in practical teacher training.

The courses are compulsory for teachers who are permanently engaged at these schools and have to be completed within 2-3 years after the first employment.

Teachers at institutions of further and higher education
Teachers at these institutions normally have a degree from an institution of higher education. They are employed on the basis of an evaluation of their academic qualifications, in most cases, with a special emphasis on their research qualifications.

Teachers in adult education
Adult education has always been in the hands of teachers from diverse backgrounds. Most teachers carry out this work as a seasonal job or as overtime work.

As mentioned earlier two-thirds of the education within this field is arranged by private promoters who often want to train their own teachers.

However, specialized subjects in adult education have as an experiment been introduced at some teacher training colleges. The Royal Danish School of Educational Studies also offers courses in adult education.

Further teacher training
Further teacher training of *folkeskole* teachers takes place at the Royal Danish School of Educational Studies, which offers shorter and longer retraining and further education courses as well as degree courses.

No such institution exists for the other types of teacher training, but SEL offers a full range of specific trade courses as well as basic and advanced courses in educational theory and practice.

As can be seen from the preceding description of the different types of teacher training they are rather different in structure and content and this makes it very difficult to go from one sector of the system to another.

The Government considers this to be a serious problem and they aim at making the system more flexible, and experiments are in fact going on in this respect.

Especially in relation to future changes within education for 16-19 year olds reforms within the training of the teachers of this group are urgent.

Numbers of teachers in different educational fields
The numbers of teachers in some of the largest educational fields in 1976-77 are shown in Table 10 below.

Youth and adult education[18]
The basic and most characteristic feature of Danish youth and adult education is the principle of popular enlightenment through liberal studies, which is based on the ideals of N. F. S. Grundtvig about the popular right to participation in and influence on cultural life in the broadest sense of the words.

	FULL-TIME TEACHERS	PART-TIME TEACHERS	
		Number of Teachers	Converted into Full-time equiv.
Primary and lower secondary school	40,000	17,000	9,900[3]
Upper secondary school and higher prep. ed.	4,300	1,400	700[3]
Vocational education and training[1]	3,700	2,700	800[3]
Courses for further education	7,000	8,000[2]	1,800[5]
Folk high schools, continuation schools, etc.	2,000[2]	–	500[2]
Leisure-time education	200[2]	30,000[2]	1,500[2]
TOTAL	57,200	59,100[4]	15,200

1. Comprises teachers at technical schools and commercial schools only.
2. Estimate.
3. When converting the figures for part-time teachers into full-time posts the duty-bound teacher hours for full-time teachers of the different categories of teachers mentioned in the table have been used.
4. Excluding teachers at folk high schools, continuation schools, etc.
5. Calculated on basis of information about the entire number of teaching hours for part-time engaged teachers.

Source: Information from the Economic-Statistical Division of the Ministry of Education.

Table 10

These principles have been normative for legislation on popular enlightenment and adult education in Denmark.

The tradition of freedom is also the basis of the Danish attitude toward state support for private schools, folk high schools, independent youth and continuation schools and for child and youth organizations, athletic associations, etc. Support in the form of public funds is given to these private initiatives regardless of the ideological background of the organizations or the promoters.

This also applies to general adult education. Two-thirds of general adult education is arranged by private promoters, of which the two largest are the Workers' Educational Association (AOF) and the Popular Educational Association (FOF).

The many different types of youth and adult education may be divided into:

(1) general youth education and youth education offering preparation for exams;
(2) voluntary youth and sport organizations;
(3) general adult education;
(4) adult education offering preparation for exams (recurrent education).

General youth education and youth education offering preparation for exams
As an alternative or supplement to the lower secondary part of the *folkeskole* education and to the general and vocational upper secondary education there are some other, different types of youth education, e.g. the municipal youth-school or one of the so-called private independent boarding schools (continuation schools, home economics schools, etc.).

The municipal youth schools
The municipal youth schools offer young people between 14 and 18 instruction in a very wide range of subjects and recreational activities.

During the late sixties and early seventies these schools developed into a supplementary source of leisure-time education and activities attended by almost 60 per cent of this age group, the majority of whom attended the regular school in the daytime.

Since implementation of the Education Act of 1975, the *folkeskole* and the municipal youth school system have worked especially closely together, particularly with regard to manual subjects but also on such subjects as geography, history and biology, making it possible to complete compulsory education after the seventh form by participating in full-time education in the municipal youth school.

It is also possible to sit for either the Leaving Examination or the Advanced Leaving Examination of the *folkeskole* in one or more subjects in connection with instruction given at municipal youth schools.

Youth school programmes also comprise basic vocational courses for young semi-skilled workers and special education for young retarded readers and for those suffering from mental or physical handicaps.

There are also special youth school programmes which are part of the effort to prevent or combat youth unemployment. These are often special courses held for youth of up to 25 years of age in order to improve their chances of obtaining employment. Special arrangements for vocational and educational guidance for this age group have been established in many places.

Continuation schools

The continuation schools are mainly intended for young people between 14 and 18 years of age. They were originally residential schools for young people — mainly from the rural areas — where they could improve the knowledge they had acquired in the *folkeskole* at an age when they were too young to enter the folk high schools. These schools now largely function as an alternative to the eighth and tenth forms of the *folkeskole*, and are chosen by many pupils who do not feel at home in the general school system.

The instruction offered at these schools corresponds to the instruction given in the *folkeskole* and most of the schools hold the leaving examinations of the *folkeskole*. Furthermore, alternative recreational activities are offered in the pupils' spare time and much weight is put upon social life in the schools.

A number of continuation schools have been established where practical work is of great importance. About half of the time is spent on theoretical instruction and the rest on work such as forming or gardening, working in the kitchen, operating a printing press, salvaging or recycling waste products, etc.

In 1978/79 continuation schools had a total of more than 10,000 students — and their popularity is clearly increasing. One reason for the rise is that more and more pupils at primary/ lower secondary school level feel the need — after an unbroken stretch of 8–9 years — for a change of environment.

Home economics schools

Home economics schools are boarding schools for young people over 16 years of age; they are similar to continuation schools, but they offer theoretical and practical instruction in the field of home economics in addition to general education courses.

However, the instruction at these schools differs somewhat from school to school. Some schools only offer instruction in needlework, while others offer a course which is part of the basic vocational education programme in the field of food industry, and which prepares students for work as assistants and supervisors in industrial kitchens.

Some schools offer further education in these fields in the form of 20 week courses.

Agricultural schools[19]
The agricultural schools are another example of private independent boarding schools within a special field.

Until recently it was a characteristic feature of the agricultural schools that they offered education within an area where there were no public alternatives. However, it is now possible to take a basic vocational education within agriculture, horticulture and forestry. The most common type of education within agriculture is, however, still the education offered by the agricultural schools.

It might appear strange to describe the courses of education offered by the agricultural schools under the heading 'youth and adult education', as the education offered at these schools is more like a traditional vocational education.

The reason for placing them in this group can be found in the historical development of these schools. Their origin is to be found in the 'free school movement' inspired by the ideas of N. F. S. Grundtvig, and originally they were considered to be an alternative or a supplement to an ordinary folk high school course for young people from rural districts, as the schools offered instruction in both general and agricultural subjects.

The schools offer various courses within the agricultural area and some general subjects. Most of these courses are part of an educational programme – the green curriculum – which has been worked out by the farming organizations, the agricultural schools and the Ministry of Education in order to ensure a satisfactory education for farmers. Successful completion of this educational programme is a precondition for receiving government financial support for the purchase and establishment of a farm.

Included in the group of agricultural schools are one dairy school and three horticultural schools.

Administration
Anyone who so wishes can take the initiative of establishing a private boarding school, and if certain rules are fulfilled (e.g. the school must be private and self-governing), the school can be approved by the Ministry of Education, and receive state grants covering up to 85 per cent of the operational cost connected with educational activities, as well as loans on favourable terms for the initial expenditure.

These rules apply to the above-mentioned continuation schools, home economics schools and agricultural schools, as well as to the folk high schools which are mentioned below.

Instruction at these types of schools is not totally free of charge. A minimum price for attendance is fixed by the Ministry of Education each year as a basis for fixing the amount of educational support which can be offered to the students who attend. It is possible to obtain both state and municipal support, depending on the income of the parents and the students.

The administration of the municipal youth schools comes under the municipal councils and the local education authorities, and no fees are charged for attendance.

Voluntary youth and sports organizations
Parallel to the institutionalized education system, non-formal education for youth and adults in leisure-time activities is for the most part provided by youth and sports associations or voluntary youth organizations. More than two thirds of all children and youth are members of these organizations, whose total number of work-hours, on a voluntary, non-paid basis, for the 7-17 year age group amounts to one quarter of that of the *folkeskole*.

The sports organizations
Today about 20 per cent of the total population of 5 million in Denmark is organized in one of four different voluntary national sports associations.

In close co-operation with the folk high schools, local sports clubs consider physical education as part of a general socio-cultural educational programme, and since the last part of the eighteenth century these clubs have been an important factor in the cultural life in the rural districts of Denmark.

Youth organizations

There are also more than 50 youth organizations offering leisure-time activities for children and youth — or representing the interests of certain groups of adolescents. Most of these organizations are based on political or religious ideas.

In addition to the very comprehensive and varied opportunities they provide, youth organizations have other common features, such as a democratic structure, which is built on the influence and participation of the members in the decision making process. The value and strength of these organizations lie among other things in the fact that participants come voluntarily, and that members experience a meaningful context in which to select, plan and perform their own activities. They become part of a process which meets the needs for being together, for development, for being accepted and for influencing one's own situation.

State support

There are two separate approaches to financial support for these organizations:

(1) According to the Football Pools Act (revised in 1976) a certain percentage of the surplus of the Danish Football Pools is given to such organizations — with four fifths to the sports associations and one fifth to the youth organizations. In 1979 the total sum of this grant was about 120 million D.kr.

(2) In 1954 the Act on leisure-time education introduced a system of public support for local youth and sports organizations and for the training of leaders.

According to the latest revised Act (1969) local public facilities (schools, etc.) must be put at the disposal of these organizations free of charge. Likewise, the organizations are guaranteed certain remunerations of the expenses of facilities which they own or rent. They get grants for leader training and employment of youth consultants.

In 1979 the government expenditure totalled about 50 million D.kr.

Expenditures from local authorities to youth and sports organizations totalled more than 450 million D.kr over and above the costs of providing the public facilities free of charge.

In spite of this public support the main part of the expenses of the organizations is borne by the organizations themselves by participants' subscriptions or fees, or by local and national fundraising campaigns.

General adult education

Folk high schools

For many years the folk high schools were used almost purely by young people from the rural areas. This situation has changed lately, one of the reasons being, of course, that the population in the rural areas has been constantly diminishing. Another reason is the growing trend for young people from the cities to apply for these courses in order to improve their knowledge in one or more fields, or — which may be said to be equally important — to spend a period concentrating on acquiring general education and information.

Folk high schools are completely free to draw up their own curricula, the sole condition for obtaining state recognition being that the education must be of a general, all-round character.

There are no entrance or leaving examinations, and no leaving certificates. The most frequent subjects are Danish, particularly Danish literature, history, social affairs, foreign affairs, foreign languages, psychology and musical appreciation.

Practical work plays an increasingly large part in the courses. Several folk high schools have specialized in physical education and sport in close connection with voluntary youth movements. In recent years special schools for retired people have been started.

There are about 85 of these residential schools, with courses varying from vacation courses of one week to regular courses of up to 10 months.

Most folk high schools receive students from the age of $17\frac{1}{2}$. However, some schools have a high age limit for entrance (18, 19, 20 and 25) and a few so-called *ungdomshøjskoler* – youth high schools – receive students between 17–19 years of age. Other schools have special courses for elderly people (*pensionisthøjskoler*).

The number of students in a year attending regular folk high school courses for 5–8 months is approximately 10,000, while the number of participants in the short courses is approximately 32,000.

Other types of general adult education

Every town and most rural districts have for many years had evening schools (*aftenskoler*) in winter for adults. The subjects taught cover a wide field. The law permits evening classes to be arranged on any subject appealing to adults in their spare time. The subjects may be general school, cultural or social, manual or vocational.

Attendance is on one, sometimes two evenings a week. Students pay an enrolment fee, plus, for certain subjects, a sum totalling about one quarter of the teacher's fee. Teachers at evening schools are only to a limited extent formally trained teachers, anyone whose qualifications are approved by the local authorities being accepted. The central and local governments contribute, according to the subjects, three-quarters or the whole of the teacher's fees, and the authorities must make premises available.

Besides evening schools proper, which have a very long tradition, many other forms of education are provided. They include evening folk high schools with a more advanced and non-vocational, non-practical slant. The subjects are restricted to the arts and social and scientific questions. Other forms of spare-time education are study circles, special education for the handicapped and vocational courses where the needs are not covered by other legislation. It is also possible to set up interest groups, e.g. with special interests in practical and arts subjects.

Lecture series can likewise be organized with public support. Grants can be obtained for various cultural arrangements, lectures, art shows, concerts, etc.

A special form of voluntary education is the university extra-mural course (*folkeuniversitetsvirksomhed*), in which representatives of the universities co-operate with educational associations throughout the country in organizing education to spread a knowledge of scientific methods and results.

Voluntary education may be arranged by private sponsors or by municipal authorities. The private groups are often organized by one or other of the large educational associations, of which the oldest, and still the biggest, is the Workers' Educational Association (*Arbejdernes Oplysningsforbund*) founded in 1924 and affiliated to the Social Democratic Party and the trades unions. The second largest is the Popular Educational Association (*Folkeligt Oplysningsforbund*), founded in 1947 on the initiative of circles close to the Conservative Party. Several other educational associations have similarly been established in more or less close association with political organizations.

There is a very large public response to the various forms of voluntary education. The annual attendance is about 600,000 (the population of Denmark is about 5,000,000).

Another aspect of education in Denmark is the increasing use of radio, TV, correspondence courses and evening school – and combinations of these. In addition, experiments have been going on with a scheme to reach sections of the population who do not normally participate in voluntary education and other leisure activities. A number of experimental models are being tested.

Administration

The overall planning and administration of general adult education comes under the Directorate for Primary and Lower Secondary Education, Youth and Adult Education and Teacher Training Colleges.

At the local level the municipal councils are responsible for the administration. They are, however, assisted by adult education boards, on which the consumers are represented.

General adult education is partly financed by the State and partly by the local authorities (each pay three-eighths of teachers' fees). Furthermore, the municipalities are obliged to find suitable premises for the teaching.

The rest of the expenses are paid by the participants.

The folk high schools are administered and financed in accordance with the rules which apply to the other types of independent boarding schools.

Adult education offering preparation for exams (recurrent education)

Courses preparing for exams at the general lower and upper secondary school level
(*den prøveforberedende undervisning*)

In order to give the people who have only received a limited general schooling an opportunity to supplement this schooling in their leisure time a new Act was passed in 1977 which made it compulsory for the counties to establish courses leading to the leaving exams of the *folkeskole* and the HF exams, as well as a number of other educational awards.

The courses are arranged in such a way that it is possible to attend them both during the day time and in the evenings and to follow courses and take exams in one or more subjects at a time, and in this way, over a period of 2–4 years, to take a qualifying course.

Tuition and education at these courses are free.

The passing of this Act is a very important renewal of adult education, as it makes it possible for anyone who so wishes to return to the educational system and to take a qualifying exam without any costs.

The courses have already proved to be a great success and they are attended by more and more people. In 1977–78, 26,000 students attended one or more course at the *folkeskole* level and 16,200 attended courses at the HF level. The last figure has risen to 24,000 in 1978–79.

Vocational adult education

A number of retraining courses for semi-skilled workers have been established under the Ministry of Labour.

The courses, which are normally residential, are run at special schools for semi-skilled workers or at commercial or technical schools. Their duration is from one or two weeks to several months.

The courses are normally highly specialized within each branch; however, general subjects are also to be found in some of the courses.

Correspondingly there is a fairly comprehensive range of supplementary courses for skilled workers.

Furthermore, under the Ministry of Education a number of further commercial and technical education and training courses for adults are arranged.

Finally, it should be mentioned that many retraining courses are arranged by the different labour and management organizations.

Participation in youth and adult education and leisure-time education
Table 11 shows the number of course places in 1976–77.

EDUCATIONAL ACTIVITY

Labour market courses		66,783
Courses for semi-skilled workers	42,209	
Retraining for up-dating skilled workers	22,263	
Retraining for redeployment	325	
Special training for young people preparing for a vocation	1,986	
Vocational courses		69,692
State controlled examination in one subject	15,628	
State controlled higher examination in one subject	8,526	
State controlled special course (diploma in specialized business studies)	35,588	
Other public vocational training	9,950	
Leisure-time education preparing for an examination		89,752
Ninth to tenth class level	57,601	
Higher prep. courses, single subjects	32,151	
High schools etc. (free schools)		16,431
Folk high schools	9,483	
Agricultural schools	3,477	
Home economics schools	2,095	
Maritime, navigation and hometrade master schools (nautical schools)	1,421	
University extension courses		28,000
Other leisure-time education		1,103,871
General leisure-time education	551,598	
Lectures	61,863	
Special education	34,988	
Vocational courses	13,244	
Youth schools	142,178	
Interest groups for children and young people (approx.)	300,000	
Other vocationally slanted courses		120,000
Employer and trade organizations	10,000	
Labour organizations	30,000	
Private promoters	30,000	
Internal firm courses	50,000	
Various public retraining and further training activities		18,000

The figures indicate the total number of course places covered in the mentioned educational activities in the course of a 12 month period. In certain cases these figures will considerably exceed the number of persons who have participated in the educational activities, as one person can participate in several courses.

Table 11

The marking system (the 13-system)

The use of the marking system in primary and secondary education (cf. executive order of
4 February 1963, section 1, sub-section 2)
Marks given according to the 13-system are divided into three main groups: excellent, average and
doubtful (0 lies below these and is very rarely given).

13:    Is given for the exceptionally independent and excellent performance
11:    Is given for the independent and excellent performance
10:    Is given for the excellent but not particularly independent performance
 9:    Is given for the good performance, a little above average
 8:    Is given for the average performance
 7:    Is given for the mediocre performance, slightly below average
 6:    Is given for the somewhat doubtful but more or less satisfactory performance
 5:    Is given for the doubtful and not satisfactory performance
03:    Is given for the very doubtful, very insufficient and unsatisfactory performance
00:    Is given for the completely unacceptable performance

The leaving examinations of *folkeskole* are voluntary for the individual pupil. No particular
mark is required for having passed one or more of the voluntary leaving examinations (*Folkeskolens Afgangsprøve* or *Folkeskolens Udvidede Afgangsprøve*), which may be taken in a number of
subjects.

In order to pass *Studentereksamen* (Upper Secondary School Leaving Examination) or
Højere Forberedelseseksamen (HF) (Higher Preparatory Examination), the sum of all the marks
received must be at least 5.5 multiplied by the number of marks, and the sum of the two lowest
marks plus the average of the rest of the marks must be at least 13.

The use of the 13-system is intended to ensure uniformity in the evaluation of achievement
at the institutions where it is in use. Generally, marks given in the *folkeskole* and intermediate
education represent the pupil's achievement seen in relation to that of the peer group.

The use of the marking system in higher education (cf. executive orders of 5 April 1971,
no. 148 and 25 November 1971, no. 503)

13	
11	very good
10	
9	
8	good
7	
6	
5	
3	less satisfactory
0	

At institutions of higher education either a total average of 6 or in other cases a mark of at
least 6 in each subject is required for passing. Marks given at institutions of higher education
represent the student's achievement in terms of standards set by the institution in question.

Further information about the requirements of any particular institution must be obtained
through that institution.

Educational support (financial assistance)[20]

Statens Uddannelsesstøtte (SU) – State Educational Support – is given in the form of scholarships and state guaranteed loans from banks and savings banks to students over 18.

The scholarships are given according to the financial need of the applicant (this is dependent upon his own economic circumstances and upon the size of the taxable income and assets of his parents, in case of applicants under 22 years of age).

State guaranteed bank-loans are granted to all applying students, regardless of their financial situation.

Support can only be given to state recognized courses of education.

Educational support is normally not available for foreigners. However, dispensation can be given under certain circumstances, e.g. if the student has been resident in Denmark for a continuous period of at least two years immediately prior to the support period, or is the child of citizens of the other member countries of the European Community, provided that these citizens are either gainfully employed in Denmark, or have been employed as such, or carry out or have carried out work in this country in accordance with the rules of the European Communities as regards the right to establishment and the exchange of services. It is, however, a condition that the children have come to Denmark in connection with the activities of their parents and are still resident here.

Important educational bodies with special tasks

The Central Council for Education (Det centrale uddannelsesråd – *CUR*)
The council was set up in 1973 as an advisory body to the Government and naturally particularly to the Minister of Education in questions concerning the entire educational system in Denmark.

The four educational councils (Sektorrådene)
The four educational councils for the basic school etc., for post-compulsory education, for tertiary education, for youth and adult education etc. were set up in 1975 to assist CUR and to advise the Ministry in their respective fields.

The members of these five councils are decision makers and researchers, and as a result the way is opened up for mutual influence within all educational sectors.

In 1975 the Minister of Education asked the CUR to work out a comprehensive plan for the Danish educational system up to 1990, which could function as a basis for information and public debate and as a guideline for politicians and the Minister of Education.

This work was carried out in close co-operation with the four sector councils and in 1978 the CCE presented a very thorough report, *Danish Educational Planning and Policy in a Social Context at the End of the 20th Century,* the *U-90* report, which has indeed become the basis for public debate as well as a useful working document and guideline for the Ministry of Education.

The National Centre for Educational Resources (Landscentralen for Undervisningsmidler)
is an institution under the Ministry of Education whose task it is to register and catalogue all educational resources; to work as a co-ordinating body between the manufacturers and the consumers of educational material; to enter into contracts with Radio Denmark, the National Film Centre, and other manufacturers concerning the production, purchase and acquisition of educational programmes; to act as a distributor of films, tapes and similar educational aids to schools and other educational institutions; and to take care of the distribution of material to the county centres (Act No. 419 of 13 June 1973).

	Number
Primary and Lower Secondary Education, etc.†	
Primary and Lower Secondary Schools‡	2,272
Real courses	35
Upper Secondary Education, etc.	
Upper Secondary School (*Gymnasia*)	113
Courses leading to the upper secondary school leaving examination (*Studenterkurser*)	12
Higher preparatory courses (*HF-kurser*)	1
Post-compulsory education and leisure-time education	
Continuation schools	118
Youth boarding schools	3
Home economics schools	21
Folk high schools and youth high schools	85
Agricultural schools	27
Vocational Training	
Technical schools	54
Commercial schools	61
Schools for marine engineering	10
Teacher Training Colleges	
Teacher training colleges (for teachers for primary and lower secondary schools)	31
Colleges for the training of teachers for kindergartens and recreation centres	26
Colleges for the training of teachers in home economics	2
Degree Courses in Engineering	
The Technical University of Denmark	1
The Danish Academy of Engineers	1
State-recognized engineering colleges	9
Universities and University Centres	
Universities	3
University centres	2
Other courses of tertiary education	
The Royal Danish Veterinary and Agricultural University	1
Dental colleges	2
Royal Danish School of Pharmacy	1
Schools of economics, business administration, and modern languages and their branches	11
Schools of architecture	2
Academies of music	5
The Danish School of Librarianship	2
The Royal Danish School of Educational Studies	1
The Danish State Institute of Physical Education	1
Schools of social work	4

Table 12: *Continued*

	Number
The Danish School of Journalism	1
Schools of Physical Therapy	6
School of Midwifery Education, State University Hospital, Copenhagen	1

† Including private free schools, *reál* schools, and schools for the handicapped.
‡ Excluding upper secondary schools and courses leading to the upper secondary school leaving examination with departments of primary and lower secondary education.

Table 12: Total number of educational institutions 1977–78

The National Library of Education (Danmarks Paedagogiske Bibliotek)
is the main library for educational theory, schools affairs, educational psychology, and the psychology of children and young people. This library is under the authority of the Directorate for Primary and Lower Secondary Education, Youth and Adult Education, Teacher Training Colleges, etc. It is administered by a head librarian.

The Danish Institute for Educational Research (Denmarks Paedagiske Institut)
works with educational research, educational development and informational service in education.

The Danish National Institute of Social Research (Socialforskningsinstituttet)
The task of the Institute is to carry out policy-oriented research on a multi-disciplinary basis investigating social conditions in Denmark including social security and social services, working conditions and the social aspects of matters affecting family and youth, and living and health conditions.

Research Secretariat (Forskningssekretariatet)
Six national research councils are in charge of the administration of state grants for research projects. The Research Secretariat assists those councils in their administrative duties, and at the same time functions as the secretariat for the Planning Council for Research.

Royal Danish School of Further Teacher Training (Danmarks Laererhøjskole)
has the responsibility of providing further education for teachers from the primary and lower secondary schools and teacher training colleges and others who are professionally on an equal footing with them, as well as of developing and utilizing scientific research with special reference to the school.

	NUMBER OF PUPILS/ STUDENTS	ANNUAL OPERATIONAL EXPENDITURE PER PUPIL/STUDENT	TOTAL OPERATIONAL EXPENDITURE PER CANDIDATE
		D.kr	*D.kr*
Pre-school class	54,981	3,700	–
Basic school, forms 1–9	700,945	10,000	–
Tenth form	51,576	15,000	–
Upper secondary school, higher preparatory courses	56,411	18,000	56,000†
Independent boarding schools	15,647‡	17,000§	–
Vocational education: §§			
Commerce, clerical trades and public administration			
Apprentices	17,872	3,000	9,000
Basic vocational education	10,326	5,000	17,000
Construction industry: Iron and metal industry			
Apprentices	40,822	6,000	24,000
Basic vocational education	13,395	13,000	60,000
Food industry and service trades			
Apprentices	6,013	7,000	21,000
Basic vocational education	2,920	14,000	65,000
Graphic industry			
Apprentices	736	8,000	33,000
Basic vocational education	1,027	21,000	100,000
Kindergarten teachers and recreation centre teachers	6,303	16,000	55,000
Social workers	1,281	18,000	–
Teacher training colleges	13,373	22,000	109,000

† Contrary to what is the case for upper secondary candidates the operational expenditure for higher preparatory candidates also comprises instruction in the tenth form of the primary and lower secondary school.
‡ Converted into per year figures.
§ Government grants.
§§ Pupil figures are 'rolling figures'.

Table 13: Unit costs in the educational system: The level of annual operational expenditure for instruction per pupil/student, and the level of total operational expenditure for instruction per candidate 1977–78

	NUMBER OF STUDENTS	ANNUAL OPERATIONAL EXPENDITURE PER PUPIL/STUDENT D.kr	TOTAL OPERATIONAL EXPENDITURE PER GRADUATE D.kr
Courses at the universities of Copenhagen and Aarhus			
Theology	1,263	17,000	290,000
Social sciences	10,040	10,000	105,000
Humanities	19,531	11,000	
UC†	13,743		380,000
UA‡	5,788		210,000
Medicine	5,948		
incl. clinical training		48,400	481,000
exl. clinical training		37,300	370,600
Natural sciences	7,414	46,000	1,050,000
Institutions of Higher Education			
Danish MSc in engineering	3,249	72,000	530,000
Danish BSc in engineering (Danish Academy of Engineers and AUC)§	1,266	40,000	190,000
Danish BSc in engineering (state-recognized engineering college)	2,206	50,000	220,000
Royal Danish Veterinary and Agricultural University	1,574	74,000	560,000
Dentist	1,150	79,000	460,000
Pharmacist	637	42,000	300,000

† UC University of Copenhagen.
‡ UA University of Aarhus.
§ AUC Aalborg University Centre.

Table 14: Unit costs in the educational system: The level of annual operational expenditure for instruction per student, and the level of total operational expenditure for instruction per graduate

Notes

1. DENMARK, MINISTRY OF EDUCATION (1978). *U-90 – Danish Educational Planning and Policy in a Social Context at the End of the Twentieth Century.* See Bibliography, 'General Overviews'. Cf. also p. 60.
2. RØRDAM, T. (1965). *The Danish Folk High Schools.* See Bibliography, 'History'.
3. In this chapter the word 'municipalities' is used to designate the most immediate government authorities, urban and rural, on the local level.
4. ENGBERG, A. (1979). *Early Childhood – and Pre-school Education in Denmark.* See Bibliography, 'Pre-School Education'.
5. Cf. Act No. 313 of 26 June 1975 on the *Folkeskole,* Section 1.
6. DENMARK. MINISTRY OF EDUCATION (1978). *Vocational Studies.* See Bibliography, 'Primary and Lower Secondary Education'.
7. DENMARK. MINISTRY OF EDUCATION (1977). *Contemporary Studies.* See Bibliography, 'Primary and Lower Secondary Education'.
8. DENMARK. MINISTRY OF EDUCATION (1978). *The Aims of the Subjects taught in the Folkeskole* (Ministry of Education's Order of 24 September 1975).
   DENMARK. MINISTRY OF EDUCATION (1979). *The Aims of the Optional Subjects of the Folkeskole* (Extracts from the Ministry of Education's Executive Order No. 658 of 28 November 1975). See Bibliography, 'Primary and Lower Secondary Education'.
9. *Folkeskolens afgangsprøver* – the Leaving Examinations of the *Folkeskole* (LE) – and *folkeskolens udvidede afgangsprøver* – the Advanced Leaving Examinations of the *Folkeskole* (ALE).
10. JØRGENSEN, I. S. (1978). *A Danish Model for Special Pedagogical Assistance.* See Bibliography, 'Special Education'.
11. DENMARK. MINISTRY OF EDUCATION (1977). *Notice concerning the Teaching of Non-Danish-Speaking Pupils in Primary and Lower Secondary Schools.* (Ministry of Education Notice No. 199 dated 8 March 1976). See Bibliography, 'Primary and Lower Secondary Education'.
12. DAHLGAARD, L. (1977). *The Financing of Private Schools in Denmark.* See Bibliography, 'Primary and Lower Secondary Education'.
13. DENMARK. MINISTRY OF EDUCATION (1977). *Recent Development and Trends in the Educational System in Denmark.* See Bibliography, 'General Overviews'.
14. DENMARK. MINISTRY OF EDUCATION (1977). *Notice of Upper Secondary Schools and Upper Secondary Courses Act.* See Bibliography, 'General Upper Secondary Education'.
15. DENMARK. MINISTRY OF EDUCATION (1979). *Curriculum Regulations for the Gymnasium.* See Bibliography, 'General Upper Secondary Education'.
16. DENMARK. MINISTRY OF EDUCATION (1978). *Vocational Education and Training in Denmark.* See Bibliography, 'Vocational Education'.
17. DENMARK. MINISTRY OF EDUCATION (1978). *Trends in the Development of the Relationship between Theory and Practice in the Danish System of Vocational Training.* See Bibliography, 'Vocational Training'.
18. Leisure-time Education (Consolidation) Act, 1975.
19. DENMARK. MINISTRY OF EDUCATION (1978). *Agricultural Education and Training in Denmark.* See Bibliography, 'Vocational Training'.
20. Changes in the legislation on educational support are expected.

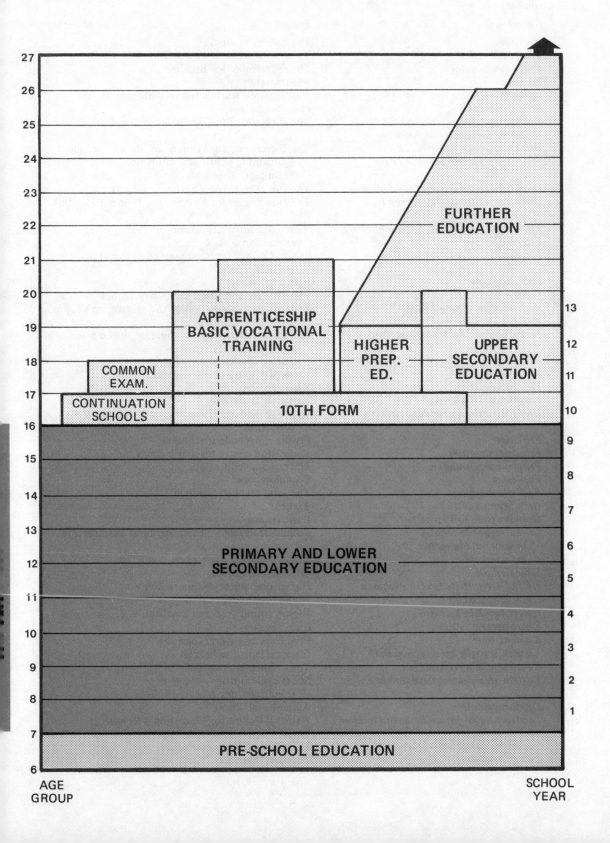

AGE
GROUP

SCHOOL
YEAR

88   DENMARK

Glossary

Danish	English
Amtsråd	The county council
Arbejdskendskab	Vocational studies (a subject in the *folkeskole*)
Byggedirektoratet	The Directorate for Building
Børnehave	Kindergarten
Børnehaveseminarium	Kindergarten teacher training college
Børnehaveklasse	Pre-school class
Direktoratet for gymnasieskolerne og højere forberedelseseksamen	The Directorate for Upper Secondary Education
Direktoratet for folkeskolen, folkeoplysning, seminarier mv.	The Directorate for Primary and Lower Secondary Education, Youth and Adult Education, Teacher Training Colleges, etc.
Direktoratet for erhvervsuddannelserne	The Directorate for Vocational Education
Direktoratet for de videregående uddannelser	The Directorate for Further and Higher Education
Efg (erhvervsfaglige grunduddannelser)	Basic vocational education
Efterskole	Continuation school
Elevråd	Pupils' Council (student council at the upper secondary level)
Folkehøjskole	Folk high school
Folkeskolen	The primary and lower secondary school
Folkeskolens afgangsprøve	The leaving examination of the primary and lower secondary school
Folkeskolens udvidede afgangsprøve	The advanced leaving examination of the primary and lower secondary school
Folketing	*Folketing* (Parliament)
Folkeuniversitet	University extra-mural courses
Forskningsråd	Research council
Forskningssekretariatet	Research Secretariat
(De) fortsatte skoleuddannelser	Upper secondary education, post-compulsory education
Friskoler	Private independent schools
Fritidsseminarium	Recreation centre teacher training college
Fritidsundervisning	Leisure-time education
Faellesfag	Common core
Faelleslaererrådet	The joint teachers' council
Gren (gymnasiet)	Branch
Grundkursus (folkeskole)	Basic course
Grundlaeggende tekniske eksamensuddannelser	Courses leading to a basic technical examination
Gymnasieskole	Upper secondary school
Handelsskole	Commercial school
HF (højere forberedelses-) eksamen	Higher preparatory examination
Husholdningsskole	Home economics school
Højere handelseksamen	Higher commercial examination
Klasselaerer	Class teacher
Klassens time	Free class discussion (period)
Klassisk sproglig gren (gymnasiet)	Classical language branch
Kommunalbestyrelsen	The municipal council
Kortere videregående uddannelser	Short-cycle further education (*i modsaetning til long-cycle f.e.*)
Landbrugsskole	Agricultural school
Landscentralen for undervisningsmidler	National Centre for Educational Resources
Linie (gymnasiet)	Line
Laengerevarende videregående uddannelse	Long-cycle further education
Laererforsamling	Teachers' assembly

Laererrådet	The teachers' council
Laererseminarier	Teacher training colleges
Laerlingeuddannelse	Apprenticeship training
Laeseplan	Guidelines to a curriculum (indicates what is to be taught)
Matematisk-fysisk gren (gymnasiet)	Mathematics–physics branch
Matematisk linie (gymnasiet)	Mathematics line
Modtagelsesklasse	Reception class (for immigrant pupils)
Musik-sproglig gren (gymnasiet)	Music–languages branch
Naturfaglig gren (gymnasiet)	Natural sciences–mathematics branch
Nysproglig gren (gymnasiet)	Modern languages branch
Obligatoriske fag	Compulsory subjects
P-fag	Practical subjects
Private skoler	Private schools
Prøveforberedende enkeltfagsundervisning for voksne	Single-subject courses prep. for an exam (for adults)
Paedagogikum	Teacher training period (practical + theoretical) for upper secondary school teachers given after the completion of a university degree
Realeksamen	Lower secondary leaving examination under the old educational system
Rektor (gymnasiet)	Headmaster
Rektor (universitet el. lign.)	Rector (university)
Restgruppen	The residual group
Samarbejdsudvalg	Joint consultation committee
Samfundsmatematisk gren (gymnasiet)	Social studies – mathematics branch
Samfundssproglig gren (gymnasiet)	Social studies – languages branch
Samtidsorientering	Contemporary studies (a subject in *folkeskolen*)
Skoleinspektør	Principal (primary + lower secondary school)
Skolekommission	The education committee
Skolenaevn	School board
Skoleplan	The school plan (indicates where schools are to be located within the municipality, boundaries of the school districts, the size and structure of the individual school and the number of teaching staff)
Skoleråd	School council at upper secondary schools
Sproglig linie (gymnasiet)	Language line
Statens Uddannelsesstøtte	State Educational Support
Studentereksamen	Upper Secondary School Leaving Examination
Svendebrev	Journeyman's test
Teknisk skole	Technical school
Tilbudsfag (folkeskolen)	Offered subjects (optional subjects which must be offered at the individual school) cf. *valgfag*
U-90	(The Report of the CUR – Central Council of Education on Danish Educational Planning in the period up to 1990)
Udvidet kursus (folkeskolen)	Advanced course
Undervisningsplan	The educational plan (the educational plan indicates the scope and content of instruction (the curriculum))
Undervisningsvejledning	Teaching guide (suggests how to teach a subject)
Ungdomsskole	Youth school
Valgfag (folkeskolen)	Optional subjects (subjects which *may* be offered at the individual school) cf. *Tilbudsfag*
Vuggestue	Day nursery
(De) videregående uddannelser	Further (and higher) education, tertiary education
Årskarakterer	Marks for the year's work

Bibliography

Where no publishers are stated the publications mentioned are published by and available through the Ministry of Education, International Relations Division, Frederiksholms Kanal 25 D, 1220 Copenhagen K, Denmark.

History

DIXON, C. W. (1959). *Education in Denmark.* Centraltrykkeriet: Copenhagen.233 pp.
RØRDAM, T. (1965). *The Danish Folk High Schools.* Det danske Selskab (in a new edition in German from 1977).
STYBE, S. E. (1979). *Copenhagen University, 500 Years of Science and Scholarship,* published by the Royal Danish Ministry of Foreign Affairs, Ill. 219 pp.

General overviews

A Survey of the Administration of the Educational System in Denmark. (1978). 43 pp. (j.nr. 91-10-1-77).
Administration of Primary and Lower Secondary Education in Denmark. (1979). 9 pp. (j.nr. 91-30-2-79).
Recent Development and Trends in the Educational System in Denmark. (1978). 18 pp. (j.nr. 91-10-6-78).
U-90 – Danish Educational Planning and Policy in a Social Context at the End of the 20th Century. (1978). Central Council of Education, Ministry of Education. 365 pp. Ill. (D.kr. 75). (Available through Schultz Boghandel, Møntergade 21, Denmark).

Statistics

DAHLGAARD, L. and MARKER, P. (1979). *Unit Costs in the Danish Educational System 1976–77, 1977–78.* Lauge Dahlgaard is Chief of Division and Preben Marker is Head of Section. 30 pp. (j.nr. 91-10-1-79).
MOLANDER, E. (1979). *Educational Statistics.* Statistical Material 1977–78 Relating to Courses (mainly under the Ministry of Education). Esbjørn Molander is in the Economic-Statistical Division. 15 pp. (j.nr. 91-13-1-79).

Pre-school Education

Children in Denmark. (1979). Edited and published by Det danske Selskab.
ENGBERG, A. (1979). *Early Childhood – and Pre-school Education in Denmark.* Agnete Engberg is an Educational Inspector. 10 pp. (j.nr. 91-31-5-79).
Starting School. (1977). Extracts from a report by the Committee appointed by the Minister of Education on 8 September 1975, on co-operation between home, pre-school, school and leisure-time activities for children in the 5–8 years group. 15 pp. (j.nr. 91-31-2-77).

Primary and Lower Secondary Education

Act on the 'Folkeskole'. (1978). (Act no. 313 of 26 June 1975, on the *Folkeskole* as amended in pursuance of Act no. 243 of 8 June 1977).
The Act on the 'Folkeskole' – in force from August 1976. (1978). (An information publication for parents). 24 pp. Ill. (j.nr. 91-16-1-77).
The Aims of the Subjects taught in the 'Folkeskole' in Denmark. (1978). (Ministry of Education's Order of 24 September 1975). 6 pp. (j.nr. 91-38-6-78).
The Aims of the Optional Subjects of the 'Folkeskole'. (1979). (Extracts from the Ministry of Education's Executive Order no. 658 of 28 November 1975). 4 pp. (j.nr. 91-38-6-79).
Circular on Foreign Mother Tongue Teachers in the 'Folkeskole'. (1978). (Primary and Lower Secondary School). (Ministry of Education's Circular of 27 January 1978). 2 pp.
Contemporary Studies. (1977). Primary and Lower Secondary School in Denmark. Guidelines to a curriculum and teaching guide. 65 pp. (j.nr. 91-38-2-78).
DAHLGAARD, L. (1977). *The Financing of Private Schools in Denmark.* Lauge Dahlgaard is Chief of Division, Economic and Statistical Division. 9 pp. (j.nr. 91-22-1-77).
Fact Sheet/Denmark Primary and Secondary Education. (1977). (Published by the Press and Cultural Relations Department of the Ministry of Foreign Affairs). 1 p. (Also available in German and French).

HELSTED, H. (1979). *The New School Act.* Henrik Helsted is Chief of Division. 10 pp. (j.nr. 91-30-2-77).

Information and Counselling. (1978). General Information about Educational Guidance and Careers. 9 pp. (j.nr. 91-46-78).

LASSEN, P. (1978). *Ethnographical Study-boxes as a Means of Inter-cultural Understanding.* Poul Lassen is an Educational Adviser. 5 pp. (j.nr. 91-38-ethn.-78).

Notice concerning the Teaching of NON-DANISH-SPEAKING Pupils in Primary and Lower Secondary Schools. (1976). (Ministry of Education Notice No. 179 of 8 March 1976). 6 pp. (j.nr. 91-30-1-77).

Provisions and Guiding Proposals Concerning the Teaching of ENGLISH as a Foreign Language in the Danish Primary and Lower Secondary School. (1978). 5 pp.

Provisions and Guiding Proposals Concerning the Teaching of FRENCH as a Foreign Language in the Danish Primary and Lower Secondary School. (1978). 2 pp.

Provisions and Guiding Proposals Concerning the Teaching of GERMAN as a Foreign Language in the Danish Primary and Lower Secondary School. (1978). 5 pp.

Provisions and Guiding Proposals Concerning the Teaching of LATIN as a Foreign Language in the Danish Primary and Lower Secondary School. (1978). 2 pp.

Resumé of Teachers' Guidance on Sexual Orientation in the 'Folkeshole'. (1971). 15 pp.

The School, the Pupil and the Parents. (1979). A guide to co-operation between the home and the School. (Extract from Ministry of Education's Teaching Guide *Skole, elev og foraeldre.* Ministry of Education 1977). 53 pp. (j.nr. 91-32-3-79).

Umwelterziehung in Dänemark. (1978). 14 pp.

Vocational Studies. (Arbejdskendskab). (1978). 7 pp. (j.nr. 91-50-1-79).

General Upper Secondary Education

Curriculum Regulations for the Gymnasium (the Danish Upper Secondary School). (1979).

Development in Danish Education of the 16 to 19 year olds 1973–1977. (1978). 7 pp. (j.nr. 91-41-4-78).

Notice of Upper Secondary Schools and Upper Secondary Courses Act. (1977). (Ministry of Education Notice No. 370 of 28 June 1977). 6 pp. (j.nr. 91-35-2-77).

The Danish Upper Secondary School System. (1977). Timetables for the *Gymnasium* and the Higher Preparatory Examination. 5 pp. (j.nr. 91-35-1-77).

Vocational Education

Agricultural Education and Training in Denmark. (1978). 9 pp. (j.nr. 91-44-Gen-78).

Trends in the Development of the Relationship between Theory and Practice in the Danish System of Vocational Training. (1978). (With special notion on the general studies in the basic vocational training system). 16 pp. (j.nr. 91-50-1-78).

Vocational Education and Training in Denmark. (1978). 46 pp. (j.nr. 91-46-78).

Youth and Adult Education

Fact Sheet/Denmark, Danes flock to adult-education classes. Published by the Press and Cultural Relations Department of the Ministry of Foreign Affairs. 2 pp. (Also available in *German* and *French*).

Leisure-Time Education in Denmark. (1978). (The Leisure-time Education, etc. (Consolidation) Act no. 383 of 14 July 1975). 31 pp. (j.nr. 91-46-1-78).

Recurrent Education in the Nordic Countries. Published by the Nordic Council of Ministers, Secretariat for Nordic Cultural Cooperation, Copenhagen. 53 pp. NU B 1977: 18 E.

The Educational Council of Youth and Adult Education Etc. (1978). Contribution to the Preparation of U-90, First Part, (Aims — Principles — Reform Proposals). 74 pp. (j.nr. 91-41-3-78).

WESTERGAARD, K. (1975). 'Educational Leave in Denmark'. Extract from: *Educational Leave in Member States,* Commission of the European Communities. Collection Studies. Social policy Series — no. 26 Brussels, August.

Co-operation, Copenhagen. 53 pp. NU B 1977: 18 E.

Teacher Training (including further teacher training)

ANDERSEN, H. (1976). *The Royal Danish School of Educational Studies.* Henning Andersen is the Rector, The Royal Danish School of Educational Studies. 14 pp.
BELVENUIT, G. (1979). *Inservice training of Teachers in the European Community.* G. Belvenuit is with the Commission of the European Communities, Education Series No. 8. November 1979 pp. 113–24 on Denmark).
Foreign Teachers in Denmark. (1976). (a) Note concerning the possibilities of employment with the Danish *Folkeskole,* i.e. The Public Primary and Lower Secondary School. 2 pp. (j.nr. 90-68-79). (b) (1977). Note concerning the possibilities of employment in the Danish upper secondary schools, upper secondary courses and higher preparatory examination courses. 2 pp. (j.nr. 90-68-79).
'General Teacher Training'. Reprint from: *Denmark, An Official Handbook* (1974). Royal Danish Ministry of Foreign Affairs, Copenhagen. 2 pp. (j.nr. 91-62-1-77).
LØVE, T. (1978). *Training of teacher–councellors for the Danish Folkeskole.* Tove Løve is a Lecturer at the Royal Danish School of Educational Studies. 6 pp. (j.nr. 91-65-2-78).

Higher Education

Aalborg University Centre, a modern university. Published by Aalborg University Centre. 6 pp.
A Survey of the Engineering Courses in Denmark. (1977). 3 pp. (j.nr. 91-73-77).
CHRISTENSEN, P. R. and SVERDRUP-JENSEN, S. 'The Aalborg University Centre'. (North Jutland, Denmark). (Extracts taken from: *Paedagogica Europae* XIII, 1978–3. 43 pp.
Fact Sheet/Denmark, Advanced education (1977). (Published by the Press and Cultural Relations Department of the Ministry of Foreign Affairs). 2 pp. (Also available in *German* and *French*).
Higher Education in the European Community, A Handbook for Students. (1979). Published by the Commission of the European Communities. 175 pp.
List of Institutions of Post-Secondary Education in Denmark. (1977). 10 pp. (j.nr. 90-11-77).
Odense University. (1978). *Information about Odense University and Rules of Admission for Foreign Students.* Published by Odense University. 6 pp.
Roskilde University Centre. (1975). Educational Programmes and Patterns. Published by Roskilde University Centre. 16 pp.
The Administration of the Institutions of Higher Education Act. (1978). (Act no. 362 of 13 June 1973, as amended in pursuance of Act no. 328 of 10 June 1976). 15 pp. (j.nr. 91-10-2-78).
The University of Aarhus. Rules of Admission for Foreign Students 1979–80. Published by the University of Aarhus. 6 pp.
The University of Copenhagen, 1978. Published by the University of Copenhagen. 51 pp. (History, Structure, Admission, Instruction, etc.).

Special Education

Circular regarding the special education in primary schools of pupils with behavioural problems and pupils suffering from emotional disturbances. (1972). (The Danish Ministry of Education's circular of 4 February 1972). 8 pp.
JØRGENSEN, I. S. (1978). *A Danish Model for Special Pedagogical Assistance.* I. Skov Jørgensen is the Superintendent of Special Education, Ministry of Education. 22 pp.
JØRGENSEN, I. S. (1979). *Early Measures against Handicaps in Children.* I. Skov Jørgensen is the Superintendent of Special Education, Ministry of Education. 34 pp. (j.nr. 91-37-2-79).
JØRGENSEN, I. S. (Ed). (1979). *Special Education in Denmark.* Det Danske Selskab, Copenhagen.
JØRGENSEN, I. S. (1974). *Special Education of Pupils with Reading Problems.* I. Skov Jørgensen is the Superintendent of Special Education, Ministry of Education. 17 pp.
JØRGENSEN, I. S. (1977). *Special Education Within the Teaching Programme of the Primary and Lower Secondary School.* I. Skov Jørgensen is the Superintendent of Special Education, Ministry of Education. 14 pp.
Special Educational Measures Within the Legislative Sphere of the Ministry of Education. (1977). 14 pp. (j.nr. 91-37-1-77).

Diverse

Central Advisory Service for Educational Building. (1977). Collection of experiences, inspection of school buildings from 1972–1976. 13 pp.

Executive Order Concerning State Educational Support to Foreigners. (1976). Ministry of Education Executive Order No. 454 of 6 September 1976. 2 pp. (j.nr. 91-16-2-77).

Measures to Combat Youth Unemployment Taken According to the Employment Plan. (1978). Published by the Ministry of Education and the Ministry of Labour. 38 pp.

Main Points of Act no. 113 of 9 April 1975, on Danish State Educational Support. (1978), 2 pp. (j.nr. 91-18-1-78).

Sex-roles and Education. (1979). By the Committee on Sex Roles and Education, Ministry of Education. 106 pp. Ill.

The Use of the Marking System (13-system). (1978). 1 p. (Also available in *German* and *French*).

Bibliography

STEWART, F. E. and FRASER, B. J. (1973). *Scandinavian education.* A bibliography of English-language materials. New York. 271 pp. (Denmark pp 37–128).

FEDERAL REPUBLIC OF GERMANY

Summary

Compulsory education begins at the age of six for all children in the Federal Republic of Germany and as a rule continues for 12 years, i.e. nine years (in Berlin and North Rhine–Westphalia ten years) of full-time education and three years of part-time education. Leaving aside pre-school education (kindergartens, reception classes, school-kindergartens), the first stage in the education system is the primary school (*Grundschule*), which is attended by all children from the first until the fourth – in Berlin, the sixth – school year.

Primary school forms the basis for the secondary schools which provide a general education: the main school (*Hauptschule*), from the fifth, or seventh, to the ninth, or tenth, school year; the intermediate school (*Realschule*), from the fifth, or seventh, to the tenth school year; and the grammar school (*Gymnasium*), from the fifth, or seventh, to the thirteenth school year. In addition, all the *Länder* are experimenting with comprehensive schools (*Gesamtschulen*), for the fifth to tenth school years.

The fifth and sixth classes of all schools providing a general education are devoted to helping and guiding pupils with regard to their future school careers. In this respect the Conference of Education Ministers has concluded an agreement on what is known as the 'orientation stage'. The introduction of this orientation stage and the associated approximation of curricula of the fifth and sixth classes of all types of school make transfers within the system far easier and postpone the decision on a school career until the seventh class. The orientation stage can also take the form of a separate phase of education, distinct from any school type, as is the case in Bremen and Lower Saxony. Secondary school education does not then begin until the seventh school year.

After nine years of full-time education most young people take a course of vocational training or find employment.

From the tenth school year onwards the general secondary schools are joined by various secondary schools with a vocational slant which, after nine years of full-time education, every young person not attending a general secondary school (intermediate or grammar school) must attend at least part-time for a minimum of three years in addition to his vocational training course or employment. After ten years of full-time education an intermediate certificate of education is obtained at an intermediate or grammar school (or a main school in some *Länder*). This certificate entitles the holder to a course of training leading to more demanding occupations or to go on to a specialized higher-grade school (*Fachoberschule*).

Provided appropriate courses are chosen and the required final examinations are passed, secondary general and vocational schools are followed by university-level education. After 12 years of school education, a young person can go on to a specialized college (*Fachhochschule*), after 13 years to a university or equivalent institute of learning. Institutes of further education and adult education offer a wide range of courses for those who have completed their education.

Instruction in schools is usually given in classes of pupils of approximately the same age. But in certain subjects (languages, mathematics, science) courses at different levels are often given from a given year onwards (generally the fifth or seventh class). Whether a pupil goes up to the next class or stays down depends on the knowledge he has acquired and his performance during the school year. Performance is assessed by a system of marks and also, in the reorganized upper school level of grammar schools, by a system of points.

The curricula of the various schools are issued by the Education Ministers of the *Länder*. They are usually drawn up in special commissions, which include teachers and experts, on the basis either of the directives or outline directives adopted by the Conference of Education Ministers or of an agreement among the *Länder*.

The university year is normally divided into semesters. Depending on the subject area chosen, a course of study takes between six and thirteen semesters.

The successful conclusion of a university course entitles the graduate to begin a second phase of training, i.e. preparation for a post as teacher, judge or any other public service occupation, or to immediate access to an occupation in the field he has studied (chemistry, medicine, psychology, commerce).

Attendance at all state schools and universities is free. The educational aids required in schools are either given to pupils free of charge or lent to them. Where they are given to pupils, their parents are sometimes required to bear a portion of the costs.

Under the Federal Promotion of Education Act pupils of secondary general and vocational schools in their eleventh and subsequent years of education and university students are entitled, subject to certain conditions, to financial assistance from the State for the period in which the course of education for which assistance has been requested can normally be completed. Such assistance is granted only if the income and assets of the pupil or student himself and of those required to support him are not sufficient to meet the cost of the course of education.

Pre-school education

The pre-school education of three to five year old children takes place largely in kindergartens. Kindergartens are independent as to their organization and educational content and are the responsibility of the local authorities or private organizations. Attendance is voluntary.

In addition, some five year old children in some *Länder* attend preparatory and reception classes. All the *Länder* have taken special pedagogical measures to facilitate the child's transition to primary level, one particular aim being co-operation between teachers at the two levels.

Children of compulsory school age but not yet mature enough to go to school attend school-kindergartens, which usually form part of the primary schools.

Special kindergartens are provided for the educationally subnormal and for physically and mentally handicapped children.

Primary school (*Grundschule*)

The lowest stage in the education system is known as the *Grundschule*, or primary school, and is attended by all children for the first four, in Berlin the first six, years of their school education. The purpose and aims of the primary school are determined by its place in the school system: providing the basis for subsequent education while as far as possible taking account of the special abilities and interests of the individual child.

At primary school children are taught to read and write German and also the basics of subjects that will be studied in greater depth later: social studies, history, geography, biology, physics and chemistry. The curriculum also includes mathematics, religious instruction (in Bremen biblical history on a general Christian basis), music, art, handicrafts or practical work, and physical education. All subjects are compulsory. The school week consists of between 20 and 30 lessons, depending on age level.

Primary school teachers obtain their qualifications by attending a university for at least six semesters (in Bremen eight semesters) followed by a period of pre-service training of between one and three years. The university course and pre-service training conclude with state examinations.

Special schools

Special schools are designed to educate and train children and young people whose physical, mental and psychic condition does not permit them to attend general schools to receive the education and training to which they are entitled.

There are the following types of special school for:

the blind;
the deaf;
the mentally handicapped;
the physically handicapped;
the sick;
the educationally subnormal;
the hard of hearing;
the visually handicapped;
children with speech defects;
children with behavioural disturbances.

With the exception of special schools for the educationally subnormal and the mentally handicapped, all special schools use the curricula of general schools (primary and main schools, intermediate schools, grammar schools), but apply teaching methods and principles adapted to the nature of the children's handicaps.

The organizational form of special schools varies according to local conditions and the nature of the handicap: separate classes in general schools (primary and main schools), half-day and all-day special schools and boarding schools.

Teachers at special schools obtain their qualifications by attending a university for eight semesters and completing at least 18 months' pre-service training. The university course and the pre-service training conclude with state examinations.

Secondary schools

General secondary schools

Main school (*Hauptschule*)

The main school is a secondary school consisting of five classes (5 to 9) (in North Rhine–Westphalia six classes (5 to 10)), or three classes (7 to 9) (in Berlin four classes (7 to 10)) where the primary school continues for six years or where there is a separate orientation stage (Berlin, Bremen, Hesse, Lower Saxony). Main school leavers usually enter working life and attend a vocational school until they have completed their vocational training, for at least three years. At the same time, since it forms the basis for subsequent forms of education, it is closely linked with the vocational school system, in which other certificates up to the university entrance qualification can be obtained.

The curriculum of main schools comprises the following compulsory subjects: German, a foreign language, mathematics, physics/chemistry, biology, geography, history, work and social studies, religious instruction, music, art, politics, physical education (and, in Bavaria, theory of education and domestic science). Mathematics and foreign languages are usually divided into courses at different levels to allow for differences in pupils' learning capacities, to enable them to obtain certificates and to facilitate the transition to other types of school leading to subsequent education. The school week consists of between 30 and 33 lessons.

Teachers obtain their qualifications by attending a university for six semesters (in Bremen eight semesters, in Berlin six or eight semesters) and completing a period of pre-service training which at present varies in form from one *Land* to another and takes between one and three years. At the end of the university course and pre-service training state examinations are taken.

Intermediate school (*Realschule*)

The intermediate school is a secondary school which, in its standard form, spans the fifth or seventh to tenth years of compulsory education. There is also a three-year form of intermediate school for main school pupils who transfer to the intermediate school after the seventh year of compulsory education. In North Rhine–Westphalia a four-year course of this kind is widespread. Similarly, the standard intermediate school in Bavaria offers a four-year course only.

The intermediate school prepares its pupils for work in which they will be called upon to show a high level of independence, responsibility and leadership, predominantly in practical occupations.

Its curriculum differs from that of the main school in offering a wider range of languages (two foreign languages, one of them compulsory) and by endeavouring to go into subjects in greater detail. The school week consists of 30 to 34 lessons.

Intermediate school teachers obtain their qualifications by reading two subjects at a university for at least six semesters (in Bremen eight semesters) and then completing 18 months of pre-service training. The university course and the pre-service training conclude with state examinations.

Grammar school (*Gymnasium*)

Gymnasium is a collective term for all secondary schools of general education which take the pupil on to the thirteenth year of education and in which, provided his performance in the thirteenth year has been satisfactory, he takes an examination (the *Abitur* examination) which, if passed, entitles him to study at a university. The final certificate obtained at some grammar schools entitles the pupil to take any course of study; in other cases, only certain subjects or groups of subjects may be read. The traditional types of grammar school concentrate on modern languages, mathematics and science, or the classical languages. They have been joined by others that specialize in the social sciences, economics, engineering, the fine arts, agriculture, domestic sciences and textile engineering. In its standard form, the grammar school comprises the fifth, or seventh, to thirteenth classes, depending on the duration of primary school education. There is also a type of grammar school to which main school pupils can transfer after their seventh year, and other types for particularly gifted intermediate and vocational school leavers.

Working people can attend evening grammar schools, at which the school-leaving certificate can be obtained after a course of at least three years, and institutes at which the university entrance examination can be taken. The principal task of the grammar school is to prepare the pupil for the university entrance examination, i.e. to give him a basic academic education. Grammar schools also prepare pupils for demanding courses of non-university vocational training.

The compulsory subjects in the fifth to tenth classes of grammar schools leading to a university course in any subject are German, mathematics, biology, geography, music, art, physical education, at least two foreign languages, history, social studies, physics and chemistry. Religious instruction is a full subject in most *Länder*. The school week consists of 30 to 36 lessons, depending on the class and the *Land*.

The upper school of the *Gymnasium* begins after the tenth class and is no longer divided up according to type of *Gymnasium*. The basic features of organization of the new form of upper school are the replacement of the class system with a system of basic courses and advanced courses and the introduction of a new form of performance appraisal, a credit system.

The pupil remains in the upper school for a minimum of two and a maximum of four years, the year being divided into six-month terms.

The curriculum is divided into compulsory and optional subjects and comprises:

a. languages, literature and art;
b. social sciences;

c. mathematics, science and technology;
d. religious instruction;
e. sport.

The school week generally consists of 30 lessons, the ratio of compulsory to general subjects being about two to one. The chief compulsory subjects are German, foreign languages, the visual arts, music, philosophy, instruction in Christianity and other religions, current affairs or history/ geography/social studies, economics, mathematics, physics, chemistry and biology. The optional subjects may be the compulsory subjects already mentioned and pedagogics, psychology, sociology, law, geology, astronomy, technology, statistics, data processing, etc.

Within these two areas a distinction is made between basic and advanced courses. Basic courses consist of two or three lessons a week. Advanced courses provide a thorough grounding and understanding in the subject and a more specialized knowledge, including possible applications of the sciences and arts. Such courses consist of at least five and usually six lessons a week. The pupil must choose two subjects at the advanced level, one of which must be a foreign language or mathematics or a natural science. The *Länder* are also free to prescribe a third advanced-level subject and, if necessary, additional links in the case of the second and third advanced-level subjects and of courses and combinations of courses.

Grammar school teachers obtain their qualifications by attending a university for at least eight semesters and completing at least 18 months' pre-service training. The university course and the pre-service training conclude with state examinations.

Comprehensive school (*Gesamtschule*)

There are at present over 200 comprehensive schools in the Federal Republic of Germany, regarded by most *Länder* as experiments in a new organizational form of the first stage of secondary education. The comprehensive schools embrace the educational concepts of the fifth to ninth, or tenth, classes of the schools in the multi-stream system. In co-operative comprehensive schools the different types of school within the multi-stream system (main school, intermediate school, grammar school) continue to exist, but under one roof and a single school administration and with co-ordinated curricula, the aim being to facilitate transfers between one type of school and another. In integrated comprehensive schools all the pupils are taught together rather than being allocated to a given type of school. Subjects are taught at different levels, enabling pupils to obtain the various final certificates of the schools in the multi-stream system (main school, intermediate school, transfer after the eleventh grammar school class). Some comprehensive schools have an upper school, usually of the grammar school type.

Comprehensive school teachers obtain their qualifications in the same way as teachers at schools within the multi-stream system. They are therefore qualified to teach in a primary school, a main school, an intermediate school or a grammar school.

Vocational training schools

Vocational school (*Berufsschule*)

The vocational school (*Berufsschule*) is a secondary school attended by young people undergoing initial vocational training (see also section on non-school vocational training, p. 00), or in employment, having left a main school or another school providing a general education, but still required to attend a vocational school. The vocational school has the task of teaching its pupils general and special subjects while taking particular account of vocational training requirements. Vocational training is divided into an initial and a specialized stage, the initial stage taking the form of a basic vocational training year (*Berufsgrundbildungsjahr*), in which instruction is given full-time throughout the year, or of a dual system of in-school and in-firm training. About 40 per cent of teaching time is devoted to the general subjects of German, social studies or current affairs, economics, religious instruction and sport. The teaching of special subjects in vocational schools is attuned to the training regulations applicable to the various occupations. The vocational school is attended part-time, on one or more days of the week, usually for a maximum of 12 lessons a week, or for several weeks at a time (block instruction). Successful pupils receive a school-leaving certificate, which is awarded without a specific examination being taken and, in combination with a vocational training certificate (skilled worker's certificate or certificate of apprenticeship), gives access to higher schools in the vocational training system (specialized schools – *Fachschulen*).

The basic vocational training year (*Berufsgrundbildungsjahr*)

By a decision of the Conference of Education Ministers taken in 1973, 'basic vocational training year' is the name given to the initial stage of vocational training, which may take the form of a full-time school year. The aim is to teach general subjects (not related to a specific occupational area) and the theory and practice of occupational areas in the form of basic vocational training. The basic vocational training year forms the basis for subsequent specialized training in the occupations allotted to an occupational area. It caters for young people who have completed their statutory compulsory full-time education. They must opt for an occupational area. The curriculum comprises a section not related to a given occupational area and a section devoted to the theory and practice of an occupational area. Provided a pupil's performance in the basic vocational training year is satisfactory, it is credited to him as the first year of vocational training in the occupations making up the chosen occupational area.

The teaching staff of vocational schools and in the basic vocational training year are divided into those who teach general subjects and the theory of special subjects and those who teach the practical side. The former obtain their qualifications by attending a university for eight semesters, taking a course of practical training, usually of one year, and completing two years of pre-service training. The university course and the pre-service training conclude with state examinations. The latter obtain their qualifications by taking a course of initial vocational training, an advanced course at a specialized school and a course of basic pedagogical training at special institutions.

Specialized vocational school (*Berufsfachschule*)

Specialized vocational schools are full-time schools designed to prepare pupils for an occupation or to train them in an occupation and also provide them with further general education. Admission is granted to those who hold the final certificate of a main school or the final certificate of an intermediate school, depending on the object of the training. The duration of courses at specialized vocational schools varies according to the occupation in which the training is given and the ultimate objective. The minimum is, however, one school year. There are many different types of specialized vocational school, examples being the commercial school, child care schools and schools for technical assistants. Training at specialized vocational schools always ends with a final examination. At two-year specialized vocational schools, to which holders of the final certificate of a main school are admitted, a final certificate equivalent to that of an intermediate school can usually be obtained. The school week consists of between 30 and 35 lessons. The teaching staff obtain their qualifications in the same way as vocational school teachers.

Higher-grade vocational school (*Berufsaufbauschule*)

Higher-grade vocational schools are attended by young people who are still at a vocational school or have completed their compulsory vocational education. They provide a general education and a grounding in technical theory that go beyond what the vocational school sets out to achieve, the final level of education being equivalent to that required for the intermediate school certificate. The whole course comprises at least 1,300 lessons. Like specialized vocational schools, higher-grade vocational schools concentrate on various areas, these being general industry, industrial technology, commerce, domestic science, nursing and social pedagogics, and agriculture.

In addition to subjects relating to a specific area, all courses at higher-grade vocational schools include German, a foreign language, history and current affairs, geography and economic geography on the cultural and social side, and mathematics, physics and chemistry on the mathematical and scientific side. The occupation-oriented subjects in all specialized areas include economics and management science.

The training of teachers is the same as that of vocational school teachers.

Specialized higher-grade school (*Fachoberschule*)

Specialized higher-grade schools comprise two age-groups (the eleventh and twelfth classes), admission being granted to holders of an intermediate school or equivalent certificate. General subjects and the theory and practice of special subjects are taught, as pupils are prepared for the qualifying examination for admission to a specialized college having university status (*Fachhochschule*).

Such schools exist for engineering, commerce and administration, domestic science, social work design, navigation, etc. Practical training is provided in the eleventh class, i.e. in the first year, on four days a week throughout the year. In addition, there are at least eight hours of teaching a week. Those who have completed a course of vocational training can omit the eleventh class. In the twelfth class (second year of the specialized higher-grade school) 30 compulsory lessons in general and special subjects are taught a week. The compulsory subjects are German, social studies, mathematics, science, one foreign language and physical education. The general subjects are the same for all specialized areas. The teaching of general subjects accounts for at least three-fifths of the compulsory curriculum.

Teachers at specialized higher-grade schools are qualified to teach at a grammar school or vocational training school or have graduated from a university in science, engineering or economics and have had several years of practical experience in their respective fields.

Vocational grammar school (*Berufliches Gymnasium*)

Admission to vocational grammar schools is gained by holders of a suitable certificate from a first-stage secondary school (an intermediate school or equivalent). Teaching is concentrated on preparing pupils for the general university entrance examination. In all the *Länder* the specialized areas of 'business science' and 'technical sciences' are offered. A range of subjects at basic and advanced level enables the pupil to acquire the knowledge he requires to study at a university. Some *Länder* also offer other specialized areas and courses.

Specialized school (*Faschoberschule*)

The specialized schools build on an initial vocational qualification and provide a vocational training in greater depth and further general education. They train medium-level specialists capable of independently managing a plant or other unit in their specialized field (e.g. the crafts, agriculture or housekeeping) and of training new recruits, or of filling higher posts with clearly defined responsibilities.

Admission to specialized schools is granted only to those who have successfully completed a course of training in a relevant occupation or have equivalent practical experience. In addition, candidates must usually be employed.

Full-time courses generally last for at least one year. Some of the principal types of specialized school are as follows:

		Length of course
a.	technical schools	4 half-years
b.	specialized schools for economics	2 half-years
c.	specialized schools for domestic science	2 or 4 half-years
d.	specialized schools for social pedagogics	4 half-years
e.	agricultural schools	2 half-years
f.	higher agricultural schools	2 half-years

The training of the teachers is the same as that of vocational school teachers.

Non-school vocational training

GENERAL

Having completed their compulsory full-time education, most 15 to 18 year olds receive their vocational training by the dual system, i.e. in the firm and at a vocational school (see diagram on p. 109).

While the *Länder* are responsible under the Constitution of the Federal Republic for in-school vocational training, the Federal authorities bear the responsibility for non-school, i.e. in-firm, and inter-company vocational training.

Non-school vocational training (initial and advanced vocational training and retraining) is governed by the Vocational Training Act of 1969, which is comprehensive and applies throughout the Federal Republic of Germany.

This Act covers the vocational training provided in industry, agriculture and comparable non-industrial institutions, particularly in public service, the liberal professions and domestic service. In-firm training is supplemented in inter-company training centres, for which various bodies are responsible (e.g. employers' associations, chambers of industry, etc.). They usually cover those aspects of training to which adequate attention cannot be devoted in the firm, but which are required by the training regulations.

VOCATIONAL TRAINING CONTRACT

The vocational training contract is concluded between the trainer (the firm) and the trainee (formerly the apprentice) on the basis of the Vocational Training Act. The content and duration of the training and the examination requirements are laid down in Federal orders (training regulations). Training takes between two and three years, but usually continues for three years. Three-and-a-half year training courses also exist, however, for example in electrical engineering. At present, training can be provided in about 460 recognized occupations.

In-firm vocational training is governed by training regulations issued by the Federal Government, and teaching in vocational schools by curricula subject to *Land* legislation.

The training regulations governing in-firm training and the framework curricula for in-school training are drawn up by a co-ordinated procedure in accordance with a 1972 agreement between the Federal Government and the *Land* governments. This ensures a close link between in-firm and in-school training.

The object of vocational training is to provide a basic training in an occupation and the skills and knowledge required for that occupation.

PLACES OF TRAINING, TRAINING STAFF

The Federal Education Act establishes the principal criteria for deciding whether a firm is suitable as a place of training, i.e. the nature of the firm, equipment and number of training places.

In-firm training is the responsibility of trainers who must satisfy certain conditions before they are deemed suitable for the task of training. As a rule, they must have successfully completed a course of vocational training, have relevant practical experience and be at least 24 years old. A further requirement is a knowledge of vocational teaching, which in various sectors is defined in trainer aptitude regulations based on the Vocational Training Act.

QUALIFICATIONS

Training in a recognized occupation concludes with a final examination. These examinations are set by the Chambers of Crafts and Trades in the case of craft occupations, by the Chambers of Industry and Trade for industrial and trade occupations, and by the Ministries of Food and Agriculture in some *Länder*, by the Chambers of Agriculture in others, in the case of occupations in agriculture.

These chambers are independently administered organizations of the various branches of industry in the form of public-law entities to which firms and companies are required to belong. They act on behalf of their respective sectors and also, as in the case of training, on behalf of the State. The final examination is designed to establish whether the examinee has the necessary skills and the required practical and theoretical knowledge and is familiar with the material taught at the vocational school and forming an essential part of his vocational training.

The Vocational Training Act calls for at least one interim examination to be held during the vocational training in accordance with the provisions of the training regulations to ascertain what progress has been made. The examination board is composed of equal numbers of the employers' and employees' representatives and at least one teacher from a vocational training school.

The examination consists of a practical, an oral and a written part. A candidate is considered to have passed the examination if his performance in the various parts is at least 'satisfactory'. A certificate showing the result achieved is awarded. The examination may be repeated twice.

Successful completion of training is a condition for beginning an occupation as a journey-man, assistant or skilled worker at corresponding collectively agreed rates of pay, for acquiring the qualification of master craftsman by taking the appropriate examination after several years of practical experience and for admission to certain specialized schools of further vocational training, evening grammar schools and special secondary schools which prepare adults for university entrance.

FURTHER VOCATIONAL TRAINING

Further vocational training is taken both in and out of school. While in-school training follows on from a successfully completed course of vocational training and appropriate practical experience and teaches the knowledge required for the performance of activities in senior positions (specialized schools), the Vocational Training Act provides for examinations in further education in the case of non-school vocational training.

These examinations, which may be set by the bodies appointed by the Vocational Training Act (i.e. the Chambers of Industry and Trade and the Chambers of Crafts and Trades for the industrial sector), must meet the special requirements of adult vocational training.

To provide a basis for systematic and uniform further training and to enable it to be adapted to technical, economic and social requirements and their development, further vocational training, including examinations and certificates, may be governed, pursuant to the Vocational Training Act, by Federal orders (further training regulations).

VOCATIONAL RETRAINING

Vocational retraining is designed to provide the qualifications required for an occupation other than that for which the initial vocational training was intended. It differs from further vocational training, which follows on from previous vocational training or practical experience, in that a completely new and different qualification is obtained. Under the Vocational Training Act vocational retraining measures must satisfy the special requirements of adult vocational training.

The second educational channel

The 'second educational channel' covers institutes of education at which working adults can obtain certificates of general education. The schools concerned are evening main schools, evening intermediate schools, evening grammar schools and special secondary schools that prepare adults for university admission.

While classes at the first three types of school are held, as their names imply, in the evenings, the pupils of the special secondary schools are prepared for university entrance in day-time courses.

Courses at evening grammar schools and special secondary schools usually take three to a maximum of four years and conclude with the university entrance examination. Admission to both types of school is confined to those who have completed a course of vocational training or can produce evidence of at least three years of regular employment. Applicants must be at least 19 years old.

The curriculum of both types of school follows the pattern of that of the upper school of grammar schools.

Teacher training

Qualified pre-school staff

Qualified staff and assistants are employed in pre-school education. The qualified staff are usually state-recognized teachers and social education staff. Most of the assistants are children's nurses.

Social education staff are trained at specialized colleges (*Fachhochschulen*) and general colleges (*Gesamthochschulen*), both having university status (also at the university proper in Bremen). Their training is governed by *Land* legislation, which requires a three- or four-year course. In the case of a three-year course, the practical training takes place after the university course has been completed. Four-year courses include two semesters of practical training.

The training is completed with the award of a degree or diploma.

Teachers are trained at specialized schools or academies, the course usually lasting three years.

In most *Länder* entrance requirements include not only a certificate of intermediate education (e.g. an intermediate school certificate) but also prior vocational training. The first two years are devoted largely to theoretical training at a specialized school, the third to practical training supervised by the specialized school or academy.

Practical training is closely linked to theoretical training during the three-year course.

Children's nurses receive two years' training at specialized vocational schools. Most *Länder* then require one year's practical experience before granting state recognition as a children's nurse.

The training of staff for pre-school education concentrates primarily on educational theory, psychology and sociology, the didactics and methods of practical social education and the education of children and young people.

School teachers

Teachers are trained in the *Länder* at *university-level institutions* (universities and teacher training, art, music and general colleges with university status). Admission for all types of potential teachers is dependent on their having passed the *university entrance examination* after 13 years of school education. In most *Länder* training is geared to a given type of school (primary and main school, intermediate school, grammar school or vocational school). In some *Länder* it is attuned to the stage of school education (primary stage, first secondary stage and second secondary stage).

The course takes six semesters for teaching posts in primary, main and intermediate schools or the primary and first secondary stages and eight semesters for posts in the second secondary stage (specialized higher-grade schools, grammar schools, vocational schools) and usually eight semesters for posts at special schools. In Bremen eight semesters of training are required for all teaching posts. For all teaching posts the course comprises basic studies in education and special studies to meet the requirements of the type or level of school.

The course concludes with the first state examination. Those who pass this examination are entitled to begin the second stage of teacher training, or pre-service training, which is oriented largely towards the practical side of teaching. Candidate teachers undergoing their pre-service training do a limited amount of teaching in certain schools and then build on the experience they have gained in seminars. Depending on the teaching post aspired to and the *Land*, pre-service training takes 12–18 months.

The pre-service training similarly concludes with a state examination (the second state examination), which opens the way to an appointment in the school service with all the rights and obligations of a teacher.

All teachers are required to attend advanced teacher training courses.

Advanced teacher training is the responsibility of special institutes set up by the Education Ministries. It is designed to keep teachers in permanent touch with advances in the sciences and to enable them to obtain qualifications to teach other subjects.

Advanced teacher training courses vary considerably in content and duration. The institutes involved therefore regularly publish their extensive programmes to permit each teacher to make his individual choice of courses. In some cases, the courses are held during the afternoon or evening in the vicinity of the school but, on the whole, the courses take some considerable time and are held at central points where the teachers are housed and fed by the institutes.

To attend courses of this kind, teachers are granted paid leave.

University teachers

University teachers (professors, lecturers) do not undergo specific training in the Federal Republic of Germany. Their appointment as university teachers does, however, depend on their satisfying requirements which are laid down in the University Framework Act and the University Acts of the *Länder*. As a rule, the requirements are:

a. the successful completion of a course of university study;
b. teaching aptitude;
c. special qualification for academic work (generally proved by the class of doctorate) or artistic work;

and also, depending on the requirements of the post, either

d. additional academic achievements (generally proved by having passed the qualifying examination for lecturing at a university) or additional artistic achievements; or
e. special achievements in the application or development of academic knowledge and methods in at least five years of practical experience.

The universities

Structure of the university system

Tasks of the universities
The university-level institutions of education (universities, technical colleges/universities and teacher training, music, art, general and specialized colleges) are devoted to the cultivation and development of the sciences and arts in their respective fields through research, teaching and study.

They prepare students for occupations requiring the application of scientific knowledge and methods or the capacity for artistic creativity. Their tasks also include encouragement of the next generation of scientists and artists and advanced studies.

Types of university

Universities (including colleges offering courses in a limited number of subject areas)
At present the Federal Republic of Germany has 67 universities, technical colleges/universities and colleges specializing in a given field.[1] These institutes offer courses in every subject (medicine, natural sciences, engineering, the humanities, law, economics, the social sciences).

The fundamental privileges of the universities include the right to conduct research, to teach, to examine students and award bachelor's degrees, master's degrees and doctorates and to grant the qualification to teach at universities.

Teacher training colleges
Most students at teacher training colleges are trained for posts in primary, main and special schools, a distinction being made between training for primary schools and training for main schools. Following the reorganization of the school system, the training is geared in some *Länder* to school stages, i.e. the primary stage (first to fourth school years) and the various types of school in the first secondary school stage (main schools, intermediate schools, fifth to tenth years of grammar schools, comprehensive schools).

In view of the research they carry out in the fields of pedagogics and specialized didactics, some teacher training colleges have the right to award degrees (in pedagogics) and doctorates of philosophy and pedagogics. In Bavaria the former teacher training colleges have been incorporated into the academic colleges. In Bremen, Hamburg, Hesse and Lower Saxony all teachers are trained at the universities. North Rhine–Westphalia incorporated teacher training colleges into its universities on 1 April 1980.

Colleges of art
The state colleges/academies for the visual arts are devoted to preliminary vocational training in the arts, it being possible in some cases to take an examination (set by the State or the individual college) in subjects such as:

architecture, sculpture, stage design, design, glass design, the goldsmith's art, pure graphic arts, applied graphic arts, interior decorating, pure ceramics, pure art, applied art, pure painting and restoration.

After eight or ten semesters at some art colleges students are awarded the title of 'master student' for special achievements. Art colleges with the appropriate departments (e.g. in the teaching of art and practical work, theory of education and philosophy) also train *art teachers* for grammar schools and in some cases for main and intermediate schools, i.e. the first secondary stage.

Apart from vocational preparation, the art colleges' sphere of activities also extends to the development and study of artistic methods.

Colleges of music

The state colleges of music train students in all fields of music such as instrumental music, singing, composition, directing and musicology. Church music departments and departments for the teaching of music also exist. The training of intermediate and grammar school music teachers is primarily the reserve of these colleges. The universities are usually concerned only with the cultivation of the theoretical study of music. Some colleges of music are also colleges of the performing arts and train students to beome actors, singers or dancers.

General colleges (*Gesamthochschulen*)

The general colleges offer courses otherwise available at the universities, technical colleges/ universities, teacher training colleges, specialized colleges and, to some extent, colleges of art. Depending on the admission requirements for the various courses and what the students wish to study and are capable of studying, they may complete their studies after a shorter period, usually three years, or a longer period, usually four years.

Germany's first *correspondence university* – a general college – has been in existence in Hagen, Westphalia, since 1975 and at present offers degree courses in three subjects as well as a wide programme of other courses and further education.

Specialized colleges (*Fachhochschulen*)

The specialized colleges came into being in 1970/71 under an agreement reached by the *Länder* of the Federal Republic in 1968. They are designed to provide a scientifically and artistically based education by means of practice-oriented teaching to qualify the graduate to act independently in his occupation. As part of their assignment, specialized colleges may carry out their own studies and research and development work.

The courses offered by specialized colleges correspond in part to those available at universities and other colleges. But studies at the specialized colleges differ from university studies in being more practice-oriented and of shorter duration and usually devoting longer periods to on-the-job training. The vocational qualifications obtained at specialized colleges differ from university qualifications accordingly. Transfers from a specialized college to a university and vice versa are in principle possible if the applicable admission requirements are satisfied.

Special forms of university

In addition to the universities and colleges described above, for which, with few exceptions, the State is responsible and which are open to anyone satisfying the requirements for admission to the course of study of his choice, there are special forms of college to which access is restricted. Since 1973 the Federal Government has maintained armed forces colleges in Hamburg and Munich. Various branches of the administration have their own colleges for the training of certain categories of civil servant in law and public administration. These colleges have hitherto accepted students only to meet the requirements of their own organizations.

Other special forms

A special university-level institution is the vocational academy, theoretical and practice-oriented vocational training being provided in the academy and in in-firm training centres (dual system).

Training at vocational academies is offered as an alternative to university-level studies in Baden–Württemberg and Schleswig–Holstein. Those who have passed the university entrance examination are eligible for admission. Courses are available in business science, technical subjects and the social services.

Training lasts three years, after which successful students become qualified business administrators, engineers or social educators (followed in each case by the letters BA = *Berufsakademie* = vocational academy).

Further information can be obtained from the Ministry of Science and Art of Baden–Württemberg and the Ministry of Education of Schleswig-Holstein (for addresses see selected bibliography at end of chapter).

University entrance requirements

The general university entrance examination
Passing the general university entrance examination gives access to the study of any subject at any university-level institute of education. The colleges of art and music usually require additional evidence of artistic talent in the subject chosen. In the case of courses in the liberal arts such evidence may in certain instances replace the general university entrance certificate. For the specialized colleges a course of practical vocational training is required.

As a rule the general university entrance examination is taken at grammar schools after 13 years of education.

The university entrance examination in specific subjects
Passing the university entrance examination in specific subjects gives access to the study of certain subjects at university-level institutions of education. The examination is usually taken after 13 years of school education by pupils who have transferred from other schools to one of the special forms of grammar school (eleventh to thirteenth years) with a vocational slant, such as grammar schools specializing in women's occupations, agriculture or technical subjects.

The specialized college entrance examination
Passing the specialized college entrance examination gives access to specialized colleges and equivalent courses at general colleges. The examination is usually taken at a specialized higher-grade school (eleventh and twelfth years) after 12 years of school education.

Special criteria for admission to university-level courses in which places are limited
The number of applicants has for some years exceeded the university places available in an increasing number of subjects, and restrictions have therefore had to be imposed. In a state treaty the *Länder* have made the following arrangements for the allocation of university places in courses to which such restrictions apply:

For the time being, up to 12 per cent of university places are reserved for cases of hardship and up to 6 or 8 per cent for foreigners. A total of 7 per cent are also reserved for students doing a second degree, for those wishing to study for occupations for which there is a particular public need and for students transferring from specialized colleges. Most of the remaining places are allocated on merit, i.e. by reference to the average mark in the school-leaving certificate. The remainder are distributed to those who have waited longest since becoming eligible for admission to a university (seniority principle).

As this procedure has resulted in excessive demands as to past performance and in excessively long waiting periods in subjects for which there are large numbers of applicants (e.g. medicine, pharmacy and dentistry), the University Framework Act provides for a 'special selection procedure' for such cases. Under this procedure university places will be allocated on the basis of the 'level of qualification', as evidenced by the school-leaving certificate, and of the results of an assessment procedure (e.g. tests, practical work and interviews), although special quotas for cases of hardship, foreigners etc. will be retained.

Accordingly, in the 1980/81 winter semester up to 30 per cent of university places in the medical faculty will for the first time be allocated on the basis of the results of a test procedure combined with the average of the marks obtained by the applicant in his university entrance examination. Other places in this faculty will be allocated by the drawing of lots, the chances of winning a place being graded according to the average of the marks shown in the school-leaving certificate.

At the same time the allocation of university places on the basis of waiting periods will be phased out.

Final university examinations

Evidence of the successful completion of a course is provided in a state examination or a university examination (giving a bachelor's degree, master's degree or doctorate). State examinations are set by state examination boards, whose members usually include university teachers. The universities are authorized by law to set university examinations.

A *state examination*, for which the State stipulates the requirements, is taken for a relatively limited number of occupations: the medical profession (doctors, veterinaries, dentists), teachers, law, pharmacy and food chemistry. In some *Länder* the final examinations at specialized colleges are set by the State.

University examinations, giving access to other occupations, vary considerably. Originally degree examinations qualifying successful examinees for an occupation could be taken at universities only in economics and the social sciences. Since about 1960 it has also been possible to obtain a master's degree in the humanities and more recently a bachelor's degree at teacher training and specialized colleges. The distinction between examinations for a bachelor's degree and examinations for a master's degree according to subject area is now no longer a standard procedure at the universities, and both types of examination can now be taken in 13 subjects, including biology, geography, education, psychology and sociology, out of the present 69 courses leading to a bachelor's degree and 58 courses leading to a master's degree.

Courses at universities, technical colleges, teacher training colleges and general colleges culminating in the state examination, a bachelor's degree or a master's degree may be continued to doctorate level.

The students

Universities in the Federal Republic of Germany do not charge German or foreign students tuition fees.

All students must pay a social contribution (in Lower Saxony a contribution to the student administration) of varying amounts up to DM 50.

Reference has already been made (see Section 0) to the possibility of obtaining education grants.

On registration every student automatically becomes a member of the student body (*Studentenschaft*) in most *Länder*. The student body has the task of safeguarding the students' educational, social and cultural interests and of maintaining inter-regional and international student relations. The student body is represented by the student parliament or the student council, which is elected by the student body for two semesters. The student parliament or student council elects the General Student Committee (AStA), the executive organ of the students' self-governing body.

All universities have students' societies and groups of many different kinds.

Gifted students can obtain financial assistance from one of many foundations.

The German Academic Exchange Service offers scholarships for foreigners. In addition, the universities make scholarships available to foreign universities under university partnership schemes.

Note

1. 'Colleges offering courses in a limited number of subject areas' is a reference not to specialized colleges with university status but to the Medical Colleges in Hanover and Lübeck, the Sports College in Cologne; the Administrative Sciences College in Speyer and the twelve Colleges of Philosophy and Theology and Church Colleges.

Selected bibliography

Das Bildungswesen in der Bundesrepublik Deutschland. Kompetenzen − Strukturen − Bildungswege (1978). Published by the Secretariat of the Permanent Conference of the Education Ministers of the *Länder* of the Federal Republic of Germany, Luchterhand-Verlag: Neuwied.

Kulturpolitik der Länder 1977 und 1978 (1979). Published by the Secretariat of the Permanent Conference of the Education Ministers of the *Länder* of the Federal Republic of Germany: Bonn.

Sammlung der Beschlüsse der Ständigen Konferenz der Kultusminister der Länder *in der Bundesrepublik Deutschland,* Luchterhand-Verlag: Neuwied.

Berufsbildungsbericht (1980). Published by the Federal Minister of Education and Science. (Sole distributors: Gersbach & Sohn Verlag in Kommunalschriftenverlag Jehle GmbH, Isoldenstrasse 38, 8000 Munich 40.)

Bildungsgesamtplan, Vols 1 and 2 (1972). Published by the Federal and Land Commission for the Planning of Education and the Promotion of Research, Stuttgart: Klett.

Berich über die Entwicklung des Bildungswesens 1976–1978 (July 1979). Drawn up in preparation for the 37th International Conference on Education, Geneva. (Obtainable from the Secretariat of the Conference of Education Ministers, 5300 Bonn, Nassestrasse 8.)

Haupttendenzen der Entwicklung des Bildungswesens der Bundesrepublik Deutschland in den Jahren 1976–1978 (July 1979). Report drawn up in preparation for the 37th International Conference on Education, Geneva. (Obtainable from the Secretariat of the Conference of Education Ministers, 5300 Bonn, Nassestrasse 8.)

Heckel/Seipp: Schulrechtskunde (1976). Luchterhand-Verlag: Neuwied and Darmstadt. 5th edition.

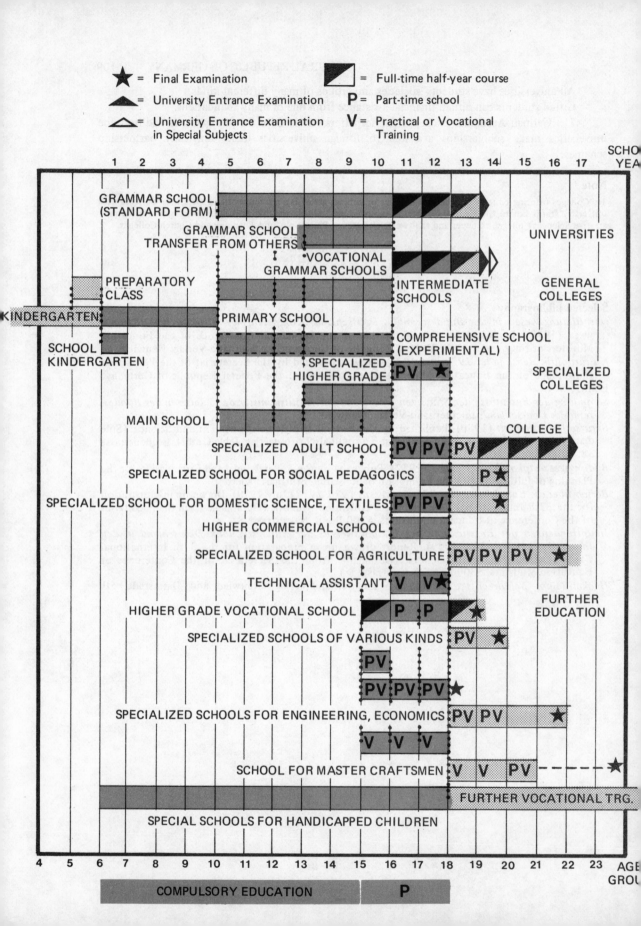

FRANCE

General principles

The Education Act No. 75 620 of 11 July 1975 redefined the aims and objectives of the French educational system, reflecting both *continuity in the principles* by which it is governed and the *need to adapt* to the development of society and the contemporary world.

The 'need for free public education, in successive stages, open to all citizens' was proclaimed in France in 1789. The laws enacted between 1881 and 1889, at the instigation of the Minister, Jules Ferry, organized public primary education with the aim of fashioning the man and the citizen. From these origins the French educational system has kept certain specific principles, laid down in the preamble to the 1946 and 1958 Constitutions: 'The nation guarantees the child and the adult equal access to education, vocational training and culture. The free and secular organisation of public education at all levels is a duty of the State'. From these principles have emerged a number of characteristics by which the French educational system differs from the other European systems:

— The rules governing the administrative and financial organization of teaching establishments, the content of the various subjects taught, the number of hours allotted weekly to each of them and the ways in which studies are certified, are based on provisions laid down at national level.

— Staff are state officials, with the exception of service and maintenance staff in pre-elementary and elementary education, who are paid by the local authorities.

— The State has the monopoly of the award of university degrees and diplomas, of the organization of examinations for the recruitment of officials or for entry into certain schools.

— Education is free in public schools and establishments. Assistance is given to families, in accordance with social criteria, for accessory expenses, by various means including education grants.

— Education is compulsory for children of both sexes living in France, from their sixth to their sixteenth year.

— Public education is secular, and religious education is not included in school curricula.[1] A day's holiday is accorded in the middle of the week, at present on Wednesdays, to allow families, if they so wish, to give their children religious education.

— Relations between the State and private educational establishments are governed by the Act of 31 December 1959 and the subsequent laws and regulations. Financial assistance is given to establishments which enter into contracts. Under the simple contract, which is the one generally concluded by private primary schools, the State takes charge of the remuneration of teachers on condition that they possess the requisite qualifications, whereas under the 'contract of association', the contract generally concluded by private secondary schools, under which the State pays the salaries of teachers and running expenses, the private school must provide education which is in conformity with public educational curricula, must employ teachers belonging to the public sector or who are bound to the State by contract, and must agree to their educational supervision by public inspectors.

The Act of 11 July 1975 reasserts the principle of the right of every child to obtain education designed to 'promote the development of his potentialities' and to 'prepare him for working life and the exercise of his responsibilities as man and citizen'. This education 'constitutes the basis of permanent education'. 'The State guarantees respect for the child's personality and the educational action of families'.

The task of the educational system is '*to promote equality of opportunity*', by making it possible 'for everyone to gain access to the various types or levels of education, in accordance with his talents' (Article 1). The Act reasserts the role played by the nursery school for children who have not reached compulsory school age in anticipating educational difficulties and compensating for inequalities. *Primary education* is given in the elementary schools; it is divided up into five successive stages. Emphasis was placed on the adaptation of education to the individual child's rate of progress, in order, as far as possible, to avoid repeating classes.

To this end, the Act also stipulates that: 'All children shall receive secondary education in colleges'. 'Colleges shall provide a common course of education, divided up into four successive stages', of which the last two may include teaching additional to the common curriculum, some of which will be preparatory to vocational training.

The Act came into force at the beginning of the 1977 academic year for all children starting the preparatory 'cycle' (first year of the elementary school) or in the sixth class (first year of secondary schooling) and subsequently for each succeeding class.

Generally speaking, the reform introduced, which concerns all levels of education, is based on three principles:

1. The institution of a *common course of education*, together with a series of *options* and *help for pupils who have difficulties*;
2. A more balanced general education adapted to the modern world, a manual and technical education and a general education in the arts;
3. The setting up, through various councils in which staff, families and pupils participate, of a genuine school community in line with the school's greater educational independence.

Administration of the education system

Two ministerial departments – the Ministry of Education and the Ministry for the Universities – share the responsibilities of the former Ministry of National Education (1932–74), which itself took over from the Ministry of Public Education (1828). *The Ministry of Education* is mainly responsible for nursery schools, primary education and general and technical secondary education (colleges, *lycées*, vocational *lycées*), some post-secondary education (preparatory classes for the *grandes écoles*, advanced technical section), for school guidance and continued education.

The Ministry for the Universities has under its authority the higher education establishments subject to the Higher Education Outline Act of 1968, together with some engineering schools and university institutes of technology.

A number of institutions for general and vocational education come under other ministries: agricultural education comes under the Agricultural Ministry, probationary schools under the Ministry of Justice, while the Ministry of Defence runs the military schools. Most ministerial departments have set up advanced schools for the training of their senior officials and technical staff.

Finally, the school medical service comes under the Health Ministry and responsibility for physical education and sports comes under the Ministry for Youth, Sports and Leisure.

The central services of the Ministry of Education (see Figure 1)
The central department of the Ministry of Education consists of:

— the Minister, the Secretary of State and their private offices;
— the inspectorate general;

- the central services of the ministry;
- the attached public establishments.

The Department is also required to seek the opinion of central advisory bodies.

The Minister, a member of the Government, is the head of the services which constitute the Ministry of Education. He directs and supervises all public educational services, with the exception of those attached to other ministries. He exercises surveillance/or supervision over private establishments which provide education coming within his province.

The Secretary of State assists the Minister in certain specified tasks (decentralization, school buildings, international affairs, etc.).

The private offices are staffed with officials chosen by the Minister or the Secretary of State. They transmit to all services directives which reflect the policy of the Minister and the Government.

The central services of the Ministry consist of:

— *The General Programming and Co-ordinating Directorate* (Direction générale de la programmation et de la coordination – *DGPC*), responsible for drawing up the general action programme of the Ministry and for co-ordinating the studies and research work required to formulate education policy and co-ordinate the measures necessary for its implementation.

— *The Schools Directorate* which deals with primary education (nursery schools, elementary schools, specialized education schools), is responsible for staff (teachers and departmental inspectors), draws up the curricula and is in charge of the vocational training of the teachers.

— *The Colleges Directorate* determines educational policy at this level, runs the premises and facilities allotted to this category of establishment, is responsible for college teaching staff (PEGC) and takes charge of their training. It is also responsible for information and guidance services and for matters of private education at all educational levels.

— *The* Lycées *Directorate*, which is responsible for organizing and managing *lycées* and vocational *lycées*, for upper secondary curricula and examinations, for apprenticeship and for continued education.

— *The* Lycée *Teaching Staff Directorate*, which engages, administers and trains the managerial and educational staff of the establishments and the *professeurs agrégés* and certified teachers who teach in *lycées* and colleges.

— *The Administrative Staff Directorate*, which is responsible for administrative and service staff of the central department and outside services.

— *The General Administration Directorate* is responsible for the organization, equipment and running of the administrative services, for the use of the resources common to the various divisions and services of the Ministry of Education, for the school institutions and grants, and for staff welfare.

— *The Equipment and Building Directorate*, which deals with all administrative and technical matters concerning school buildings.

— *The Finance Directorate*, which draws up the budget and co-ordinates its implementation, keeps the general accounts and is responsible for liaison with the Budget Minister and the Prime Minister (civil service).

Three services and one unit

Computer and statistical studies service;
International affairs service;
Information service and
Unit for cultural work in the school environment
These carry our their specific activities.

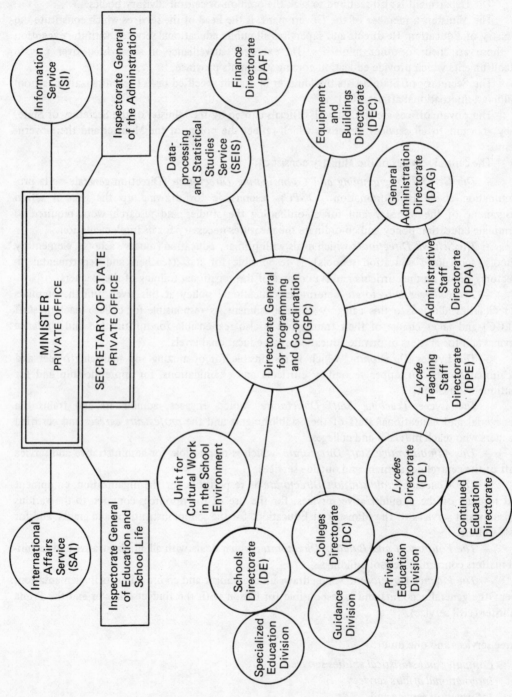

Figure 1 Organization of the central administrative department of the Ministry of Education

The administrative staff and general administration divisions and the computer and statistical studies and international affairs services are also available to the Ministry for the Universities.

The inspectorates general perform a variety of tasks in the services and educational establishments: supervision of operations and staff, but also, and more particularly, surveys, animation, liaison, studies, co-ordination and adaptation. There are two categories of inspectors general:

– *Inspectors general for public education* (inspecteurs généraux de l'instruction publique – *IGIP*) inspect the teaching given in the various subjects. They may also deal with the general aspects of the life of the school community or be given 'particular assignments' by the Minister;

– *Inspectors general of the National Education Administration* (inspecteurs généraux de l'administration de l'éducation nationale – *IGAEN*) have administrative and financial duties. They may perform these duties in the services and establishments of the Ministry for the Universities, as for those coming under the Ministry of Education.

The supervision and assessment of 'school life' are carried out by a joint group (IGIP and IGAEN).

The central advisory bodies are:

– *The Supreme National Education Council* which is composed of representatives of the administration and users and staff of the educational system. It has advisory functions on all matters of national interest concerning education. It also has judicial powers in disciplinary matters.

– *The General and Technical Educational Council*, which is consulted on rules, curricula, examinations, etc.

– *The Joint Technical Committees and Joint Administrative Boards*, which take part in the management of services and staff in the framework of the general civil service staff rules.

– *The Advisory Vocational Boards* are responsible for liaison with representatives of industry and the professions (employers and employees) and for the development and organization of technical education. Questions concerning several or all advisory vocational boards are dealt with by the Inter-vocational Advisory Board.

In addition, the specialized councils attached to other ministries are consulted as and when necessary. This is the case, for example, of the Council for Youth, Popular Education and Sport or of the National Council for Higher Education and Research.

Regional and local administration of education

The administration of the outside services of the Ministry of Education plays a particular part in the general system of the regional and departmental services of the State. There are two reasons for this:

(1) In the first place, most aspects of the management of the educational system do not fall within the scope of the promotional and co-ordinating duties of the state civil services exercised by the *préfets* of the *départements* and regions. The rules adopted in 1964 provided for:

– allocation of building subsidies to local authorities, which, in the majority of cases, own the educational premises;

– management of funds used to subsidize school transport services;

– management of school social welfare funds payable to families (grants and sundry assistance);

PARIS

VERSAILLES   CRÉTEIL

LILLE

AMIENS

ROUEN

CAEN

REIMS

NANCY - METZ   STRASBOURG

RENNES

ORLÉANS - TOURS

DIJON   BESANÇON

NANTES

POITIERS

LIMOGES   LYON

CLERMONT

GRENOBLE

ACADÉMIES
DES ANTILLES
ET DE LA GUYANE

GUYANE

BORDEAUX

GUADELOUPE

MARTINIQUE

TOULOUSE   MONTPELLIER   NICE

AIX-MARSEILLE

RÉUNION

DE LA CORSE

Map of the Academies, 1979

- allocation of the resources of the apprenticeship tax;
- contractual relations between the State and private education;
- generally speaking, all managerial action which brings together the educational system and local authorities.

(2) Secondly, the Ministry of Education has at its disposal a highly organized regional service (26 metropolitan Academies) (see map on p. 116), with the main part of the decentralized powers (since 1962), which has helped to strengthen this level of the administration directed by a *Rector*.

The departmental level is administered by Academy inspectors, in the name of the Rector; this level is less well endowed than the rectorate level.

However, under the policy of administrative decentralization, it is planned to establish gradually a better balance between these two administrative levels.

It should be noted that this situation is different from that of the other administrative branches of the State, for which the regional side is generally concerned with studies and programming, whereas the managerial tasks are carried out by the departmental directors.

An effort has, however, been made gradually to make the limits of the Academies coincide with those of the regional action areas. At present, this objective has been attained in all regions except three (Ile de France, Rhône-Alpes and Provence, Alpes, Côte d'Azur), which have two or three academies.

Administrative structure of the academy (see Figures 2 and 3)

The Rector, academy services.

In each of the 27 Academies, the Minister of Education is represented by a Rector.

The Rector is a senior official appointed by the Cabinet; he must hold a state doctorate.

The powers of the Rector, head of the Academy administration, have been strengthened by decentralization measures taken since 1962. Furthermore, the Rector has kept certain functions in the affairs of the two ministerial departments which, in the recent past, were part of the national educational system:

- the universities;
- youth, sports and leisure.

In primary education, the Rector opens and closes schools and classes; he appoints teachers and takes the severest disciplinary measures.

This situation is now changing, however, since it has been announced by the Minister and the Secretary of State that, in accordance with the Government's policy to increase administrative decentralization, decisions concerning the management of pre-school and elementary education would have to be taken up at *département* level; the Rector will only intervene to allocate resources between the *départements* within his province, at a fixed rate.

In secondary education, the Rector is responsible for the administration and general surveillance of the establishments in educational, administrative and financial matters. He shares out between them the posts which have been put at the Academy's disposal. He appoints and dismisses certain categories of staff, in particular college teachers of general subjects (*professeurs d'enseignement général de collège* – PEGC) and assistant teachers. He has responsibilities in the management of staff and is the authority for incurring certain staff and operational expenditure.

He oversees the private educational establishments and supervises those which have concluded a contract with the State. He awards grants, organizes examinations and presides over Academy councils and boards. He has powers in matters concerning youth and sports.

In higher education, the Rector is 'Chancellor of the universities of his Academy'. He represents the Minister for the Universities in the statutory bodies of these establishments. He co-ordinates higher education and other branches of education, in particular teacher training.

The following serve as advisers to the Rector:

- *The Chief Inspector of Technical Education* (inspecteur principal de l'enseignement technique – *IPET*)
- *the Academy Delegate for Continued Education* (délégué académique à la formation continué – *DAFCO*)
- *The Head of the Academy Information and Guidance Service* (service académique d'information et d'orientation – *SAIO*), director of the regional delegation of the ONISEP;
- *the regional engineer, adviser on school and university buildings*;
- *the regional medical inspector*, medical adviser;
- *the welfare officer*, welfare adviser.

In addition, the following assist the Rector for matters within their special fields:

- *the Director of the Regional Centre for Educational Documentation* (centre regional de documentation pédagogique – *CRDP*);
- *the Chief Inspector, Regional Director for youth, sports and leisure.*

The Rector has at his disposal the following advisory bodies:

- *the Academy Council*, which has administrative, legal and disciplinary functions;
- *the Academy Board for the school card*;
- *the Regional Grants Board*, etc.;
- a number of joint administrative boards and joint technical committees for staff management.

An Academy covers several *départements*. In each *département*, the *Academy inspector* is the director of the services of the *département*, which he administers in the name of the Rector.

The Academy inspector, director of the education services of the *département*, is selected from among persons holding the highest university degrees (doctorate, *agrégation*) or from among senior staff of *lycées* and teachers' training schools.

The role of the Academy inspector, director of the education services of the *département*, was strengthened as a result of measures for administrative decentralization in primary and secondary education.

In pre-elementary and elementary education, the director of the education services of the *département* has wide functions, concerning in particular the management of primary school teachers and their training. These functions were strengthened in 1979 through the introduction of several measures for administrative decentralization.

In secondary education, the director of the education services of the *département* assists the Rector in the administrative and financial supervision of *lycées* and colleges and in staff management.

Besides these functions, the director of the education services of the *département* has wide powers with regard to private education (surveillance and supervision, conclusion of contracts) and with regard to the other branches of education: youth, sports, permanent education, medical supervision, specialized education, out of school work, etc.

The director of the education services of the *département* may have the following officials attached to him:

- *an assistant Academy inspector*;
- département *inspectors of national education* (inspecteurs départementaux de l'éducation nationale – *IDEN*), who inspect public and private schools, nursery schools, elementary schools and specialized education schools. The *département* inspectors are recruited by competitive examination. They assist the Academy inspectors in the management of primary school teachers. They supervise the running of schools and classes. For this purpose, they maintain all necessary contacts with local councillors. They make a considerable contribution to the pedagogical aspects of education and the further training of primary school teachers;
- *the information and guidance inspector*, who co-ordinates departmental activities in this sphere and in particular the activities of the information and guidance centres (*Centres d'information et d'orientation* – CIO);
- *the inspectors of technical education.*

There are also, in many *départements*, Département *Educational Documentation Centres* (Centres départementaux de documentation pédagogique – *CDDP*), which take over from the regional educational documentation centres.

Among the advisory bodies at *département* level, should be mentioned:

- *the* Département *Council for Primary Education*, which has educational, administrative, legal and disciplinary functions. It plays an important part in private education (litigation and opening of private schools). It can take certain disciplinary measures against private primary school teachers and may impose a teaching ban against public and private teaching staff;
- *the* Département *Grants Board*, etc.

The bill on the extension of the responsibilities of local authorities now under discussion in Parliament (tabled at the beginning of 1979) provides for the institution of a single advisory body with wide functions in each *département* at *département* level.

Administration of schools

The final link in the administrative apparatus is the school. Pupils in the public education system are spread among more than 62,000 nursery and primary schools and 7,200 secondary schools (4,700 colleges, 1,100 *lycées* and almost 1,400 vocational *lycées*).

The heads of schools (*directeur*), colleges (*principal*) and *lycées* (*proviseur*) are public officials whose responsibilities are both administrative and educational. They are assisted in their task by statutory bodies: school council, establishment council.

In *nursery and elementary schools*, school heads are responsible for running their schools efficiently and organizing the life of the school community. They report on their work to the academic authorities.

They organize the teachers' timetable after consulting the teachers' council. They form educational teams. They assign pupils to different classes and groups. They help with teaching, particularly by advising young teachers. They are responsible for relations between school and the local authority. They see that the school rules are applied.

Every school has a teachers' council, a parents' committee and a school council.

– *The teachers' council* is composed of the school head (chairman) and all the school's teachers. It gives its opinion on the organization of the service. It is also consulted on problems concerning school life;

– *The parents' committee* is composed of the elected representatives of the parents;

– The teachers' council and the parents' committee may meet jointly as the *school council.*

120   FRANCE

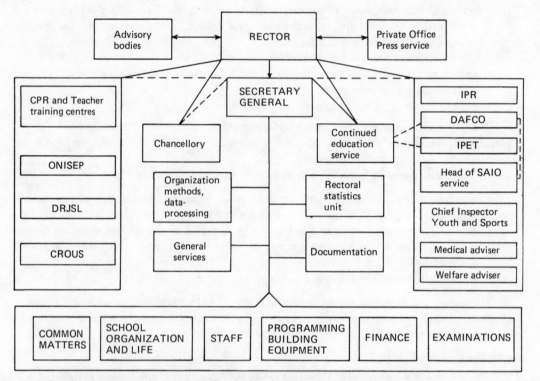

DAFCO: *Délégué académique pour la formation continue* (Academy delegate for continued education)

Chief of SAIO Service: *Service académique d'information et d'orientation* (Academy information and guidance service)

CRDP: *Centre régional de documentation pedagogique* (Regional centre for educational documentation)

ONISEP: *Office national d'information sur les enseignements et les professions* (National office for information on education and on trades and professions)

DRJSL: *Direction régionale de la jeunesse, des sports et des loisirs* (Regional division for youth, sports and leisure)

CROUS: *Centre régional des oeuvres universitaires et scolaires* (Regional centre for university and school works)

IPR: *Inspecteur pédagogique regional* (Regional inspector of education)

IPET: *Inspecteur principal de l'enseignement technique* (Chief inspector, technical education)

Figure 2 An example of the organization of a rectorate

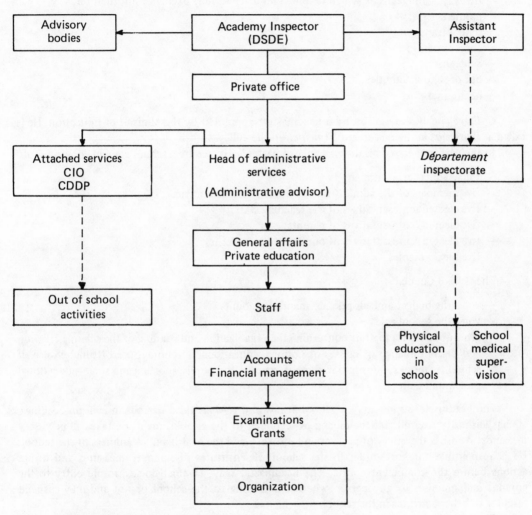

CIO   *Centre d'information et d'orientation*
       (Information and guidance centre)
CDOP   *Centre départemental de documentation pédagogique*
       (*Département* centre for educational documentation)

*Figure 3 An example of the structure of an Academy Inspectorate (*Département *education services)*

The chair is then taken by the school head.

The school council is consulted on the following.

- the school rules;
- the ways and means by which families and teachers may exchange information;
- nature classes;
- school transport;
- child minding;
- canteens;
- out-of-school activities;
- health matters.

Colleges and lycées are run by a headmaster[2] appointed by the Minister of Education. He is called a '*Proviseur*' in the *lycées* and '*Principal*' in the colleges.

In the performance of his duties the headmaster is assisted by a school council composed of:

- the headmaster, chairman;
- five members of the administrative authority and the services;
- five elected representatives of the teaching staff;
- five elected representatives of parents;
- five elected representatives of pupils (two in colleges);
- five local notables.

The School Council:

- votes the budget and adopts the financial accounts;
- votes the school rules;
- gives opinions on matters concerning the organization and running of the school: creation and discontinuance of classes or options, educational autonomy, use of time, choice of school textbooks, information of staff, parents and pupils, sporting and socio–educational programmes, etc.

The headmaster represents his school at law and *vis-à-vis* third persons in civil proceedings. He has authority over all staff belonging or seconded to the establishment. He takes all necessary measures to ensure the safety of persons and property and the health and cleanliness of the school. He is responsible for good order in the school. He institutes disciplinary measures and brings actions before the competent courts. The headmaster may, in emergencies, forbid entry to the grounds and premises to any person whether belonging to the school or not and may suspend teaching or other activities in the school.

The headmaster is helped in his task by an assistant who, if the headmaster is absent or prevented from performing his duties, assumes his responsibilities, including the chairmanship of the school's statutory bodies.

Various councils take part in the *life of the school community*:

- *the teachers' council* is composed of all the teachers of a class. This council meets every quarter to assess the results and aptitudes of pupils and to advise them in their work. It draws up a school report for every pupil and makes proposals for his or her guidance in consequence. The guidance advisor may participate in the work of the teachers' council;
- *the class council* discusses proposals made by the teachers' council. Two representatives of the pupils (class delegates) and two representatives of parents take part. The class council makes proposals for the pupils, particularly at the end of the third class. The education advisor, the guidance advisor, the welfare officer, the doctor and the nurse also

serve as members of the council when they have personal knowledge of the case of one or several pupils of the class;

— the education councils are composed of teachers of the same subject and are designed to promote the co-ordination of the teaching programme.

In the school community the representation of parents and pupils is of particular importance:

— *the parents' associations* are composed of the pupils' parents; they participate through their elected representatives in the school council. The *parents' delegates* also participate in the class councils and the Disciplinary Council;

— *The class delegates* are pupils elected by their fellows (two per class). They take part in the class councils and elect their representatives to the school council.

Funding of educational expenditure

The rules for allocating expenditure between the two main financial agents, the State and the local authorities, are as follows:

This is of course a very simplified breakdown. Since the characteristic of the French system for funding educational expenditure is that the contributions of State and local authorities complement each other, the rules governing the allocation of financial costs are necessarily complex.

Very broadly, the breakdown of state expenditure charged to the budget of the Ministry of Education in 1979 is shown in Table 3.

Structure of education

Education during the compulsory school period is open to all children of both sexes.

Pre-elementary and elementary education

(1) *Pre-elementary education* is for children from two to six years old. It is given either in nursery classes or, if there are none, to children over five years old in the infant sections of elementary schools.

The education given helps to develop the child's personality in all its forms, to train the child in the use of his various methods of expression and to prepare him for the education given later in the elementary school, without ever anticipating the work which will be done at that level (reading, writing, for example).

The nursery school plays an important role in the early detection and educational treatment of handicaps. Thus one of the four measures included in priority action programme No. 13, to 'ensure equality of opportunity through education and culture' (1976–80), is aimed, under the VIIth Plan, at the extension of pre-school education: in 1978–79 all children from four to five

| | STAFF | RUNNING COSTS | BUILDINGS | SOCIAL WELFARE | |
				TRANSPORT	GRANTS
State	Teaching staff 100%		State subsidy	State subsidy (63% on average)	School attendance grants (56,000 beneficiaries)
Local authorities	School upkeep and service staff	School running costs borne by local authorities	Local authority owner and contractor	Cost shared with families	At the initiative of the local authorities

Table 1: Nursery and elementary education (public)

years old attended pre-school establishments; the percentage for three year olds was 87 per cent (plan target 92 per cent) and for two year olds 30.7 per cent (target 45 per cent).

It should be pointed out that women teachers in nursery schools (there are still very few male teachers) have the same training and the same status as elementary school teachers.

(2) *Elementary education* must give children who have turned six in the calendar year, and, in exceptional cases, children who have turned five before 1 September of the current calendar year, a practical knowledge of spoken and written French, counting and simple arithmetic. It should enable them to acquire the rudiments of knowledge through a range of stimulation activities contributing to scientific, technical, artistic and physical education.

Education in the primary school consists of five successive stages organized in three cycles, the preparatory cycle, elementary cycle and intermediate cycle.

In order to foster steady progress and, as far as possible, to avoid repeating classes, provision is made for adaptation courses in the early stages of learning: reading, writing and arithmetic. This help can be given, in accordance with the needs of the pupils and for varying lengths of time, in all subjects or in only one of them. It must be fitted into the teacher's ordinary work and the time allotted to the subject. Special catching-up classes may also be organized, but only as an exceptional measure and for a short period of time. Finally, the teacher may have recourse to psycho-educational aid groups (*Groupes d'Aide Psycho-pédagogique* – GAPP) for more specific rehabilitation or support. The GAPPs are usually made up of a school psychologist and two rehabilitation specialists.

Children who cannot keep up with ordinary schooling, owing to physical or mental mal-adjustment, are put, after consultation of the *Special Education Boards* either into an adaptation class attached to the nursery or elementary schools, or into specialized classes attached to the schools for the mentally deficient, for children with motor and sensory handicaps or for children with behavioural disorders, or into highly specialized establishments when they suffer from particularly severe handicaps.

Secondary education

Secondary education comprises:
Education in colleges open to pupils who have completed the intermediate school cycle. The *lycées* continue the education given in the colleges by developing the pupils' general culture and specialized knowledge.

The *colleges* take in pupils who have completed the intermediate cycle of the elementary school. The pupils are assigned to classes formed, without any differentiation, for the school year.

	STAFF	RUNNING COSTS	BUILDINGS	SOCIAL WELFARE TRANSPORT	GRANTS
State	All establishments are, in principle, national	State subsidy to running costs accounts for about $\frac{2}{3}$ of expenditure	State subsidy (about 80% of costs)	State subsidy (63% on average)	1,745,000 beneficiaries in 1979 (+ free education in colleges)
Local authorities	In principle no compulsory contribution to staff costs	Contribution of $\frac{1}{3}$	Municipalities owners and contractors *de jure* since 1962	Contribution of municipalities and families	Supplementary grants by *départements*

Table 2: Secondary education (public).

EXPENDITURE ON THE PUBLIC EDUCATION SYSTEM	SOCIAL WELFARE IN EDUCATION	STATE ASSISTANCE TO PRIVATE EDUCATION
58,993 million francs	4,840 million francs	8,722 million francs
	(Finance Bill 1979)	

Table 3

Attendance at colleges is for four years. It is divided up into two two-year cycles. The *cycle d'observation* (sixth and fifth classes) and the *cycle d'orientation* (fourth and third classes).

To help children who have difficulties and to reduce the number of repeated classes, there is a weekly support class (included in the teacher's working hours and scheduled in the timetable) for each of the three basic subjects taught in the sixth and fifth classes: French, mathematics and a modern language. It is in addition to the common weekly timetable of 21 hours, which is supplemented by three hours of physical education and sport.

As well as this support work, there is *intensive* work for pupils who have no difficulty in keeping up with the lessons given.

The curricula include the traditional subjects (French – mathematics – modern languages – history and geography – natural sciences – art education) to which have been added new subjects such as elementary economics, physical sciences and manual and technical education.

In addition to the subjects in the *cycle d'observation* curriculum, the *cycle d'orientation* includes optional subjects; either Latin, Greek, or a second modern language on the one hand, and scientific options on the other.

Pre-occupational classes and *classes in preparation for apprenticeship* have also been maintained to enable older pupils, in particular those who have completed the *cycle d'observation* and who appear to want to take up a job at the end of compulsory schooling, to prepare for the choice of an occupation. On completing these classes, pupils may either: take up working life, acquire a vocational training (through an apprenticeship served alternatively under a supervisor and in an apprentices training centre) or enter a vocational *lycée* to prepare a vocational aptitude certificate.

Adaptation classes are also held for handicapped children or children suffering from slight mental deficiency. The *special education sections* (*sections d'éducation speciale* – SES) give these pupils a sufficient general and technical education to allow them to hold down a job. There are also more specialized schools which may take adolescents whose handicaps are of a type or severity demanding special educational or therapeutic treatment.

At the end of the third class, the colleges issue a certificate testifying to the education acquired during the time spent in them.

Teaching in colleges is given by teachers specialized in the various subjects. Most of them belong to two categories: general college teachers (level first cycle of higher education, competitive examination and training in a regional centre) who teach two subjects, and certified teachers (licence + competitive examination + training in a regional education centre) who teach a single subject.

The *lycées*

The education given in the *lycées* is an extension of the education given in the colleges. It is designed to foster the general culture and specialized knowledge of the pupils. This education is given for the most part outside the period of compulsory education. It may include some vocational training and may serve as a preparation for further education.

– Vocational training of adults	105,000
– National employment fund	14,000
– Employment-training contracts	42,000
– National arts and crafts conservatory (Paris)	33,000
– National Tele-education Centre	115,000
– Vocational training fund (agreement and causes for social advancement)	
• oral courses	421,000
• postal courses	33,000
• employment pact agreement	58,000
• special agreements for overseas *départements*	13,000
• collective action	18,000
– Courses for young national service conscripts	42,000
Total	894,000

(of which there are the following numbers in courses now being set up
with the participation of the Ministry of Education and of the universities)

– Social advancement courses:	
• subsidized courses	47,000
• recognized courses	217,000
– National Arts and Crafts Conservatory (Paris)	33,000
– National Tele-education Centre	115,000
Total	412,000

Source: Secretariat General, vocational training. Data processing and statistical studies department *Education and training tables* (retrospective statistics 1967–68/1976–77).

Table 4: Continued vocational training: numbers trained in the year 1976–77

– *The vocational* lycées (lycées d'enseignement professionnel – *LEP*) at present provide courses leading to a vocational aptitudes certificate (*Certificat d'aptitude professionnelle* – CAP) after three years, or, after two years, to a vocational studies certificate (*Brevet d'études professionnelles* – BEP). These courses provide training at the clerical or skilled-worker level (level V of the official French classification into six levels of occupational qualifications.) However, the CAP course is more specialized in conception than the BEP course.

In future, the *preparatory classes* will take pupils on completion of the fifth class, for two years, followed by a period of vocational training proper, leading to the CAP. On completion of the second year of the preparatory class, pupils can obtain the college certificate by arrangements adapted to their curricula.

– *The* lycées. The 'long' period of education given in the *lycées* comprises either a three-year course leading to the national secondary education *baccalauréat* diploma (the *baccalauréat* may include certification of a professional qualification in a specified technical branch – the two first years of the course constitute the *cycle de détermination*, followed by a final year of specialization) or a three-year course leading to the national technical diploma (*Diplôme national du brevet de technicien*) which mentions a specific vocational field.

Some *lycées* have specialized sections (about 100 classes) for children with motor handicaps or visual or aural deficiencies.

Teaching in the *lycées* is given by *professeurs agrégés* (master's degree + competitive examination + one year's teacher training) or by certified teachers. The LEPs employ various categories of teacher to provide general and vocational teaching.

Higher education

The *universities* provide general or specialized courses open to candidates who either hold the secondary education *baccalauréat*, have passed a special university entrance examination, held in accordance with national regulations, or have a French or foreign diploma recognized, under national regulations, as the equivalent of or substitute for the *baccalauréat*.

These courses in general comprise three study cycles:

— the first cycle, lasting two years, leads to a general university studies diploma. The teaching is designed to develop in students aptitudes and knowledge giving competence in expression and performance and an understanding of the contemporary world. It also provides for the study and use of scientific concepts and methods. This cycle includes compulsory and optional subjects;
— the second cycle, also lasting two years, gives a high level scientific education preparing students for working life and professional responsibilities. These studies lead to the licence and the master's degree;
— the third cycle courses are designed to give students a more thorough knowledge of their chosen special subject and a mastery of the rigorous methods of reasoning and experimentation required both in professional work and in scientific research and advanced teaching. These studies lead to one of the following diplomas:

  — third cycle doctorate (in three years),
  — doctorate in engineering, restricted to certified engineers (in three years),
  — specialized higher studies diploma (one year),
  — State doctorate.

Advanced technical courses are given by technical establishments which come under (in particular) the Ministry for the Universities, for example the university institutes of technology which give two year courses leading to the university diploma in technology, the national institutes for applied sciences, the national polytechnics, etc.

The advanced technical sections in the *lycées* on the other hand, which prepared students for the various advanced technical certificates, come under the Ministry of Education.

The public or private grandes écoles, attached to the various ministries or private bodies turn out engineers or commercial or technical executives. The courses last in general from two to five years.

Entry to the schools is by competitive examination and, in certain cases, requires two to three years' study after the *baccalauréat* in the *lycée* classes which prepare pupils for the *grandes écoles*.

Continued education

The participation of the school in continued education, which has been expanding since 1971, is helping to get the school apparatus out of its restricted sphere by mobilizing teachers and equipment and by its contribution to the implementation of training programmes for adults, employees and others. In 1977, in listening hours, the schools of the Ministry of Education carried out 82.9 per cent of the work financed from public funds and 18.9 per cent of the work financed by industry.

Furthermore, in the case of teacher training, one year courses were formerly organized for teachers in industry, in order to familiarize them with the industrial world and enable them to transmit the knowledge so acquired to their colleagues and to the young people in their classes. This very expensive experiment has been discontinued but will be resumed in another form, that of short courses soon after initial training and during professional life.

This link with the working world is also being strengthened through a national employment pact, introduced in 1977 and since renewed, for improving the placing of young people in jobs in the difficult conditions which now prevail in the labour market. This pact, between the State and industry, provides for the organization of practical courses, of employment-training contracts and training courses for young people from 18 to 26 years of age. Education contributes to the training work done under this head.

Entry, guidance and selection procedure

At the end of the elementary school pupils automatically go on to the first year in college.

At the end of the *cycle d'observation* in colleges, as at the end of the *cycle d'orientation*, the teachers' council, after ascertaining the wishes of families, make proposals as to whether the pupil goes to a higher class or repeats the same class. The proposals are discussed by the class council and are then notified to parents, who can appeal against the decision. At the end of college schooling and in the light of the wishes of families and the decisions regarding the pupils' future, the Academy inspector, director of departmental education services, assigns the pupil to a place in an establishment.

At the end of secondary schooling, pupils sit for the *baccalauréat*, which officially constitutes the first general and undifferentiated higher education diploma.

Some universities make access to certain courses of study subject to standards of attainment which they lay down. Others accept candidates without the *baccalauréat*, who can take their higher education courses in accordance with the university's own special arrangements.

It should also be remembered that the *grandes écoles* and the primary and secondary teachers' training centres put up a limited number of places for competitive examination.

The following diagram of the French educational system shows the academic route followed by students and the stages and courses of study leading to the final diplomas.

Education in figures

Because of the size of its budget (18 per cent of the national budget) and staff (more than 950,000) and the number of pupils in public and private schools, colleges and *lycées* (almost 12.4 million), the Ministry of Education ranks high among the French ministerial departments.

French population	53.4 million
Working population	21.0 million
Total school population	12.4 million
Education budget 1979 or 3.41 per cent of the gross national product and 17.6 per cent of the state budget	80,873 million francs
Universities budget 1979	13,139 million francs

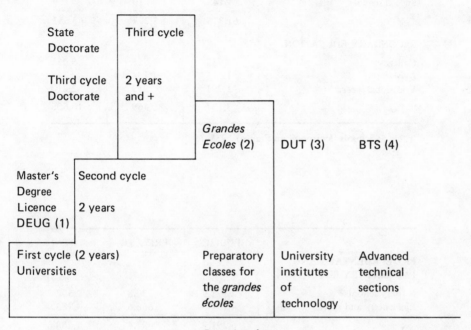

Baccalauréat

(1) DEUG: *Diplôme d'études universitaires et générales* (University and general studies diploma).
(2) The length of the course of studies varies from one *grande école* to another. The courses usually lead to the degree of Engineer. On leaving these schools a number of pupils attend post-university institutes. Finally, a large number of pupils attend university courses and obtain university degrees (masters degrees and doctorates).
(3) DUT: *Diplôme Universitaire de Technologie* (University diploma in technology). This diploma opens the way to professional life. A certain number of persons with this diploma continue their studies either in the *grandes écoles* or in the universities.
(4) BTS: *Brevet de Technicien Superieur* (Advanced technician's certificate).

	PUBLIC	PRIVATE	TOTAL
PRE-ELEMENTARY AND ELEMENTARY EDUCATION			
Nursery schools	14,974	323	15,297
Elementary schools	46,257	6,935	53,192
Special schools	145	19	164
	61,376	7,277	68,653
SECONDARY EDUCATION			
Colleges	4,735	1,316	6,051
Lycées	1,111	1,234	2,345
Vocational *lycées*	1,291	919	2,210
	7,137	3,469	10,606

Table 5: Schools (Metropolitan France) 1978–79

	PUBLIC	PRIVATE	TOTAL
PRE-ELEMENTARY AND ELEMENTARY EDUCATION			
Nursery schools	2,171.9	330.8	2,502.7
Elementary and special schools	4,119.3	666.6	4,785.9
	6,291.2	997.4	7,288.6
SECONDARY EDUCATION			
Colleges	2,671.7	587.6	3,259.3
Lycées	887.0	257.4	1,144.4
Vocational *lycées*	598.1	163.1	761.2
	4,156.8	1,008.1	5,164.9
OVERALL TOTALS	10,448.0	2,005.5	12,453.5
Percentage	83.9	16.1	100.0

Table 6: Pupils (Metropolitan France) 1978–79

	TAKEN	PASSED
Secondary *baccalauréat*	225,969	154,081
Technical *baccalauréat* (qualification level IV)	97,400	59,800
Occupational studies certificate (qualification level V)	121,000	75,400
Occupational aptitude certificate (qualification level V)	403,900	229,647

Table 7: Examinations public and private education (Metropolitan France) 1979

Pre-elementary and elementary education (1978/79)

Nursery and infant classes	66,390
Elementary classes	169,154
Special education classes	19,697
Replacement and supply teachers (various)	34,080
	289,321

(74.5 per cent of primary school teachers are women)

Secondary education (including auxiliaries) 1978/79

Colleges	158,275
Lycées	72,740
Vocational *lycées*	47,768
	278,783

(55 per cent of secondary school teachers are women)

Table 8: Teaching staff (public education)

	EDUCATION	ACCESSORY ACTIVITIES	TOTAL EDUCATION	PROPORTION OF EACH FUNDING SOURCE
Education and universities ministries	37,436	3,642	41,078	52.0%
Other ministries	6,385	5	6,390	8.1%
Common costs†	7,125	591	7,716	9.8%
Total central public administrative departments	50,964	4,238	55,184	69.9%
Local authorities	8,110	1,939	10,049	12.7%
Various local administrative departments‡	397	–	397	0.5%
Total local public administrative departments	8,507	1,939	10,446	13.2%
Industry	2,629	119	2,748	3.5%
Households	2,680	7,627	10,307	13.1%
Miscellaneous	190	90	280	0.3%
TOTAL EXPENDITURE	64,952	14,013	78,965	100.0%

† Mainly cost of civil pensions.
‡ Chambers of trade, of agriculture, of commerce and of industry.

Table 9: Funding of educational expenditure in 1974 (ordinary expenditure + capital expenditure)

Notes

1. With the exception of those parts of the national territory which were restored to France in 1919.
2. The 'headmaster' may of course be a 'headmistress'. However, for convenience, the masculine title and pronoun are used.

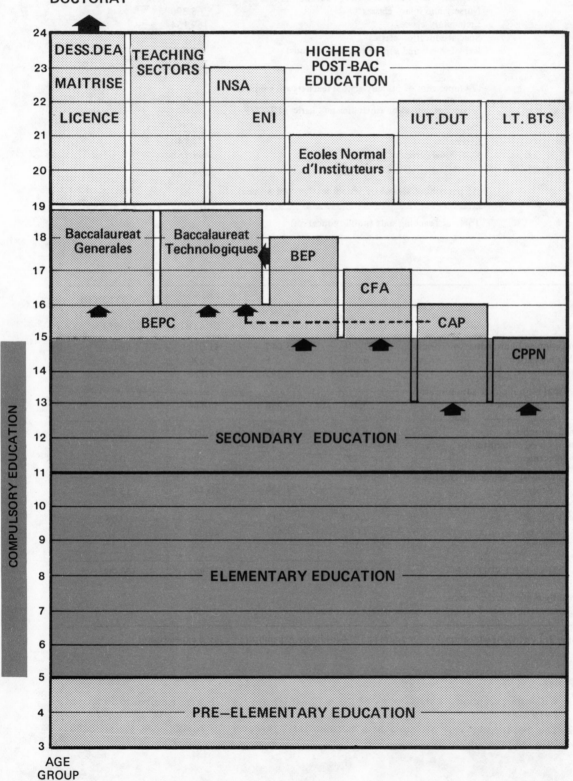

AGE
GROUP

Acronyms and abbreviations

	French	*English*
CFPT	*Centre de Formation de Professeurs Techniques*	Training Centre for Technical Teachers
ENNA	*Ecole Normale Nationale d'Apprentissage*	National Apprenticeship School
UER	*Unité d'Enseignement et de Recherche*	Education and Research Unit

(Medicine, dentistry, pharmacy, sciences, literature and arts, social sciences, applied mathematics, law, economic sciences, economic and social administration)

DESS	*Diplôme d'Etudes Supérieures Spécialisées*	Advanced Specialized Studies Diploma
DEA	*Diplôme d'Etudes Approfondies*	Advanced Studies Diploma
DEUG	*Diplôme d'Etudes Universitaires Générales*	General University Studies Diploma
CPGE	*Classes Préparatoires aux Grandes Ecoles*	Preparatory classes for the Grandes Ecoles

(1 or 2 years)

INSA	*Institut National des Sciences Appliquées*	National Institute for the Applied Sciences
ENI	*Ecole Nationale d'Ingenieurs*	National Engineering School
EN	*Ecole Normale*	Competitive examination
IUT	*Institut Universitaire de Technologie*	University Institute of Technology
DUT	*Diplôme Universitaire de Technologie*	University Technology Diploma
LT	*Lycée Technique*	Technical *Lycée*
BTS	*Brevet de Technicien Supérieur*	Advanced Technicians' Certificate
Bac	A: Philosophy – literature	
	B: Social economics	
	C: Mathematics – physics	
	D: Mathematics – natural sciences	
	E: Mathematics and technology	
Bac de technicien	F: 11 special subjects: Engineering, electronics, electro-technology, civil engineering, physics, chemistry, biological sciences, medico-social sciences, building equipment, micro-technology, music.	
	G: 3 special subjects: Administrative techniques, quantitative management techniques, commercial techniques	
	H: Data-processing	
BT	*Brevet de Technicien*	Engineer's certificate
BEP	*Brevet d'Etudes Professionnelles*	Occupational studies certificate (possibility of joining the long cycle through an adaptation First)
CAP	*Certificat d'Aptitude Professionnelle*	Vocational Aptitude Certificate (possibility of joining the long cycle through a special Second)
CFA	*Centre de Formation d'Apprentis*	Apprentices' Training Centre
CPA	*Classe Préparatoire à l'Apprentissage*	Class in preparation for apprenticeship
CPPN	*Classe Pré-professionnelle de Niveau*	Pre-vocational Class
CM2		Intermediate Course second year
CM1		Intermediate Course first year
CE2		Elementary course second year
CE1		Elementary course first year
CP		Preparatory course

Bibliography

Works on education in France
The list below contains only a small number of the reference works on education in France.

The educational system in France. Collection of Practical Guides of the CNDP – 1978.

Reform of the Educational system. Collection of rules and regulations. Official Gazettes, Brochure No. 1434. 1978.

Education in the elementary school. Ministry of Education. Publisher CNDP — 1978.

MINOD, J. (1977). *Management of secondary schools.* Berger Levrault.

Glossary of terms used in the administration of education. National Institute for School and University Administration — 1974.

Teachers and democratic development

NORVEZ, A. (1977). *Numbers of secondary school teachers and future needs.* National institute for democratic studies. *Collection Travaux et Documents.* Cahier No. 82 PUF 1977.

JOIN-LAMBERT, C. (1978). *Apprendre l'école.* Calmann Levy.

Collection educational sciences. Published by the ESF. A series of works have been published under the general title 'questions–answers on', dealing with: the nursery school — preparatory courses — elementary courses — intermediate courses — entry into the sixth class — schooling for the children of migrants — physical education and sport — short technical education — the *lycées* (the latter to be published in due course).

BARRE, R. and BOURSIN, J.-L. (1974). *From secondary to higher education.* Documentation Française.

French university institutions – present position. Collection Notes et Etudes Documentaires No. 4424–4425–4426 (1977) — publisher: Documentation Française.

Higher education (short course) in France — Notes et Etudes Documentaires No. 4001 — Documentation Française — 1973.

History of education

GRUSON, P. (1978). *The State as teacher.* Mouton — School of advanced studies in the social sciences.

PROST, A. (1977). *Education in France (1800–1967).* Armand Colin.

ZELDIN, T. (1978). *History of French Passions.* Encres.

Useful addresses

Ministère de l'Education
110 rue de Grennelle, Paris 7è   Tel. 550 10 10

Ministère des Universités
61/65 rue Dutot 75732 PARIS CEDEX 15   Tel. 539 25 75

Service des Etudes Informatiques et Statistiques (SEIS)
58 boulevard du Lycée 92170 VANVES   Tel. 554 95 25

Office National d'Information sur les Enseignements et Professions (ONISEP)
46 rue Albert PARIS 13è   Tel. 583 32 21

Centre d'Etudes et de Recherches sur les Qualifications (CEREQ)
9 rue Sextius Michel 75732 PARIS CEDEX 15   Tel. 577 10 04

Institut National de Recherche Pédagogique (INRP)
29/31 rue d'Ulm 75230 PARIS CEDEX 05   Tel. 329 21 64

Centre National de Documentation Pédagogique (CNDP)
29 rue d'Ulm PARIS CEDEX 05   Tel. 329 21 64

Agence Nationale pour le Développement de l'Education Permanente (ADEP)
21/23 rue de la Vanne 92120 MONTROUGE CEDEX   Tel. 657 11 88

Office National des Universités et Ecoles Françaises
96 boulevard Raspail PARIS 6è   Tel. 22 50 20

IRELAND

Introduction

Due to the zeal of Irishmen who had studied in Britain and who had come under the influence of
the western British Church, monasticism took root in Ireland in the early years of the sixth
century. Later, the monasteries became centres of learning which attracted not only Irish youths
but students from abroad as well. Particular attention was paid to the Scriptures and to the
writings of the later Christian Fathers. The students used styli on waxed tablets, while the more
accomplished scribes devoted skill and care to the transcription of the Gospels and other books.
The work was at first in Latin, but in time the monks began to write in Irish as well. Though most
of the surviving manuscripts are of a late period, many of them embody traditions and literature
transmitted through the monasteries from a much earlier time. The Fili, a body strongly attached
to the ancient language, composed Irish poetry in metres deriving from Latin hymns, and
assembled the Brehon Laws. Writers and poets produced prose romances and historical tales, as
well as reconstructing the great pagan epics, so that Ireland was the first nation north of the Alps
to produce a vernacular literature.

From such schools as Clonard, Clonmacnois and Bangor, missionaries went overseas and
made a noteworthy contribution to civilization in a Europe that had been overrun by the
barbarian invaders of the Roman Empire. They brought back with them that combination of
vernacular and Christian learning represented abroad by such Irish scholars as the geometer,
Virgilius of Salzburg, and the philosopher, John Scotus Eriugena.

Partly as a result of the Norse incursions, Ireland's contribution to European education
declined between the ninth and the eleventh centuries. Hardly had the Norse threat been overcome
when the Normans arrived; this invasion marked the beginning of that continuous struggle for
survival as a nation which lasted down to the present century and impeded the development of a
national culture.

From the days of Henry II to those of Henry VIII, rivalry between the Irish and the
Norman-English hindered educational progress. During this period, when the great European
centres of learning were being developed as universities, Irish students were not readily admitted
to the better schools within the walled towns of the English colony, or *Pale,* while Englishmen
were often excluded from the monasteries controlled by the Irish. Beyond the Pale, education was
provided by monastic schools attached to the convents of the mendicant orders; in these,
promising youths might learn Latin and make some progress in the trivium and quadrivium (the
two branches of medieval learning, comprising respectively: grammar, rhetoric and logic;
arithmetic, geometry, astronomy and music).

Beyond the Pale, also, there was a highly developed system of bardic schools, which were a
distinctive feature of Gaelic civilization. These were secular institutions devoted to the study of
Gaelic literature with special emphasis on metrical composition. In them, bards received formal
training for what was considered to be the exalted and highly professional career of the man of
letters; this was an exclusive calling, protected by the ordeal of initiation. The *Ollamh,* or chief
poet, had to know by heart a large number of romances, including the two hundred and fifty
'prime stories' — combinations of novel and epic, prose and poetry, ranging over a highly-
formalized series of conventional themes, such as destruction of fortified places, courtships, feasts,

water-eruptions, navigations and so on. The bardic schools were maintained in part by the gifts of the students, but depended mainly on the generosity of local rulers. Since, however, the bards were regarded as inimical to English rule, from Tudor times onwards government policy aimed at their suppression. When the military conquest of the country was effected in the sixteenth century, many of the chiefs fled to the Continent and, deprived of their patronage, the hereditary families of poets and teachers also took refuge abroad, or were absorbed into the peasantry. Cromwell's campaign, and the widespread plantation that followed it, marked the end of the bardic schools. Something of their tradition lived on in the 'Courts of Poetry' which, though little more than gatherings at which poetry was discussed and recited, helped to keep alive the craft of verse-making down to the nineteenth century.

The dissolution of the great abbeys under Henry VIII ushered in a new era of positive intervention by the English State in education. Hereafter there was to be a carefully-planned state system of schools, aimed at assimilating the Irish people to English culture and the new religion. This policy was to be maintained with varying emphasis and intensity for the next three hundred years. These aims were unacceptable to the mass of the people.

The Penal Laws against Catholic education were circumvented, in part, by the founding of Irish colleges at Louvain, Lisbon and Salamanca. At home, the later Penal period was the era of the hedge-schoolmaster. Hedge-schools were so called because the master had to teach out of doors, since a householder might suffer distraint for harbouring him. The hedge-school curriculum was often quite extensive; based on the 'three R's', it might include history, geography, book-keeping, surveying and mathematics. Devotion to the Classics persisted; it is said that fluent speakers of Latin could be met with in parts of the country.

With the hedge-schoolmaster is linked the 'poor scholar', usually a promising pupil who, having obtained basic education at his local hedge-school, travelled to others in search of further knowledge, depending the while on the hospitality of the peasants. Hedge-schools first appeared in the seventeenth century, and flourished in the eighteenth; their popularity was due to the willingness of an already impoverished people to make sacrifices for their children, and to their co-operation with the teachers. In the second half of the eighteenth century, the rise in population and the relaxation of the Penal Laws resulted in a considerable increase in the number of hedge-schools. In 1824, there were 7,600 independent 'pay schools' under lay Catholic teachers: of these, the majority were hedge-schools. They were tolerated, but received no state assistance, and were usually conducted in huts or cabins. In sharp contrast were the endowed schools, mainly Protestant in character, such as those of the Erasmus Smith Foundation and the schools of the Kildare Place Society; these received parliamentary grants up to 1831, when the grants were transferred to the newly-introduced system of national education, upon which the present system of primary education is based.

The authority of the State in education is vested in the Minister for Education, who is a member of the Government and responsible to *Dail Eireann*. The Minister's administrative agency is the Department of Education, the staff of which – administrative and technical – are civil servants. At the head of these is the Secretary, and there are six Assistant Secretaries, each in charge of a major administrative division of the Department in primary and post-primary fields. The Department also deals with the universities and other institutions of higher education, the National Library, National Museum, National Gallery and various organizations of a cultural nature.

The fundamental principles underlying the educational system are set forth in Articles 42 and 44.4 of the Constitution of Ireland. The State acknowledges that the primary and natural educator of the child is the family and that parents are free to provide this education in their homes, in private schools, or in schools recognized or established by the State. The State, however, as guardian of the common good, requires that the children receive a certain minimum education, moral, intellectual and social. The State 'shall provide for free primary education' and, when the public good requires it, shall provide other educational facilities or institutions. Legislation providing state aid for schools shall not discriminate between schools under the management of different religious denominations, nor be such as to prejudice a child's right to attend a state-aided school without attending religious instruction in that school. Thus, in the Articles dealing with education, the Constitution safeguards the rights of parents, especially in the matter of religious and moral formation, as well as the natural and imprescriptible rights of the child.

The Department of Education, therefore, provides for education free of charge in primary and second level schools and it gives substantial aid to universities and other institutions of third-level education. Education at the primary level is given, for the great majority of children, in state-supported schools known as 'national' schools (the term 'national' as used in Ireland has its origins in the system of national education introduced in the nineteenth century). Second-level education is provided in secondary, vocational, comprehensive and community schools and to a very minor extent in some regional technical colleges. The Department of Agriculture is responsible for agricultural education in certain second-level schools: these schools do not come within the jurisdiction of the Department of Education.

School attendance

Attendance at schools is compulsory for children between the ages of six and fifteen years. Ireland is, however, virtually unique among European countries in that it makes provision in public primary schools for all children from the age of four. The majority of pupils transfer to second-level schools at about twelve years of age. The normal duration of the second-level course of study is five years, consisting of a three years' junior course and a two years' senior course.

Curriculum

The curricula being pursued in Irish schools reflect the basic philosophy of Irish society, its Christian code of values and its national aspirations. Even before political independence was achieved the restoration of the Irish language was seen as a legitimate function of the school system and is at present a basic aim of Irish education.

Responsibility for school curricula is the prerogative of the Department of Education. Towards the end of the 1960s it was decided that educational interests within and without the Department should be consulted with a view to bringing the educational approaches in the primary school into line with modern thinking on the nature of the child and his learning needs. A committee of school inspectors was given the task of designing an appropriate curriculum within these terms. In 1971 the introduction of the 'New Curriculum for Primary Schools' was launched – the principles and practice of which were set forth in a substantial two-part curriculum hand-book. The task of on-going evaluation of the New Curriculum was entrusted to the Curriculum Unit of the Department of Education. At the post-primary level the Department exercises control over curricula, but syllabi Review Committees which are representative of a wider spectrum of interest in the field of education are established to assist in the preparation or modification of courses of study in the various subject areas. At the same time there is an awareness not only of the problem of transition from primary to post-primary school but also of the specific difficulties which confront the young person who leaves the school system at the end of the junior post-primary cycle. The matter of integration of curricula at post-primary level is at present being actively pursued, while the question of transition from primary to post-primary school is being investigated by a special committee set up by the Minister for Education to advise him in this regard.

Students, as a rule, follow a three-year junior post-primary course leading to either the Intermediate Certificate or the Day Vocational Group Certificate of the Department of Education. It is noted that a large percentage of students leave full-time education at the end of the junior cycle and while many may return to the educational system through apprenticeship courses and adult education programmes, nevertheless it is thought that special attention ought to be paid to the specific needs of these young people. Towards this end, pre-employment courses which have a strong vocational bias were devised with the general aim of bridging the gap between the values and experiences which are normally part of the educational process and those current in the adult world of work. In addition to pre-employment courses there has been established, as a pilot programme, the transition year project which is a one-year inter-disciplinary course and is directed towards the intellectual, social and emotional maturation of the young pupil. It is conceived primarily as an introduction to adult education and to *éducation permanente*.

Curriculum evaluation and investigation of standards generally is the responsibility of the Department of Education and is carried out by the Department's Inspectorate. Such evaluation is a condition precedent to the successful implementation of curricular proposals or modifications at all levels and argues for the existence of soundly-based systems of educational research. Until recent years educational research in Ireland was neither well organized nor well supported. Studies in historical and other aspects of Irish education had been made by individual scholars but there had been a lack of systematic investigation into educational problems. Neither had research been a conspicuous feature of the education departments of Irish universities, due principally to the limitations of staff and their concern with pedagogical training rather than the broader study of education. In more recent years, however, the picture has changed and there is now not only a greater awareness of the need for educational research as a fundamental of educational and especially curricular development, but also greater financial and other support for such research. The principal thrust has come from the work being done by the Educational Research Centre in St Patrick's College of Education, on the one hand, and from the investigation of linguistic methods being conducted by *Institiúid Teangeolaíochta Éireann* (The Irish Linguistic Institute) on the other. As well as the work done by these two institutes other studies have been carried out by the Department of Education's Inspectorate, Psychological Service and Curriculum Unit, by the Curriculum Development Unit of Dublin University and by the Shannon Curriculum Development Centre. Many innovations in both teaching methods and curricular content have come from these studies. Much of the momentum of educational development in Ireland has been generated by the publication in 1966 of *Taighde ar Oideachas* (*Investment in Education*), a comprehensive study of the economic and sociological aspects of the country's education. Coupled with this survey in the extent of its influence is the Report of the Commission on Higher Education 1960–67.

In the Department of Education there is a resource centre which allocates grants to the schools for the purchase of educational hardware. It is also responsible for publications relating to the curriculum and for the preparation of certain teaching aids.

Teacher Centres are a recent development of the supporting structures. Their function is to provide help for the teachers in the form of resource material, professional advice, lectures, seminars, courses etc.

At primary and at post-primary levels the Department's Inspectors visit the schools regularly in order to evaluate standards.

The great majority of junior post-primary pupils are presented for the Group Certificate Examination and/or the Intermediate Certificate Examination. Although the purpose of these examinations is pupil certification, in practice, their effect is that both schools and pupils work towards standards of achievement prescribed by the Department.

Pre-school education

Education is compulsory and free for children from six to fifteen years of age. As already stated education is provided in the public national schools for all children from the age of four. Consequently while there are a small number of private nursery schools the majority of children receive their primary education from the age of four in a single primary school or in a group of such schools on a single site.

About 3 per cent of pupils attend private nursery and primary schools which are frequently associated with private secondary schools. These are fee-paying institutions, ineligible for state subsidy.

Primary education

When the system of national education was set up in 1831 a Board of Commissioners was established to assist in the provision of elementary schools and in the supplying of existing elementary schools with trained teachers and suitable textbooks. It remains the accepted practice in Ireland that the State does not normally conduct schools, but makes provision for education by enabling other parties to do so. Hence the national schools were, in origin, voluntary parochial schools established by the various religious authorities, and the manager of a national school was usually the local clergyman of the religious denomination to which the majority of children attending that particular school belonged. However, as already stated, the Rules for National Schools under the Department of Education do not discriminate between schools under the management of different religious denominations nor may they be construed so as to affect prejudicially the right of any child to attend a national school without attending religious instruction at that school.

Boards of Management for national schools were established in 1976. The Boards comprise representatives of the Patron of the school, the teachers and the parents of children attending the school. The Board of Management of each individual school is charged with the direct government of the school, the appointment and removal of teachers on individual contracts subject to the Minister's approval, the disbursement of school funds and the conducting of the necessary correspondence.

All national schools receive financial support from the State, which pays up to 90 per cent of the cost of building and equipment and 75 per cent of the maintenance costs, together with the teachers' salaries in full. Local contributions supplement the state expenditure on building, equipping, renovating and maintaining the schools. The Department of Education exercises a large measure of control over the operation of the schools, the curriculum and the qualifications of the teachers as set out in the Rules for National Schools under the Department of Education.

There is a free school transport service for children who reside 5 km or more from the nearest school (3 km for pupils under 10 years).

The new curriculum for primary schools which has already been mentioned postulated as a basic aim the purpose of enabling the child to live a full life as a child, and of setting him on the road to a full and useful life as an adult in society. Intrinsic to such a design was a process of harmonious development to be achieved through the operation of an integrated curriculum which, eschewing subject-barriers and curricular differentiation, would be characterized by unity, flexibility and, above all, relevance to the social, intellectual, cultural, physical, and economic environment of the pupil.

There is no formal terminal examination on the primary education cycle: the former 'Primary Certificate Examination', which was compulsory after 1944, was discontinued in 1967. A cumulative record card, furnished by the principal teacher of the school, testifies to the pupil's having completed the sixth standard programme, and provides an assessment of the pupil's progress. This card is transmitted to the authorities of the second-level school at which the pupil subsequently enrols.

Special education
Special educational provision is made for handicapped children through measures ranging from residential and day special schools and special classes in ordinary schools to itinerant teacher services and home tuition. Particulars of the main categories of pupils for whom this provision is made, the form it takes and the number of children involved are given in the table below. In Ireland as elsewhere there is a recognition that full integration of handicapped children must be considered as the first option in individual cases but that options including that of complete segregation by special provision must also be kept open. Special education is administered mainly by the Primary Education Branch of the Department of Education and forms part of the national school system. The schools are conducted either by a religious body or by a voluntary body concerned with the particular handicap (e.g. Spina Bifida Association) and as in the case of other national schools there is a Board of Management representative of all the parties involved. The Department pays teachers' salaries and the cost of transport and gives grants towards the cost of building, equipping and operating schools. Through its inspectorial service, the Department maintains control over the standards of education in special schools and classes.

The Department of Health is responsible for the provision of boarding, day-care, psychological, medical and para-medical services for children attending special schools and classes.

At second level, the handicapped may continue their education in the special school in which they have pursued the primary course. In second-level schools there are at present limited arrangements by way of instruction in special classes; plans are being made to extend this provision. In recent years a new development has taken place featuring the integration of physically handicapped children with other children in certain second-level schools.

CATEGORY OF HANDICAP	TYPE OF PROVISION	NO. OF PUPILS
Blind and partially sighted	2 schools There is a Visiting Teacher Service on a national basis	139
Deaf and hard of hearing	4 schools Visiting Teacher Service	819 1,000 (approx.)
Physically handicapped	7 special schools 10 schools in hospitals Special provision in 3 second-level schools Home tuition	447 242 60 42
Mildly mentally handicapped	31 schools 157 classes	3,394 2,135
Moderately mentally handicapped	29 schools	2,117
Emotionally disturbed	14 schools	451
Multipli-handicapped	1 school	29
Specific reading disability	1 school	53

Table 1: Educational provision for handicapped pupils 1979

Teachers are recruited for work with the handicapped from the general body of first- and second-level teachers, mainly the former. Special post-graduate diploma courses, financed by the Department of Education, are provided for teachers of handicapped pupils.

Second-level education

The second-level schools catering for children in the age-range 12–19 years, include:

(a) secondary schools;
(b) vocational schools;
(c) comprehensive schools; and
(d) community schools.

Secondary schools came into being in the following way. From 1570 onwards, there existed in Ireland statutory provision, from diocesan revenues, for secondary schools. In that year, 'An Act for the Erection of Free Schools' was passed by the Parliament in Dublin, which provided that 'there shall be from henceforth a free school in every diocese of this realm of Ireland, and that the schoolmaster shall be an Englishman or of the English birth of this realm'. The diocesan schools thus legislated for were of the secondary grammar school type. Further state provision for secondary education was made later. In 1614, and thereafter, five Royal Free Schools were established in Ulster from endowments forming part of the lands confiscated from the native Irish in the Plantation of Ulster. This type of public provision by royal endowment was continued by Charles II, who issued charters for the establishment of two Royal Schools in Leinster. Another notable group of schools founded and maintained by public endowment were the Erasmus Smith Grammar Schools, at Drogheda, Galway, Tipperary and Ennis, so called after a Cromwellian who obtained large tracts of Irish land confiscated after the insurrection of 1641. Various other schools and groups of schools were founded and maintained by private endowment, or through funds provided by corporations and municipal bodies. All the schools under these various headings were Protestant, catered for the ascendancy minority, and were intended to strengthen state policy in its aim of preserving and extending English ways and English power in Ireland.

After the Reformation, the fortunes of Catholic schools varied according to the measure of the effectiveness of state control and the rigour with which state policy was applied. During the sixteenth and seventeenth centuries, Catholic grammar schools managed to survive and even to flourish, especially in the towns. In this period, some 20 colleges for Irish Catholic students were founded on the Continent, mainly to educate candidates for the priesthood. From the end of the seventeenth century onward, state control became effective over the whole of Ireland, and Catholic education could be carried on only furtively, and under difficult conditions, as a consequence of the implementation of a severe penal code aimed at the economic and cultural subjection of the nation.

Towards the end of the eighteenth century, the Penal Laws, under pressure of enlightened and patriotic Protestant opinion, began to be relaxed. Under the Relief Act of 1782, Catholic schools and teachers were countenanced by law, under certain conditions. This led at once to the foundation of Catholic secondary schools. Throughout the nineteenth century, various types of schools were founded by religious orders of priests, brothers and nuns, providing some kind of secondary education. Progress was slow, as these schools were entirely private and unendowed, and did not receive state aid or recognition. By 1871, only 12,274 Catholic pupils, out of a Catholic population of over 4 million, were receiving what could be termed a secondary education; at the same time, 11,896 Protestant pupils, out of a Protestant population of a million and a quarter, were receiving a secondary education at various types of state-endowed schools.

The first state provision for general secondary education came with the Intermediate Education Act of 1878. This Act established the Intermediate Education Board for Ireland, whose duty, as defined by the Act, was to provide secular intermediate (i.e. secondary) education:

(1) by instituting and carrying on a system of public examinations;
(2) by providing payment for prizes and exhibitions, and giving certificates to successful students;
(3) by providing for the payment to managers of schools complying with the prescribed conditions, of fees dependent on the results of public examinations;
(4) generally, by applying the funds placed at the disposal of the Board, provided that no examination be held in any subject of religious instruction, nor any payment made in respect thereof. The Act made no change in the status of schools; the state-endowed schools retained their endowments as well as receiving the payments specified in the Act. All other schools (the vast majority, in fact) were privately owned and managed. The examinations held by the Board were in three grades, junior, middle and senior. Exhibitions and prizes were available, on a competitive basis, to candidates in each of the three grades.

After the establishment of *Saorstat Eireann* the Intermediate Board was abolished (1923). A new system of secondary education, with a new programme, followed on the Intermediate Education (Amendment) Act, 1926. The secondary system became the concern of the new Department of Education; changes in various regulations had the effect of broadening the curriculum, improving teaching methods and the conditions of teachers, and, in general, freeing the schools from the constricting effects of a system in which the provision of educational needs was largely governed by money grants dependent on success in examinations. The new programme replaced the junior, middle and senior grades by two certificate examinations, the Intermediate Certificate and the Leaving Certificate.

The development of *vocational schools* resulted from the organization of technical and craft education in Ireland, which is comparatively modern; it developed as a result of voluntary movements in cities and towns, mainly for the teaching of art. In the mid-nineteenth century Bianconi founded the Mechanics Institute at Clonmel. In 1848, a School of Design in Art was founded in Cork, and four years later a School of Art was established in Limerick at the instance of the Athenaeum Society. Of special significance was the founding in Dublin, 1867, of the Royal College of Science, to supply courses of instruction related to the sciences of industry; particularly mining, argricultural, engineering and manufacturing operations.

In England, a Department of Practical Art had been set up under the Board of Trade, in 1852, to foster general elementary instruction and to give assistance to schools in which art was taught. This was taken over by the Privy Council Committee on Education, and became the Department of Science and Art, with the task of distributing, in Ireland as well as in Britain, the annual Parliamentary Vote for instruction in these subjects. Aid was given in national and secondary schools, and also in evening schools and technical institutions; there were grants for building and apparatus, and payments on the results of examinations as well as scholarships and prizes. The Technical Instruction Act of 1889 empowered the local authorities to levy a rate in aid of schemes for technical or manual instruction, and to appoint committees to act on their behalf in administering such schemes. Schools were eligible for grants under the Act, provided they were open to the public, the premises were suitable, the teachers satisfactorily qualified, and the curriculum approved by the Department. After 1892, the Department of Science and Art contributed towards technical instruction a direct grant equal in amount to the sum contributed by the local authority. However, the monies available were still inadequate to provide an efficient system of technical instruction. As a result of the recommendation of the 'Recess Committee' of inquiry into Ireland's agricultural and industrial resources, the Department of Agriculture and Technical Instruction came into operation, by Act of Parliament, in 1900. Besides granting increased sums to encourage the teaching of science and allied subjects in national and secondary schools, the Department proposed state-subsidized schemes for instruction in art, technology and science in urban areas, and in manual instruction, rural industries and domestic science in rural areas. These schemes, if acceptable to the local authorities, were to be administered by committees set up by them, and would be organized and aided by them. The Act was a success in practice, and 49 local committees were set up. Permanent technical schools were established in the larger urban centres; instruction in the rural areas was provided mainly by itinerant teachers who gave short intensive courses in woodwork and domestic economy. In all areas, instruction was confined to afternoon and evening classes; whole-time day classes were few. A training school for teachers of domestic economy was maintained at Kilmacud in Co. Dublin; and courses of higher scientific and technical instruction were given at the College of Science and the Metropolitan School of Art.

After the Department of Education had assumed responsibility for the educational services, a commission was appointed in 1926 to inquire into, and advise on the system of technical instruction in relation to the requirements of trade and industry. The principal recommendations made by the commission were embodied in the Vocational Education Act of 1930. Of special significance for the future was the observation in the commission report that, for many boys and girls there was 'a period of idleness or of indefinite educational purpose from the age of 14 years or so', with the view expressed that 'a proper system of continuation education is of vital importance, and its organization should be undertaken without delay'. The Act enjoined on every Vocational Education Committee the duty of establishing and maintaining in its area a suitable system of continuation education, and of supplying, and aiding the supply of, technical education. Provision was made for compulsory attendance at continuation or technical courses in areas designated by the Minister.

It soon became evident that the most satisfactory manner of dealing with the problem was to establish permanent central schools at which full-time courses would be available. In due course some 300 such schools were in operation. The curriculum, if it were to have practical value, could not be a uniform one applicable alike in city, town and country; hence different types of courses were organized. By arrangement with ecclesiastical authorities, religious instruction was provided in all schools. The most typical courses were, for boys, the junior technical course and the junior rural course, and for girls, the junior domestic science course and the junior commercial course.

The junior technical course was intended to cater for boys aiming at skilled manual employment and requiring some kind of technical knowledge, while the junior rural course was slanted towards agriculture. Junior domestic science prepared girls for occupations requiring manual skill, more especially in all that appertains to care of home and family; the commercial course catered largely for prospective book-keepers, typists and business employees. Pupils at the end of a two-year course were expected to have reached the standard of the Day Vocational Certificate, awarded on the results of an examination conducted by the Department. This certificate was widely accepted as evidence of qualification for certain types of employment. When, in later days, vocational education was integrated into a wider and more comprehensive post-primary system, it was decided to retain the Day Vocational Certificate.

In 1967 the free education scheme for second-level pupils was introduced leading to a major expansion of second-level enrolment and inevitably the advent of comprehensive education and an awareness of the need for an increasing emphasis on technical education. Fifteen *comprehensive schools* have been provided in Ireland. The comprehensive schools were regarded as experimental and the experience gained thereby led to the establishment in 1972 of the first *community school.*

In the year 1978 the distribution pattern was as follows: 532 secondary schools with 11,241 teachers catered for 196,855 pupils; 246 vocational schools employed 4,463 teachers to provide for an enrolment of 68,915; 15 comprehensive schools in which 502 teachers were engaged and which were attended by 8,083 pupils; 26 community schools with 896 full-time teachers in charge of 13,975 pupils.

Second-level programme

It can be said that the several distinctive types of institution, traditional and modern, operating in the domain of second-level education have this in common: that without exception they have been shaped or modified by the demand for equality of opportunity, the purpose being to ensure not merely that all young people have access to second-level schooling, but that the courses offered be suitable to their individual aptitudes and abilities. In addition, the interests of the individual as well as those of the community suggest a balance between the numbers of pupils receiving an academic-type education and those receiving an education with a technical bias.

Hence the emphasis has been on a broad curriculum in each school centre, which in practice means that the centre must be sufficiently large to provide varied and comprehensive syllabi. A town in which there are one or more second-level schools is regarded as a school centre. Where schools of different types already existed in close proximity to each other, they have been encouraged to pool their resources, thus affording the pupils a wider curricular choice than any one of these schools, operating independently, could hope to offer. The programme of instruction is prescribed by the Department and the schools are inspected by Department inspectors. The programme involves two phases:

(a) *Junior level* (usually of 3 years' duration) leading to the *Intermediate Certificate.* This certificate testifies to the completion of a balanced course of general education suitable for pupils who discontinue full-time education at about sixteen years of age, and, alternatively, to the fitness of pupils for entry on more advanced courses of study;

(b) *Senior level* (of 2 years' duration) based on a *Leaving Certificate* programme designed to equip the student for immediate entry into society, or for a course of further study at a university or other institution of further education. Curricular choice in the Leaving Certificate was expanded in the seventies through the introduction of subjects of a work-related character including building construction, engineering workshop — theory and practice — mechanics, technical drawing, economics, accountancy and business organization, in addition to the more academic language, science and social studies subjects.

Secondary schools

As a result of their historical development secondary schools are privately owned institutions conducted by boards of governors, religious communities (mainly Catholic) or individuals. Provided they qualify for recognition by the Department of Education they receive considerable financial assistance through grants in respect of each eligible pupil and the payment of over 90 per cent of the salaries of the staff of the schools. The State also contributes 80 per cent of the cost of building and equipping secondary schools. A capitation grant is paid to all secondary schools in respect of each recognized pupil. In addition a special supplemental grant is paid in respect of each recognized pupil to all schools which do not charge tuition fees, and under this arrangement all but a very small percentage of secondary schools offer free education. In the case of Protestant secondary schools a block grant towards tuition costs is paid to their Secondary Education Committee which administers and distributes the grant to individual pupils.

The secondary school programme must include instruction in specified subjects with a syllabus approved by the Minister for Education. The subjects and syllabi are published annually in the Department's *Rules and Programme for Secondary Schools*. Two courses are followed at secondary schools, i.e. the Intermediate Certificate Examination course and the Leaving Certificate Examination course. The results of the Certificate Examinations are shown in the form of grades (each representing a percentage range of marks) and each candidate is awarded a certificate of the grades obtained by him at the examination.

Vocational schools

As will be seen from the development of vocational education, Vocational Education Committees whose members are elected by the local authorities are the appropriate authorities prescribed by legislation to manage and operate vocational schools. These schools provide second-level programmes of instruction with a bias towards instruction in practical subjects. They also provide evening courses for adults in a very wide variety of subjects.

The State provides some 90 per cent of the total finances for vocational schools, the balance being met from the funds of the local authorities.

Vocational school students are prepared for the Day Vocational Certificate examination after a two-year course; this certificate covers four main areas: manual instruction, commerce, home economics and rural science. The courses are so designed as to enable the pupil who remains at school for another year to qualify for the Intermediate Certificate.

In recent years vocational schools have become involved in the Leaving Certificate course with a predictable emphasis on those practical subjects and applied sciences which accommodate the demands of industry and business. Students who proceed to the Leaving Certificate frequently have entry to a technical or technological college as their objective.

Comprehensive schools

These were established in areas where adequate facilities for post-primary education were not available. The comprehensive schools combine secondary-academic and secondary-vocational education in one curriculum which offers each pupil the type of education best suited to his preference and potential. Early selection and rigid streaming are eschewed and a systemized career guidance service is available in each school. They are managed by Boards of Management representative of the Vocational Education Committee of the area, the diocesan religious authority (Roman Catholic or Protestant, as appropriate) and the Minister for Education. They are financed from central government funds. It is not intended to establish any further comprehensive schools.

Community schools

Frequently the result of amalgamation of existing secondary and vocational schools and the successor to the comprehensive school, the community school seeks to involve the local community to an ever-increasing degree in the educational activities of the area, and to make further provision for adult and general part-time education. Existing second-level schools have been amalgamated to form a community school mainly to create a school unit which would be large enough to provide a varied curriculum. The development of community consciousness is a prime objective; hence the school amenities – the playing fields, the halls, the gymnasia – are freely available to the community outside school hours. As is the case with the comprehensive school the community school, in accord with the purpose of creating a unified post-primary system of education, offers a full range of courses leading to the Day Vocational Certificate, Intermediate and Leaving Certificate qualifications.

Community schools are administered by Boards of Management consisting of representatives of the secondary school managers, the Vocational Education Committee, the teaching staff and parents of the pupils attending the school. They are financed from central government funds.

Teacher education

Primary: At the request of the Minister for Education the Higher Education Authority prepared a report on teacher training in 1970. This Report was considered by a Planning Committee set up by the Minister and the recommendation concerning the establishment of a Teaching Council was accepted by him. As an initial step in the revision and improvement of the existing system the training course for primary teachers was extended from two to three years, commencing in 1974, and each of the six colleges of education for the training of primary teachers established an arrangement with an appropriate university institution under which trainee teachers follow an approved university course leading to the award of a Bachelor of Education degree on its successful completion. Other university graduates may qualify as primary teachers on completion of a one-year post-graduate diploma course at the colleges of education.

Post-primary: Post-primary teachers from two major categories: (1) teachers of general subjects, who must be university graduates; and (2) teachers of specialist subjects who must hold recognized teaching diplomas or degrees awarded as a result of their having successfully completed training courses in colleges of art, home economics, etc.

There are two colleges of education for the training of teachers of home economics and one — Thomond College of Education — concerned with the training of post-primary teachers of specialist subjects, e.g. physical education, woodwork, metalwork, building construction, rural science, etc. Courses in the home economics colleges are of three and four years' duration and courses at Thomond College of Education are of four years' duration except for 'trade' entrants to metalwork, woodwork and building construction for whom courses are of three years' duration. The majority of teachers in secondary schools have university degrees plus a Higher Diploma in Education acquired during a one-year course at post-graduate level in a university; so have most of the teachers of academic subjects at vocational, comprehensive and community schools.

The number of students at teacher training institutions (excluding the Education Departments in Universities) in 1978/79 was as follows:

— primary school colleges of education: 2,705
— vocational teacher training colleges: 199
— home economics teacher training colleges: 167
— Thomond College of Education: 175

Regional technical colleges

There are, in all, some nine regional technical colleges in Ireland. Their function is to educate for trade and industry over a wide spectrum of occupations, ranging from craft to professional level, notably in engineering and science, but also in commercial, linguistic and other specialities.

Regional technical colleges are specially concerned with providing courses aimed at filling gaps in the industrial manpower structure, particularly in the technician area. It is then the endeavour of a regional technical college to respond sensitively to the operational needs of the region. But this very purpose postulates a process of continued adaptation to social, economic and technological change — a consideration that rules out a final fixed pattern of courses. In any event, some of the whole-time courses on offer are local in their appeal, and are meant to be taken up by students within an approximate 10 mile radius of the college.

Originally the colleges catered for Leaving Certificate students interested in technical subjects; but, as demand for their more specialized services grew, the Leaving Certificate courses were, in the majority of cases, transferred to adjacent vocational schools. The colleges at the present time cater for four main sectors of education:

(i) *Craft apprenticeship and craft-based technician courses.* Apprentices in trades designated under the Trade and Apprenticeship Act are released to colleges on a day-release or a block-release basis during their apprenticeship. In addition, colleges cater on a similar basis for telecommunications technicians, for a variety of other technical grades, and for a number of non-designated and service trades. Whole-time courses are available in the Galway and Cork Colleges for the hotel and catering trades.

(ii) *Middle and higher-level technician courses.* These courses are generally for students of a Leaving Certificate or equivalent standard of attainment. They provide for the education and training of technicians in engineering, science and business studies, and in the various specializations arising out of areas such as civil, electrical, electronic and mechanical engineering, architecture and construction, applied chemistry and applied biology, marketing, accountancy, middle-management, etc. In a number of colleges there are courses of similar level in hotel and catering studies and in art and design. The qualification available after a two-year course of study is a National Certificate. Students may then or later proceed to a further year's study which leads to a National Diploma. Diploma-level courses are generally of a more specialized nature, and in many cases reflect the predominant industrial activity of the region where they are located.

(iii) *Professional (degree-level) courses.* Such courses are confined in the main to the Dublin Colleges of Technology and the National Institutes of Higher Education. A degree-level course in hotel and catering management is offered in the Regional Technical College, Galway.

(iv) *Adult part-time courses.* The colleges provide a very wide range of such courses organized on an evening, a day-release or an intensive short-course basis. The majority of such courses are of a vocational or employment-related nature. Courses of this type can be undertaken to meet the needs of particular industries or industry groupings.

In the case of regional technical colleges, course standards are assessed and certificates and diplomas awarded by the National Council for Educational Awards. It is possible for students under certain conditions to proceed from national certificate/diploma courses to degree-level courses in the National Institute for Higher Education, Limerick, and in the Dublin Colleges of Technology. Exemptions are also available in certain related university courses for those who wish to transfer to the university sector. Students who complete their certificate course in one college may transfer to another college for diploma-level studies if the speciality they require is not catered for in their original college. Courses are so co-ordinated as to facilitate this type of transfer. Certificate and diploma courses are mainly full-time courses, but can be made available on an equivalent part-time basis to meet the needs of students already in employment.

Third-level

There are two universities – the National University of Ireland and the University of Dublin. Both are self-governing institutions but each receive State grants to meet operational expenses and also grants for capital purposes. The National University of Ireland is organized on a federal basis but the individual colleges enjoy a large measure of autonomy. The three constituent University Colleges are Dublin, Cork and Galway. St Patrick's College, Maynooth, an ecclesiastical college which now admits lay students, is a recognized college (as distinct from a constituent college) of the National University. In 1975 the National University granted recognized college status to Colleges of Education for the training of primary school teachers. The University of Dublin consists of one college – Trinity College, Dublin. The term 'recognized college' is used for a number of institutions of higher education which are associated with the National University of Ireland. Their courses must be approved by the senate of the university for the award of degrees and other qualifications of the university.

The referendum proposal contained in the Seventh Amendment of the Constitution Act was approved by the people in July, 1979. This amendment of the Constitution has opened the way for legislation to dissolve the National University of Ireland and establish its constituent colleges as independent universities. The Bill for the purpose of such reorganization is in course of preparation.

There is an independent medical school, the Royal College of Surgeons in Ireland, attended by approximately 730 students (1977/78) many of whom came from abroad. In the academic year 1977/78 there were about 25,500 students in attendance at Irish universities. Generally speaking, entrance qualifications are related to the Leaving Certificate curriculum. About 83 per cent of the capital and recurrent expenditure of the universities is provided from state funds. The state subsidy per student in 1977/78 was £1,340. Fees are payable by the students; but in the year 1977/78 more than 28 per cent of the students were holders of grants.

In 1972 a National Institute for Higher Education was established in Limerick, geared both to degree-level and non-degree level students, and providing courses – many of them module-type – in management, administration and a wide range of technologies. A similar institute, the National Institute of Higher Education, Dublin, will accept students from the school year 1980/81. The National College of Art and Design, which has its immediate origins in the Metropolitan School of Art, which in turn derived from 'a little academy or school for drawing and painting' which the Dublin Society decided to establish in 1746, provides educational services in the domain of art, crafts and design (including the training of teachers of art).

The National Council for Educational Awards (NCEA), is the validating authority for degree-level as well as non-degree level qualifications in third-level non-university institutions generally.

There is no uniform policy on the admission of overseas applicants to colleges of higher education, either at the universities or elsewhere. Competence in English, written and oral, is part of the entry requirement for most colleges. The university institutions reserve the right to restrict the number of students entering first-year undergraduate courses. In practice there are more applicants than places for all courses but in general a student from outside Ireland is more likely to be accepted for a degree course in arts (excluding social science), science, agriculture, law and commerce/business studies.

All applicants for admission to one of the university colleges must be eligible for matriculation in a group of six subjects from a matriculation programme. In the case of non-Irish applicants these six must include English, a language other than English and, in most cases, mathematics.

Adult and community education

Provision for adult education – consisting of part-time day courses and part-time evening courses – has for a long time constituted a very significant element in the responsibilities of the Vocational Education Committees. The numbers participating in adult education courses in community and comprehensive schools have increased progressively since the establishment of these schools.

The universities, the colleges of technology and the regional technical colleges are also actively involved in the provision of adult education courses. The constituent colleges of the National University of Ireland in Cork, Dublin, and Galway have separate adult education or extra-mural departments serving the requirements not only of the immediate neighbourhood but also of more remote areas. St Patrick's College, Maynooth, has also become involved, and offers diploma courses in adult and community education. The colleges of technology in Dublin have always been associated with such activities and the regional technical colleges also make a valuable contribution in their respective areas.

Several voluntary agencies receive state grants in respect of adult education activities. Examples are the Dublin Institute of Adult Education, the College of Industrial Relations, Dublin, *Muintir na Tíre, Macra na Tuaithe,* the Irish Countrywomen's Association and the National Youth Council of Ireland. AONTAS – the National Association of Adult Education, consisting of statutory and voluntary organizations – also receives a state grant.

From the school year 1979/80 adult education organizers are being appointed throughout the country in conjunction with the Vocational Education Committees. These organizers will discharge functions of an organizing and co-ordinating nature including liaison with all appropriate community interests.

The school psychological service

Established in 1965, the school psychological service set its sights early on the emerging and evolving needs of a rapidly developing 'open society', and on the new demands being made on pupils and teachers. It became a corner-stone of policy that the service should, as far as possible, function as an integral element of the support and services generally available to schools for handicapped children provided by the regional health boards including the school medical service and the assessment services for the purpose of furthering all aspects of pupil development, and so of enabling pupils to achieve their full potential in the community. The service is regionally organized; in several areas there are community-based services which operate at both primary and secondary education levels.

The psychological service is concerned with individual and group developmental counselling, with the diagnosis and remediation of learning difficulties, the development of appropriate programmes and curricula, the implementations of changing structures within the school organization and so on. The psychological service has been involved in the provision of basic and in-service training courses for remedial teachers and guidance counsellors.

Initiated and maintained by the Department of Education, the school counselling service effectively assists students in the domain of curriculum choice, and also provides information on career and further educational opportunities. The service works in liaison with the National Manpower Placement Services of the Department of Labour, and facilitates as far as possible the transition of the 15 to 19 age group from the school to the working environment.

School transport

A school transport system has existed in one form or another since 1909 when authority was given for the establishment of school transport van (horse-drawn) services where a national school was closed and its pupils transferred to another, e.g. as a provision which would facilitate the closure of uneconomic schools. Transport continued to be confined mainly to children living in districts where the national schools had been closed, until 1955 when a scheme was introduced permitting the provision of transport services where they were considered necessary to enable national school children to attend school regularly. A state grant of at least two-thirds of the cost of running a service was provided in all cases, the remainder of the cost being met by local contribution.

Free transport to post-primary schools was introduced with the advent of free post-primary education in April 1967, with the aim of ensuring that a child's right to equal opportunity for education would not depend on his parents' circumstances and where he lived in relation to where suitable education could be provided. The post-primary scheme gave free transport to second-level pupils who lived three or more miles from a centre in which free post-primary education was available. The organization and administration of these services was given to *Córas Iompair Éireann,* the national transport company, acting as agents of the Minister for Education. It has been from the beginning a comprehensive countrywide scheme, serving every post-primary centre in the country.

At that time services for national school children were also made free of charge and the arrangements for the provision of the services transferred also to *Córas Iompair Éireann.* The effects of this and of the implementation of the policy of amalgamation of small schools are reflected in the growth of numbers of children on primary school services.

The number of primary school children with transport increased from 2,200 in May 1967 to over 11,000 in September 1967 and to 65,300 by September 1978. The number of post-primary children with free transport has grown from 53,000 in March 1968 when the free post-primary education scheme was still at an early stage, to over 92,000 in September 1978.

Transport is provided either on the ordinary public bus and train services operating throughout the country or on special school bus services. When special school services are necessary, *Córas Iompair Éireann* either employ buses financed by the Department of Education, with ownership vested in the Company as agents of the Minister for Education, or contract with private transport operators. The Company also uses a small number of its own vehicles.

For children who do not qualify for free transport but can be accommodated on the special school services by using spare capacity, term tickets are available at very low rates. At present about 15,000 pupils travel as fare-payers on these services.

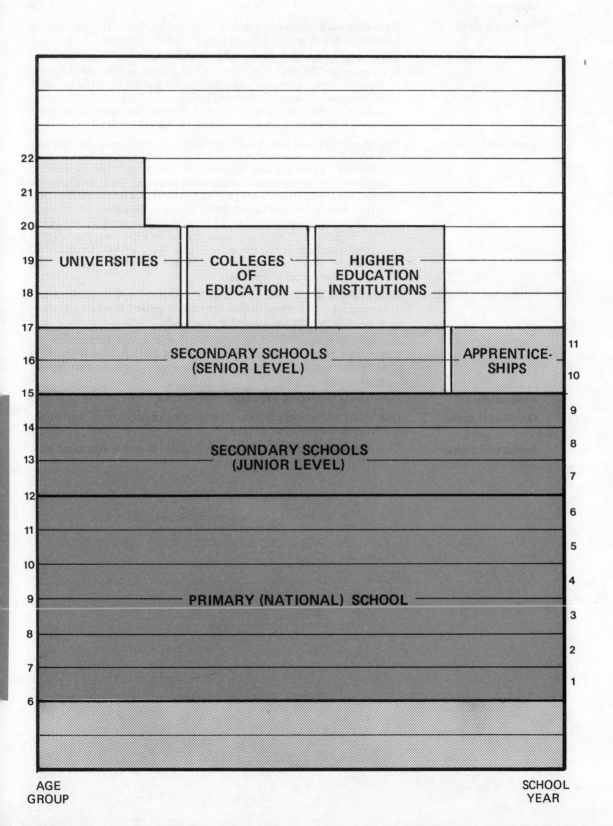

AGE
GROUP

SCHOOL
YEAR

Glossary

National schools	State-supported primary schools originating from the system of national education introduced in the nineteenth century.
Secondary schools	These schools are recognized in accordance with the Rules and Programme for Secondary Schools. They are financially aided by the State through capitation and other grants and through the payment of incremental salary to a recognized quota of teachers. As a consequence of the introduction of the free education scheme the great majority of the schools are paid grants in lieu of tuition fees.
Vocational schools	In each country and city, vocational schools operate under the management of a Vocational Education Committee elected by the local authority. They provide second-level education courses with an emphasis on practical or vocational subjects. They also provide specialized technical training for particular trades or professions, and offer evening courses for adults in a very wide variety of subjects. Pupils in the age-group 12 to 15 years follow courses leading to the Day Vocational Certificate, generally taken after two years, or to the Intermediate Certificate after a three years' course. A substantial number of vocational schools also provide courses leading to the award of the Leaving Certificate.
Comprehensive schools	Established in the 1960s to provide a comprehensive curriculum and serving local communities through local Boards of Management these schools were built and funded by the State.
Community schools	Schools which arose out of the experiment with comprehensive schools, are built to serve a local community and meet the needs formerly served by separate secondary and vocational schools, and are funded by the State.
Denominational	Catering for persons of a specific religious faith.
Constituent college	One of the colleges which forms the teaching and research organs of the National University of Ireland.
Recognized college	Used for a number of institutions of higher education associated with the National University of Ireland.

ITALY

Introduction

Legal basis

The Italian educational system is made up of:

    (a) a state school organization;
    (b) a training organization entrusted to the Regions in the field of vocational education;
    (c) a series of private schemes, parallel to the state school organization and the regional training organization.

The difference between the state schools and the other types of education lies in the fact that only the State is authorized to issue education certificates valid for the whole national territory, which confer the right to compete for all posts in public administrations and are required for acquiring qualifications in all the liberal professions (e.g. medicine, architecture, engineering, etc.).

The term 'state school' is more restrictive than the term 'public school' because schools managed by local authorities (provincial and municipal administrations) are also to be regarded as public.

As a rule the Regions do not manage schools proper, but vocational training courses, which are also public. The diplomas obtained through these courses are valid for trades and professions throughout the national territory.

Non-state schools, that is, the public ones of local authorities and the private ones, can be granted 'legal recognition' if in the judgement of the state administration they show that they offer sufficient educational and teaching safeguards, and if they undertake to follow the programmes of study laid down by the State: this means that the pupils of such schools have the same legal status as the pupils of the state schools, and hence their course of study has the same value in law as that of the pupils of the state schools.

Administrative organization (see Figures 1 and 2)

The state school organization and the non-state public and private school organization are headed by the Ministry of Public Education.

The Minister of Public Education and his Under-Secretaries (each of whom is normally delegated by the Minister to handle a part of school administration) have under them a number of directorates-general. These are:

    — Directorate-General for Primary (Elementary) Education;
    — Directorate-General for First-grade (Intermediate) Secondary Education;
    — Directorate-General for Classical, Scientific and Teacher Training Education;
    — Directorate-General for Technical Education;
    — Directorate-General for Vocational Education;
    — Directorate-General for University Education;
    — Directorate-General for Non-State Schools;
    — Directorate-General for Personnel;

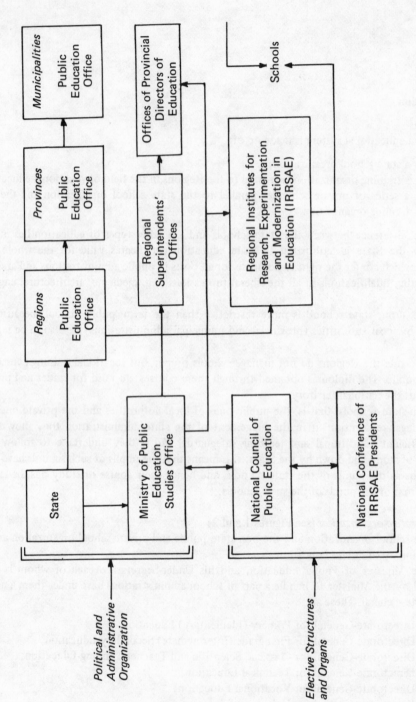

Municipalities
Public Education Office

Provinces
Public Education Office

Regions
Public Education Office

State

Offices of Provincial Directors of Education

Regional Superintendents' Offices

Regional Institutes for Research, Experimentation and Modernization in Education (IRRSAE)

Schools

Ministry of Public Education Studies Office

National Council of Public Education

National Conference of IRRSAE Presidents

Political and Administrative Organization

Elective Structures and Organs

Figure 1

there are also the following inspectorates-general:

- Inspectorate for Nursery Schools;
- Inspectorate for Artistic Education;
- Inspectorate for Physical Education.

The Ministry of Public Education possesses a body of central inspectors who are responsible for inspecting the activities of all state and non-state schools.

Also located in the Ministry of Public Education are the Office of Studies and Programming (responsible directly to the Minister), which supervises research and experimentation, and the Directorate-General for Cultural Exchanges, which looks after cultural and educational relations with other countries.

All proposals for legislative measures and proposals for administrative measures of major importance must, before being published, be submitted for an opinion to national elective administrative organs, namely:

- The National University Council;
- The National School Council (see below).

The Ministry of Public Education operates in the country at large through the Regional Superintendents' offices, whose powers are limited to school buildings and relations with the IRRSAE (Regional Institutes for Research, Experimentation and Modernization in Education) and the offices of the Provincial Directors of Education, which are responsible for the whole of the ordinary administration of nursery schools, elementary schools and intermediate schools (competitions for staff appointments, salaries, career development, pensions, etc.) and for surveillance over all the other types of schools. The Provincial Directors of Education are assisted, through mandatory but non-binding consultations, by the Provincial School Councils. To each Provincial Education Director's office is attached a body of technical inspectors who are responsible for inspecting the activities of nursery, elementary and intermediate schools.

School organization

The school calendar

The school year is fixed at 215 days and begins around 15 September. Lessons end around 10 June and are followed by examinations. Within the school year there are two holiday breaks:

- the Christmas holiday (22 December to 3 January);
- the Easter holidays (about one week);

and also several one-day holidays. The school week is always six days long. Timetables vary according to the type of school.

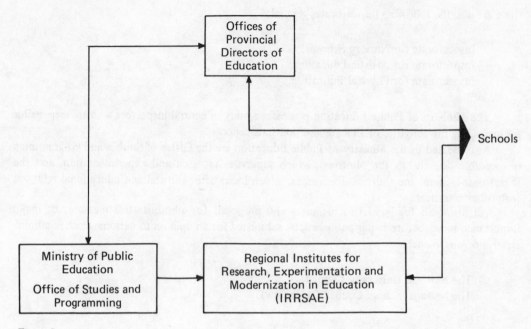

Figure 2

The pupils

Over the past 20 years the school population in the 3–5 year age group has doubled; that in the 6–10 year age group has remained more or less steady; that in the 11–14 year age group has trebled; that in the 15–18 year age group has quadrupled; and, lastly, that in the 19–22/23 year age group has quintupled (see Table 1).

The universities represent a quite specific situation, characterized by a 'stop/go' rhythm, which seems to show a tendency towards restrained growth (for example, in the academic year 1978/79 there were about 6,000 registrations fewer than in 1977/78).

The teachers

Teachers actually employed number 713,000 (1977 census), of whom 27,208 are in nursery schools (as against 11,615 in 1973), 258,974 in elementary schools (225,805 in 1973), 245,553 in lower intermediate schools (215,781 in 1973) and 197,081 in higher secondary schools (153,805 in 1973) (see Table 2).

The trend towards an increasing preponderance of women on teaching staffs, typical of the Italian teaching body, has practically come to a halt in recent years, the heaviest concentration of women teachers still being found in the lower grades of school. This is due essentially to the growing difficulties on the labour market, which impel many male graduates to take up teaching owing to the lack of professional alternatives.

TOTAL NUMBER OF PUPILS

School years	School units	Classes	Male and Female	Female	Pupils registered for first year	Pupils re-doing a year	Pupils awarded leaving certificate
Nursery Schools							
1952–53	13,561	23,541	1,012,238	509,925			
1962–63	18,508	31,436	1,232,602	610,164			
1970–71	23,922	44,622	1,586,785	777,874			
1971–72	25,630	49,839	1,619,773	793,432			
1972–73	27,224	55,767	1,686,392	823,128			
1973–74	28,044	56,555	1,734,710	850,313			
1974–75	28,620	50,574	1,767,612	866,077			
1975–76	29,397	63,434	1,822,527	892,143			
1976–77†	28,978	62,553	1,789,024	—			
1977–78†	29,478	63,335	1,321,744	—			
1978–79†	29,762	66,786	1,854,219	—			
Compulsory Schooling							
Elementary schools							
1952–53	33,181	234,812	4,445,314	2,108,454	1,150,648	715,892	596,975
1962–63	41,390	272,873	4,330,098	2,094,893	924,249	511,353	679,566
1970–71	37,091	281,336	4,840,761	2,343,852	1,061,599	350,037	841,126
1971–72	36,173	281,604	4,913,382	2,380,569	1,006,013	289,597	880,966
1972–73	35,356	284,780	4,964,595	2,380,569	985,481	263,096	897,561
1973–74	34,583	286,451	4,963,389	2,407,616	944,232	221,732	910,040
1974–75	33,982	287,141	4,922,920	2,389,527	919,956	189,585	999,191
1975–76	33,233	284,625	4,833,415	2,348,516	918,162	143,873	964,411
1976–77†	32,867	278,368	4,741,650	—	882,512	—	985,809†
1977–78†	32,001	277,766	4,651,051	2,259,908	875,362	103,502	937,332
1978–79†	31,524	270,034	4,584,300	—	847,253	—	—

Intermediate schools

1952–53	3,374	32,044	963,926	339,774	370,135	—	198,148
1962–63	8,653	53,927	1,594,111	683,221	668,144	220,976	388,795
1970–71	8,942	100,180	2,167,539	1,012,264	858,389	182,216	603,208
1971–72	9,193	105,753	2,286,850	1,071,589	883,692	169,855	644,101
1972–73	9,437	110,557	2,421,799	1,140,117	931,586	178,576	707,695
1973–74	9,656	115,606	2,530,461	1,196,050	958,121	175,180	729,421
1974–75	9,781	118,264	2,628,758	1,248,459	990,963	189,055	777,071
1975–76	9,827	123,062	2,778,597	1,321,447	1,062,751	155,896	782,403
1976–77†	9,949	125,963	2,869,120	—	1,048,240	—	801,085
1977–78	9,970	128,337	2,938,791	1,405,196	1,054,476	202,954	862,878†
1978–79†	9,956	128,298	2,932,615	—	1,035,870	—	—

Higher Secondary Schools

1952–53	2,533	19,449	460,003	173,342	144,015	—	76,438
1962–63	4,490	36,269	929,033	350,788	302,468	88,244	133,089
1970–71	6,308	65,233	1,656,117	688,775	483,911	109,405	312,197
1971–72	6,397	70,914	1,732,178	727,460	53,112	130,685	330,673
1972–73	6,549	75,394	1,820,458	773,740	526,674	129,607	343,492
1973–74	6,682	80,508	1,915,857	829,282	564,015	132,328	352,761
1974–75	6,772	83,533	1,990,649	871,217	579,249	131,494	370,990
1975–76	6,825	88,931	2,096,582	929,813	607,926	117,234	401,407
1976–77†	6,882	92,167	2,189,183	—	625,629	—	406,616
1977–78	6,987	95,783	2,269,934	1,041,704	653,712	160,734	432,624†
1978–79†	7,010	98,073	2,334,766	—	701,371	—	—

† Provisional data.

Table 1: The development of the school system

Type of school	Established teachers	Non-established teachers	Craft teachers	Total teachers	Annual average increase
Nursery schools					
1972–73		11,615		11,615	43.5
1973–74		16,007		16,007	37.8
1974–75	15,024†	4,783		19,807	23.7
1975–76				23,341	17.8
1976–77				27,208	16.6
Elementary schools					
1972–73	211,870	13,935		225,805	4.5
1973–74	226,405	10,114		236,519	4.7
1974–75	230,045	10,940		240,985	1.9
1975–76	230,887	11,979		242,886	0.8
1976–77	255,763	3,074		258,842	6.6
1977–78	253,870	5,104		258,974	0.1
Lower intermediate schools					
1972–73	67,837	147,944		215,781	
1973–74	68,920	156,038		224,958	
1974–75	168,831	59,380		228,211	
1975–76	169,079	70,185		239,264	
1976–77	161,648	75,647		237,295	
1977–78	158,277	87,276		245,553	
Higher secondary schools					
1972–73	43,766	95,253	14,786	153,805	10.3
1973–74	43,967	101,670	14,169	159,806	3.9
1974–75	99,141	52,451	14,350	165,942	3.8
1975–76	101,877	58,581	14,975	175,433	5.7
1976–77	101,589	68,487	49,579	189,659	8.1
1977–78	99,548	76,647	20,886	197,081	3.9
Total state teachers					
1972–73	323,473	268,747	14,786	607,006	7.9
1973–74	339,292	283,829	14,169	637,290	5.0
1974–75	513,041	127,554	14,350	654,945	2.8
1975–76	–	–	14,975	680,904	4.0
1976–77	–	–	–	713,004	4.7

† Data of the Ministry of Public Education.
Source: Prepared by CENSIS from ISTAT data.

Table 2: Teaching staff in state schools according to legal status and type of school

The percentage data illustrating the halt in the trend towards the employment of increasing numbers of women teachers are as follows:

- 1973/74 elementary schools 82.8 per cent
- 1976/77 elementary schools 83.2 per cent
- 1973/74 lower and higher intermediate schools 56.2 per cent
- 1976/77 lower and higher intermediate schools 56.2 per cent.

Expenditure on education

The Italian system of public education covers altogether a band of users ranging in age from 3/4 to 22/23 years (see Figure 2). The users of the school and university service (1978/79 data) number over 12,000,000, distributed as follows:

- nursery school: 1,854,219
- elementary school: 4,584,300
- intermediate school: 2,932,615
- higher secondary school: 2,334,766
- university: 756,922

The incidence of public expenditure on education and culture in relation to net national income has remained at around 6.6 per cent (6.7 per cent in 1977). In 1978 public expenditure on the item 'education and culture' totalled 11,891.6 thousand million lire, representing an increase of about 15 per cent on the previous year. On the other hand, the incidence of state expenditure on education in relation to aggregate state expenditure has declined (11.5 per cent in 1978), having remained steady at around 13.5 per cent in the previous three years. The decline is found to be more marked if account is taken of the fact that expenditure on education has also fallen in relation to aggregate state revenue, decreasing to 12.6 per cent in 1978 as compared with 15.2 per cent in the previous years (see Table 3). Between 1970 and 1978 the expenditure of the Ministry of Public Education rose from 2,043.2 to 7,525.9 thousand million lire (up 268.3 per cent) and in 1978 alone it increased by 10.1 per cent as compared with approximately 28 per cent for the previous two years. The budget of the Ministry of Public Education is heavily dominated by expenditure on staffing (about 92 per cent). Over the last eight years average expenditure per pupil has shown an appreciable increase: for example, a pupil in vocational education now costs the State over one million lire a year, a pupil in intermediate school 775,000 lire and a pupil in technical education almost 850,000 lire (see Table 4).

The nursery school

Nursery or infant schools cater for children of both sexes aged between 3/4 and 5/6 years and in law take the following forms:

- religious private nursery schools
- lay private nursery schools
- municipal public nursery schools
- state public nursery schools.

The state public nursery school

Instituted on 9 March 1968, state public nursery schooling is established as a public-service structure for all children of Italian citizens and pursues aims of 'education, development of the children's personality, assistance and preparation for participation in compulsory schooling, rounding off the work of the family. Attendance is free of charge and optional'.

It is normally composed of three sections corresponding to the age of the children: 3/4, 4/5, 5/6 years, each of which may not have less than 15 or more than 30 children registered/attending. The minimum weekly timetable is 42 hours over six days a week, and the schooling is in operation for not less than 10 months a year.

The teaching programme is at present regulated – as regards objectives and contents – by 'guidelines' prepared by a commission of experts and introduced under the 1969 Act. With the establishment of state nursery schooling, school attendance has shown a considerable increase,

Years	PUBLIC EXPENDITURE†					Percentage incidence on net national income at market prices	Average public expenditure per capita (lire)
	State	Regions‡	Provinces§	Municipalities	Total		
1970	2,680.3	25.2	69.0	294.8	3,069.3	5.8	57,381
1971	3,145.5	33.2	82.9	349.1	3,610.7	6.2	67,073
1972	3,246.7	35.9	100.6	444.6	3,827.8	6.0	70,651
1973	3,730.0	44.2	127.8	526.2	4,428.2	5.9	81,034
1974	4,422.4	213.7	127.6	656.2	5,419.9	6.0	98,222
1975	5,266.4	293.9	164.8	742.3	6,467.4	6.3	116,226
1976	6,304.4	354.3	196.8	958.5	7,814.0	6.1	139,501
1977	8,406.9	505.2	231.2	1,212.4	10,355.7	6.7	183,863
1978§§	9,422.8	650.0†§	293.7	1,525.1	11,891.6	6.6	210,099

† State expenditure is net of contributions to local authorities for state public education provided by the municipalities and provinces; in the case of local authorities the figures relate only to current expenditure.
‡ From 1974 onwards the contributions to the ordinary regions and the expenditure of the autonomous provinces are included.
§ From 1974 onwards the expenditure of the autonomous provinces is excluded.
§§ Provisional data.
†§ Estimate.

Source: ITALY. MINISTRY OF THE BUDGET AND ECONOMIC PROGRAMMING (1979). General report on the economic situation of the country (1978). Rome.

Table 3: Public expenditure on education and culture, according to spending authority (thousand million lire). Years 1970-78

Grade of education	1970	1971	1972	1973	1974	1975	1976	1977	1978	Index numbers (base: 1970 = 100)
Nursery schools	339.7	224.0	238.5	241.8	280.9	282.1	333.0	454.7	493.3	145.2
Elementary education	134.0	155.0	164.3	211.4	253.9	275.8	342.7	453.9	517.3	386.0
Intermediate education	231.7	277.8	293.7	351.3	429.3	497.1	594.3	750.7	775.7	334.6
Classical, scientific and teacher training education	201.6	261.0	263.2	308.0	381.4	375.7	515.5	604.2	651.4	323.1
Technical education	307.7	303.5	345.6	405.6	450.7	476.6	614.9	740.4	839.5	272.8
Vocational education	418.0	424.3	477.7	540.9	583.3	632.6	783.1	991.5	1,111.7	266.0
University education	491.2	470.5	464.9	631.7	668.3	759.6	823.6	1,042.7	1,086.0	221.1

Table 4: Average final expenditure of the Ministry of Public Education per state school pupil in the various grades of education (thousands of lire). Years 1970-78

rising from 57 per cent (1970) to 72 per cent (1979) of children in the 3–5 years age group (see Table 5). In absolute figures the statistical data for the year 1978/79 are as follows:

	Percentage of children	
Pupils registered	*in the 3–5 year age group*	*Teachers*
1,854,000	72.3 per cent	111,061†

† In 1979 the 'helpers', who previously played a subordinate role, were also put on the teacher establishment: they may be estimated to number around 10,000.

Recruitment of staff for the state nursery schools (the only kind of school in which the teachers have rights and duties regulated by the law) is by competition under the rules applicable to all the teaching staff of state schools.[1] Under the most recent provisions there are two forms of competition: (1) a qualifying course of varying duration (not less than six months, with at least 200 hours of teaching, for personnel taken on *de facto* as 'temporary teachers' or 'engaged temporarily'); (2) a competition consisting of an examination before a state commission, followed by a year of in-school practice, directed by a team and concluding with a second examination, upon which enrolment on the establishment is dependent.

The elementary school

The elementary school is today the basic initial structure of the Italian school system. Elementary schooling is free of charge, lasts five years, caters for the 6–11 year age group and represents the first phase of compulsory schooling.

Organization of teaching

Under Act No. 1254 of 24 December 1957 elementary schooling is split into two 'cycles', the first of which is made up of the first and second classes, while the second consists of the third, fourth and fifth classes. Movements from one class to another are based upon assessments made by the class teachers themselves. At the end of the five years, and subject to the passing of an examination, the elementary school leaving certificate is obtained.

The programmes of study currently in use are still those issued on 14 June 1955 (Act No. 503). They have a dual function: (1) laying down rules; and (2) providing guidelines. They lay down rules (which indeed are binding) as regards the degree of preparation which pupils must

	STATE SCHOOLS		NON-STATE SCHOOLS		TOTAL	
Years	*Number*	*%*	*Number*	*%*	*Number*	*%*
1972–73	289,446	+ 46.1	1,387,936	−2.8	1,686,382	+ 4.1
1973–74	365,374	+ 26.2	1,369,336	−1.3	1,734,710	+ 2.9
1974–75	443,778	+ 21.5	1,323,336	−3.3	1,767,612	+ 1.9
1975–76	512,623	+ 15.5	1,309,904	−1.1	1,822,527	+ 3.1
1976–77	575,153	+ 12.2	1,213,871	−7.3	1,789,024	−1.8
1977–78†	633,239	+ 10.1	1,188,505	−2.1	1,821,744	+ 1.8
1978–79†	693,796	+ 9.6	1,160,423	−2.4	1,854,219	+ 1.8

† Provisional data.
Source: ISTAT data.

Table 5: Trend of pupil numbers in nursery schools (1972–78)

attain; they provide guidelines as regards methods of teaching (which is unrestricted). In the first 'cycle' education is based on the teaching of reading, writing and counting. In the second 'cycle' the content of the education is arranged under specific subject heads, such as:

religion (Catholic, introduced into the state schools in virtue of the 1929 Concordat between the Italian State and the Catholic Church)[2]

— moral, civic and physical education;
— history;
— geography;
— science;
— arithmetic and geometry;
— Italian language;
— drawing and writing;
— singing;
— manual and practical work.

The teachers qualified to teach in elementary schools are those entering the profession from the four-year teacher training institutes.

Since 1971 (Act No. 820) full-time schooling from 8 a.m. to 4 p.m. five days a week and from 8 a.m. to 1 p.m. on Saturdays has been in operation on an experimental basis and in schools expressly requesting it. This scheme has involved introducing into the curriculum the study of additional subjects and specific kinds of instruction (activities concerned with linguistic expression, musical activities, artistic activities, technological activities, etc.) which are mostly carried on in the afternoons and are always conducted by elementary-school teachers.

A further substantial change in the organization of elementary schooling concerns the appraisal of scholastic merit: the traditional 'grades' have been abolished and replaced by analytical and rounded assessments (for each pupil); these assessments are transcribed on to personal cards, which take the place of the school reports.

Legal basis
Originally in the hands of the municipalities, elementary schooling was brought under the State in 1912, and since 1933 it has been governed by uniform regulations covering the whole of the national territory. At present it is organized under a centralized administrative system (see *Administrative organization* section), as modified, however, by the introduction in 1974 of the collegial organs (see section on *The democratic management organs in the school system*).

Elementary schooling is administered in school groups (comprising several schools), directed by a local director of education, who is a graduate or holds a university diploma in 'school supervision', and is recruited exclusively from among established elementary-school teachers.

Elementary-school attendance, which remained steady from the early sixties, has undergone a continuous decline in recent years: between 1974 and 1979 the fall was around 7 per cent, the total number of children attending having dropped from a peak of 4,964,595 in 1972/73 to 4,584,300 in 1978/79. Over the last five years the number of registrations for the first class had dropped 10.3 per cent because of the falling birth-rate (see Table 6).

The intermediate school
Intermediate schooling is three-year post-elementary education catering for the 11–14 year age group and being the final phase of compulsory schooling. With the reform of 1962 (Act No. 1859) it is single intermediate schooling free of charge for everyone (in accordance with the stipulations

	School units	Classes	TOTAL NUMBER OF PUPILS Male/Female	Female	Pupils registered for the first year	Pupils re-doing a year	Pupils awarded leaving certificate
			Elementary schools				
1952–62							
Absolute fig.	+ 2,789	+ 38,058	− 91,112	+ 2,685	−244,416	−220,299	+ 97,970
%	+ 7.3	+ 1.6	− 2.0	+ 0.1	− 21.2	− 30.8	+ 16.4
1963–73							
Absolute fig.	− 6,034	+ 11,557	+ 634,497	+ 312,848	+ 61,232	−248,257	+ 217,995
%	−14.6	+ 4.2	+ 14.6	+ 14.9	+ 6.6	− 48.5	+ 32.1
1974–79							
Absolute fig.	− 2,759	−16,107	−379,389		− 96,979		
%	− 8.0	− 5.6	− 7.6		− 10.3		

Table 6: Development of elementary and intermediate schools, by periods of time: 1952–62, 1963–73, 1974–79

of the Constitution of the Italian Republic, Article 34). Its purpose is to prepare pre-adolescents for entry into working life and society.

Organization of teaching

New teaching programmes have been in operation for a little over a year (since 9 February 1979). These confer equal status on all subjects and all forms of teaching, lay down general objectives and contents and abound in methodological indications in that they lay down the principle of the programming by the Class Council of educational routes, taking account of the various cultural levels of the pupils.

The subjects taught are:

— religion (same remark as under 'elementary school');
— linguistic education;
— education in history, civics and geography;
— education in a foreign language;
— education in mathematics, science and health;
— artistic education;
— technical education;
— musical education;
— physical education.

As a rule, each school must not have more than 24 classes, the size of which may vary between 25 and 30 pupils.

In addition to the school buildings the municipalities must provide the equipment for the buildings and look after their general upkeep.

As a part of compulsory education, intermediate schooling is non-selective in character; the repeat examinations have been abolished and replaced by multi-disciplinary 'catching-up courses' and 'support courses' for pupils in difficulty, to be taken in the second half of the school year and with a maximum duration of 160 hours of lessons.

In intermediate schools, as in elementary schools, the 'grades' awarded to pupils by individual teachers have been finally abolished. They have been replaced by the 'assessment card', which in content and method is very similar to the one in use in elementary schools.

At the end of the three-year period pupils passing a final examination obtain the intermediate school leaving certificate, which provides access to the courses of higher secondary education.

After a strong expansion over the past 25 years (from 963,926 pupils in 1952/53 to 2,938,791 in 1977/78), attendance at intermediate schools is now tending to drop appreciably, mainly on account of the falling birth-rate: in 1978/79 as compared with 1977/78 registrations fell by about 6,000 in total and by 19,000 for the first class, representing reductions of 0.4 per cent and 0.7 per cent respectively (see Table 7).

The higher secondary school

Higher secondary schooling is post-compulsory education which is not free of charge, catering by and large for users in the 14–19 year age group. At present in all its forms it provides access to all university faculties; however, while the classical, scientific and artistic schools do not confer professional qualifications, all the other types of schools issue a professional-qualification diploma, which provides access to the intermediate professions.

The secondary school system consists of five kinds of school, comprising 20 basic types:

1. *Grammar school education of two types:* classical grammar school and scientific grammar school;
2. *Teacher training education of two types:* teacher training institute and teacher training school;
3. *Technical education of eight types:* agricultural, commercial, surveying, nautical, industrial, women's, business and tourism institutes;
4. *Vocational education of six types:* agricultural, industrial, maritime, commercial, hotel, women's vocational institutes, each of which is split into a large number of specialities (over 100 altogether);
5. *Artistic education of two types:* artistic grammar school and art institute (the latter split into 23 speciality sections).

Historically, there has been a distinction between the technical institutes, which offer a five-year course in preparation for the near-professional grades in the public services, industry and

	PERCENTAGE AVERAGE ANNUAL INCREASES	
	Total number registered	*Registered for the first year*
Between 1950/51 and 1960/61	+ 7.0	+ 5.9
Between 1960/61 and 1970/71	+ 4.4	+ 3.7
Between 1970/71 and 1973/74	+ 5.1	+ 3.6
Between 1973/74 and 1974/75	+ 3.9	+ 3.3
Between 1975/76 and 1976/77	+ 3.3	− 1.8
Between 1977/78 and 1978/79	− 0.4	− 0.7

Source: Prepared by CENSIS from ISTAT data.

Table 7: Trend of school attendance in intermediate schools

commerce, and the vocational institutes which offer shorter courses preparing technicians and skilled workers for the various sectors of the economy. But this distinction is now becoming blurred: the vocational institutes also in many cases have five-year courses that permit entry to universities.

About three-quarters of the young people reaching the requisite academic standard (intermediate school leaving certificate) enter the various channels of higher secondary education, with a higher proportion in the south of the country (77.2 per cent for 1978/79) than in the north (69.5 per cent for 1978/79) (see Table 8). Under the Decree of the President of the Republic No. 416 of 1974 all the higher secondary school establishments are granted administrative autonomy in regard to their school operating expenditure (articles 2 and 25).

Grammar school education

The classical grammar school

The classical grammar school (*liceo classico*) provides a five-year course (14–19 years), the first two years of which constitute classical high school (*Ginnasio*), although today with the abolition of the examinations for admission to the first grammar school year, the grammar school 'cycle' may be regarded as a single course of study.

Type of school	1975/76	1976/77	1977/78	1978/79
	Absolute figures			
Vocational institutes	347,593	367,426	399,345	417,097
Technical institutes as a whole:	932,603	989,668	1,030,206	1,038,940
– industrial technical institutes	314,670	312,303	304,897	498,821
– commercial technical institutes	391,897	439,933	476,434	499,212
– technical institutes for surveyors	127,847	133,061	134,409	134,860
Teacher training schools and institutes	198,426	201,023	206,299	217,962
Scientific grammar schools†	373,614	391,729	389,777	394,832
Classical grammar schools	190,874	188,978	187,282	194,200
Art institutes and artistic grammar schools	54,072	55,359	57,023	57,785
TOTAL	2,096,582	2,189,183	2,269,934	2,334,766
	Percentages			
Vocational institutes	16.6	16.8	17.6	17.9
Technical institutes as a whole:	44.4	45.2	45.4	45.1
– industrial technical institutes	15.0	14.3	13.4	16.8
– commercial technical institutes	18.7	20.1	21.0	21.5
– technical institutes for surveyors	6.1	6.1	5.9	5.8
Teacher training schools and institutes	9.5	9.2	9.1	9.3
Scientific grammar schools†	17.8	17.7	17.2	16.9
Classical grammar schools	9.1	8.6	8.2	8.3
Art institutes and artistic grammar schools	2.6	2.5	2.5	2.5
TOTAL	100.0	100.0	100.0	100.0

† Including language grammar schools.
Source: Prepared by CENSIS from ISTAT data.

Table 8: Distribution of pupils by type of higher secondary school

The subjects taught are as follows:

- religion (same remark as under 'elementary school');
- Italian language and literature;
- Latin language and literature;
- Greek language and literature;
- foreign language and literature (mainly English and French);
- history;
- philosophy;
- geography (for high school), natural sciences, chemistry and astronomical geography (for grammar school);
- mathematics;
- physics;
- history of art;
- physical education.

The hours of teaching vary from class to class: 27 hours for high school classes, 28 hours for the first and second grammar school years and 29 hours for the third.

The classical grammar school provides access to all university faculties, including (since 1969) the teacher training faculty. The teaching programmes in operation today are still those of 1952.

The scientific grammar school

The scientific grammar school is a five-year course (14–19 years) which originated in the conversion in 1923 of the physics and mathematics section of the technical institutes.

At present the scientific grammar school is split into a two-year period and a three-year period without any examination between them.

The subjects taught are:

- religion (same remark as under 'elementary school');
- Italian language and literature;
- Latin language and literature;
- foreign language and literature (mainly English and French);
- history;
- philosophy;
- geography (for the two-year period), natural sciences, chemistry, astronomical geography (for the three-year period);
- physics;
- mathematics;
- drawing;
- physical education.

The weekly number of lesson hours is distributed as follows: 25 for the first class, 27 for the second class, 28 for the third class, 29 for the fourth class and 30 for the fifth class. There are only slight differences between the two types of grammar school as regards programmes and hours: in the classical grammar school 19 hours a week are devoted to the humanities and 7 to scientific subjects; in the scientific grammar school 17 hours a week are devoted to the humanities and 8 to scientific subjects.

The scientific grammar school, like the classical grammar school, provides access to all university faculties. The programmes used likewise go back to 1952.

Teacher training

The teacher training institute

This provides a four-year course (14–18 years), whose purpose is to prepare young people for the profession of elementary school teacher.

Since the end of the Second World War the third and fourth classes have been required to do teaching practice ('apprenticeship'), which has to be performed in elementary classes under the guidance of a graduate in the theory of education ('apprenticeship' instructor), assisted by the local director of education at the elementary school where the practice is performed.

The subjects taught are:

— religion (same remark as under 'elementary school');
— Italian language and literature;
— Latin language and literature;
— foreign language (mainly English and French);
— philosophy and theory of education;
— psychology;
— history and geography;
— natural sciences, chemistry and astronomical geography;
— mathematics and physics;
— drawing and history of art;
— choral singing;
— physical education;
— a musical instrument (optional).

The weekly timetable is as follows: 32 hours for the first class, 33 for the second, 31 for the third and 30 for the fourth.

The diploma awarded at the end of the four-year course is a qualification for elementary school teaching and is a qualifying certificate of study for admission to the teacher training faculty of Italian universities.

Since 1969 all holders of the teacher training institute diploma may register (Act No. 910 on liberalization of access) in all university faculties once they have completed (successfully) a preparatory course lasting a full school year at a higher secondary school.

The teacher training school

Teacher training schools provide a three-year post-compulsory course of study (14–17 years) at the end of which the diploma of nursery-school teacher is obtained. Access is either through an admission examination for candidates who hold only the elementary school leaving certificate or upon application for candidates holding the intermediate school leaving certificate.

The subjects taught are:

— religion (same remark as under 'elementary school');
— Italian language and literature;
— theory of education;
— history and geography;
— mathematics, book-keeping and natural sciences;
— hygiene and child care;
— music and choral singing;
— home economics and domestic work;
— modelling and drawing.

In addition, there is a parallel 'apprenticeship' course to be followed in the second and third years. One or more nursery-school classes are attached to each school.

Technical education

The technical institutes (see beginning of section, p. 00, category 3)
These are five-year schools (14–19 years), highly vocational in character and with the declared aim of training young people for careers in the public service, industries, crafts and commerce, and precisely because of this specific aim the actual legal framework of the technical institutes has been affected more than any other by the radical economic and social changes that have occurred in the country.

At the present time (as already stated) there are eight basic types of technical institute, of which five go back to the old order of 1931 and three have been added in recent times: the women's technical institute, the technical institute for tourism and commerce and the technical institute for accountants and foreign correspondents.

The programmes of study in use today go back to 1961 (revision of the 1936 programmes).

The wide range of subjects and specialities is distributed over the five years in such a way that the theoretical subjects (e.g. mathematics, physics, science, etc.) are most heavily concentrated in the first two years and the applied/vocational subjects (e.g. topography, book-keeping, etc.) in the final three years.

The teaching timetable is the heaviest, in quantitative terms, of all the timetables of higher secondary schools; whereas at grammar schools the teaching hours never exceed (on average) 30 a week, in the technical institutes they may be as high as 40 a week.

Following the 1969 liberalization of access to the universities holders of technical-institute diplomas may register in any university faculty, including the faculties of foreign languages and those of the Institute of Oriental Studies in Naples.

State vocational education

The vocational institutes
These were created around 1950 for the purpose of preparing, through short training courses, technicians and skilled workers for the various sectors of the economy, and are today the most effective branch of the whole secondary school system.

Until a few years ago these institutes did not provide any form of access to the universities: today most of them have five-year courses which allow such access. Each of them was set up under a specific presidential decree and not, like all the other institutes, under a general Act.

As previously stated, there are six types, each of which is split into a large number of sections or 'channels' covering 2, 3 or at most 4 years, the number of hours of theoretical/ practical lessons being around 40 a week.

The general picture is as follows:

- the vocational institute for agriculture has 16 sections, each lasting 2 years;
- the vocational institute for industry has 57 sections, lasting from 2 to 4 years;
- the vocational institute for maritime activities has 7 sections, lasting from 2 to 3 years;
- the vocational institute for commerce has 6 sections, lasting from 2 to 3 years;
- the vocational institute for the hotel business and tourism has 6 sections, lasting from 2 to 4 years;
- the women's vocational institute has 20 sections, lasting from 2 to 3 years.

In addition to the vocational subjects for the various specialities, the programmes include a single general discipline; general culture and civics.

Admission to the state vocational institutes is by means of the intermediate school leaving certificate or through an admission examination in the case of candidates not holding the appropriate qualification and over 14 years of age.

Under the Act of 27 October 1969 experimental fourth-year and fifth-year courses (previously mentioned) were set up, at the end of which students are required to take the state examination for the vocational matriculation diploma, which is valid for admission to any university faculty. The programmes and timetables of the experimental courses are laid down from time to time by the Minister of Public Education, after consultation with the National Council of Public Education.

The subjects common to all sections are:

— religion (same remark as under 'elementary schools');
— Italian language and literature;
— history;
— civics;
— physical education.

Artistic education

The art institute

This is at present split into no less than 23 specialized sections or 'channels', each of which has courses lasting from three to five years. Students in the art institutes, as in the state vocational institutes, are able to attend two-year courses extending the period of study to five years, and thus, after passing the matriculation examination, acquire the right of access to university faculties. Art institutes also provide access to the Academy of Fine Arts and to the profession of teacher for 'drawing' in secondary education establishments.

The artistic grammar school

This is a four-year school split, after a common two-year period, into two sections:

(a) one preparing for the study of painting, sculpture, decoration and scene-painting in the schools of the Academy of Fine Arts; and
(b) the other preparing for study in the faculty of architecture and for art-teaching in intermediate schools.

Since the liberalization of access to university in 1969 all students who have passed the matriculation examinations and successfully completed a preparatory year (see under *Teacher training institute* on p. 168) have the right of access to all university faculties.

The organization of studies and the subjects taught remain as they were in 1926.

In addition to the specialized disciplines, the programmes include the following cultural subjects:

— literature and history;
— history of art;
— mathematics and physics;
— natural history, chemistry and geography.

The Universities

Universities and higher institutes have full autonomy in teaching and administration, although under the law they are subject to the supervision of the organs of the State and specifically of the Ministry of Public Education.

Universities and higher institutes may also be established by public and private bodies.

The state universities, 36 in total, and catering for 92 per cent of university students in Italy, receive a financial contribution from the State. The independent (private) universities are not entitled to any financial aid but, depending upon circumstances and needs, may apply for and obtain state financial contributions.

Administrative organization and teaching structure

The organs responsible for governing a university are: the Rector (or the Director in the case of higher institutes), the Academic Body, the Academic Senate, the Administrative Council, the Faculty heads and Councils.

The Rector (or Director in the case of higher institutes), who is elected by all the established academic staff (Academic Body) and holds office for three years, chairs the Academic Senate, which is the governing body composed of all the Faculty heads. Faculty Councils, which up to 1973 were composed solely of the established academic staff, now also include academic staff of different standing and representatives of the junior teaching staff.

Representatives of the students, in numbers not defined by the law, may also participate in Faculty Councils, but only with the right to speak.

In the teaching sphere, Faculty Councils co-ordinate the programmes of the courses, fix the timetable for lectures and set up specialization courses and advanced study schools.

Under the Act of December 1969 'on the liberalization of study plans' all students registered at a university are entitled to draw up a plan of study differing from those laid down by the teaching regulations of the individual faculties provided that they adhere to the disciplines actually taught and the number of subjects laid down by the law. Once approved by the Faculty Council the study plan drawn up by the student is valid for all purposes.

The existing university faculties are:

— medicine and surgery	6 years
— teacher training	4 years
— mathematical, physical and natural sciences	4 years
— law	4 years
— literature and philosophy	4 years
— engineering	5 years
— economics and commerce	4 years
— political sciences	4 years
— architecture	5 years
— pharmacy	4 years
— foreign languages and literature	4 years
— agriculture	4 years
— higher institute of physical education	3 years
— fine arts	4 years
— nautical institute	4 years
— industrial chemistry	4 years
— social and statistical sciences	4 years
— institute of oriental studies	4 years

University population

After the decline in new registrations recorded in the previous two academic years (1976–77), there was an appreciable revival of demand in the last academic year (1978/79), first-year registrations rising from 235,069 in 1977/78 to 242,848 in 1978/79, an increase of 3.7 per cent. It would seem, however, that the university population, while reaching the point of complete saturation with almost 1,000,000 students registered (756,922 attached to specific courses plus 240,000 unattached), has stabilized midway between 'reduced congestion and further growth'.

Of the total population, about one-third attend regularly, one-third work normal hours in full-time employment and one-third are in an intermediate situation (casual work, black-economy work, spasmodic attendance; many are prepared to give up their studies if they find a steady job). This state of affairs is providing increasingly strong arguments in favour of adopting more flexible forms of education: evening classes and home study (correspondence courses, multi-media courses, TV, radio, etc.).

The trend of the numbers of students doing courses in the various faculties is shown in Table 9.

FACULTY	68/69	76/77	77/78	78/79
Mathematics, physics and natural sciences	60,096	81,456	79,693	76,263
Pharmacy	5,993	21,716	22,337	21,913
Medicine and surgery	44,127	158,383	156,803	149,673
Engineering	39,676	67,408	66,542	63,194
Architecture	9,867	47,631	46,255	45,780
Agriculture	5,405	15,879	18,930	20,008
Veterinary science	1,247	8,699	10,162	11,125
Economics and commerce	84,068	51,271	59,491	67,320
Political sciences	7,144	27,889	26,295	24,304
Law	33,393	101,078	100,262	100,915
Literature and philosophy	52,001	73,331	70,359	72,476
Teacher training	66,730	78,024	78,113	73,409
Other faculties or institutes	5,932	25,356	27,583	30,542
TOTALS	415,649	758,130	762,825	756,922

Table 9: Student numbers by faculty

The annual outflow of graduates (77,151 in 1978) increased by 19.5 per cent between 1972 and 1978, whereas the number of students registered for the first year rose by 13.2 per cent (see Tables 10 and 11). Over the same period there was also an increase in the number of unemployed graduates looking for their first job (a rise of around 15 per cent between 1977 and 1978), statistics which show how the waiting period in the transition from education to working life has lengthened.

School buildings

Responsibility for the construction of school buildings is shared between local authorities and the State.

Responsibility rests with the municipalities for nursery schools, elementary schools and intermediate schools and for higher secondary schools (classical, scientific and teacher training) and with the provinces for technical and vocational education.

The Regions are responsible for buildings in respect of vocational training courses directly managed by themselves.

University building is entirely in the hands of the State.

Faculty	1975/76	1976/77	1977/78	1978/79†	% VARIATIONS		
					1975/76–1976/77	1976/77–1977/78	1977/78–1978/79
Medicine and surgery	33,354	31,982	27,725	25,454	− 4.1	−13.3	− 6.4
Teacher training	28,948	27,354	26,670	27,410	− 5.5	− 2.9	2.8
Mathematical, physical and natural sciences	29,149	28,250	27,316	27,244	− 3.1	− 3.3	− 0.3
Law	36,821	36,754	35,868	38,545	− 0.2	− 2.4	7.5
Literature and Philosophy	24,200	22,198	22,572	24,520	− 8.3	1.7	8.6
Engineering	20,503	19,340	18,056	18,540	− 5.7	− 6.6	2.7
Economics and Commerce	21,260	24,446	27,413	30,873	15.0	12.1	12.6
Political sciences	11,580	10,713	9,209	8,789	− 7.5	−14.0	− 4.6
Architecture	12,659	13,273	11,241	11,305	4.8	−15.3	0.6
Pharmacy	6,733	6,817	6,443	6,186	1.2	− 5.5	− 4.0
Foreign languages and literature	3,234	4,070	4,367	4,568	26.5	6.8	4.6
Agriculture	5,904	6,639	7,858	7,526	12.4	18.4	− 4.2
Physical education	2,894	3,465	4,134	4,992	19.7	19.3	20.7
Veterinary science	2,543	3,109	3,369	3,539	22.2	8.4	5.0
Other faculties (oriental studies, social sciences, statistics, industrial chemistry, nautical and banking studies, maritime studies, economic and social sciences)	2,654	2,847	2,828	2,857	7.3	− 0.7	1.0
TOTAL	242,436	241,277	235,069	242,848	− 0.5	− 2.6	3.7

† Provisional data.
Source: Prepared by CENSIS from ISTAT data.

Table 10: Students registered for the first year, by faculty (1976–79)

Recruitment of staff

The teaching staff of the nursery schools still come from the three-year teacher training schools, access to which is through the intermediate school leaving certificate, or from the four-year teacher training institutes. The four-year teacher training institutes still provide training for elementary school teachers. The staff of the secondary schools (lower and higher) come from the universities. A university degree is essential for participation in the procedure whereby teachers are enrolled on the staffing lists of the state school administration. This procedure has undergone many changes in recent years. At present it is regulated by a very recent Act (1980), which provides for:

(a) a competition based on written and oral examinations and practical tests;
(b) a competition based solely on academic and teaching qualifications.

Candidates passing the competition tests are enrolled on the staff provisionally and complete in the classes assigned to them a year of teaching 'apprenticeship' supervised by a commission of experts. At the end of that year, if the judgement of the commission is favourable, their enrolment is confirmed.

University staff is at present recruited by means of national competitions based on academic qualifications alone in the case of established academic staff, on academic qualifications and on

	1967/68	1972/73	1975/76	1976/77	1977/78	1978/79
Scientific	17.5	15.0	14.2	13.9	13.8	13.2
Medical	8.3	14.4	13.8	13.2	11.8	10.7
Engineering	12.7	14.4	14.4	14.2	13.1	18.9
Agricultural	1.6	2.2	3.5	4.0	4.8	4.5
Economic	22.5	15.3	16.8	17.9	18.6	19.2
Legal	6.1	12.5	14.1	14.3	14.3	15.1
Literature	9.2	9.3	9.1	9.0	9.4	9.9
Teacher training	19.7	15.5	12.2	11.3	11.5	11.5
Diplomas	2.4	1.4	1.9	2.2	2.7	3.0
TOTAL	100.0	100.0	100.0	100.0	100.0	100.0

Source: Prepared by CENSIS from ISTAT data.

Table 11: First-year registrations: percentage compositions by group of graduate courses (some typical years between 1968 and 1978)

Inter-class council (elementary school)
First case: second class, with six sections

Parents   (6) ○○○○○○
Teachers   (6) ●●●●●●
Director   (1) ⊗

Inter-class council (elementary school)
Second case: First cycle, with four first
               and four second classes

Parents   (8) ○○○○○○○○
Teachers   (8) ●●●●●●●●
Director   (1) ⊗

Inter-class council (elementary school)
Third case: overall, with two first, two second,
               two third, two fourth, one fifth classes

Parents   (9) ○○○○○○○○○
Teachers   (9) ●●●●●●●●●
Director   (1) ⊗

Class council (intermediate school)

Parents   (4) ○○○○
Teachers   (all) ●●●
Headmaster (1) ⊗

College of teachers
(elementary and secondary schools)

Teachers   (all) ●●●
Director or headmaster   (1) ⊗

Teacher Assessment Committee
First case: up to 50 teachers

Teachers   (2) ●●
Director or headmaster   (1) ⊗
+ 1 temporary teacher

Teacher Assessment Committee
Second case: over 50 teachers

Teachers   (4) ●●●●
Director or headmaster   (1) ⊗
+ 2 temporary teachers

Class council (higher secondary and artistic school)

Students   (2) □□
Parents   (2) ○○
Teachers   (all) ●●●
Headmaster (1) ⊗

All the Councils shown here as examples are chaired by the Director or Headmaster

Table 12

interview in the case of associate academic staff or researchers. Act No. 28 of 1980 and the Decree implementing it contain transitional rules for regularizing the legal position of staff at various academic and teaching levels who were taken on by universities following the university expansion which occurred over the previous decade.

The democratic management organs in the school system

The collegial organs

Under Decree of the President of the Republic No. 416 of 31 May 1974 collegial organs – school, district, provincial, regional and national – were set up for the whole Italian state public education system.

These are school management structures designed to bring about 'participation in the management of the school, transforming the school into a community interacting with the wider social and civic community'.

The group (elementary schooling) and institute (lower/higher secondary schooling) collegial organs (see Table 12)

These are:

(1) The Class or Inter-class Council;
(2) The College of Teachers;
(3) The Group or Institute Council (and the Board);
(4) The Teacher Assessment Committee.

The Class or Inter-class Council

This is a completely new organ for elementary schools; it is composed *ex officio* of all the teachers of the class (in the case of lower and higher intermediate schools) or of the same group of classes (in the case of elementary and nursery schools), plus the elected representatives of the parents (one parent per class for the Inter-class Council and four parents per class for the Class Council), and is chaired by the headmaster or local director of education.

It has the following consultative tasks:

— it makes educational and teaching proposals (e.g. experimentation) to the College of Teachers;
— it expresses its opinion to the College of Teachers on the textbooks to be used by the pupils;
— it establishes relations with the parents.

The College of Teachers

The College of Teachers is composed exclusively of all the teachers in the school (whether on the established staff or not) and is chaired by the headmaster or local director of education. It has a variety of powers, many of which are decision-making:

— it looks after the running of the classes in the teaching sphere (programming and inter-disciplinary co-ordination);
— it decides on the choice and adoption of textbooks;
— it organizes the up-dating of the teaching staff;
— it adopts programmes of experimentation with teaching methods;
— it examines the general behaviour of the pupils.

Its consultative powers include the following:

— it makes proposals to the headmaster or local director of education on the formation of classes;
— it makes proposals concerning the school timetable;
— it makes proposals to the Minister of Public Education concerning experimentation with innovations in the structures.

In addition to the above, the College of Teachers is charged with electing from among its members:

(a) the teachers responsible for assisting the headmaster or local director of education, the first one elected assuming the duties of 'deputy' to the headmaster or director;
(b) the teacher representatives on the other school collegial organs (Group or Institute Council and Assessment Committee).

The Group or Institute Council (and the Board)

This is an entirely new organ in Italian schools. It has only one *ex officio* member: the headmaster or local director of education, all the other representatives – teachers, parents and pupils (the latter only in the case of the higher secondary schools) – are elected by the respective groups. The Institute or Group Council (for schools of up to 500 pupils) is normally composed of 14 representatives, comprising six teachers, six parents, one non-teacher and the headmaster or local director of education. The Council is chaired by a parent and its term of office is three years.

The powers of the Group or Institute Council are nearly all of an administrative and financial nature, powers as regards teaching being of secondary importance.

In fact, at the decision-making level, the Council takes decision on:

— the budget estimates;
— the final budget;
— expenditure on teaching equipment for the school;
— supplementary activities (visits, study trips, etc.);
— relations with other schools;
— cultural, sporting and recreational events and activities;
— welfare activities.

The Institute or Group Council is flanked and assisted by a small body with an absolute majority of school staff: the Board. This is an organ composed of the headmaster or local director of education, the school secretary, one teacher, one non-teacher and only two parents.

The Board's tasks are:

— to prepare the work of the Council;
— to draft the budgets;
— to implement the decisions of the Council;
— to give its opinion to the head of the school regarding the convening of the Parents' Assembly.

The Teacher Assessment Committee

This is the organ which upon request prepares the assessment of the services of the teachers employed. In the past this function was performed by the institute head. The Committee is made up exclusively of teachers (from two to four according to the total number of teachers) and the headmaster or local director of education, who chairs it. The opinion of this organ is essential for the appointment or non-appointment of teachers to the established staff.

NB. In addition to the institute or group collegial organs mentioned, there are the Parents' Assembly and the Parents' Committee. These bodies are not, however, regarded as true school management organs inasmuch as they have no legal authority over school organization.

The collegial organs at the district level
Under the Decree of the President of the Republic No. 416 of 1974 the territory of each Italian Region is subdivided into 'school districts' (a zone is a district if it has a population of up to 200,000 inhabitants) with a view to 'bringing about the democratic participation of the local communities and the social forces in the life and management of the school'. The Act provides for the presence of all grades of schools – from elementary to higher secondary – within the territory of a district. The district management organ is the District School Council, elected every three years.

The District School Council
This is the only collegial structure in which the majority of the membership comes from outside the school organization.
It is in fact composed of:

- 4 headmasters or local directors of education (including one from a non-state public school);
- 6 teachers (including one from a non-state public school);
- 7 parents (including one from a non-state public school);
- 3 employed workers (chosen by the trade union organizations);
- 2 self-employed workers (chosen by the trade union organizations);
- 1 entrepreneur (chosen by the Chamber of Commerce);
- 2 representatives of cultural bodies;
- 7 representatives of the municipal administration;
- 7 students from higher secondary schools (including one from a non-state public school);
- 2 representatives of the non-teaching staff;
- 3 representatives of the provincial administration.

The District Council has few decision-making powers and confines itself to making proposals and submitting opinions to the Provincial Director of Education and to the regional and municipal organs.
District Councils take decisions on:

- the rules of procedure of the Council itself;
- the annual budget;
- the investment of the funds covering its own running costs.

The collegial organs at the provincial level (see Table 13)
These are:

- the Disciplinary Councils for teachers and non-teachers in all grades of schools;
- the Supervisory Commissions;
- the Provincial Administrative Council;
- the Provincial School Council.

Provincial School Council First case: less than 100,000 pupils, less than 100 school units, less than 10,000 teachers (42 members)	Representatives Chamber of Commerce (1)	▼
	Representatives self-employed workers trade unions (1)	✪
	Representatives employed workers trade unions (3)	✪ ✪ ✪ ✪
	Parents (4)	○○○○
	Representatives Provincial Education Office (1)	✪
	Non-teaching staff state schools (1)	▼
	Teachers non-state schools (2)	● ●
	Teachers state schools (19)	●●●●●●●●●● ●●●●●●●●●
	Headmasters non-state schools (1)	★
	Local directors of education (1)	★
	Headmasters intermediate schools (1)	★
	Headmasters higher secondary schools (1)	★
	Regional representatives (1)	★
	Provincial Public Education Adviser (1)	▢
	Municipal representatives (3)	★ ★ ★
	Provincial Director of Education (1)	☼
Provincial School Council Second case: over 300,000 pupils, over 300 school units, over 30,000 teachers (66 members)	Representatives Chamber of Commerce (2)	▼ ▼
	Representatives self-employed workers trade unions (2)	✪ ✪
	Representatives employed workers trade unions (6)	✪ ✪ ✪ ✪ ✪ ✪
	Parents (7)	○○○○○○○
	Representative Provincial Education Office (1)	✪
	Non-teaching staff state schools (3)	▼ ▼ ▼
	Teachers non-state schools (3)	● ● ●
	Teachers state schools (30)	●●●●●●●●●●●● ●●●●●●●●●●●●●●●●●●
	Headmasters non-state schools (1)	★
	Headmasters state schools (5)	★ ★ ★ ★ ★
	Regional representatives (1)	☆
	Provincial Public Education Adviser (1)	▢
	Municipal representatives (3)	☆ ☆ ☆
	Provincial Director of Education (1)	☼
	The Chairman is electred from among the members	
Executive Board of the Provincial School Council	Other members (4)	◙ ◙ ◙ ◙
	Teachers (4)	○○○○
	Provincial Director of Education (Chairman) (1)	✪

Table 13

The Provincial School Council has a three-year term of office and is composed of freely elected representatives and *ex officio* members.

Ex officio members are:

— The Provincial Director of Education;
— 3 representatives of the municipal administrations in the Province;
— 1 representative of the Regional Council.

National Council of Public Education	Headmasters non-state schools (1)	★
	Local directors of education (2)	★ ★
	Headmasters artistic schools (1)	★
	Headmasters higher secondary schools (1)	★
	Headmasters intermediate schools (1)	★
	Technical inspectors (3)	☼ ☼ ☼
	Teachers non-state schools (3)	●●●
	Teachers Italian schools abroad (1)	●
	Teachers schools of artistic education (3)	●●●
	Teachers higher secondary schools (11)	●●●●●● ●●●●●
	Teachers intermediate schools (14)	●●●●●●● ●●●●●●●
	Teachers elementary schools (14)	●●●●●●● ●●●●●●●
	Teachers nursery schools (4)	●●●●
	Non-teaching staff (3)	▼ ▼ ▼
	University academic staff (2)	◪ ◪
	Central administration staff, managerial (1)	⊗
	Central administration staff, non-managerial (1)	⊗
	Representatives CNEL (5)	⊡⊡⊡⊡⊡

The National Council of Public Education is chaired by the Minister

Table 14

The following are elected members:

- representatives of the headmasters and teaching staffs of the state and non-state schools;
- representatives of non-teaching staffs;
- representatives of the provincial administration offices;
- representatives of the pupils' parents;
- representatives of the economic and working world.

The Provincial School Council expresses opinions and makes proposals to the Minister of Education and to the regional school organs on questions concerning:

- the use of school services;
- school buildings.

Decision-making powers, which are rather limited for this organ too, concern approval of:

- programmes and plans for permanent (continuing) education;
- programmes of adult education;
- criteria for the use of school buildings and installations outside normal school hours.

Collegial organs at the regional level

The only collegial organ set up at the regional level, and one which is not really concerned with management, is the Regional Institute for Research, Experimentation and Modernization in Education (IRRSAE). These institutes are responsible for organizing and conducting the updating of teachers' and permanent education and recurrent education courses.

The representatives on this collegial structure are chosen by government organs, the State, the universities, research centres, trade union organizations, trade associations and local authorities (provincial and municipal administrations).

	1975/76				1976/77				1977/78			
	North	Centre	South	Italy	North	Centre	South	Italy	North	Centre	South	Italy
Agriculture	21,263	4,129	9,963	35,355	22,021	3,678	4,646	30,345	18,112	5,989	5,118	29,219
Industry	64,063	15,869	21,832	101,764	53,547	11,676	22,622	87,845	53,933	14,980	17,729	83,642
Services	80,873	19,150	13,662	114,045	73,746	19,912	18,275	111,933	75,989	22,397	11,534	109,870
TOTAL	166,199	39,508	45,457	251,164	149,314	35,266	45,543	230,123	148,034	40,316	34,381	222,731
Percentage composition by economic sector												
Agriculture	12.8	10.5	21.9	14.1	14.7	10.4	10.2	13.2	12.2	14.8	14.9	13.1
Industry	38.5	40.2	48.0	40.5	35.9	33.1	49.7	38.2	36.4	28.7	51.6	37.6
Services	48.7	49.3	30.1	45.4	49.4	56.5	40.1	48.6	51.4	55.4	33.5	49.3
TOTAL	100.0	100.0	100.0	100.0	100.0	100.0	100.0	100.0	100.0	100.0	100.0	100.0
Percentage composition by geographical area												
Agriculture	60.1	11.7	28.2	100.0	72.6	12.1	15.3	100.0	62.0	20.5	17.5	100.0
Industry	62.9	15.6	21.5	100.0	61.0	13.3	25.7	100.0	64.5	14.3	21.2	100.0
Services	70.9	17.1	12.0	100.0	65.9	17.8	16.3	100.0	69.2	20.3	10.5	100.0
TOTAL	66.2	15.7	18.1	100.0	64.9	15.3	18.8	100.0	66.5	18.1	15.4	100.0

Sources: Prepared by CENSIS from ISTAT data.

Table 15: Numbers of persons registered for extra-school vocational training courses, by economic sector and geographical area (1975/76–1977/78)

Collegial organs at the national level (see Table 14)

The National School Council
This is composed of 71 members, distributed as follows:

- 47 teachers from state schools of every kind and grade;
- 3 teachers from non-state schools;
- 3 headmasters;
- 2 local directors of education;
- 3 technical inspectors;
- 3 non-teachers from state schools;
- 2 members of administrative staffs;
- 1 director from non-state schools;
- 2 representatives of the Higher Public Education Council;
- 5 representatives of the economic and working world.

The National School Council has a five-year term of office and is chaired by the Minister of Public Education.

Its functions are mainly consultative and non-binding. It expresses opinions on:

- legislative questions (laws, decrees, circulars);
- programmes of experimentation with structures (financial expenditure);
- matters relating to the legal status of staff;
- the annual trend of the Italian education system.

Extra-school vocational training (regional)
Extra-school vocational training has always been an educational channel quite different from state schooling. It is characterized by a 'short and flexible' training route (generally two or three years) leading finally (at least in theory) to economically active and productive life.

Extra-school vocational training is under the direct control of the Regions (established in Italy in 1972) and still represents a training sector of considerable size (particularly in Northern Italy) and of considerable importance (especially in commerce and services, which account for 50 per cent of the total number of courses and students).

The following quantitative data can be cited (up to 1978):

- 11,500 courses;
- over 222,000 students;
- about 50,000 teachers.

It should be noted that in recent years the sector of extra-school vocational training has been showing a downward trend in Southern Italy in both the industrial and the craft sections (see Table 15).

The courses for workers
A novel feature of education in Italy is the experiment with the so-called '150 hours'. Under the employment contract of 1973 workers in the engineering and chemical industries were given the opportunity (subsequently extended to all other categories of workers) of having 150 hours of paid leave (for the whole term of the contract – three years) to catch up on and complete compulsory schooling (= three-year intermediate school leaving certificate).

From this sprang the organization and introduction by the Ministry of Public Education of evening courses for workers at state public schools, covering 450 hours, with teaching procedures and subject contents showing a different approach from those of the ordinary intermediate school.

These courses are attended by workers in regular jobs and by unemployed persons, women in the home, clerical workers, etc. over 18 years of age.

After six years of experimental operation, the following data are available (see Table 16):

— 400,000 persons have obtained the intermediate school leaving certificate of the compulsory education system;
— around 4,000 courses a year are being provided;
— the courses are attended by 80–90,000 persons a year.

Adult education

In Italy, as in the other EC countries, the demand for education from adult workers who have had little schooling is increasing considerably all the time. The following trends in permanent (continuing) education are accordingly discernible:

— further extension of the anti-illiteracy campaign and popular education sector (around 180,000);

	WORKERS PARTICIPATING					
Regions	*1974*	*1975*	*1976‡*	*1977*	*1978*	*1979§*
Piemonte	3,030	5,955	9,360	10,506	10,376	10,090
Liguria	293	869	1,375	1,618	1,466	1,447
Lombardia	3,865	6,498	11,251	11,381	10,753	10,015
Trentino-Alto Adige	161	355	1,028	1,695	1,195	952
Veneto	810	2,530	4,153	4,642	4,545	4,190
Friuli-Venezia Giulia	253	635	1,153	918	1,134	1,194
Emilia-Romagna	915	2,823	4,742	5,542	4,289	4,024
Marche	57	1,026	1,817	1,924	1,847	1,827
Toscana	739	2,151	3,755	4,534	2,959	3,744
Umbria	–	984	1,360	1,027	904	969
Lazio	2,023	6,016	7,957	9,136	7,705	7,807
Campania	1,007	3,737	10,466	12,041	10,305	12,102
Abruzzi	–	374	680	1,001	885	985
Molise	90	148	741	672	543	617
Basilicata	–	361	322	531	566	778
Puglia	528	1,496	4,329	5,512	5,001	5,532
Calabria	–	237	2,400	3,025	2,033	3,990
Sicilia	356	2,318	7,356	9,724	11,396	14,283
Sardegna	110	304	3,016	3,938	3,641	3,821
Nord	9,327	19,665	33,237	36,302	33,758	31,912
Centro	2,819	10,177	14,889	16,621	14,415	14,347
Sud e Isole	2,091	8,948	29,310	36,444	35,470	42,108
Italy	14,237	38,790	77,436	89,367	83,543	88,367

† At about three months after the beginning of the courses.
‡ Estimated on the basis of 20 pupils per course.
§ On the basis of the 1978 pupils/class estimate.

Source: Prepared from data of the Ministry of Public Education.

Table 16: Trend of participation in state courses for completion of compulsory schooling †

- the numbers of worker/evening students in the technical institutes have increased (about 50,000);
- a 're-entry' tendency has been observable among adults in the vocational training courses run by the Regions (about 90,000);
- the number of university students who, apart from studying, have full-time jobs has increased (250–300,000).

In aggregate, the number of adults at present engaged in educational and 're-entry' activities (catching-up courses, retraining courses, language classes, correspondence courses, etc.) is around 700,000.

Notes
1. Under a very recent Act, male candidates, previously debarred, may now also compete for teaching posts in nursery schools.
2. The children's parents may request exemption from these lessons.

Bibliography:
AUGENTI, A. (1973). *Problemi di economia dell'educazione (Economic problems of education)*. Florence: Le Monnier.
BARBAGLI, M. (1974). *Disoccupazione intellettuale e sistema scolastico in Italia (Unemployment among intellectuals and the educational system in Italy)*. Bologna: Il Mulino.
CANESTRI, G. and RECUPERATI, G. (1976). *La scuola in Italia dalla legge Casati a oggi (Italian education from the Casati Act to today)*. Turin: Loescher.
DE SIMONE, F. and SALAZAR, M. (1975). *La nuova scuola italiana (The new Italian school system)*, 2 vols. Milan: Giuffrè.
D'ALESSANDRO, V., RICCOBONO, L. and RUSCELLO, R. (1969). *Indagine sulla scuola del pre-adolescente (Inquiry into pre-adolescent schooling)*. Florence: La Nuova Italia.
FADIGA ZANATTA, A. L. (1976). *Il sistema scolastico italiano (The Italian school system)*. Bologna: Il Mulino.
GIUGNI, G. (1976). 'Le 150 ore per il diritto allo studio dei lavoratori' ('The 150 hours and the workers' right to study'), in *Annali della P.I.* XXII, no. 2.
GOZZER, G. (1973). *La riforma della secondaria superiore (The reform of higher secondary education)*. Rome: COINES.
PREDIERI, A. and DOLCE, G. (1975). *Scuola e Stato (Education and the State)*. Florence: La Nuova Italia.
Various (1973). 'Scuola e regioni' ('Education and the Regions'). Special number of the review *Scuola e Città*, XXIV, nos. 7–8.
Various (1976). 'I nuovi organi collegiali della scuola (1970–76)' ('The new collegial school organs, 1970–76'), in *Annali della P.I.* XXII, no. 2.
Various (1974). 'Nuove strutture della scuola italiana' ('New structures in Italian education'), in *Annali della P.I.*, no. 2.
Various (1975). 'I decreti delegati' ('The delegated decrees'), *Parva Lex.* Rome.

Statistical Sources
CENSIS (centro studi investmenti sociali) (1 January 1980). *La situazione educativa del Paese (The country's educational situation)*, nos. 327–8, Year XVI.
CENSIS (15 April 1980). *Progetti pilota CEE per la transizione tra scuola-lavoro (EEC pilot projects on the transition from education to working life)*, nos. 334–5, Year XVI.
CENSIS (15 July 1979). *Instruzione ed economia (Education and economics)*, no. 318, Year XV.
CENSIS (15 March 1979). *Diplomati, laureati e mercato del lavoro (Diploma-holders, graduates and the labour market)*, no. 310, Year XV.
CENSIS (1 April 1979). *Situazione e dinamica dei laureati in attesa de prima occupazione (Situation and prospects of graduates awaiting their first job)*, no. 311, Year XV.

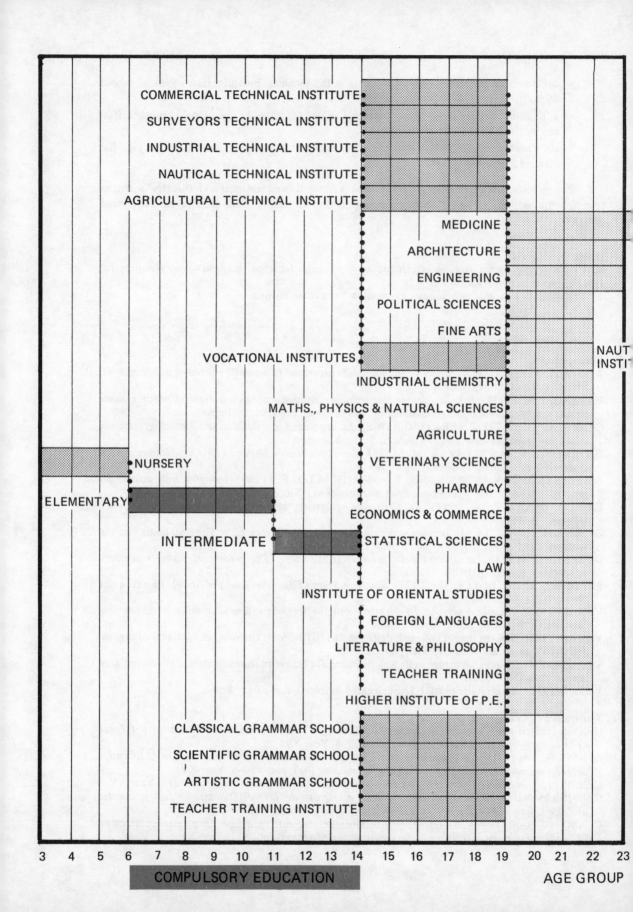

COMMERCIAL TECHNICAL INSTITUTE
SURVEYORS TECHNICAL INSTITUTE
INDUSTRIAL TECHNICAL INSTITUTE
NAUTICAL TECHNICAL INSTITUTE
AGRICULTURAL TECHNICAL INSTITUTE

MEDICINE
ARCHITECTURE
ENGINEERING
POLITICAL SCIENCES
FINE ARTS

VOCATIONAL INSTITUTES

INDUSTRIAL CHEMISTRY

MATHS., PHYSICS & NATURAL SCIENCES

AGRICULTURE

VETERINARY SCIENCE

PHARMACY

NURSERY

ECONOMICS & COMMERCE

ELEMENTARY

STATISTICAL SCIENCES

INTERMEDIATE

LAW

INSTITUTE OF ORIENTAL STUDIES

FOREIGN LANGUAGES

LITERATURE & PHILOSOPHY

TEACHER TRAINING

HIGHER INSTITUTE OF P.E.

CLASSICAL GRAMMAR SCHOOL
SCIENTIFIC GRAMMAR SCHOOL
ARTISTIC GRAMMAR SCHOOL
TEACHER TRAINING INSTITUTE

NAUT
INSTI

3 4 5 6 7 8 9 10 11 12 13 14 15 16 17 18 19 20 21 22 23

COMPULSORY EDUCATION

AGE GROUP

LUXEMBOURG

Introduction

The Ministry of Education is responsible for pre-school, primary, post-primary and higher education.

The advisory bodies include:

1. *The Higher Committee for Education*, whose task is

    (a) to study general problems relating to education and teaching;

    (b) to give opinions on questions submitted to it by the Ministry of Education;

    (c) to present the Ministry of Education with its own proposals, suggestions and information relating to educational problems and reforms or new legislations which it considers appropriate in schools and training outside schools.

The Higher Committee for Education meets at the request of either the Ministry of Education or its chairman, or at the written request of at least one-third of its members.

The Higher Committee for Education may consist of up to 42 members, appointed by the Ministry of Education for a renewable term of two years. Duties will be shared according to Article 10 of the rules of procedure of the Committee. The Committee's executive consists of the chairman and deputy chairman, the secretary-general and assistant secretary-general – both of whom are responsible for writing reports. The executive has a maximum of 10 members, appointed directly by the Ministry of Education. The other committee members are appointed by the Ministry of Education and proposed by the various authorities concerned, so that there is:

one representative of the clergy;
one representative of the Ministry of Sport;
one representative of the Ministry of Health and of the Environment;
one representative of the Ministry of Family Affairs;
one representative of the Ministry of the Interior;
three representatives from post-primary education boards of directors;
one representative of the Board of Inspectors;
four post-primary teachers' representatives;
three primary and pre-school teachers' representatives;
four parents' representatives;
two representatives of school sports associations;
two representatives of school cultural associations;
two representatives of industry;
one representative of private denominational education.

The Committee and its executive are assisted by an administrative secretary appointed by the Minister from among the staff of the Ministry of Education.

The Committee may sometimes – if the Minister agrees – enlist the services of experts on the subject it is required to study.

With the Minister's agreement, the Committee may set up joint study committees with organizations dealing with educational problems. The Committee devises its own rules of procedure which are then approved by the Minister of Education.

2. *Schools Committees*

Each municipality has a schools committee, headed by the burgomaster as chairman, or his delegate chosen from the local council. It includes a churchman, proposed by the leading church official and appointed by the Minister of Education (he may delegate the priest in charge of another parish to substitute for him during visits by the committee to schools in that parish) and three lay members appointed by the local council. In municipalities with 3,000 or more inhabitants, there are five lay members. If possible, one lay member should be a father, another a mother, of children attending a local primary school. Apart from these requirements, the council may choose any resident aged 25 or over, living in the municipality, and possessing full civil and political rights. No teacher may be a member of the committee.

The schools committee must meet at least twice a year: in the month following the return to school after the summer holidays and in January. At least twice a year a member of the teaching staff, designated each year by the local teaching body, is invited to the committee's meetings, in an advisory capacity, as is the school doctor or one of the school doctors, designated by the local council.

The schools committee changes every time the local council changes, one month after the councillors have been officially installed. Members may be re-elected. When a vacancy arises among the members it appoints, the council must find a replacement within one month. Members elected in their capacity as parents of pupils must leave the committee once they cease to fulfil this requirement. All members elected as replacements serve out their predecessors' terms. Procedures for electing the teachers' delegate are laid down by Grand-Ducal regulation.

The committee chooses its own secretary.

This committee is particularly concerned with ensuring that class time-tables are observed in primary schools; with ensuring that attendance is good and that absences are discouraged, and ascertaining that all children of school age are enrolled at the appropriate schools. It is responsible for informing the local authorities of necessary repairs to school premises and furniture requirements; it will also indicate to the local council and the inspector anything it considers useful or in the interests of primary education, and will assist with the organization of supplementary school activities and projects such as libraries, collections, school meals and gardens, etc.

3. *Federations and Associations of parents of primary, post-primary and further higher education pupils*

These are advisory groups. For example, there are two delegates from the most representative parents' associations on the committee set up to deal with the allocation of financial support from the State for students in further higher education.

Statistics

The number of pupils in intermediate level education – technical and vocational – from 1975 to 1979 is shown in Table 1.

Appropriations for education cover not only expenditure on all forms of public education, but also on training young people. Their allocation is shown in Table 4.

Pre-school education

Nursery education is optional for four year-olds and compulsory for five year-olds.

The Law of 5 August 1963, which makes schooling compulsory for nine years from the age of six, also emphasizes the fact that nursery education should not involve formal teaching.

	Boys	Girls	Total
1975/76	8,177	5,778	13,955
1976/77	8,327	6,128	14,455
1977/78	8,865	6,517	15,382
1978/79	9,034	6,663	15,697

Table 1: Pupils in intermediate level education

Of these, the numbers in full-time and part-time education were:

	Boys	Girls	Total
1975/76	5,739	5,187	10,926
1976/77	6,077	5,468	11,545
1977/78	6,575	5,702	12,277
1978/79	6,667	5,735	12,402

Table 2: Full-time education

	Boys	Girls	Total
1975/76	2,438	591	3,029
1976/77	2,250	660	2,910
1977/78	2,290	815	3,105
1978/79	2,367	928	3,295

Table 3: Part-time education

(in millions of Luxembourg francs)

	1978	%	1979	%	1980	%
General expenditure	90.7	1.8	103.0	2	105.7	1.8
Pre-school and primary education	2,057.7	42	2,193.1	40.6	2,389.2	41
Secondary and intermediate-level education	1,405.0	28	1,749.5	32	1,721.9	30
Vocational training	975.4	20	941.2	17.4	1,077.5	18.6
Agricultural training	61.9	1	73.6	1.4	80.8	1.4
Higher education	80.0	1.2	89.9	1.6	100.0	1.6
Special education and training outside schools	304.2	6	306.5	5	326.5	5.6
TOTAL	4,974.9		5,456.8		5,801.6	

Budgets for 1978, 1979, 1980:

(in millions of Luxembourg francs)

1978: 33,352 (general account)   education: 4,975 = 14.9%
1979: 36,292 (budget)   education: 5,457 = 15%
1980: 39,014 (draft budget)   education: 5,802 = 14.8%

Teachers, lecturers and administrative staff in all types of public educational institutions in Luxembourg are state officials and hence natives of Luxembourg. Maintenance staff, particularly cleaning women, are mainly foreigners.

Public education in Luxembourg is free in all types of educational establishment. Pupils pay no fees. The Ministry of Education awards grants to deserving pupils, to pupils who are deserving and in need, as well as to those who are simply in need.

Table 4: Allocation of educational funds

Both nursery and primary education are run by the local authorities, subject to the approval of the higher authority.

Primary education

The basic law on primary education in the Grand Duchy dates back to 10 August 1912 and the most recent, which provides for nine years of compulsory schooling and sets up a special three-year unit of complementary classes to follow the first six years of primary education, to 5 August 1963. These complementary classes are intended to complete the children's basic grounding and to develop their scholastic skills and those that will enable them to choose a profession. There are also special classes and special schools for children with education problems or other handicaps.

Primary schools

Ordinary primary schools, which cater for 6 to 12 year-olds, are state-run, free, and in most cases, co-educational.

The following subjects are taught:

i   religious instruction or ethics;
ii   Luxemburgish, French and German;
iii arithmetic;
iv   national history, the local environment, geography and natural science;
v   painting and drawing, writing, craft, music and physical education.

Every term, marks are awarded on the basis of written work done in class, homework and oral participation.

Complementary classes

These are for all pupils who complete their primary school studies but do not go on to any other form of post-primary education. They last three years. Pupils from various communes may be grouped together in regional schools.

The syllabus contains:

i   general subjects – religious instruction, French and French correspondence, German and German correspondence, arithmetic, civics, history, geography, natural science, art, music and physical education;
ii   for boys – craft (woodwork and metalwork);
iii for girls – domestic science (nutrition, cookery, home economics, textile technology, needlework, laundering, cleaning and ironing, care of the sick and babycare).

Pupils who make a success of year nine (complementary classes) are awarded the end-of-primary certificate.

Special education

There are also special primary classes for children of school age who are educable, but not in an ordinary group. Here are some of the specialized public and private establishments in the Grand Duchy:

i   special education centres for mentally retarded children;
ii   schools for sick and delicate children;
iii the speech therapy centre;
iv   the institute for spastics and anarthritics;
v   the institute for the visually handicapped.

Middle school (intermediate or lower secondary) education – technical and vocational courses
The seventh year common course, the eighth year middle school (technical and vocational) course and the ninth year middle school (technical) courses in building, mechanics, tools, electro-technology, fine arts, ancillary medical preparation, chemistry, hotels and catering and vocational courses in metalwork, electricity, woodwork, building, hairdressing, fashion, nutrition, graphic art, sales and commerce, will gradually be altered to bring them into line with the observation/pre-specialization unit of secondary technical education (years seven, eight and nine).

Middle school (intermediate or lower secondary) education
These classes, which are free, were set up to provide the right sort of general grounding for young people more particularly suited for lower- and medium-grade work in the public and private sectors. They are open to pupils who have completed the six years of primary education and passed an entrance examination. The course is a five-year one divided into two units – unit one, which lasts three years and leads to a certificate of completion of compulsory schooling, and unit two, which lasts two years and is divided into the following three sections:

i   administration and commerce, leading to the department of administration and commerce at the technical *lycée* school of business and management or an equivalent school abroad;
ii   technology and industrial studies, leading to the institute of higher technology or an equivalent school abroad;
iii biology and social studies, leading to certain ancillary medical courses.

Middle school studies end with the middle school completion certificate, which mentions the course studied and entitles the holder to sit the entrance examination for lower grade civil service work.

Unit two of the middle school education will gradually be altered to bring it into line with unit two of secondary technical education.

Technical and vocational courses
There are two types of vocational and technical courses in the Grand Duchy – full-time courses and apprenticeships plus day release. All candidates must have completed the sixth year of primary education, after which they take a two-year course of full-time education (seventh year common curriculum and eighth year technical or vocational).

Technical courses
In this branch, the eighth year class is common to all sections, but students have a number of possibilities in year nine – the departments of fine arts, crafts, technical studies, hotels and catering, chemistry, commerce, ancillary medical preparation and agronomy.

1. The department of fine arts offers three years of basic training (years 9, 10 and 11), leading to the fine arts end-of-course diploma, and one year of specialization (year 12), leading to the higher certificate of proficiency in art (CAFAS) in one of the following: fine arts, painting, sculpture and ceramics; graphic art and advertising; interior decoration and design.
2. The craft department has five sections – carpentry and cabinet-making, wrought iron work, painting, sculpture and ceramics. The course is a three-year one, beginning in year nine, and leads to an end-of-course diploma equivalent to the certificate of vocational proficiency (CAP).

3. The technical studies department has four sections – building, mechanics, electrotechnology and machine tools. Here again the course is a three-year one beginning in year nine and leading to an end-of-course diploma equivalent to the CAP in the relevant profession.

   Holders of this final examination in electrotechnology and holders of CAPs in that or allied subjects can go on for a further two years to obtain the diploma of technician in electrotechnology.

4. The school of catering trains staff to work in the hotel and catering trade. It is open to students in year nine who have either successfully completed two years of post-primary training or passed an entrance examination. This is a full-time course of study lasting three years, each of them followed by 10 weeks of practical work in a hotel or restaurant in the Grand Duchy. There is an end-of-course diploma and a CAP, holders of which can either set up their own hotels or restaurants or go on to specialist courses to obtain the diploma of master caterer.

5. The chemistry department is also a three-year course that starts in year nine. At the end of year 11, students take the end-of-unit one examination to obtain their certificate of assistant chemist. They can then go on to unit two, a two-year course leading to the diploma of chemical technician.

6. The commerce department offers a two-year course of full-time study starting in year nine. In the second year, students specialize in company management or secretarial skills after which they take the CAP theory examination which opens the way for a final year of practical work in a firm, ending with the CAP practical examination. Students who successfully complete year 10 can go on to the preparatory class at the technical *lycée*/school of business and management (see p. 191).

7. The department preparing for ancillary medical careers runs a three-year course starting in year nine. At the end of year 11, students can sit an entrance examination to go to schools of nursing attached to hospitals.

8. Boys can choose between agronomy and agriculture. The course offered by the department of agronomy is a five-year one and the final examination entitles the holder to a diploma in agricultural studies and opens the way to unit two – two further years of study leading to the qualification of agricultural technician.

   The structures of technical education will gradually be altered to bring them into line with the structures of the middle school unit of secondary technical education.

Vocational courses (apprenticeships)

After following the seventh year common curriculum, pupils opt for either vocational or technical studies. Apprenticeships proper start after year nine in a full-time course of vocational education, i.e. once the candidate has completed his compulsory schooling. Apprenticeships are available in all branches of industry, craft and commerce.

An average apprenticeship lasts three years. Training is along sandwich course lines – i.e. practical work in the firm alongside theory in the classroom. In certain highly technical careers (electrotechnician and car mechanic, for example), the first two years are replaced by full-time schooling. Apprenticeships lead to a CAP.

In some branches, where less theoretical knowledge is required, apprentices may train for a certificate of manual proficiency (CCM) and then go to evening classes and sit the final apprenticeship theory examination.

The structures of vocational education will be altered gradually to bring them into line with those of the middle school unit of secondary technical education.

Training for ancillary medical careers

These courses are open to pupils who:

    (a) get through the examination at the end of the three-year preparatory course;

    (b) hold a middle school end-of-course certificate (biology and social studies);

    (c) have made a success of year three of secondary general education and passed a short promotion examination.

The nursing course is a three-year one involving both theoretical (1,500 hours) and practical (3,600 hours) work. It leads to the Luxembourg state nursing diploma, a basis for most subsequent special courses.

Luxembourg offers the following further courses for trained nurses: a child care course (one year), psychiatric nursing (one year), midwifery (two years), nurse-anaesthetist (24 months), assistant radiology medical technician (18 months), assistant surgical medical technician (18 months) and assistant laboratory medical technician (clinical biology, micro-biology, pathological anatomy, medical chemistry, blood transfusion or health chemistry – all 18 months). The structures of this branch of education will be adapted gradually to bring them into line with unit three of secondary technical education.

The technical lycée/*school of business and management*

Candidates who hold the end-of-course diploma from the middle school (administration and commerce) or have successfully completed year three of secondary education do not need to sit an entrance examination. Holders of CAP examinations in commercial subjects are eligible after one year's preparatory study and an entrance examination. The course lasts two years, after which the school awards its final diploma – which is equivalent to the secondary school leaving certificate for admission to medium-grade posts in administration.

The educational structures of the *lycée* will be altered gradually to bring them into line with the structures of unit three of secondary technical education.

Secondary technical education

In accordance with the Law of 21 May 1979 on the organization of vocational training and secondary technical education, the Ministry for Education embarked on a series of experiments in years seven and eight of secondary technical education, at the beginning of the 1979–80 school year.

This law will be implemented within five years of taking effect.

Pupils can enter secondary technical education at the end of year six of primary education, provided they pass the entrance examination.

Secondary technical education, with identical courses for girls and boys, prepares pupils for higher technical courses, and for jobs, by providing them with general, social, technical and vocational training.

There are three units of secondary technical education:

    (1) a three-year observation/pre-specialization unit;

    (2) a second or middle unit, with both a full-time technical course and a part-time vocational course for apprentices, usually lasting three years;

    (3) an upper unit of two years, providing comprehensive training and leading to the diploma of technician or the certificate of completion of secondary technical studies.

Pursuant to the Law of 21 May 1979, the following establishments offering post-primary courses of education:

Ecole des Arts et Métiers	
Collège d'Enseignement Moyen	
Centre d'Enseignement Professionnel de l'Etat	Luxembourg
Ecole de Commerce et de Gestion	
Ecole Hôtelière Alexis Heck	Diekirch
Collège Nic. Biever	Dudelange
Ecole Professionnel de l'Etat	Esch-sur-Alzette
Collège d'Enseignement Moyen et Professionnel	Ettelbruck
Institut de l'Enseignement agricole	
Collège d'Enseignement Moyen et Professionnel de l'Est	Grevenmacher
Collège d'Enseignement Moyen	Mersch
Collège de Pétange	Pétange
Collège d'Enseignement Moyen et Professionnel du Nord	Wiltz

are now technical *lycées* with the following names:

Lycée technique des Arts et Métiers	
Lycée technique Michel Lucius	
Lycée technique du Centre	Luxembourg
Lycée technique Ecole de Commerce et de Gestion	
Lycée technique Alexis Heck	Diekirch
Lycée technique Nic. Biever	Dudelange
Lycée technique d'Ettelbruck	Ettelbruck
Lycée technique agricole	
Lycée technique d'Esch-sur-Alzette	Esch-sur-Alzette
Lycée technique Jos. Bech	Grevenmacher
Lycée technique de Mersch	Mersch
Lycée technique Mathias Adam	Pétange
Lycée technique du Nord	Wiltz

The observation/pre-specialization unit

The accent in the seventh year is on general training. Language teaching at this level covers Luxemburgish, French and German.

In year eight, the aim is to build on the bases acquired in the previous year. All pupils also have to follow a certain number of pre-specialization courses.

In year nine, options are included in the syllabus, so pupils' timetables begin to reflect the tastes and skills that will determine the departments they go into in unit two.

At the end of unit one, all pupils get a certificate of completion of compulsory schooling. Where appropriate, this also mentions that the holder has successfully completed the observation/pre-specialization unit.

The middle unit

Unit two, which usually lasts three years, consists of two separate courses – a vocational one and a technical one.

The vocational course is divided into two:

i   three years' part-time study in the classroom alongside practical work in the firm;
ii a mixed formula involving one year of full-time study plus two of combined theory and
    practice or two years' full-time study plus one combined theory and practical.

The technical course involves full-time study as preparation for various professions. It lasts three years, the third one of which is mainly practical and can be done at the school or in agriculture, craft, commerce or industry. If year three is done in a firm, the candidate has to sign a contract for the course and register it with the relevant trade organization. The professions involved here are listed by a Grand Ducal regulation drawn up in the light of the opinion of the trade organizations concerned.

Unit two vocational and technical courses lead to an apprenticeship completion examination conferring a certificate of vocational and technical proficiency (CATP).

This final examination in both vocational and technical subjects is part theory and part practice and organized on a national basis. No distinction is made between the various branches. The results of the theoretical and practical work completed during the course of the middle unit may be partly taken into consideration. The CATP theory examination is at the end of year two of the middle unit.

The CATP vocational and technical theory examinations are equal and confer the same rights. The same is true of the practical examinations.

The student who passes the apprenticeship completion examination can go straight on to the corresponding courses in the upper unit of secondary technical education, under conditions laid down by Grand Ducal regulation.

The vocational course
Students following the vocational middle unit course may study in one of the following departments:

i   craft;
ii industry;
iii commerce;
iv hotels, catering and services;
v   agriculture.

The vocational syllabus contains the following compulsory components:

– a general programme of languages, arithmetic, civics, hygiene, book-keeping and
  correspondence;
– a programme of the relevant vocational theory and practice.

The theoretical end-of-apprenticeship examination is at the end of year 11. In year 12, students get a thorough knowledge of the practical side of their subject, in the school and in the firm, as preparation for the final practical examination.

A Grand Ducal regulation lays down the conditions of study and practical training and the arrangements for the practical examination.

Students who get through the theory examination can move on to the corresponding classes of the upper unit of secondary technical education, on conditions laid down by Grand Ducal regulation.

In some professions, named by Grand Ducal regulation, students whose in-course results suggest they will not achieve the relevant vocational goals within the time-limits laid down by the law are still allowed to sit the practical examination.

These students get a certificate of manual proficiency (CCM) if they pass this examination (including the oral theory test).

Holders of the CCM can sit the written theory examination later if they have followed adult education courses.

The technical course
Students on the technical course in the middle unit can study in one of the following branches:

   i   craft and industrial training (sections for building, mechanics, machine tools, electro-technology and chemistry);

   ii ancillary medical and social studies (sections for home economics, preparation for careers as ancillary medical workers and special education instructors and studies for education instructors);

   iii art;

   iv administration and commerce;

   v   hotels and catering (sections for hotel work, cookery and services);

   vi agriculture.

Further departments and sections may be set up by Grand Ducal regulation.

The technical course contains the following compulsory components:

   — a common curriculum comprising religious instruction or ethics, languages, mathematics, physics, chemistry, contemporary history, physical education and sport;

   — a programme of the relevant vocational theory and practice;

   — a compulsory programme of options.

Grand Ducal regulations can, if necessary, alter the specifications and introduce additional compulsory subjects, options and voluntary courses.

In the middle unit technical course, pupils who successfully complete years 10 and 11 do not need to sit the theory examination and can move straight on to the corresponding classes of the upper unit of secondary technical education on conditions laid down by Grand Ducal regulation.

Students wishing to sit the final practical examination must have completed a year 12 course of practical training in the firm or the school. This twelfth year practical part of the technical course is, as far as possible, integrated with the twelfth year practical part of the mixed formula vocational course.

Unit three (the upper unit)
This comprises two years of full-time study in one of three departments:

   i   administration (sections for management and secretarial studies);

   ii general technical education;

   iii technician's training (sections for agriculture, art, biology, chemistry, electrotechnology, civil engineering, mechanics, hotels and catering).

Further departments and sections may be set up by Grand Ducal regulation.

The syllabus comprises:

   (a) a common curriculum of general subjects – French, German and a third language (obligatory option), physical education and sports, civics, contemporary history, economics and social science;

(b) scientific studies – mathematics, physics and chemistry;

(c) technology and practical work, possibly involving practical courses in public and private sectors.

Grand Ducal regulations lay down the subjects which are compulsory and those which can be studied as options in each section. They also decide on the importance of given subjects in each class and lay down syllabuses and weekly timetables in the light of the particular aims of each section.

Grand Ducal regulations can, where necessary, introduce extra compulsory subjects or options.

Ministerial regulations can, where necessary, introduce voluntary courses.

The vocational theory and the practical training syllabuses and the programme of options are devised with the help of the relevant professional organizations.

The upper unit of secondary technical education leads to a national examination for which the syllabus and any other arrangements are laid down by Grand Ducal regulation.

Any candidate who is not an upper unit student but has followed equivalent courses of study recognized by the Ministry for Education can also sit this examination.

Successful candidates from departments i and ii above are awarded the secondary technical completion certificate, specifying the course followed and the subjects tested and stating that the holder has enough knowledge to enable him to embark on higher technical or university courses in his special subject.

Candidates from department iii are awarded the diploma of technician, stating the course followed and the subjects tested.

Standard diplomas are drafted by the Ministry for Education.

Adult education in vocational subjects
The aim here is to:

i help people with vocational qualifications to extend their basic training or to adapt it to technical trends and to the needs of the economy;

ii give people who completed their compulsory schooling without getting any qualifications the opportunity of obtaining elementary vocational training via an accelerated training scheme;

iii give wage-earning and independent workers the opportunity to prepare examinations for diplomas and certificates covered by the Law of 21 May 1979 on the organization of secondary technical education.

Certificate of master craftsman
After five years' work as a CATP-holder, candidates of 24 and over may sit their master craftsman's certificate – either by taking one major examination or a number of partials. Preparation for this may be made either during the course of one year or at weekends over three years.

The higher school of labour studies
This was founded in 1946 and reorganized in 1963. It provides workers with additional training in legal, economic, political and social matters via classes on labour laws, social legislation, industrial medicine, safety and hygiene in the firm, vocational guidance and economics and finance.

Preparing adults for CATP examinations
The aim here is to give people the opportunity to change professions and work for the final apprenticeship examinations in various branches of craft, industry, commerce and the services sector.

The courses include:

    i   theory classes at the Lycée technique du Centre in Luxembourg and, where necessary, at other secondary technical establishments;

    ii   practical work experience.

The theory classes include:

   — groundwork for specialized vocational training;

   — specialized vocational training.

    Candidates wishing to follow the theory classes must be at least 18 years of age and be able to produce written evidence of the periods, type and quality of their professional activity. No special studies are required.

    The Government Commissar for final apprenticeship examinations decides whether candidates should pass, on the basis of proposals from a special committee appointed by the Ministry for Education.

Secondary education

1. The essential aim of secondary education is to provide thorough general training as a preparation for higher study at the university. There are classical studies courses and modern studies courses and all take seven years.

    Boys and girls follow identical syllabuses. Secondary education of this kind is dispensed in these establishments:

    i   Athénée de Luxembourg;
    ii   Lycée classique de Diekirch;
    iii   Lycée classique d'Echternach;
    iv   Lycée de garçons de Luxembourg;
    v   Lycée de garçons d'Esch-sur-Alzette;
    vi   Lycée Robert Schuman de Luxembourg;
    vii Lycée Hubert Clément d'Esch-sur-Alzette;
   viii Lycée Michel Rodange de Luxembourg.

Lower school secondary education is also provided in the following schools:

    Lycée technique Mathias Adam, Pétange;
    Lycée technique Nic. Biever, Dudelange;
    Lycée technique du Nord, Wiltz;
    Lycée technique Jos. Bech, Grevenmacher.

    Pupils can embark upon courses of secondary education once they have completed six years of primary study and passed the relevant entrance examination.

    2. The seven-year secondary course is divided into two units:

(a) unit one, the lower school course, consisting of the one-year observation class (in which the only languages studied are Luxemburgish, French and German) plus two other classes;

(b) unit two, the upper school four-year course.

    When children go into the second year of the secondary school, they opt for classical studies (Latin) or modern studies (English).

The classical studies course divides up as follows in the first year of unit two:

(a) Latin-languages;
(b) Latin-science – with a choice of either mathematics or natural science or economics.

Pupils who opt for sections (a) or (b) can choose between English language and literature and Greek language and literature.

The modern studies course divides up as follows in the first year of unit two:

(a) modern languages;
(b) modern languages-science – with a choice of mathematics, natural science or economics.

3. Secondary studies lead to a secondary education completion certificate in one of the following groups of subjects:

(a¹) Latin-languages: French, German, English or Greek, Latin, philosophy, history and political economy.
(a²) Modern languages: French, German, English, fourth modern language, philosophy, history and political economy.
(b) Latin-science and modern languages-science (mathematics): two of the following three languages – French, German and English; philosophy; political economy; mathematics I; mathematics II; physics and chemistry.
(c) Latin-science and modern languages-science (natural science): two of the following three languages – French, German and English; philosophy, political economy, mathematics, physics, chemistry and biology.
(d) Latin-science and modern languages-science (economics): French, German, English, philosophy, history, mathematics, economics I, economics II.

Candidates are examined on the syllabus studied during their final year in the secondary school.

Successful candidates are awarded the secondary education completion diploma, specifying the department of study and the relevant section and options.

Students who hold this diploma can then go on to study at the university.

The institute of higher technology (IST)
The institute of higher technology was set up in the Grand Duchy in application of the Law of 21 May 1979. It has three departments:

  i   mechanics;
  ii   electrotechnology;
  iii civil engineering.

The course is a three-year one leading to an examination for which the programme and other arrangements are laid down by Grand Ducal regulation.

Successful candidates are then qualified technical engineers.

Holders of the end-of-technical education diploma are admitted to the first year courses at the IST.

The conditions of admission for students who have diplomas from other seven-year courses of secondary general or technical education are laid down by Grand Ducal regulation.

The entrance requirements and arrangements for moving up from one year of study to the next are also laid down by Grand Ducal regulation.

The teacher training institute

This institute, in Luxembourg–Walferdange, trains primary and nursery school teachers. The course is a two-year one of practical study and theory leading to a certificate of educational proficiency.

Since September 1971, acting on a decision by the Government Council, the institute has been offering two basic courses – a primary teaching course and a nursery course. This is pursuant to the Law tabled on 7 July 1971 (Parliamentary Document No. 1535). The pre-school course was made official by the Law of 18 August 1973 on the training and classification of nursery school staff.

Candidates are admitted to the institute on the basis of their results at the end of their secondary school studies in Luxembourg or European establishments.

The institute also runs a further course for trained teachers wanting to work in special schools and classes for mentally handicapped and spastic children.

The institute has:

i   a clinical psychology service, run with the help of neuro-psychiatrists, psychologists, orthopaedic specialists and specialized instructors;
ii   an educational psychology service;
iii   an educational resource centre.

Primary education is dispensed in both state and private schools. Both types of school – including nurseries, primary schools proper and the complementary and special classes – are inspected by the education authorities.

Primary education is supervised by both the commune and the State. In the latter case, responsibility for this is on the shoulders of the Minister for Education and, at his request, of the education committee and the inspectors. Local supervision is carried out by the local authorities and the school committee. Religious classes are supervised by the head of the relevant church.

It should be noted that a draft law:

i   reforming teacher training and
ii   setting up an institute of higher education

is likely to be voted at the next parliamentary session.

This law provides for:

nursery and primary teacher training courses, lasting four semesters, to be run at the teacher training institute. Candidates wishing to follow this course must, in particular, hold a Luxembourg secondary school completion certificate (or a recognized foreign equivalent) and one of the certificates of study issued by the university pursuant to Articles 8 and 12 of the Law of 18 June 1969 on higher education and the recognition of foreign university qualifications. They must sit an entrance examination and be classified in order of results. Teacher training shall include two probationary semester organized by the institute and four semesters of preparatory study in the institute itself.

Adult education for teachers and instructors shall include retraining, advanced and specialized courses and activities.

Secondary education in Luxembourg is provided by teachers of arts subjects, science, economics and social science, art, physical education and music.

Under Article 1 of the Grand Ducal Regulation of 21 February 1976, which lays down the criteria for approval of foreign degrees and qualifications in *lettres* (arts subjects), for admission to the training course for secondary school teachers, the expression *lettres* is defined as covering languages and literature, history, geography and philosophy.

Under Article 1 of the Grand Ducal Regulation of 18 December 1970, laying down criteria for the approval of foreign degrees and qualifications in sciences for admission to the training course for secondary school teachers, the term *sciences* is used to mean mathematics, physics, chemistry, biology and geology.

No foreign higher education final diploma in arts or sciences can be approved unless a foreign or Luxembourg secondary leaving certificate is held, in accordance with the current Luxembourg regulations. Foreign final diplomas submitted for approval should be recognized degrees in the country of origin, or give access to either the teaching profession or to practical teacher training period.

Diplomas submitted for approval should represent completed studies in either arts or sciences, of at least four years or eight semesters or 12 terms.

A final diploma should represent studies covering one or more subjects in either the sciences only or the arts only, in accordance with the definition of these fields in the country where the diploma has been obtained.

Subjects should basically be those taught in secondary schools in Luxembourg in accordance with current laws and regulations. As far as approval of foreign qualifications and degrees is concerned, the system in Luxembourg applies to the following degrees:

- philosophy and arts
- physical sciences and mathematics
- natural sciences (chemistry and physics)
- law
- medicine
- dentistry
- veterinary medicine
- pharmacy.

It is therefore necessary for prospective teachers of both arts and sciences to have this approval.

Under the Law of 25 August 1971, which establishes the post of teacher of economics and social science in secondary education establishments, a prospective teacher should:

(a) hold a secondary leaving certificate from Luxembourg or a recognized foreign equivalent, in accordance with current regulations in Luxembourg;

(b) hold a final diploma issued by an institute of higher education recognized by the state in which it operates, representing four years' study of economics, commerce, social or political sciences, as described in the register of diplomas established by the Law of 17 June 1963, designed to protect higher education qualifications;

(c) have completed a teacher training course of at least two years and have passed an examination at the end of it;

(d) be capable of teaching a number of lessons to be determined by Grand Ducal regulation.

In accordance with the Grand Ducal Regulation of 24 July 1972 which lays down the conditions for training and appointing art teachers in secondary schools, a prospective teacher should:

(a) hold a secondary leaving certificate from Luxembourg or a recognized foreign equivalent in accordance with current Luxembourg regulations;

(b) have completed a course of at least four years' teaching-based art studies, at a foreign university-level institution, recognized by the state in which it operates;

(c) hold a diploma entitling him to teach art in the official secondary education system of the country where it is issued, or admitting him to a teacher training course in this subject;

(d) have completed a teacher training course, and passed an examination at the end of it, enabling him to teach in secondary and higher education.

In accordance with the Grand Ducal Regulation of 24 July 1972 which lays down the conditions for training and appointing physical education teachers in secondary schools, a prospective teacher should:

(a) hold a secondary leaving certificate from Luxembourg or a recognized foreign equivalent in accordance with current Luxembourg regulations;

(b) have completed a course of at least four years' teaching-based physical education studies at a foreign university-level institution, recognized by the state in which it operates;

(c) hold a diploma entitling him to teach physical education in the official secondary education system of the country in which it is issued, or admitting him to a teaching course in this field;

(d) have completed a teacher training course and passed an examination at the end of it, entitling him to teach in secondary and higher education.

In accordance with the Law of 24 July 1973 which establishes the post of teacher of music in secondary education establishments, a prospective teacher should:

(a) hold a secondary leaving certificate from Luxembourg or a recognized foreign equivalent in accordance with current Luxembourg regulations;

(b) have completed a teaching-based music course of at least four years at a foreign university-level institution, recognized by the state in which it operates;

(c) hold a diploma entitling him to teach music in the official secondary education system of the country in which it is issued or admitting him to a teacher training course in this field;

(d) have completed a teacher training course and passed an examination at the end of it, entitling him to teach in higher and secondary education.

In accordance with the Grand Ducal Regulation of 25 April 1974 laying down the syllabus of courses and examination procedures for the general secondary education teacher training course, scientific and teacher training courses and the conditions for appointing teachers of arts subjects, sciences, economics and social science, art, physical education and music, cover the following subjects:

General subjects:

1. adolescent psychology;
2. educational sociology;
3. school structures and legislation on secondary education;
4. general methodology.

Special subjects:

1. methodology of the various branches of teaching.

The courses on general subjects are taken by all students. Each student also takes courses on the methodology of his own subject. Syllabuses of the above subjects are worked out in detail by the Ministry for Education, with the advice of the educational training department.

Tests are written or oral
All tests are assessed by at least two examiners and marked out of ten. In deciding final results and grading of candidates, the average mark obtained in general subjects and the mark obtained in methodology are taken into equal consideration.

Examination decisions, including those concerning the eligibility of candidates, are taken by those responsible for the courses, and there is no right of appeal.

Successful candidates must have a total of at least 12 marks for the general section and the special section, or at least five marks for each section. Candidates who do not succeed in obtaining a total of at least 12 marks have to retake the section in which they failed to obtain at least five marks. Retaking in part may be limited to one or more subjects in the general section.

Candidates who fail to obtain five marks in both the general and the special sections have to retake all examinations.

Technical and vocational state education in Luxembourg covers

- secondary teachers
- teachers with engineering degrees
- teachers with degrees in architecture
- vocational teachers
- instructors.

Under the Grand Ducal Regulation of 30 September 1968 which lays down the conditions for admission to training and for the appointment of teachers with degrees in engineering or architecture in technical and vocational education establishments, applicants for these posts should hold a secondary leaving certificate from Luxembourg or an equivalent recognized by the Ministry for Education.

They should also hold a diploma in architecture or engineering of recognized university standard in the country of issue. The diploma should be included in the register of diplomas set up in accordance with the Law of 17 June 1963 for the protection of higher education qualifications. Appointment of teachers with degrees in engineering or architecture follows the completion of a period of teaching practice in a technical or vocational education establishment designated by the Ministry for Education, and leading to examination. The training period consists of teaching itself, and a period of working for one or more firms or public authorities.

Under the Grand Ducal Regulation of 6 September 1968 laying down the conditions for admission to teacher training and the appointment of vocational teachers to technical and vocational education schools or colleges, applicants wishing to take the examination admitting them to training must fulfil the following conditions. Trainee vocational teachers are divided into three groups:

A. general subjects;
B. technical drawing and design;
C. technical science.

A. Candidates wishing to become vocational teachers in group A must hold a Luxembourg secondary leaving certificate and have completed six university semesters or six semesters at a technical school or at a vocational teacher training institute, or four semesters at a teacher training institute followed by two semesters of higher education abroad.

B. Candidates wishing to become vocational teachers in group B must hold a Luxembourg school leaving certificate (classics and modern section) and have completed six semesters at a university-level technical institution, an academy of fine arts, an art school, a technical school or a vocational teacher training institute.

C. Candidates wishing to become vocational teachers in group C must hold either a diploma in technical engineering from the Technical School of Luxembourg or a foreign equivalent recognized by the Ministry of Education, and have completed four semesters at a technical school or vocational teacher training institute; or hold a Luxembourg school leaving certificate (classics section B or modern section B) and have completed either six semesters at university or six semesters at a university-level technical school, higher technical school or vocational teacher training institute.

Group A – general subjects – covers the following options:

— arts subjects
— physical sciences and mathematics
— biology
— chemistry.

Examinations for admission to training courses in the following subjects have been suspended since 15 September 1975:

— arts subjects
— biology
— chemistry.

The university
The Luxembourg university centre was set up by the Law of 18 June 1969 on higher education and the recognition of foreign qualifications and the Law of 11 February 1974 on the university statutes. It runs university courses in three different departments and there are two departments offering training courses in addition to this.

The departments running university-level courses are:

i   law and economics;
ii   arts and humanities;
iii science.

These departments offer first year university courses that are in line with the syllabuses of universities in the neighbouring countries.

Law and economics
These courses correspond to the demands of the first year of law and economics in France (i.e. the DEUG in law, economics, economic and social administration) and to the Belgian syllabus covered in the two years of *candidature* in law.

The department also offers a short (two-year) course of practical law and economics for students interested in retraining or in entering their chosen profession more quickly.

Arts and humanities

The department has the following sections:

i   philosophy and psychology;
ii   classical philology;
iii   Romance studies (French and Italian);
iv   German;
v   English;
vi   history;
vii   geography.

Courses in the department are intended for students wishing to become secondary school teachers.

Science

The science department offers courses that are in line with the first-year requirements in the faculties of medicine, pharmacy and science in foreign universities.

Courses are designed to cover the syllabuses currently being studied in those universities traditionally attended by students from Luxembourg – who thus follow the compulsory classes and options selected in the light of the university they expect to go to in the second year.

There are four sections in this department:

i   medical studies (ME);
ii   pharmaceutical studies (PH);
iii   chemistry and biology (CB or DEUG – science of nature and life);
iv   mathematics and physics (MP or DEUG – science of structures and matter).

Students may follow courses in any one of these sections.

Holders of the Luxembourg secondary school completion certificate (Latin or modern studies) or any recognized foreign equivalent may enrol for regular courses. The administrator of the relevant department may also give permission for students with another end-of-secondary diploma and anyone else with enough knowledge to follow the courses properly to attend on an unofficial basis.

Students who get through the Luxembourg university course can sign on for second year courses at foreign universities (third year law courses in Belgium) and obtain equivalent diplomas for their national qualifications.

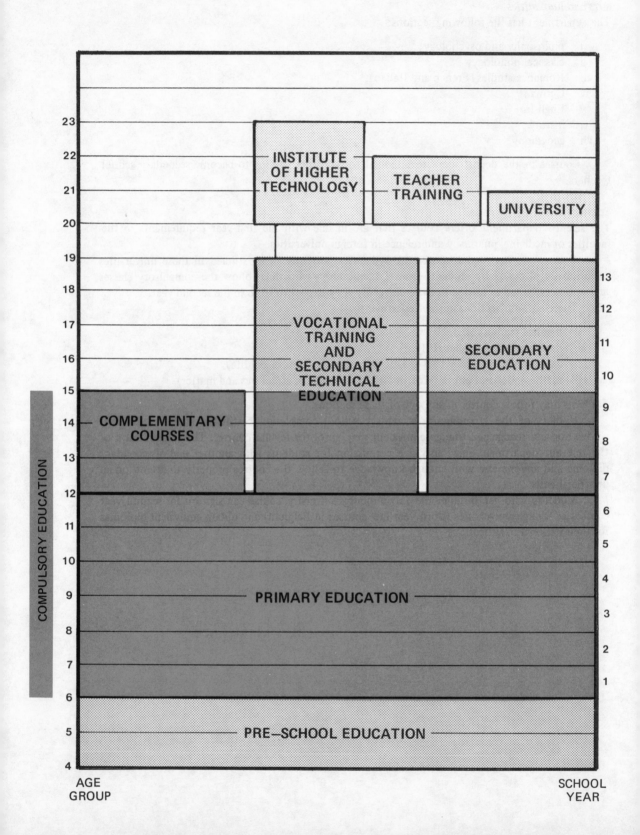

INSTITUTE
OF HIGHER
TECHNOLOGY

TEACHER
TRAINING

UNIVERSITY

VOCATIONAL
TRAINING
AND
SECONDARY
TECHNICAL
EDUCATION

SECONDARY
EDUCATION

COMPLEMENTARY
COURSES

PRIMARY EDUCATION

PRE–SCHOOL EDUCATION

COMPULSORY EDUCATION

AGE
GROUP

SCHOOL
YEAR

NETHERLANDS

Introduction

Historical development

Before the sixteenth century little is known about the existence of schools or any kind of educational system in the Netherlands. An important boost was the founding of the universities of Leyden (1575), Groningen (1614) and Utrecht (1636). In the nineteenth century the first national school laws were passed. In 1848 a provision in the Constitution stated that the giving of education should be free. Although the founding of a school no longer needed the permission of the Government, the champions of denominational education were not satisfied as yet. The expense of establishing and running the schools still had to be borne by the parents. This remained a burning issue in Dutch politics until 1917, when the relevant article of the Constitution was amended and public and private primary schools were put on an equal financial footing. This parity now applies to all schools. In spite of the fact that the School Struggle (*School strijd*) was fought over the issue of denominational schools, the Constitution allows freedom of education for people of every persuasion. All private schools are eligible for maintenance from state funds, provided they comply with certain statutory conditions relating to their establishment and operation. There is no difference between the quality of teaching and the qualification obtained in public and private schools. This – putting on an equal footing public and private education – is unique in the world, and deeply cherished by the Dutch population. It is of course undeniably true that it does lead to a great degree of compartmentalization. Education in the Netherlands is regulated by a number of Education Acts. These have undergone constant revision, or have even been replaced altogether so as to coincide with the development of the views held on education among the people. Most important recently has been the passing of the Secondary Education Act (1963). The underlying principle of this Act was that there should be more attention paid to equal opportunity for all pupils. The aforementioned Act attempted to attain this goal among other things by the introduction of the bridge-year (*brugklas*) between primary and secondary education.

Pupils have here the opportunity to switch from different school-types without losing a year. Developments in secondary education are moving more and more towards a comprehensive-type school. A special feature of Dutch education has always been the large amount of preparatory vocational education and apprenticeship-training taking place under the responsibility of the schools instead of industry. The Apprenticeship Act (1966) regulates this type of education so that the apprentice can also take part in general and practical training courses.

Administration

The Constitution lays down the Government's obligations with regard to education, which is defined as 'a subject of constant solicitude'. The Minister of Education and Science bears responsibility for education by looking after legislation concerning education and its implementation. There are secretaries of state, who have their own field of responsibility. All are accountable to Parliament. The Minister of Agriculture and Fisheries looks after agricultural training.

The Education Council, instituted by law, is responsible for advising the Ministers on bills, reform and the renewal of the education system and the implementation of various laws.

Public education is run either by the State or the municipalities. Parents' committees exist but have not any administrative role. Private education is run by private organizations. An Act on Compulsory Education stipulates that parents have the obligation to ensure that their children attend school for a number of years. Compulsory education starts at the beginning of the school year (1 August) in which the child reaches the age of 6 years and 8 months. Compulsory full-time education ends if the minor has been attending school for a period of 10 years, or has reached the age of 16 years. Since January 1975 the Act has been amended to make part-time education compulsory during the first year following full-time education. Pupils have to attend certain institutes for part-time education for a period of two days per week for one year. The intention of the Act was to make part-time education compulsory for another year.

Fees

Parents are exempt from paying school fees for children attending nursery schools, primary schools, special schools, and secondary schools (only the first four years).

School fees for children attending secondary school after the first four years are a maximum of 500 guilders per year. The assessment is made by the inspector of taxes on the basis of the income tax and wealth tax payable. The number of children in the family attending school are taken in account.

The same arrangements apply to higher vocational education. At universities and *hogescholen* tuition fees have to be paid for the first four years only (Dfl. 500). Registration fees (100 guilders) have to be paid annually.

Qualifications needed to teach in the Netherlands

Generally speaking it is not permitted to teach at a Dutch school with a foreign teaching qualification. Exceptions exist only for some teaching qualifications in secondary schools.

Foreign students: admission

Everyone wishing to study at a Dutch institution of university standard must be admissible to the Dutch university examinations. Holders of a non-Dutch diploma must first obtain a Dutch ministerial decree or declaration showing their admissibility.

The number of non-Dutch nationals that can be admitted to courses in veterinary science, medicine and dentistry, is severely limited.

Pre-primary education (*kleuteronderwijs* = k.o.)

Pre-primary education in the Netherlands is organized in accordance with the Pre-primary Education Act which came into force on 1 January 1956.

Generally speaking a child can be admitted to a pre-primary school on the day he becomes 4 years old and must leave the school as soon as he reaches the age of 7. Although pre-primary education is not compulsory, 93 per cent of all 4 year olds and about 97 per cent of 5 year olds attend a pre-primary school.

Pre-primary education is completely free of charge. The parents themselves are allowed to choose the pre-primary school they wish their child to attend.

Normally the children attend the school for three hours in the morning from Monday to Friday and for two hours in the afternoon on Monday, Tuesday, Thursday and Friday. The total holidays amount to about 12 weeks per year.

The pre-primary school does not undertake to teach the children in the usual sense of the word.

Each school has a play and work programme. Experiments are going on to achieve the complete integration of pre-primary education with primary education.

Primary education (*lager onderwijs* = l.o.)
Primary education is compulsory. On 1 August of the year in which a child reaches the age of 6 years and 8 months that child is required to attend primary school. In addition children can be admitted to primary school on 1 August each year, provided they have reached the age of 6 years before 1 October of the calendar year in which they are admitted. Primary education lasts for six years; each year consists of a minimum of 1,000 hours (although 880 hours are regarded as adequate for the first two years). Compulsory schooling thus consists of six years' primary education and four years' secondary education.

Primary education is organized in accordance with the Primary Education Act of 1920. Primary education is directed towards the best possible continuous development of the pupils, taking into account at the same time the individual differences manifested by the pupils as they pass through successive development stages. The form teacher is responsible for all subjects. There are very few specialist teachers in primary schools, except those teaching physical education.

Each pupil must show that he has made satisfactory progress each year; where this is not the case the year must be repeated.

Special education (*buitengewoon onderwijs* = bu.o.)
Special education is organized in accordance with the Special Education Decree of 1967. Special education consists of pre-primary, primary and secondary level. The children requiring special education belong to two different categories:

- children with sensorial, physical or mental handicaps or children with behavioural problems;
- children whose parents' jobs take them from place to place: people living on barges or in caravans, fairground workers.

The first category is by far the largest and within this category the largest group comprises backward and imbecile children, who are difficult or very difficult to teach. The minimum age for entry to special education is for each of these categories 3 years and the maximum age for attendance is 17 or in special cases 20 years of age.

This category comprises schools for children falling into the following categories: hard of hearing, deaf, children with speech defects, blind and partially sighted, physically handicapped, children in homes for the chronically sick, delicate children, epileptics, backward children (with learning difficulties), imbecile children (with severe learning difficulties), the educationally sub-normal living in homes, severely maladjusted children, children living in institutional care and children in schools attached to institutes where mental disturbance is studied and treated, children with learning difficulties and behavioural problems, children with multiple handicaps. The second category consists of only pre-primary and primary level. The maximum age for entry to this category is 15 and in very special cases 18 years.

Mobile schools are organized for the children of fairground workers.

Decisions of admission to special education are made by a special committee. The committee consists of the head of the school to which admission is being sought, a medical specialist and a psychologist or educationalist; there may also be other members.

At the present time more than 5 per cent of all school pupils are attending special education courses.

Secondary education (*voortgezet onderwijs* = v.o.)

General features
Secondary education comprises all forms of education after primary school, with the exception of the universities. The most important forms of secondary education are:

— *voorbereidend wetenschappelijk onderwijs* (v.w.o.) = pre-university education;
— *algemeen voortgezet onderwijs* (a.v.o.) = general secondary education;
— *beroepsonderwijs* (b.o.) = vocational education.

The Secondary Education Act (WVO), which is also sometimes known as the Mammoth Act, and which came into force in 1968, contains rules on these forms of education and the schools in which they are offered.

The purpose of this Act is to introduce a coherent set of educational provisions for secondary education. Various instruments are available for this purpose, e.g. a planning procedure to ensure state support for new schools. The internal structure is also taken care of by the provisions concerning the first secondary school year, known popularly as the bridging class (*brugklas*), which provides pupils with easier access to the second year of more than one kind of school. In this way it is possible to postpone the final choice of a school for a year.

The Act allows the forming of *scholengemeenschappen* (school-groups), along the lines of the comprehensive schools in the United Kingdom and Sweden. A *scholengemeenschap* is, according to the Act, one school (one administration, one supervisory board), which includes various kinds of schools, e.g. a general secondary school and a vocational school, or a school for pre-university education and a general secondary school. At least one of the schools included in a *scholengemeenschap* must be a secondary school.

There are also evening schools and part-time courses corresponding to practically every type of secondary school and leading to equivalent diplomas.

Admission to schools for secondary education is generally determined by an admission committee, set up by the schools' governing authorities. (The admission committee consists of the principal and teachers of the school/schools for secondary education. Heads of the schools for primary education can also be members of the committee. Before deciding or advising on admission, the admission committee consults the report, which the head of the school for primary or special education has prepared.)

For admission to schools for pre-university education and to h.a.v.o. schools pupils must demonstrate their ability to follow the courses for which they are applying. Ability is tested in at least one of the following ways:

(a) an entrance examination (set up by the school teachers with at least Dutch and arithmetic as compulsory examination subjects);
(b) a special class (attached to the school where at least 16×50 min. and not more than 32×50 min. lessons are given by the school teachers);
(c) an appraisal of knowledge and ability spread over at least the whole of the pupil's last year at primary school;
(d) a psychological test.

*Pre-university education (*voortgezet wetenschappelijk onderwijs = v.w.o.)*
These schools fall into three types: the 'gymnasium', the 'atheneum' and the 'lyceum'. All three offer a six year course leading on from primary school. The schools provide preparation for university studies. The difference between a 'gymnasium' and an 'atheneum' is, that in the 'gymnasium' teaching must be provided in Latin and Greek, while no such teaching is offered at an 'atheneum'. However, an 'atheneum' can receive permission to provide teaching in Latin. The 'lyceum' is a school which combines a 'gymnasium' and an 'atheneum' with a common first year of studies.

After the fourth or fifth year of studies both the 'gymnasium' and the 'atheneum' divide their pupils into A and B streams. The main subjects in the B streams at both kinds of school are mathematics and science; the main subject in the A stream at the 'gymnasium' is classical languages and in the A stream in the 'atheneum' modern languages and economics.

Each stream leads up to a final examination in seven subjects, five of which are compulsory and two are selected by the candidate. The five compulsory subjects are as follows:

Gymnasium A stream: Dutch, Greek, Latin, one modern language (French, German or English) and one subject from history, geography or economics;

Gymnasium B stream: Dutch, Greek or Latin, one of the above mentioned modern languages, mathematics and one subject from physics, chemistry or biology;

Atheneum A stream: Dutch, two of the above mentioned modern languages, history or geography and economics;

Atheneum B stream: Dutch, one of the above mentioned modern languages, mathematics and two subjects from physics, chemistry or biology.

All the subjects referred to can also be optional subjects – with the exception of Latin and Greek at an atheneum – for each of the four streams, together with Frisian.

More subjects are taught than appear in the lists of examinations. For example there are compulsory classes in social studies, physical education and various cultural subjects. In addition the school can offer classes in various subjects, for example Russian, Spanish, Esperanto, Hebrew, religious studies, cultural history of Christianity, philosophy, etc. In 1973 it became possible to organize 'gymnasia', 'atheneums' and 'lyceums' on an unstreamed basis with the final examination containing the same number of compulsory subjects and the candidate being offered a free choice of five (four at an unstreamed 'gymnasium') of the seven examination subjects. Dutch language and one of the modern languages referred to are always compulsory subjects. An unstreamed 'gymnasium' must always include at least one of the classical languages in the final examination. This type of school is becoming increasingly popular.

In 1978 about 45 per cent of pupils engaged in pre-university education already attended an unstreamed school of this type.

*General secondary education (*algemeen voortgezet onderwijs = *a.v.o.)*
There are two levels in this kind of education: lower and upper level. Each level follows on directly from primary education. The (*middelbaar algemeen voortgezet onderwijs* = m.a.v.o.) schools for general secondary education, lower level, offer a four-year course. Some schools also offer a three-year course, with a simpler curriculum. The final diploma from a m.a.v.o. school or section gives access to the schools for senior secondary vocational education; the final diploma of the four-year m.a.v.o. school can give access to the fourth year of the schools for general secondary education, upper level (*hoger algemeen voortgezet onderwijs* = h.a.v.o.).

The h.a.v.o. school offers a five-year course. The h.a.v.o. diploma gives access to the schools for higher vocational education. Pupils attending the a.v.o. schools are given – as at the v.w.o. schools but at a different level – a broad basis for later vocational training. The pupils receive instruction in their mother tongue, two or three modern languages (French, German, English), history, geography, social studies, mathematics, physics, chemistry, biology, physical education and one or more cultural subjects. The school can include more subjects in its programme. The final examination includes six subjects (five for the three-year m.a.v.o. section), the subjects being Dutch, one of the modern languages referred to and three or four optional subjects, chosen by the candidate. The options are: the non-compulsory modern languages, Frisian, history, geography, mathematics, physics, chemistry, biology, commerce and one cultural subject.

*Vocational education (*beroepsonderwijs = *b.o.)*

General features

Vocational education in the Netherlands is divided into eight main groups, most of them organized at three levels, viz. junior secondary (*lager beroepsonderwijs* = l.b.o.), senior secondary (*middelbaar beroepsonderwijs* = m.b.o.), and higher vocational education (*hoger beroepsonderwijs* = h.b.o.).

Technical training which prepares for technical occupations and nautical education, preparing for the inland shipping services, the Rhine service, service at sea and in the fishing industry.

Domestic science education provides general and practical preparation for domestic management as well as for the welfare and service occupations.

Agricultural education provides pupils for work in agriculture, farming and market gardening, food technology, the organization and maintenance of parks and forests and green areas in general.

Trade education prepares pupils for careers, independent or otherwise, in trade, commercial and service industries.

Commercial education provides pupils with training for a career in business or in government or semi-government bodies.

Teacher training gives pupils at a senior secondary level preparation for work as pre-primary school teachers and at higher level for work as primary and secondary school teachers.

Socio-pedagogic education, offered only at senior secondary and higher level, prepares pupils for careers in youth work, adult education, cultural work, social work, community organization, personnel work, child care, health care, librarianship and journalism and for other careers in this area.

Art education only at higher level prepares pupils for careers in all branches of the arts: music, dancing, stage, variety, the art industry and the cinema.

Under particular conditions the junior secondary vocational education diploma provides access to the senior secondary vocational level and the senior secondary vocational diploma provides access to the higher level.

*Junior secondary vocational education (*lager beroepsonderwijs = *l.b.o.)*

Junior secondary vocational education plays an important role in the Dutch education system, since about 30 per cent of young people leaving primary school go on directly to junior secondary vocational education. All junior secondary vocational education courses last for four years. The first two years are almost totally devoted to general subjects and the last two years to vocational preparation.

The junior secondary technical schools (*lager technisch onderwijs* = l.t.o.)

These are the largest group. All pupils have a choice of examination courses at three levels, A, B and C (in ascending order of difficulty). If they take three examination subjects at C level they are able to pass on to schools for general secondary education, lower level, and schools for senior secondary vocational education.

Technical education at junior secondary level also includes individual technical education (*individueel technisch onderwijs* = i.t.o.), intended for pupils in need of more individual attention, because of their learning difficulties or social circumstances. Pupils who obtain their diploma after completion of this kind of course are able to receive further training in industry under the Apprenticeship Act.

Nautical training offers courses in the following areas: seamanship, engineering, work on barges. Here too it is possible to pass on to senior nautical training.

Junior secondary domestic science schools (*lager huishoud-en nijverheidsonderwijs* = l.h.n.o.)
These are largely attended by girls. Here too there is a choice of examination courses at three levels. After obtaining passes in two examination subjects at C level it is possible to go on to senior secondary domestic science schools and senior secondary socio-pedagogic schools (*middelbaar huishoud-en nijverheidsonderwijs* = m.h.n.o./*middelbaar sociaal pedagogisch onderwijs* = m.s.p.o.) (or with passes in three examination subjects at C level in the preparatory higher vocational education course (*voorbereidend hoger beroepsonderwijs* = v.h.b.o.).

As in the case of the individual technical education referred to above, individual domestic science education (*individueel huishoud-en nijverheidsonderwijs* = i.h.n.o.) is intended for children who require more individual forms of teaching, because of their learning difficulties or social circumstances.

Junior secondary agricultural education (*lager landbouwonderwijs* = l.l.o.)
This covers instruction in agriculture, horticulture and forestry together with agricultural technology. The examination syllabus and the opportunities for access to other courses are the same as those for junior secondary technical education.

Instruction can also be given at schools with a simplified curriculum, intended for children who need more individual teaching because of their learning difficulties and their social circumstances (*individueel landbouw onderwijs* = i.l.o.).

Schools for junior secondary trade education (*lager middenstandsonderwijs* = l.m.o.)
These have developed considerably over the last 15 years. The examination syllabus and the opportunities for access to further courses are the same as for junior secondary technical education.
Junior secondary commercial education (*lager economisch en administratief onderwijs* = l.e.a.o.)
This is more generally based than at the tradesmen's schools. The l.e.a.o. is the most recent form of junior secondary vocational education. The examination syllabus and the opportunities for access to further courses are the same as for junior secondary technical education.

In addition to full-time courses there are a large number of part-time courses intended in particular for older persons, who wish to prepare themselves for the tradesmen's exam, which is a legal prerequisite if one desires to set up in business.

Senior secondary vocational education (middelbaar beroepsonderwijs = *m.b.o.*)
Students who have obtained an appropriate junior secondary vocational education diploma in an appropriate combination of subjects, or who hold a m.a.v.o. diploma may be admitted to senior secondary vocational education courses. The length of the course varies from area to area and can last for a maximum of four years.

Technical education at senior secondary level (*middelbaar technisch onderwijs* = m.t.o.)
This is given in schools with a four-year course. The third year is a practical year, which is supervised by the school. These schools are intended to train the middle management for industry.

Nautical education at senior secondary level covers training as mate or master, mariner and ship's engineer on small trading vessels, deep sea tugs and larger fishing vessels. Normally the course lasts for two years.

Domestic science education at senior secondary level (*middelbaar huishoud-en nijverheidsonderwijs* = m.h.n.o.)

This covers seven different courses:

— the interim general link courses (one or two years; preparation for other forms of senior secondary vocational education (m.b.o.) leading to qualifications in the care and welfare sectors);
— child and youth care (two or three years);
— dressmaking (two years);
— tailoring (one year; follow-up course to the course in dressmaking);
— training class (one year; supplementary training in general domestic science for girls who have completed general secondary education);
— preparatory training for higher vocational education (v.h.b.o.) (three years; acts as a link between l.b.o. and h.b.o.);
— household management (three years; preparation for middle management functions, for example running the domestic affairs of an institution).

Some schools offer a two-year training course for chemists' assistants, doctors' and/or dentists' assistants.

Agricultural education at the senior secondary level (*middelbaar landouw onderwijs* = m.l.o.)
This includes training courses in agriculture, horticulture, forestry and plant and food technology. The courses last between two and four years.

Senior secondary trade education (*middelbaar middenstandsonderwijs* = m.m.o.)
This includes senior retail trade schools (three years) and senior hotel restaurant and catering training courses (four years including one year practical training).

Senior secondary commercial education (*middelbaar economisch en administratief onderwijs* = m.e.a.o.)
This is divided into five sectors each lasting for three years. These are as follows:

— administrative section;
— commercial section;
— secretarial section;
— management section;
— optional section.

In addition there is an experimental tourist section.
Students holding a m.a.v.o. diploma or who have completed three years h.a.v.o. or v.w.o. can be admitted to the pre-primary teachers training course.
This course lasts for four years and is divided into a three-year course providing training as a teacher for a pre-primary school and a part-time course, which provides training as a senior pre-primary school teacher. Only those holding a diploma from the full-time course are admitted to the part-time course. This diploma also provides entry to the training courses for primary school teachers.

Senior secondary socio-pedagogic education (*middelbaar sociaal pedagogisch onderwijs* = m.s.p.o.)
This includes the following:

— training as a family welfare worker;
— training as an old persons' welfare worker;
— training as sports organizer;

- occupational therapy schools;
- training courses in labour policy and staff management;
- training in the social services;
- organizational training;
- training as youth organizers;
- training in cultural work;
- training in work therapy.

Full-time and/or part-time courses are available, which last for two or three years.

In addition to the kinds of vocational education referred to above, which are organized in accordance with the WVO, there are four other kinds of vocational education.

Apprenticeship training

Apprenticeship training is organized in accordance with the 1966 Apprenticeship Act. Under this Act the apprentice receives practical training from his employer in a specific occupation and at the same time follows supplementary general and vocational training in a school.

The characteristic of the apprenticeship system is the fact that an agreement is concluded according to which the apprentice receives training from a supervisor in the performance of a specific occupation, while at the same time he engages in supplementary general and theoretical vocational training at a school. A student generally undertakes training under the apprenticeship system after attending an l.b.o. course but there are also openings for those students who have engaged in a different form of secondary education. There are two sorts of training: primary and continued. Primary training lasts for at least two years, continued training lasts for at least one year.

The supplementary training is given in schools established for this purpose or in special departments of l.b.o. schools. Courses are generally given on one day per week. There are also evening classes.

At the end of the course an examination is taken including a practical and theoretical section. The apprentices who have only passed in the practical section can obtain a diploma attesting their practical skill. An apprentice must be aged under 27 years.

Educational institutes for early school-leavers and for young adults

The aim of these institutes is to provide training for those young people who have left full-time secondary education, and who may or may not have found work.

The educational institutes for early school-leavers are intended to give educational assistance to young people who may or may not have already obtained a job and are no longer engaged in full-time education. Training courses of this kind are given separately to boys and girls and are divided into two age groups: 15–18 year old and 17–27 year old. These courses are not exclusively directed towards intellectual training as such, but primarily towards the development of the individual and the provision of help with problems encountered by young people in their daily lives: the relationships with others, with society, in their work, in their leisure time, in marriage, etc. Courses take place during working time and also in the evening.

There are therefore two categories of institutes:

- institutes exclusively intended for the 16–18 year old, who are working and who attend an institute twice a week. The participation of this group has risen sharply in the last few years through the introduction of compulsory part-time education. The expenses of these institutes are completely reimbursed by the State;
- centres for young adults, 17–25 year old (who do not fall into the compulsory part-time

education category). These are usually evening schools and are financed partly by the State, the province and the municipality.

Correspondence courses

Correspondence courses offer an opportunity to study at all levels for those who for various reasons are not in a position or are not prepared to engage in other kinds of education. In 1977 about 194,000 students were engaged in such courses, which are organized by private institutions. In order to improve the level of teaching and to protect the consumer a statutory regulation has been introduced concerning the qualifications of the teachers, the quality of the courses and the level of work of the participants, the content of the written agreement, the examinations and the diplomas and the extent to which advertising may be undertaken. The authorities do not subsidize correspondence courses.

Adult education and retraining

Workers who are unemployed or threatened with unemployment can register with the regional employment bureau and sign up for a course at an adult vocational training centre.

Courses at these centres are free of charge and last from between four and 12 months according to the subject chosen and the abilities of the candidate. During this period each candidate receives payment to compensate for loss of earnings at a level corresponding to the minimum wage. The training methods in these centres are comparable with the methods of programmed training on the modular pattern: the student carries out practical work which involves some theoretical elements. Most of these centres provide training in at least three trades within the building industry and seven within the metal-working industry (of which two are electronics and automobile engineering). Each of these courses begins with one of the two following basic courses: metal-working or building.

At the end of the course a diploma is issued which shows the duration of the course and the subject in which it was taken.

Higher education (*hoger onderwijs* = h.o.)

Higher vocational education *(*hoger beroepsonderwijs *= h.b.o.)*

There are a number of structural differences between h.b.o. on the one hand and university education (*wetenschappelijk onderwijs* = w.o.) on the other. The first of these is that the universities have always aimed at concentrating various subject areas within one institute. On the other hand, the h.b.o. institutions represent a wide diversity of types of school, which have largely come into being within the course of the present century. As a result the subjects within this sector are divided between a number of institutions with a separate administration in each case.

The second difference is, that whereas the university system is based on the principle that a student is able to devote the whole day to study and research, the vocationally based h.b.o. system also enables people who are already working to engage in part-time education.

The number of students in each sector shows the social significance of the h.b.o. system. In 1977, 10,228 students completed their university studies, while 21,331 students completed their h.b.o. studies.

Higher technical education (*hoger technisch onderwijs* = h.t.o.)

This trains students from v.w.o., h.a.v.o. schools and even from m.b.o. schools for the higher and middle management of small or medium-sized undertakings. The students are required to have an adequate knowledge of the basic subjects, mathematics, physics, chemistry and biology.

Students who have completed their studies at a h.t.o. school can in some cases use short part-time courses to specialize in the subject in which they are engaged in industry, the service sector or the public service.

The higher technical education system includes the higher technical schools, the schools for laboratory workers and the schools for higher nautical education.

Higher technical schools (*hoger technische school* = h.t.s.)

There are 29 day and evening higher technical schools with 22,000 students registered in 1978 and offering the following subjects: automobile engineering, building contracting, management, architecture, chemistry, chemical technology, textiles, computer technology, economic management technology, electrical engineering, physical engineering, advanced computer studies, surveying, mechanical engineering, civil engineering, metallurgy, physics, processing technology, naval architecture, transport technology, transport studies, aircraft design.

The full-time course lasts for four years including the training periods outside the school and the projects for the final examination.

The evening course lasts for five years, in some cases preceded by two preparatory years. According to the requirements, specialization is at the student's option. The diploma confers a legal right to use the title of *ingenieur* (*ing.*).

The final level of studies reached by these practically trained engineers is comparable with the final level of studies reached by the more theoretically trained engineers from the universities of technology.

Schools for laboratory technicians

There are 24 full-time and evening schools for laboratory technicians with 13,000 registered students in 1978, divided between medical studies, chemistry, physics, zoology and botany. The courses are at present divided into three levels, i.e. h.b.o. level A lasting for two years, h.b.o. level B lasting for three years and the schools for higher education in the physical sciences (*hoger natuurwetenschappelijk onderwijs* = h.n.w.o.) lasting for four years, all full-time including the practical training spent outside the schools, but under the supervision of the training institute. The emphasis on practical knowledge and the broadening and widening of knowledge in the theoretical subjects is responsible for the division into levels. The evening courses, h.b.o. A and h.b.o. B, last for three and four years respectively. In the foreseeable future all existing laboratory technicians training courses are to be re-organized within institutes for three-year higher laboratory technicians training.

Higher nautical education

There are nine higher nautical schools with a total of 3,500 students in 1978, offering courses for mate, ship's engineer and radio officer on board large foreign-going vessels.

The basic training courses comprise:

- for mates: the four-year higher technical school structured training, navigation section, and the two-year BS course (B level, S *stuurman* = mate);
- for ships' engineers: the four-year higher technical school structured training, ships engineering section and the two-year BM course (B level, M *machinist* = ship's engineer);
- for radio officers: the two-year ship's radio communication training course.

These training courses also involve a preparatory year for students who have completed a m.a.v.o. school (mathematics and physics or chemistry as one of the subjects for final examination).

All the courses referred to lead up to a final school examination – under state supervision – and a diploma from the school.

The higher technical school structured course – a four-year course, including a supervised training trip during the third year, of which the student keeps a written record – leads up to the (lowest) state diploma as a skilled seaman, third mate on commercial vessels, or the state diploma A as ship's engineer on production of the school diploma; the higher state diplomas can be obtained after experience at sea without any further study or examination, and on application for the (highest) state diploma as first mate, or state diploma C as ship's engineer.

The BS and BM courses for mate and ship's engineer have always consisted of a primary theoretical training, leading up to a final school examination – not subject to state supervision – and a school diploma, followed by several years' experience at sea and then a number of intermittent continuation courses leading up to state examinations and a qualifying state diploma as mate or ship's engineer. On production of the school diploma for the two-year training in ship's radio communication, the general radio officer's certificate (State Certificate) can be obtained.

At one of the higher nautical schools there is also the possibility of training for the state aircraft engineer's certificate.

The higher domestic science education system (*hoger huishoud-en nijverheidsonderwijs* = h.h.n.o.) This includes the school for applied domestic science education which offer a course lasting four years. These schools aim at giving both theoretical and practical preparation for careers in the running of the day-to-day affairs and domestic management of hospitals, old people's homes, recreation centres, etc. and in organizations for household information.

In order to obtain admittance to these courses the minimum requirement is the h.a.v.o. diploma or an m.b.o. diploma or a diploma of preparatory training in higher vocational education (v.h.b.o.).

Higher agricultural education (*hoger landbouw onderwijs* = h.l.o.) This is divided between: agriculture, tropical agriculture (with a course lasting three years), horticulture, food technology, forestry and soil technology, market gardening and landscaping. In general students are admitted with a diploma from a senior agricultural or horticultural school or a h.a.v.o. diploma.

The diploma from the higher agricultural school gives access to the University of Agriculture at Wageningen and the veterinary department of the University of Utrecht.

The two higher hotel and catering schools
These prepare students for management functions in the hotel, cafe and similar industries (director, manager, assistant manager, staff manager in hospitals, etc.); the courses last three years. Admission to the first year of studies is open to those holding at least the h.a.v.o. diploma or the m.m.o. or the m.e.a.o. diploma.

The schools for higher commercial education (*hoger economisch en administratief onderwijs* = h.e.a.o.)
These have a course lasting three years, except for the department of computer science, where the course lasts four years.

Admission is open to those holding the h.a.v.o. diploma (with a specified set of subjects) or the m.e.a.o. or m.m.o. diploma.

At the end of the first year the student chooses between various subject areas, as follows:

– industrial administration;
– trade and commerce;

- economics and law;
- industrial computer science;
- communications.

Other departments and specialities are in preparation (accountancy department with two specialities, brokerage, higher retail trade studies, management).

There is also a school for higher recreational and tourist studies (h.e.a.o. school with a special curriculum) with a course lasting three years.

Teacher training (*opleiding onderwijzend personeel*)

TEACHER TRAINING FOR PRIMARY SCHOOLS (*ONDERWIJZERSOPLEIDING*)

Teacher training for primary schools is given at teacher training colleges (*pedagogische academies* = p.a.s) and comes under the h.b.o. system. The course lasts three years. The training was originally divided into two parts: the first lasted for two years leading up to the teacher's diploma and the second lasting for one year leading up to the full primary school teaching certificate (senior teacher). Students were admitted with a h.a.v.o. diploma or a pre-primary school teacher's diploma A. Students completing the first part successfully were admitted to the second part. At the present time, the teacher training colleges only train pupils for the full primary school teacher's certificate. The course lasts for three years. The final certificate gives holders the opportunity of being admitted to certain university courses. A teacher's certificate enables them to teach at a primary school. Holders of the full primary school teacher's certificate are able to become heads of primary schools.

All primary school teachers can carry on studying and engage in a specialization, for example, in order to obtain a certificate in the teaching of handicapped children.

Primary school teachers can obtain the Montessori certificate (course A) after one or two years' part-time training. They can then go on to take part in the B course for one year, provided they are in addition fully qualified primary school teachers.

TEACHER TRAINING FOR SECONDARY SCHOOLS (*LERARENOPLEIDING*)

Teacher training for secondary schools is divided in the following manner:

- teacher training old style for secondary schools;
- the new teacher training for secondary schools.

The teacher training courses old style provides pupils with training in two kinds of subjects: general and vocational. These two subjects are subdivided as follows:

- training in general subjects:
  - teacher training course for secondary schools, lower level (third grade level);
  - teacher training course for secondary schools intermediate and higher level (second and first grade level);
  - handicrafts and music;
  - university courses (first grade level);
- training for the vocational subjects:
  - technical education;
  - nautical education;
  - domestic science education;
  - agricultural education.

The holder of a first grade certificate is in principle entitled to teach in that subject throughout the secondary education system. A person who has obtained a second grade certificate is not entitled to teach in all kinds of secondary schools, but in more than is the holder of a third grade certificate.

The teacher training courses old style for secondary schools, lower level (l.o. *akte*) are offered as evening classes at teacher training colleges. The course usually lasts two years.

Courses old style for secondary school teacher certificates intermediate and higher level (*MO-A en MO-B akten*) are given by universities and *hogescholen* (institutions of equivalent standard) and by non-university institutes. In this latter case the courses generally take the form of evening classes. The total period of studies is between six and seven years and leads to a first grade certificate. In order to gain admission the student must have completed at least h.a.v.o. In a number of subjects, the secondary school teacher certificate is divided into two sections. For both the A certificate and the B certificate the course lasts between three and four years. The A certificate is a second grade certificate only.

No secondary school teacher's certificate is awarded for handicraft, but instead the student receives the state diploma in handicraft which is comparable as regards qualifications for teaching and length of studies. The admission requirements are all the same. The conservatoria offer the possibility of training for examinations for the A and B music teacher certificates.

In most subjects in university education, a doctoral diploma entitles the holder to teach throughout the secondary education system. The doctoral diploma confers a teaching qualification, providing the graduate has attended lectures on general educational theory at the university for one year, has attended lectures on teaching methods for his subject and has completed about 60 hours of teaching practice.

The training of teachers for vocational subjects is mainly in the form of evening courses. Generally speaking, the course lasts five years and is open to holders of a m.a.v.o. diploma or a certificate of general development (*Opleidingsbewijs Algemene Ontwikkelings* = OBAO).

A number of courses in special h.n.o. subjects for girls were terminated when sections for domestic science, health care and social studies were introduced under the new teacher's training courses. Some courses leading up to these certificates still exist.

In 1970 experiments began on the full-time training of teachers for the second and third grade certificates. The main features of these courses are:

- the training is professional, i.e. the student is prepared for the teaching profession. This means that both the subiect element and the vocational training are of great importance;
- multiple certificate. Each student studies a combination of main subject and a related subsidiary subject. The main subject is studied to second grade level, the subsidiary subject is only studied to third grade level. At the end of his studies, the student receives a second grade teaching certificate for both subjects.

The course lasts four-and-a-half years for the second grade level and four years for the third grade level. On entry the student must already have completed a v.w.o. course or a h.a.v.o. course.

Higher socio-pedagogic education (*hoger sociaal-pedagogisch onderwijs* = h.s.p.o.)
This covers a very varied set of subjects at a number of institutes. Most of the courses last for four years including practical sessions.

These include social academies, training schools for youth leaders in the field of youth training, adult education, cultural or social work, community development, personnel work, residential welfare work, child care and other socio-pedagogical occupations. There are also part-time courses to train pupils for positions in the fields of labour market policy and personnel management work and for social work. Schools of librarianship and documentation provide training in two sections, both leading up to an examination. The first section lasts for two years and the second for one year.

The school of journalism provides a three-year course.

The school of educational and careers guidance work offers a course which lasts for three years and four months.

Admission to all these courses is open to holders of a h.a.v.o. or equivalent diploma.

The h.s.p.o. also includes the four-year training at the academy of expression by word and gesture and the training as spiritual advisor/humanistic training worker at the humanistic training institute.

In certain cases, the h.s.p.o. diploma gives access to university studies in certain subjects.

The h.s.p.o. system also covers courses in nursing and courses for qualified nurses who wish to qualify further for leading positions or the teaching of nursing, as well as courses for paramedical occupations such as physiotherapy, speech therapy, hearing therapy and dietetics.

In art education there is no division into junior secondary level, senior secondary level or a higher level. It includes four types of courses, the fine arts, music, theatre and architecture.

Admission to the schools of fine arts is open to those holding a h.a.v.o. diploma or equivalent preliminary training and with creative aptitude. In general the course lasts for five years. There are a large number of specialist subjects. Under this heading there also come the Academy of Industrial Design, the School for Museum Assistants and the Film and Television Academy.

For admission to the conservatories a h.a.v.o. diploma is also required together with the necessary musical ability and singing or playing skills. In general the course lasts between five and six years. It is possible to train as: practising musician (instrumental or vocal), music teacher (instrumental or vocal), and for the practical diploma together with a number of unspecified specializations. Professional music training is given at the conservatories, the music academies, the Church Music Institute and the Carillon School.

Theatre education prepares students to become practising artists and teachers in the sectors of dance, mime, drama and the cabaret. To be admitted to either of these courses a student must not only hold a h.a.v.o. diploma, but also give evidence of adequate talent and skill. Depending on the student's aptitude the course lasts for an average of four years, but can last up to six years.

The schools of architecture offer further studies for people who have completed higher technical studies in architecture.

University education (wetenschappelijk onderwijs = *w.o.*)

In the Netherlands university education is organized in accordance with the University Education Act (WWO) of 22 December 1960 and the University Administration (Reform) Act (WUB) of 1970. There are two kinds of academic institution which differ in form only; the universities and the *hogescholen* (institutions of equivalent standard). A university has at least three faculties, which must always include a faculty of medicine or a faculty of mathematics and natural science.

There are four state universities in the Netherlands, one municipal university, two private universities and one university *sui generis*.

The four state universities are: the University of Leiden (1575), the University of Groningen (1614), the University of Utrecht (1636) and the University of Rotterdam (1973). The University of Limburg (1976) is *sui generis*, because it merely has a faculty of medicine at present. We then have the Municipal University of Amsterdam (1632).

The private universities are: the Free or Protestant University of Amsterdam (1880) and the Catholic University of Nijmegen (1923).

There are five *hogescholen* in the Netherlands, i.e. the three universities of technology in Delft, Eindhoven and Enschede; the university of agriculture at Wageningen and the Katholieke Hogeschool in Tilburg (specializing in economics, legal studies and social studies). There are also seven theological colleges, whose degrees are recognized by the authorities.

Students who are holders of the pre-university education certificate are eligible for admission to the universities and equivalent institutions.

The certificate of skill as fully qualified primary school teacher gives the holder the right of admission to studies in psychology, pedagogics and adult education. A diploma from the higher agricultural school gives the holder access to studies in veterinary science and agricultural science. A higher technical school diploma gives access to studies at a technical university in the subject corresponding to the previous higher technical school training. The holder of a diploma from a social academy can take examinations in one of the social sciences.

The only admission requirement for persons who have already reached the age of 25 is an entrance examination. Where there are any problems concerning capacity, a placement committee allocates first-year students according to subject and on the basis of a fixed plan between the university institutions.

Entrance to some subjects is restricted, admission being decided in accordance with the system of 'weighted lotteries', i.e. a combination of drawing lots and taking certain criteria into consideration. University studies are generally organized in three stages, the first of these is the one-year general preliminary stage which is followed by the studies for the candidate's qualifications, which generally last from one to two years.

Finally there follows the two to three year period of studies for the doctoral examination.

Successful completion of the doctoral examination gives the student the right to use the title of *doctorandus* (*drs.*) and if one studies law the title of *meester* (*mr.*). The student then has the opportunity of writing a thesis to obtain the title of doctor (*dr.*).

A graduate of a university of technology similarly has the right to use the title *ingenieur* (*ing.*).

Graduates in some subjects also have the opportunity of going on to take a post-graduate course to qualify as doctor, chemist, dentist or veterinarian. In such cases the *doctoraal diploma* is not sufficient.

Not all education comes under the Minister of Education and Sciences. Agricultural education comes under the jurisdiction of the Minister of Agriculture, while the Minister of Defence is responsible for military education.

In 1977 about 132,000 students in higher education were registered, of which about 30 per cent were women.

Other figures (concerning further studies, etc.) are unavailable.

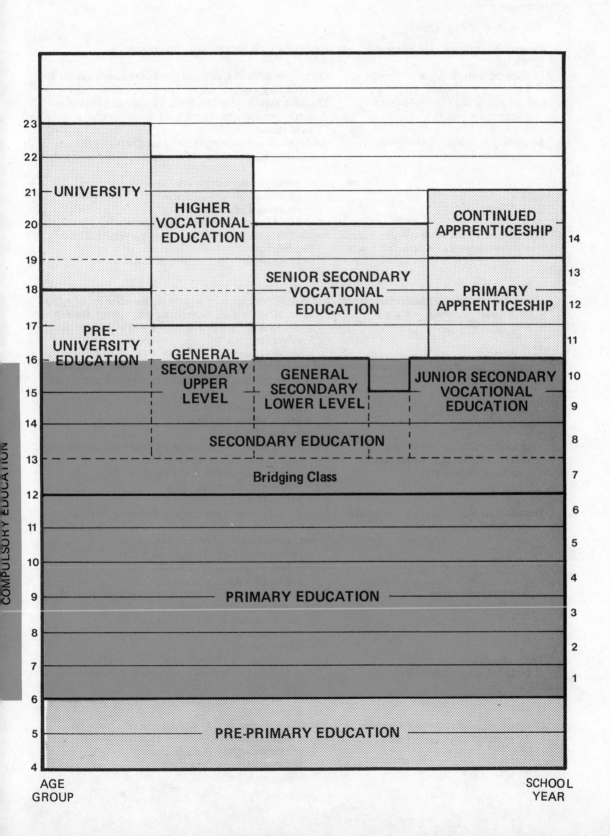

AGE
GROUP

SCHOOL
YEAR

COMPULSORY EDUCATION

Glossary

Explanatory list of terms

Pre-primary education (*kleuteronderwijs* = k.o.) — Pre-primary education, not compulsory.

Primary education (*lager onderwijs* = l.o.) — Primary education (six years), the common basis for all secondary education.

Special education (*buitengewoon onderwijs* = bu.o) — Special education for children, who for any reason are unable or unfit to attend a school for primary education.

Secondary education (*voortgezet onderwijs* = v.o.) — All forms of education after the six years of primary education, excluding university education, divided into:
— pre-university education;
— general secondary education;
— vocational education;
— other forms of secondary education.

Pre-university education (*voorbereidend wetenschappelijk onderwijs* = v.w.o.) — Secondary education preparing for university studies divided into:
— gymnasium;
— atheneum;
— lyceum.

General secondary education (*algemeen voortgezet onderwijs* = a.v.o.) — Secondary education of a general character being a final form of education, as well as a preparation for further non-university education. It is given at two levels:
— lower (m.a.v.o.);
— upper (h.a.v.o.).

Vocational education (*beroepsonderwijs* = b.o.) — All education preparing for an occupation, including teacher training and excluding university education, at three levels:
— junior secondary (l.b.o.);
— senior secondary (m.b.o.);
— higher (h.b.o.).

Technical education (*technisch onderwijs*)/Nautical education (*nautisch onderwijs*) — Technical education preparing for technical and nautical occupations, both at three levels:
— junior secondary (l.t.o., i.t.o.);
— senior secondary (m.t.o.);
— higher (h.t.o.).

Domestic science education (*huishoud- en nijverheidsonderwijs*) — Education providing general and practical preparation for domestic management as well as for the welfare and service occupations, at three levels:
— junior secondary (l.h.n.o., i.h.n.o.);
— senior secondary (m.h.n.o.);
— higher (h.h.n.o.).

Agricultural education (*landbouwonderwijs*) — Education preparing for agricultural or horticultural occupations, at three levels:
— junior secondary (l.l.o., i.l.o.);
— senior secondary (m.l.o.);
— higher (h.l.o.).

Trade education (*middenstandsonderwijs*) — Education preparing for occupations in trade, commercial and service enterprises, at three levels:
— junior secondary (l.m.o.);
— senior secondary (m.m.o.);
— higher (h.m.o.).

Commercial education (*economisch en administratief onderwijs*) — Education preparing for occupations of a business economics and office nature, at three levels:
— junior secondary (l.e.a.o.);
— senior secondary (m.e.a.o.);
— higher (h.e.a.o.).

Socio-pedagogic education (*sociaal-pedagogisch onderwijs*)	Education preparing for occupations in youth work, adult education, cultural work, social work, community organization, personnel work, child care, health care and journalism and for other careers in this field, at two levels: – senior secondary (m.s.p.o.); – higher (h.s.p.o.).
Art education (*kunstonderwijs*)	Education preparing for occupations in the different branches of the arts, at one level: – higher.
Teacher training (*opleiding onderwijzend personeel*)	Education qualifying teachers for the teaching profession, at three levels: – senior secondary (k.l.o.s.); – higher (p.a./l.o.-, m.o.-, n.o.-akten/n.l.o.); – university. Teacher training comprises teacher training for pre-primary schools (k.l.o.s.), teacher training for primary schools (p.a.) and teacher training for secondary schools (l.o.-, m.o.-, n.o.-akten/n.l.o./university courses).
Apprenticeship training (*leerlingwezen* = l.w.)	Practical training by an employer in a specific occupation with supplementary general and vocational training in a school.
Educational institutes for early school-leavers (*vormingswerk werkende jongeren* = v.w.j.)	Education and training for young people (age-group 15 to 18), who may or who may not have already obtained a job, and are no longer engaged in full-time education.
Centres for young adults (*vormingswerk jong volwassenen*)	Non-formal education for young adults (age-group 17 to 27).
Correspondence courses (*schriftelijk onderwijs*)	Education or training given mainly by correspondence courses.
Higher education (*hoger onderwijs* = h.o.)	Higher education comprises higher vocational education, including teacher training and university education.
University education (*wetenschappelijk onderwijs* = w.o.)	Education, which prepares for independent practice of learning, for the occupation of positions in society for which an education at university level is either desirable or necessary, and which improves the grasp of the coherence of the sciences.

Alphabetical list of acronyms

	Dutch	English
a.v.o.	*algemeen voortgezet onderwijs*	general secondary education
b.o.	*beroepsonderwijs*	vocational education
bu.o.	*buitengewoon onderwijs*	special education
h.a.v.o.	*hoger algemeen voortgezet onderwijs*	general secondary education, upper level
h.b.o.	*hoger beroepsonderwijs*	higher vocational education
h.e.a.o.	*hoger economisch en administratief onderwijs*	higher commercial education
h.h.n.o.	*hoger huishoud- en nijverheidsonderwijs*	higher domestic science education
h.l.o.	*hoger landbouwonderwijs*	higher agricultural education
h.m.o.	*hoger middenstandsonderwijs*	higher trade education
h.n.w.o.	*hoger natuurwetenschappelijk onderwijs*	higher (technical) education in the physical sciences
h.o.	*hoger onderwijs*	higher education
h.s.p.o.	*hoger sociaal-pedagogisch onderwijs*	higher socio-pedagogic education

	Dutch	*English*
h.t.o.	hoger technisch onderwijs	higher technical education
i.h.n.o.	individueel huishoud- en nijverheidsonderwijs	junior secondary domestic science education, individualized
i.l.o.	individueel landbouwonderwijs	junior secondary agricultural education, individualized
i.t.o.	individueel technisch onderwijs	junior secondary technical education, individualized
k.l.o.s.	kleuterleidster opleidings-school	teacher training for pre-primary schools
k.o.	kleuteronderwijs	pre-primary education
l.b.o.	lager beroepsonderwijs	junior secondary vocational education
l.e.a.o.	lager economisch en administratief onderwijs	junior secondary commercial education
l.h.n.o.	lager huishoud- en nijverheidsonderwijs	junior secondary domestic science education
l.l.o.	lager landbouwonderwijs	junior secondary agricultural education
l.m.o.	lager middenstandsonderwijs	junior secondary trade education
l.o.	lager onderwijs	primary education
l.o.-akte	lager onderwijs-akte	teacher training course old style for secondary schools, lower level
l.t.o.	lager technisch onderwijs	junior secondary technical education
m.a.v.o.	middelbaar algemeen voortgezet onderwijs	general secondary education, lower level
m.b.o.	middelbaar beroepsonderwijs	senior secondary vocational education
m.e.a.o.	middelbaar economisch en administratief onderwijs	senior secondary commercial education
m.h.n.o.	middelbaar huishoud- en nijverheidsonderwijs	senior secondary domestic science education
m.l.o.	middelbaar landbouwonderwijs	senior secondary agricultural education
m.m.o.	middelbaar middenstandsonderwijs	senior secondary trade education
m.o.-akte	middelbaar onderwijs-akte	teacher training course old style for secondary schools, intermediate and higher level
m.s.p.o.	middelbaar sociaal-pedagogisch onderwijs	senior secondary socio-pedagogic education
m.t.o.	middelbaar technisch onderwijs	senior secondary technical education
n.l.o.	nieuwe lerarenopleiding	teacher training new style for secondary schools
n.o.-akte	nijverheidsonderwijs-akte	teacher training course old style for secondary schools, intermediate level
p.a.	pedagogische academie	teacher training for primary schools
v.h.b.o.	voorbereidend hoger beroepsonderwijs	preparatory higher vocational education
v.o.	voortgezet onderwijs	secondary education
v.j.v.	vormingswerk jong volwassenen	centres for young adults
v.w.j.	vormingswerk werkende jongeren	educational institutes for early school leavers
v.w.o.	voorbereidend wetenschappelijk onderwijs	pre-university education
w.o.	wetenschappelijk onderwijs	university education

UNITED KINGDOM

England and Wales

Introduction

Historical background

Current education in England and Wales presents a considerable diversity of provision. Schooling is compulsory between the ages of 5 and 16 and this is provided by a large state or public sector (free), a small but socially influential private or independent sector (fee-charging), and a small state-aided sector run by voluntary – mainly religious – bodies. Within the public system itself there is also considerable variation. This range of diversity is largely due to the way in which schooling in England and Wales has evolved.

Before 1870 teaching was provided by independent schools and by schools run by voluntary – mainly church-based – bodies. This never reached a large proportion of the child population and by the latter half of the nineteenth century it had become inadequate in the face of the industrialized society's need for a literate and numerate populace. In 1870 Parliament passed an Education Act which initiated a system of public education to supplement the previous provision. This dual basis of provision has continued in a modified form to the present day. The Act established Local School Boards with the task of providing elementary or primary education in their areas and raising finance from local rates (property taxes), school fees and national taxes. From the beginning therefore, state education in England and Wales was organized on a local basis, and this degree of localization has also contributed to the present diversity of the system.

Education still had to answer national needs, however, and in 1900, in response to growing pressure for a national coordinated system of education under the direction of a single authority, a Board of Education was set up. Then in 1902, the School Boards were abolished and the task of providing education was handed to local government in the form of the County Borough Councils who were to work in conjunction with the Board of Education. The Act of 1902 also introduced public secondary education for the first time. In 1918, at the close of the First World War, the power of central government in regard to the local education authorities (administered by local government) was strengthened, and the school leaving age was raised to 14. During the years between the wars there was no innovative development, but secondary education was being consolidated.

In the closing stages of the Second World War a large body of social legislation was drawn up to prepare Britain for the post-war era. Among this was the Education Act of 1944, a significant step forward, which required the local education authorities to provide a three-tier system of primary, secondary and further education, with a substantial element of secondary education for all. The Act, reflecting the growing importance attached to education by the Government, replaced the Board of Education with a Ministry of Education and appointed a Minister of Education. He was given certain statutory powers and was made ultimately responsible for the maintenance of minimum standards. The Act also provided for the raising of the school-leaving age first to 15 and then to 16, aims which were achieved in 1947 and 1972 respectively.

The 1944 Act envisaged a tripartite system at secondary level with secondary modern schools, grammar schools and technical schools. Only a few technical schools were built, however, and consequently a binary system came into effect. On the basis of an examination at the age of 11 it was decided whether individual children should proceed from primary school to a grammar school (with a more academic curriculum) or a secondary modern school (with a more practical, less theoretical curriculum). During subsequent years dissatisfaction grew with this binary system and some local education authorities abolished selection at 11. In the 1960s the policy of the government changed towards one of favouring an education system in which all the children of secondary age in a particular neighbourhood were educated at the same school, a 'comprehensive school'. In 1976 an Education Act empowered the Secretary of State for Education (the Minister had been made Secretary of State in 1964) to direct local authorities to reorganize their secondary education along comprehensive lines.

Many authorities complied, but in 1979 there was a change of government and the new Government repealed the Act of 1976 while there were some authorities still to comply. Thus provision in the secondary sector exhibits a considerable amount of diversity across the country with independent schools, voluntary-aided schools, grammar schools, secondary modern schools, and comprehensive schools all currently in operation.

Administration

Unlike some highly centralized European systems the English education service is distinctive in its distribution of responsibility between central government, local government and the teaching profession. The instrument of central government is the Department of Education and Science, at the head of which is the Secretary of State for Education and Science. He or she is a member of the government of the day and has overall responsibility for education in England and for universities throughout England, Wales and Scotland. The Secretary of State is usually assisted by several Ministers. Responsibility for schools and non-university education in Wales rests with the Secretary of State for Wales who is also a member of the government.

The Department is concerned almost entirely with the formation of national policies for education rather than with executive functions. It is responsible for controlling educational building and the supply, training and pensions of teachers, but it does not lay down schools' curricula nor does it run the schools and colleges. It is also responsible, however, for maintaining minimum national standards of education and in this it is assisted by members of Her Majesty's Inspectorate, who monitor the efficiency of schools and colleges and provide Ministers with specialist advice. The money disbursed by the Department is only a small proportion of the total public spending on education, but it does play an important part in determining the block grant of money given by central government to local government.

Local government administers education through the local education authorities, of which there are 105 in England and Wales. These are responsible for over 85 per cent of national spending on education. Some 60 per cent of their educational expenditure they receive directly from central government, but the remainder they raise from the rates (local property taxes). The local education authorities administer the routine working of the education service, it being their duty to provide and run the schools and colleges in their areas and to employ teaching and ancillary staff. A Chief Education Officer is in charge of each local education authority's administration and he or she is assisted by professional and administrative staff. Control of the secular curriculum rests with the local authority, or in the case of voluntary and independent schools with the school managers or governors, but the choice of text books and timetable is usually left to the headmaster of the school with the content and method of day-to-day teaching being decided by the individual teacher. A considerable degree of autonomy is enjoyed, therefore, by local authorities, headmasters and teachers.

Whilst the system places much responsibility in the hands of the local education authorities and the schools, the 1944 Education Act empowers the Secretary of State to intervene if, locally, a statutory duty has not been carried out or if there has been in his opinion an unreasonable exercise of power. If an authority wishes to establish a new school or to cease to maintain an existing one, or if it wishes to alter the character or significantly enlarge the premises of a school, it is required under the Act to present its proposals to the Secretary of State, who has the power to approve or reject them.

In addition to this administrative pattern there is a wide range of consultative bodies upon which the Department and the local education authorities draw for advice. These include the Schools Council, the National Foundation for Educational Research, the Technicians Education Council, the Business Education Council, the Standing Committee of University Vice-Chancellors, the Council for National Academic Awards, and many others. The Schools Council is an independent but official body set up by the Secretary of State in 1964 to develop and monitor new curricula and public examinations in all subjects in primary and secondary schools in England and Wales. It has sponsored a large number of curriculum development projects. The National Foundation for Educational Research maintains a Register of Educational Research and produces a wide range of publications and psychological tests. Several of these consultative bodies may co-operate on a single project.

When the government feels there is an area of particular concern a Committee of Inquiry is set up to collect evidence and make proposals upon that area. Each Committee compiles a Report which is generally known by the name of the chairman of the Committee. The most important of these have been the Newsom Report (on independent schools), the Plowden Report (on primary schools), the Robbins Report (on full-time higher education), and the Warnock Report (on education for the handicapped).

In recent years there has been a growth of pressure groups which campaign for and promote particular educational aims. Amongst these are the Confederation for the Advancement of State Education, the Campaign for Nursery Education, and teachers' and students' unions. At a local level many individual schools also have parent–teacher associations or PTAs which bring together in regular meetings the local community and the teaching staff.

Pre-school education

Children may enter nursery schools and classes from the age of 2 although they are not normally admitted until they are 3. In 1972 the White Paper *A Framework for Expansion* set out the long-term goals which, when realized, will provide nursery education mainly on a part-time basis for all those children of 3 and 4 years whose parents wish them to benefit from it. At present nursery provision is far from complete and varies from area to area.

In 1978 there were 593 publicly maintained nursery schools in England and 70 in Wales together with approximately 11,500 privately-run playgroups affiliated to the Pre-School Playgroups Association (PPA), a voluntary organization.

The school day at the nursery schools lasts from 9 a.m. to 3.30 or 4 p.m. and it includes the opportunity for rest after the mid-day meal for those in full-time attendance. In 1978 some 34,000 children were attending a nursery school in the morning or the afternoon only in England, compared with 14,000 who were attending full-time. In Wales some 2,190 children attended nursery schools part-time in 1978, and 1,770 attended full-time. There are no formal lessons but indoor and outdoor play is guided by a teacher using a variety of materials. Every nursery school has a qualified head teacher and qualified assistant teachers. In addition to the provision in nursery schools there were some 3,614 nursery classes attached to primary schools in 1978 in England, providing for 29,000 full-time pupils and 123,000 part-time pupils. In Wales there were 756 nursery classes attached to primary schools in 1978 providing for 7,000 full-time pupils and about 9,200 part-time pupils. Each nursery class is staffed by the equivalent of a full-time nursery assistant as well as a teacher. The staffing ratio in nursery classes is 10.4 to 1 taking account of both teachers and nursery assistants.

Primary education

Education is compulsory between the ages of 5 and 16. During this period children usually spend six years at the primary stage and five years in a secondary school. About half the primary schools in England and Wales take the complete age range 5–11 years and are divided into two departments: there is an infant department for pupils between the ages of 5 and 7 and a junior department for pupils between 7 and 11 years of age. There are also separate infant and junior schools each with their own head teacher.

As an alternative to the infant/junior pattern an increasing number of local education authorities in England are establishing 'first' schools for pupils aged 5–8 or 5–9 and middle schools for pupils aged 8–12 or 9–13 years. There are a few 'combined' schools for pupils aged 5–12 or 5–13 and one or two middle schools which cater for 10–13 or 10–14 year olds.

Schools catering for the children of primary age are concerned with the general development of children and they aim to meet the current needs of their pupils as well as to prepare them for the next stage of education. They seek to provide a programme which promotes individual growth, both intellectual and physical, and throughout the primary stage high priority is given to teaching children to read, to write and to calculate. Great importance is also attached to social development and to the establishment of sound personal relationships. For infants and juniors the curriculum includes art, craft, physical education, music, religious education and studies which incorporate aspects of science, history and geography.

The differences between the infant/first school stage and the junior/middle schools stage are mainly ones of teaching approach, and depth and range of the studies undertaken. With the younger pupils the early stages of reading, writing and mathematics are introduced using materials which are familiar and relevant to the children, and the work includes many opportunities for experimenting with sand, water, clay, bricks and paints; for listening to stories and music and for imaginative play. For older children, although the approach continues to be characterized by inquiry, attention is increasingly given to the development of skills and concepts within subject areas.

Most primary schools of England and Wales are supported from public funds and maintained by local education authorities. They are usually co-educational. Maintained primary and secondary schools are of two types: county schools and voluntary schools.

Most voluntary schools were originally provided and are run by the religious denominations. They are of three kinds: controlled, aided and special agreement schools. Two-thirds of the managers of controlled schools are nominated by the local education authorities, who also bear all costs. At aided schools, the local education authorities appoint one-third of the managers, pay the teachers and meet the general cost of running the school, but up to 85 per cent of the approved expenditure may be reimbursed by the Department of Education or the Welsh Office as appropriate. For special agreement schools, of which there are none in Wales, similar reimbursement of approved expenditure is available from the Department of Education and Science; one-third of the managers are appointed by the local education authority, who also pay between a half and three-quarters of the cost. These three kinds of schools together constitute over a third of the schools maintained by the local authorities. Most of the voluntary schools in England and Wales are Church of England schools, Church in Wales schools and Roman Catholic schools.

A particular problem for schools in Wales is that of language. Wales is a bilingual country and it is government policy that local education authorities (in Wales the County Councils) should arrange for Welsh to be taught and used as a medium of teaching according to the needs and linguistic characteristics of particular areas, as well as the wishes of parents. Where Welsh is commonly spoken, it is the aim to enable pupils to develop a command of the language which will allow them to enter fully into the life of their community. In such areas, schools have developed naturally along bilingual lines – both English and Welsh being used as teaching media. In Anglicized areas 'designated' bilingual schools have been established over the past 30 years in response to a still-growing demand from parents. In January 1979 there were 64 such schools, 11 secondary and 53 primary.

Special education

Special education is provided for children needing it for any handicap, physical or mental. Regulations made by the Secretaries of State define ten categories of handicapped pupils:

- deaf children;
- partially hearing children;
- blind children;
- partially sighted children;
- physically handicapped children;
- educationally subnormal children;
- epileptic children;
- delicate children;
- maladjusted children;
- children suffering from speech defects not due to deafness.

Every local education authority has a duty to ascertain which children in its area require special educational treatment and to provide it, either at ordinary schools, special schools or otherwise. It is the Department's policy that no handicapped child should be sent to a special school who can be satisfactorily educated in an ordinary school. For example, children suffering from dyslexia and partially hearing children may attend a special class attached to their ordinary school, sharing as far as they can in the work and activities of their contemporaries.

But for many children – 131,525 in England as at 1 January 1978 – attendance at ordinary schools is impossible. For them, there are 1,591 special schools, including 142 hospital schools. In Wales, 5,739 pupils attend 71 special schools and three hospital schools. Moreover, local education authorities are developing new types of schools, for example, schools for aphasic children, for autistic children, and also reorganized schools for the blind and the deaf.

About 7.5 per cent of the special schools are under voluntary management. They receive some grant aid from the Department of Education and the Welsh Office, but are maintained primarily from the local authorities; the parents are not charged.

The main societies providing children's homes are the following:

- the Roman Catholic Church;
- the Church of England;
- Dr Barnardo's;
- the National Children's Home;
- the Shaftesbury Society;
- Royal National Institute for the Blind;
- Royal National Institute for the Deaf;
- the Spastics Society;
- National Society for Autistic Children;
- Invalid Children's Aid Association.

Handicapped children do not normally begin school before the age of 5, but there is an increasing awareness that early special educational treatment is important.

Registered pupils at special schools may not normally leave before the age of 16; there are a number of special schools where pupils may stay until they are 18 or 19 and take examination courses. There are three establishments for the further education and training of the blind and nine for the physically handicapped. Any further vocational training is the responsibility of the Department of Employment and Productivity. The special schools all have small classes with a generous ratio of both teaching and child-care staff, many of whom have taken specialist courses for work with handicapped children. Therapeutic services such as physiotherapy, speech therapy, psychiatric help and paediatric attention are also associated with special schools.

Secondary education

School types

Secondary education in England and Wales is provided at different types of schools. According to their financing, we may first of all distinguish between three types of schools:

1. The most important group is that of secondary schools maintained by local education authorities: the majority are comprehensive schools but they include 'grammar schools', 'modern schools' and a few 'technical schools'.
2. A small number of schools receive grants direct from the Department of Education and Science or from the Welsh Office: they are known as 'direct grant grammar schools'.
3. Independent secondary schools, known misleadingly as 'public schools', receive no grants from public funds, but all are open to inspection.

The maintained system of secondary education which developed from the 1944 Education Act was strongly influenced by the preceding White Paper, recommending that there should be three types of secondary school to be known as 'grammar', 'modern' and 'technical' schools.

But at the time of the 1944 Act there were a few local education authorities who were against the idea of selective education and who, when building new schools, established them as comprehensive schools.

By January 1979, there were in England:

254 grammar schools for children selected as suitable for an academic education;
536 modern schools originally designed to give a general education with a practical bias;
19 technical schools;
3,203 comprehensive and middle schools deemed secondary providing all types of education for all or most of the children in a district, from the least to the most intellectually able, and usually covering full secondary age range from 11 to 18.

By January 1978 there were in Wales:

15 grammar schools;
21 modern schools;
no technical schools, and
213 comprehensive schools.

Several forms of comprehensive schooling are now in operation:

— the system of orthodox comprehensive schools with an age range of 11 to 18;
— 'two-tier' systems with pupils transferring at 11 to junior comprehensive schools and at 13 or 14 to upper schools;

- comprehensive schools with an age range of 11 to 16; combined with sixth form colleges for pupils over 16;
- middle schools for pupils from 8-9-10 to 12-13-14 years of age followed by comprehensive schools for pupils from 12-13-14 to 18 years of age.

There are also forms of schooling which are not fully comprehensive. A few other secondary schools comprise bilateral or multi-lateral schools, providing two or three types of secondary education, although in separately organized streams. Other schools cannot be classified precisely.

Independent schools in England number about 2,200 and in Wales 64, of which about 42 per cent offer boarding accommodation. The system whereby certain independent schools were granted 'recognized as efficient' status has been discontinued and independent schools are now classified as 'registered' schools.

In the main, independent schools are divided into those which cater for pupils of between 5 and 11-13 years and those which provide for pupils between 11-13 and 18 years of age. It is in the latter category that most of the famous 'public' schools, such as Eton, Winchester and Harrow are found.

Independent schools are essentially independent of grants from both central and local government and fees are charged at these schools for tuition and for any boarding facilities.

The Direct Grant Grammar Schools (Cessation of Grant) Regulations 1975 came into operation in 1975 and gave effect to the Labour Government's intention of ending the system of direct grants to grammar schools in England and Wales. Schools were given the choice of either entering the maintained sector as comprehensive schools or of becoming fully independent. Fifty-one of the 170 direct grant grammar schools declared their intention of entering the maintained sector as comprehensive schools; most of these have already done so and the remainder are expected to do so by 1981/82. Grant ceased to be payable from the educational year 1976/77 in respect of new pupils admitted to schools which are not entering the maintained sector and these schools will become fully independent by 1981.

The Conservative Government which took office in May 1979 intend, subject to legislation, to restore the direct grant principle by introducing a scheme of Assisted Places which will enable academically able children from less well-off homes to attend independent secondary schools of high academic standard. The scheme, which is expected to start in 1981/82, will be one of remission of tuition fees funded by central government subject to a means test, and is expected to benefit about 12,000 pupils a year.

The long-term changeover to a comprehensive system of secondary education has rapidly accelerated. By 1979 there were over 3,300,000 pupils in 3,823 comprehensive schools, covering over 85 per cent of the secondary school population in England. In Wales in 1978 there were over 223,000 pupils in 213 comprehensive schools covering 92 per cent of the secondary school population. The 1979 Education Act passed by the new Government has removed the compulsion on LEAs to reorganize their secondary schools on comprehensive lines. It will now be for each authority to determine the best pattern and provision for its area.

Curricula in maintained secondary schools

In some areas children moving from primary to secondary schools are still selected, according to their level of academic attainment, for education in different types of school. Grammar schools provide a mainly academic course to selected pupils from the ages of 11 to 18; secondary modern schools provide a general education with a practical bias up to the minimum leaving age of 16, although their pupils can stay on beyond that age. Comprehensive secondary schools have now been established in most areas and admit pupils without a test of ability. Comprehensive schools normally offer a wide range of courses with both an academic and non-academic bias. Legally, the curriculum is the responsibility of the local education authorities and school governors; in practice, decisions about curriculum content and teaching methods are usually left to head teachers and staff. A wide range of subjects is taught including English, Mathematics, Science, Humanities, Environmental Studies and Modern Languages. In addition, many schools offer courses in Engineering, Architecture, Economics and Commercial subjects.

There are many notable curricula developments, some of which are designed to deal with two questions:

— the effect of examination pressures on syllabuses;
— and the courses needed as a result of the raising of the school-leaving age.

Recently curriculum development projects have included integrated science, integration of the humanities, history, geography, moral education, mathematics and careers education and guidance.

An important problem is that of the instruction of the English language to immigrant children. Local education authorities have used a variety of methods to teach English as a second language. In some areas special immigrant language centres have been set up where children from several schools are brought together for intensive language training, either full or part-time. In other areas children are withdrawn from their normal classes to receive special help in small groups.

Secondary school examinations

Although there is no national leaving examination, secondary school pupils and others may take the *General Certificate of Education* (*GCE*) or the *Certificate of Secondary Education* (*CSE*).

GENERAL CERTIFICATE OF EDUCATION
The General Certificate of Education examinations are conducted by eight independent examining bodies, most of which are connected with universities. They were introduced in 1951 to replace the former School Certificate and Higher School Certificate examinations. The General Certificate of Education provides a convenient level of minimum qualifications for entrance to higher education. The examination results are used to assess candidates by most universities other than Oxford and Cambridge, where colleges set their own entrance papers.

These examinations are set at two levels, Ordinary ('O') and Advanced ('A'). The Ordinary-level papers are usually taken at the end of the five year course in the secondary school and are designed for the top 20 per cent of the ability range. Advanced-level papers are usually taken after a further two years' study in the sixth form, i.e. the highest class in secondary education.

There are no compulsory subjects at either level and candidates may take as many or as few subjects, and as many times, as they wish. They do not need to take the same subject at both Ordinary and Advanced levels. A candidate who fails to gain a pass at Advanced level may be awarded an Ordinary-level pass on his Advanced-level paper. Since 1975 Ordinary-level results have been recorded in five grades (A–E), the top three grades (A–C) being above the former pass/fail boundary. Performance below grade E is unclassified and the results are not recorded on the Certificate.

At Advanced level, passes are awarded in five grades: A, B, C, D and E. In addition Advanced-level candidates may take Special ('S') papers which are normally set on the same syllabus as the basic Advanced-level papers but contain questions of a more searching kind. Only candidates whose basic Advanced-level papers are graded A, B or C are eligible to have their work on S-papers taken into account. These candidates may be given a supplementary grading of 'distinction' or 'merit' based on their performance on the S-papers. Candidates are not normally expected to take S-papers in more than one subject and are not allowed to take them in more than two.

The examinations are open to any suitable candidates whether they are attending school or not.

The normal minimum age of entry is 16. There is no upper age limit. There are over 50 main subjects to choose from at Ordinary level and Advanced level and many more subsidiary ones. Besides the normal academic subjects they include art, music, handicrafts, domestic science, technical and commercial subjects.

Two Advanced levels are normally the minimum qualification for entry to universities in England and Wales, but three Advanced levels are usually necessary since entry is competitive. Entry qualifications for full-time and sandwich courses in national and regional colleges are the same as for universities except that students with a good Ordinary National Certificate are admitted alongside students with Advanced-level passes. For colleges of education the minimum is usually five Ordinary levels; in practice about one-third of the entrants have two Advanced levels and another third have one.

CERTIFICATE OF SECONDARY EDUCATION

The Certificate of Secondary Education was introduced in 1965, and is intended for those children who are around the average in terms of ability for their age group. The examination is on a single-subject basis and is normally taken by pupils completing five years of secondary education. There is no pass-or-fail verdict: pupils are awarded one of five grades, or are ungraded, in each subject they take. Grade 1 represents a standard equivalent to a pass at Ordinary level in the General Certificate of Education (grades A–C). The information given on the certificate is of help to employers in placing young people in jobs and as an entry qualification for young people who seek further education in technical and other colleges. The examination is administered by 14 regional boards. Papers are based on the normal work of secondary schools. They vary from area to area and may vary from school to school, but the standard of certificates is comparable on a national basis. Work done by candidates during their final school year may be taken into account.

Since the inception of the Certificate of Secondary Education, the number of passes at the highest grade has increased steadily, as the popularity of the examination has grown. The annual number of GCE Ordinary-level subject passes in England has increased from 1.2 million in 1968 to 1.6 million in 1978. In Wales the annual number of GCE Ordinary-level subject passes awarded by the Welsh Joint Education Committee's examining board has risen from 71,888 in 1968 to 87,360 in 1978. Four out of five pupils now leave school with a graded examination result in at least one subject. Similarly, the number of school-leavers obtaining two or more Advanced levels in England has risen from 73,600 in 1968 to 96,200 in the year 1977/78. In Wales it has risen from 4,510 in 1968 to 4,980 in 1977/78.

INTERNATIONAL BACCALAUREATE

The International Baccalaureate, which can be taken in English or French (with the possibility of other languages being used for individual subjects) is now recognized for admission to higher education in most countries. The curriculum's basic principles are a broad general education and a wide choice of subjects. Courses leading to the International Baccalaureate can currently be followed in 13 educational institutions in the UK, comprising maintained and independent secondary schools, further education establishments and a college of education.

Technical and further education

Technical and further education is provided by establishments of further education after the completion of compulsory education, which means from the age of 16 on. The curriculum of the last years of compulsory education usually is not of a specifically vocational character, although it may have some vocational relevance. Courses in further education establishments cover a wide variety of predominantly, but not solely, vocational subjects and are provided at all academic levels. They may be attended by full-time, by part-time (many of them apprentices) and by sandwich students (whose periods of study at college alternate with periods of practical training in industry). The proportion of young people aged 16–18 in England and Wales in 1977/78 who were still in school was 17.7 per cent. The proportion of the 16–18 age group in England and Wales in some form of full-time education in 1977/78 was 30 per cent. The courses are provided in some 620 major establishments of various types and levels which, with some exceptions, are maintained by local education authorities. The major establishments of further education include the poly-technics and institutions with a variety of titles such as 'technical college', 'college of further education' and 'college of art'. In addition, there are over 6,300 Adult Education Centres providing courses of a mainly non-vocational character.

Further education establishments

Some of these provide mainly part-time courses in non-advanced work (up to GCE A level or Ordinary National Diploma) while others offer in addition part-time and full-time courses of advanced or higher education for students starting at 18 or 19.

For operatives, apprentices and intending craftsmen, these colleges offer part-time technical courses of three to five years leading to the examinations of the City and Guilds of London Institute and the Joint Committees. Among the most popular subjects are engineering in various forms, building and commercial subjects.

Entry to technician courses may be direct from school with qualifications at the Ordinary level of the General Certificate of Education, or after a one- or two-year part-time general course designed to assess the particular abilities and aptitudes of students without such qualifications.

Technician courses provided by the City and Guilds of London Institute are largely practical in content and are designed to match closely the industrial requirements of the student. They operate mainly on a part-time or 'block-release' basis: students on 'block-release' courses are released by their employer for periods of several weeks' study at colleges.

The National Certificate courses (part-time) and National Diploma courses (full-time and sandwich) of Joint Committees (on which Education Departments, Professional bodies and teachers are represented) are more academic in content than the majority of technician courses and cover a wider range of technical subjects. The courses are offered at two levels: Ordinary and Higher.

The Ordinary National Diploma and the Ordinary National Certificates are roughly comparable in standard to the Advanced level of the General Certificate of Education and are acceptable to some higher education establishments as alternative entry qualifications. Of the two, however, the Ordinary National Diploma provides a greater coverage, as it also involves more study time. The Higher National Certificate and the Higher National Diploma are higher education qualifications.

Existing examinations and qualifications for technicians, at present provided by the City and Guilds of London Institute and the Joint Committees, are being progressively replaced by those of the Technician Education Council. This body was established in 1973 to provide a unified national system of courses for technicians leading to a common standard which is widely recognized. The Business Education Council (established in 1974) has a similar role in respect of business courses.

Further education and industrial training

The further education establishments have always provided a wide variety of courses designed to meet the training needs of all sectors of industry. The Industrial Training Act 1964 resulted in arrangements for the joint planning of further education courses and training programmes. The Employment and Training Act 1973 led to the establishment of the Manpower Services Commission, which is responsible for training to meet the needs of industry and to meet the needs of individuals. The establishments play a major role in these activities and proposals, and there is close co-operation between the further education service and bodies responsible for industrial training.

Polytechnics

In 1966 Her Majesty's Government decided to concentrate public sector higher education within the further education system by forming from some 60 leading colleges of technology, commerce and art, 30 major institutions of a national character, to be known as 'polytechnics'. The planned total was completed in 1973. The polytechnics are primarily teaching institutions and they have close links with business and industry; one of their distinctive characteristics is the wide range, both in the composition of the teaching body and in the type and level of course offered.

Their students include many people in employment attending on a part-time or block-release basis, as well as full-time and sandwich students. In 1977/78 there were some 118,000 full-time and sandwich course students attending polytechnics. There is a wide variety of courses and qualifications in higher education. There are the two-year Higher National Certificates and the two- and three-year Higher National Diplomas, administered in the same way as Ordinary National Certificates and Ordinary National Diplomas, in a wide range of technical subjects and business studies. Within their more limited field, Higher National Diplomas are recognized as approaching the level of a pass degree. Higher National Certificates, because of the time limitations, are more narrowly based.

Higher National Certificates and Higher National Diplomas are being gradually replaced by awards of the Technicians Education Council and the Business Education Council, a process which should be complete by the early 1980s. Other courses include the Diploma in Higher Education, gained after two years' full-time study, introduced in 1972. It is a qualification in its own right but it may provide an alternative route to a degree (students can often transfer to a degree course), teacher training or other professional training. While equivalent in standard to the first two years of a degree course, Dip HEs are less specialized and many are organized on a modular basis. They are validated by the Council of National Academic Awards or by universities.

Apart from courses leading to first and higher degrees and to other important sub-degree qualifications, the polytechnics also provide courses leading to the examinations of major professional bodies.

Most degree courses in polytechnics are validated by the Council of National Academic Awards (CNAA), which was established in 1964. It awards degrees and other qualifications comparable in standard with those granted by universities to students who complete approved courses of study or research in establishments which do not have the power to award their own degrees. Courses are examined in detail before being approved as suitable for leading to a CNAA award.

At the beginning of the academic year 1977-78, in the United Kingdom as a whole, there were 1,031 CNAA first-degree courses and 156 post-graduate courses. Of the undergraduate courses, 29 per cent were sandwich courses, 54 per cent were full-time and 17 per cent part-time courses. A total of nearly 99,400 students were enrolled for these first-degree courses. The Council's awards and those of the Open University (see p. 242) have taken over many of the functions of the London University External Degree.

An increasing number of polytechnics are offering 'modular' degrees. These enable students to choose a number of courses (or 'modules') that relate either to a single subject and thus to specialization in a well-defined area of study, or to a combination of courses which, when taken together, constitute a broader, more generalized education.

In addition to technician courses, polytechnics also provide courses in business and management studies. These courses lead to CNAA degrees, Higher National Diplomas and Certificates in Business Studies, and to Diplomas in Management Studies.

Colleges of art

The non-advanced art and design courses which often lead to regional or college diplomas are largely vocational. Courses known as foundation studies are designed to develop the students' interest and skill in art and design and serve as a preparation for entry to higher and more extended courses. Following a Report, published in 1974, on 'Vocational Courses in Art and Design', a committee for art and design has been established under the auspices of the Technicians Education Council (TEC) to provide a national validating system for vocational courses in art and design.

At advanced level about 46 colleges/polytechnics are approved by the Council for National Academic Awards to offer three- and four-year full-time courses leading to the award of the CNAA degree of BA (Honours) Art and Design. Many students will have completed a foundation course but also require an appropriate combination of General Certificate of Education Advanced- and Ordinary-level passes. Several post-graduate courses are avilable leading to CNAA MA degrees.

The largest provider of post-graduate level work in art and design is the Royal College of Art which has, since it received its Royal Charter in 1967, the power to grant its own degrees.

Independent further education

Local education authorities are responsible, under the Education Act 1944, for providing courses of further education with the aim of enabling people to attain the highest qualifications to which their abilities may entitle them. Further education is also provided at a few direct-grant institutions, including the one national college and certain agricultural colleges, and at a number of independent colleges.

Finally a great number of further education courses are run by private colleges. These independent colleges are not, like independent schools, required to register with the Department of Education and Science or the Welsh Office, but they may apply for 'recognition as efficient'. The largest group of recognized colleges are those teaching English to foreign students; they belong to the Association of Recognized English Language Schools. The other recognized colleges comprise a miscellaneous group including schools of art and architecture, drama, speech and music, commerce, domestic science, wireless telegraphy and nautical studies. In 1977/78 the recognized colleges had about 16,200 full-time and 840 part-time students.

Correspondence colleges with an estimated annual enrolment of around 650,000 students belong in the majority to the Association of British Correspondence Colleges. In 1969 a Council for the Accreditation of Correspondence Colleges was established. This body is financed by the colleges themselves but from September 1977 has received an annual grant from the Department of Education and Science to be used to strengthen the Council's administration and also to encourage the new or continued accreditation of colleges, particularly those which might otherwise find it difficult on financial grounds to become or continue as members. The Council sets and makes known a voluntary code of standards for all aspects of postal tuition and grants accreditation to those colleges which conform to such standards.

The National Extension College, founded in 1963, prepares students for a variety of courses using a combination of correspondence, broadcasting and direct week-end teaching. In 1976-77, this College had approximately 10,000 students, about 40 per cent of whom worked on General Certificates of Education Ordinary- and Advanced-level subjects. Others study a variety of subjects, including courses leading to external degrees of London University.

Fees and grants

As most further education establishments are either maintained or aided from public funds, tuition fees are moderate and often remitted for young people under 18 years of age.

Many full-time students are helped by awards from local education authorities which are assessed to cover tuition fees and a maintenance grant, but parents who can afford to contribute towards the cost are required to do so. There are also some awards available from endowments, and bursaries awarded under schemes organized by particular industries or companies for the most promising of their young workers.

Teacher training

Qualifications of teachers

Teachers are appointed by local education authorities or school governing bodies or managers. They are not civil servants. Teachers in maintained schools, except for a small number of student teachers and instructors, must be approved as 'qualified' by the Department of Education and Science. Before January 1970 all graduates and holders of certain specialist qualifications were qualified to teach by virtue of their degree or specialist qualification. Graduates who gained their first degree after 31 December 1969 are not accepted as qualified teachers in maintained primary or special schools unless they have satisfactorily completed a one-year course of professional training at a teacher training institution. Graduates who gained their first degree after 31 December 1973 are not accepted as qualified teachers in any maintained schools unless professionally trained. However, graduates wishing to teach mathematics or science in secondary schools are exempted for the time being from this training requirement because of the shortage of teachers in these subjects.

There are four colleges of technical education which train teachers for further education and technical colleges. Many teachers in further education institutions have not taken courses of teacher training.

There is no formal training for university teachers, who are generally appointed for academic achievement. But many universities have now instituted short courses in university teaching methods, especially for newly appointed lecturers.

Organization of training

There is no prescribed distinction between the training and qualifications required of teachers for primary schools and for secondary schools. Once a teacher has been awarded qualified teacher status, he can in theory take a post in any school, primary or secondary. However, students are trained for teaching particular age ranges of children, and usually teach children within those age ranges.

TEACHER TRAINING INSTITUTIONS

In the academic year 1977/78 there were 118 teacher training institutions in the public sector of which 95 consisted of former colleges of education and 23 were polytechnics. Some two-thirds of these institutions were maintained by local authorities and the remainder by the Churches or other voluntary bodies. Teacher training was provided also at 30 university departments of education. In addition, there were three local authority maintained colleges of education (technical) which, with one of the polytechnics, catered for the training of teachers of technical subjects in establishments of further education. The teacher training system is, however, being contracted and restructured to provide for a reduced school population resulting from the decline in births between 1965 and 1977. Some colleges of education have merged with one another or with another establishment, while others have been closed. Numbers of initial training students have remained fairly steady in universities but have fallen in the public sector from 114,000 in 1972/73 to 61,000 in 1977/78. It is planned that on the completion of reorganization in 1981 the number of training institutions in the public sector will have been reduced to 76, with a total of some 43,350 places, and that eight colleges with about 3,350 places will have been merged with universities. Nearly 10,400 of the total of 46,700 teacher training places for 1981 have been allocated for in-service training and induction work.

There are two main ways in which students can obtain qualified teacher status:

i   By direct entry on to a three or four year course leading to a Bachelor of Education (BEd) ordinary or honours degree, for which entrants are normally required to hold the same qualifications as for entry to any degree – that is five passes in the GCE of which two are at Advanced level. These courses are available in most colleges and polytechnic departments, and in a few universities.

ii By taking a degree other than the BEd, and then completing a post-graduate certificate of education lasting one year. These courses are available at most colleges and in polytechnic and university departments of education.

In a few cases four year BA or BSc courses are available which include education as a major study, as well as teaching practice, and which lead to a teaching qualification.

Because graduates have already completed at least three years of subject studies in their degree, the post-graduate courses concentrate mainly on professional training – professional studies, educational theory and periods of teaching practice. Three and four year courses usually include in addition subject studies which may vary in number and depth according to the age range which the student intends to teach. Some courses are concurrent – that is, subject studies and professional and educational studies continue throughout the course. A number of courses are, however, consecutive in structure – that is, academic studies are taken in the earlier part of the course, professional studies being concentrated on at a later stage. Students may enter a Dip HE course, lasting two years, for which two Advanced-level passes are required on entry, and then transfer to either a BEd or some other degree, or they may take a common first year course and then decide whether to complete a BEd or other degree. These arrangements permit not only a later date for commitment to teaching, but a greater integration between teacher training and other courses of higher education which can increase the range and improve the standard of the academic studies available.

For students training to teach as specialists in secondary schools, or as semi-specialists in middle schools, major adacemic studies in the BEd course are pursued to a substantial level, though in general this is somewhat lower than would be expected for a BA or BSc honours degree. The total demands of this part of the course, together with studies in the theoretical and professional aspects of education are, however, very considerable, and in the area last mentioned there is normally a searching exercise in the form of a prolonged dissertation or inquiry. For those preparing to be primary school teachers the course is also demanding; while it sometimes requires pursuit of a major academic study as with secondary training, it often replaces this study by intensified professional studies. These are in some courses rigorously assessed and, while this is less true of others, there is a general trend towards preparing primary teachers with greater emphasis on the development and assessment of skills.

The post-graduate courses include education and professional studies, curriculum methodology and supervised teaching practice, the last taking up about one-third of the course.

The content generally is orientated towards the age ranges the graduates intend to teach. As far as the curriculum aspects are concerned, for those wishing to teach in the primary and middle years attention is given to a fairly broad coverage and those preparing for work in secondary schools usually take methodology studies in two subjects. The structure of the courses varies. There is some tendency towards thematic and integrated approaches which attempt to achieve a cohesive programme with close inter-relationship between theory and practice.

TRAINING OF TEACHERS OF HANDICAPPED PUPILS

Teachers in special schools, with certain exceptions, are required to have qualified teacher status. Teachers of blind, deaf or partially hearing children must also possess one or more other qualification required by the Secretary of State and must obtain one of these qualifications within three years of taking up a post in a special school, and before taking up a post in a partially hearing unit. Most of the courses leading to these additional qualifications require one year's full-time in-service study, although the Diplomas of the College of Teachers of the Blind and the National College of Teachers of the Deaf are gained through part-time study while teaching in a special school. Manchester University's Department of Audiology also offers a four-year BA course combining a study of deafness, teacher training and the special qualifications. The pattern of training for teachers of mentally handicapped children differs from that prevailing in other special educational fields, in that one-year post-graduate and three- or four-year undergraduate initial training courses are available at colleges or departments of education, which in addition to general preparation for teaching include a substantial element of special educational work and relevant practical experience in special schools.

A wide variety of in-service courses exists for teachers who are already qualified and who are working, or intend to take up work, with handicapped children. These vary from the very short course to the one year full-time course, and from the general course aimed at preparing teachers to work with a wide range of disabilities to the specialist course related to a particular handicap.

INDUCTION TRAINING

It has long been recognized that new teachers need to continue their training after taking up their first appointment, not because their initial training is in any way inadequate, but because certain aspects of teaching can be imparted only after a teacher has assumed full responsibility in a post. The Government envisages a build-up to 25 per cent release (i.e. one quarter of each teacher's time), comprising a lightened teaching load and school- and centre-based training for all new teachers. It has made provision in the 1979/80 Rate Support Grant for induction programmes for 2,000 new teachers. Further provision, however, may be affected by national expenditure restrictions.

IN-SERVICE TRAINING

The great majority of in-service courses in England and Wales are short courses organized locally by education authorities. There is also a national programme of short courses, organized by HM Inspectorate, which bring together for periods of from two to ten days groups of teachers with relevant experience for discussion of teaching techniques and fresh approaches to the curriculum. Longer courses leading to advanced qualifications (usually a degree or diploma awarded by a university or by the Council of National Academic Awards) are provided mainly in university departments or in other higher education institutions. Such courses can be either full-time or part-time. Teachers attending full-time courses are normally seconded to them on full pay by their employing local education authority.

There are also about 550 teachers' centres which are financed and organized by local education authorities. Their main function is to bring groups of teachers together to study curriculum developments.

University education

In the past ten years the historical divisions between the various branches of the post-school educational system have become less rigid and recent developments make it likely that this process will continue. The higher education system includes not only the universities, but also colleges responsible for the training of teachers (see p. 237), the polytechnics, responsible for technical and commercial education (see p. 235), and the colleges of art (see p. 236). The introduction in 1974 of a new type of course lasting two years and leading to a Diploma of Higher Education will assist this process of considering the higher education system as a whole.

Universities

The universities are in principle autonomous institutions. The Government exercises its responsibilities in relation to the universities through the University Grants Committee. This is an all United Kingdom body and consequently there are references in this section to universities in Scotland and Northern Ireland as well as England and Wales. Government funding covers over 90 per cent of the universities' recurrent expenditure and over 90 per cent of their capital expenditure. There are now 45 universities in the United Kingdom (including the Scottish and Northern Ireland universities) and the Open University, to which separate reference is made on p. 242, compared with 17 in 1945. There are now about 288,000 full-time and sandwich course students in universities in the United Kingdom.

Historically, the development of universities in the United Kingdom may be considered in four stages:

1. Universities founded before 1600, two of which are English (Oxford and Cambridge), four of which are Scottish (St Andrews, Glasgow, Aberdeen, Edinburgh).
2. Universities with their origins between 1800 and 1950, i.e. the universities of London, Durham, Manchester, Leeds, Liverpool, Bristol, Sheffield, Birmingham, Reading, Nottingham, Exeter, Southampton, Leicester, Hull, Newcastle and the University of Wales, and also Dundee (in Scotland) and Queens Belfast (in Northern Ireland).
3. Universities founded since the end of the Second World War in 1945, i.e. the universities of Keele, Sussex, East Anglia, York, Essex, Lancaster, Kent, Warwick, and also Stirling (in Scotland) and Ulster (in Northern Ireland).
4. Eight former Colleges of Advanced Technology (Surrey, Aston, Bradford, Bath, Brunel, Loughborough, City University of London, Salford) and two former Scottish Central Institutions (Heriot-Watt, Strathclyde), which have acquired university status since 1963. The former Colleges of Advanced Technology at Chelsea and Welsh College (Cardiff) also amalgamated with London University and the University of Wales respectively.

The University College at Buckingham is an independent institution which does not draw on public money. It opened in 1976 and its courses, which last two years, lead to a licence.

There are no denominational universities in England and Wales, access being open to all, irrespective of religious views, and none being subject to control by a religious denomination.

Studies and degrees

The general entrance requirements of British universities are at least five passes in the General Certificate of Education, including two at Advanced level (see p. 232). Prospective candidates for nearly all the universities must apply through the Universities Central Council on Admissions (UCCA). Despite the recent expansion programmes the number of qualified applicants continues to exceed the number of university places available. It is estimated by UCCA that in 1977 about 80 per cent of those able and willing to accept a place if offered (described by UCCA as 'the real field' of applicants) obtained places.

Over 95 per cent of home full-time undergraduate students in universities in 1977/78 received grants. Most awards are made by local education authorities or, in Scotland, by the Scottish Education Department, though some are made by the Ministry of Defence, Industry etc. Post-graduate students can receive awards from the Department of Education and Science, Scottish Education Department, one of the five Research Councils or, for some courses, local education authorities.

In 1977/78 about 46 per cent of students lived in colleges or halls of residence, 35 per cent were in lodgings or flats, and about 16 per cent lived at home.

University degree courses generally extend over three or four years, though in medicine, dentistry and veterinary science five or six years are required. Staff/student ratios in UK universities are estimated at about 1:9. The proportion of women as students at university has increased from 27.4 per cent in 1967 to 34.8 per cent in 1977. The titles of degrees may vary from one university to another. In most universities, the first degree in arts is the BA (Bachelor of Arts) and in the sciences BSc (Bachelor of Science). At Oxford and Cambridge the first degree is called a BA whether the course leading to it is in arts or science subjects. In the five older Scottish universities, the MA (Master of Arts) is the first degree in the arts faculty; and BSc in science. Other degree titles include BArch. (Bachelor of Architecture), BEng. (Bachelor of Engineering), and BVSc (Bachelor of Veterinary Science).

A post-graduate student may undertake one or more years' guided study or research leading to post-graduate qualifications.

Masterships (such as MA, MPhil, LLM) are usually awarded after at least one or two years' study, except, as noted above, at the five Scottish Universities where the MA is the first arts degree, and at Oxford and Cambridge, where the MA is available to all holders of the BA without further examination, provided a certain period – seven years at Oxford, five or six at Cambridge – has elapsed since the students' first entry into the university.

Several universities also award a BPhil (Bachelor of Philosophy) as a post-graduate research degree.

Doctorates are of two main kinds: the PhD (Doctor of Philosophy), which is awarded after at least two or three years' study, on the basis of a thesis embodying original research, and higher doctorates, such as DSc (Doctor of Science), LLD (Doctor of Laws), and DLitt (Doctor of Literature) which are usually awarded in recognition of an outstanding contribution to a particular field.

At most universities there are two kinds of degree: an 'honours' degree which is taken by most students and which is traditionally more specialized, and an 'ordinary' or 'general' degree, which usually covers a wider range of subjects. In recent years, the content and arrangement of many honours courses has broadened considerably. Some universities offer a wider range of optional subjects; others have joint honours courses in arts in which two main subjects are studied at the same level. This trend is especially noticeable in the new universities. At Keele all students have to study both arts and sciences for an honours degree; the first year consists of common 'foundation studies'. Another type of degree which is being introduced into some universities is the 'modular' degree, which allows a student to choose whichever courses he would like to study, provided that they are generally relevant to each other. Frequently, the courses provided by the technological universities are 'sandwich' courses, combining academic study at the university with training in industry.

University teaching combines lectures, practical classes in scientific subjects and small-group teaching in either seminars or tutorials. The form of examination taken at the end of the degree course, of the year or of the module, is traditionally a written test, supplemented, where appropriate, by oral examinations.

Extra-mural education

The universities take an active part in providing courses in adult education for the general public. Some 30 universities have departments of adult education or 'extra-mural' studies. Some courses are organized by the universities in close association with district councils of the Workers' Educational Association (WEA), a voluntary organization which also employs some full-time organizing tutors and a large number of part-time tutors. As a general principle no formal academic qualifications are prescribed for admission to these classes, nor do they lead to degrees, diplomas or certificates. Most courses are in art subjects or concerned with contemporary social problems, but increasing attention is given to science subjects.

There are four types of courses: three year 'tutorial' classes (with individual supervision by specially appointed teachers), one year 'sessional' classes, long 'terminal' classes (10 to 12 meetings) and short 'terminal' classes (6 meetings) of a less intensive character.

In 1977/78 158,000 students registered for courses organized by extra-mural departments in England and Wales. Grant-aid by the Department of Education and Science and Welsh Office is normally at a rate not exceeding 75 per cent of teaching costs. The Universities Council for Adult Education (UCAE) provides the channel through which the universities are represented on the Council of the National Institute of Adult Education (England and Wales). This Council provides a focus for formulation of common policy on extra-mural education.

The Open University

In common with other British universities the Open University has been established by Royal Charter as an independent institution authorized to confer its own degrees. It received its Charter in 1969 and launched its first courses in 1971; the academic year is from January to December. Unlike other universities, however, the Open University does not receive its grant through the University Grants Committee but is directly funded by the Department of Education and Science.

The Open University has an entirely new entrance policy, operating on a 'first come, first served' basis, and no formal entrance qualifications are required. With a small number of exceptions, students are aged 21 or over and there is no maximum age limit. Students study part-time in their own homes, largely from correspondence texts and broadcast programmes on television and radio.

The University provides for three levels of study: undergraduate, post-graduate and post-experience. Undergraduate courses lead to BA (Ordinary) or BA (Honours) degrees. Courses are of four levels – foundation, second, third and fourth – and lead to the award of full or part credits. Two credits must be at foundation level, the remainder at any of the higher levels. For an honours degree two credits must be at third or fourth levels. In all, six full credits are needed for an ordinary degree and eight for an honours degree, but students may have up to three exemptions in respect of previous studies. Each full credit course is spread over an academic year and credit awards are based on continuous assessment and examination results. Students may enrol for a maximum of two credit courses per year, but most are expected to take five years to secure an ordinary degree or six years for an honours degree. Foundation courses normally require attendance at a one week summer school. In 1978 about 59,000 students registered for undergraduate courses.

Post-experience courses are taken outside the degree programme but are at a comparable level to undergraduate ones, and give an opportunity to students to extend their knowledge for career purposes or to acquire knowledge of a new field. In 1978, about 7,000 students registered for such courses. Higher degrees available at the Open University are Bachelor of Philosophy, Master of Philosophy and Doctor of Philosophy.

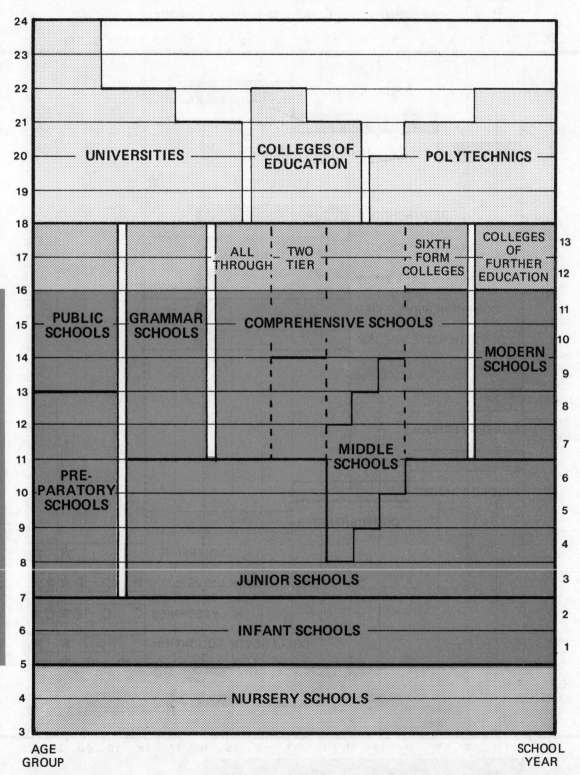

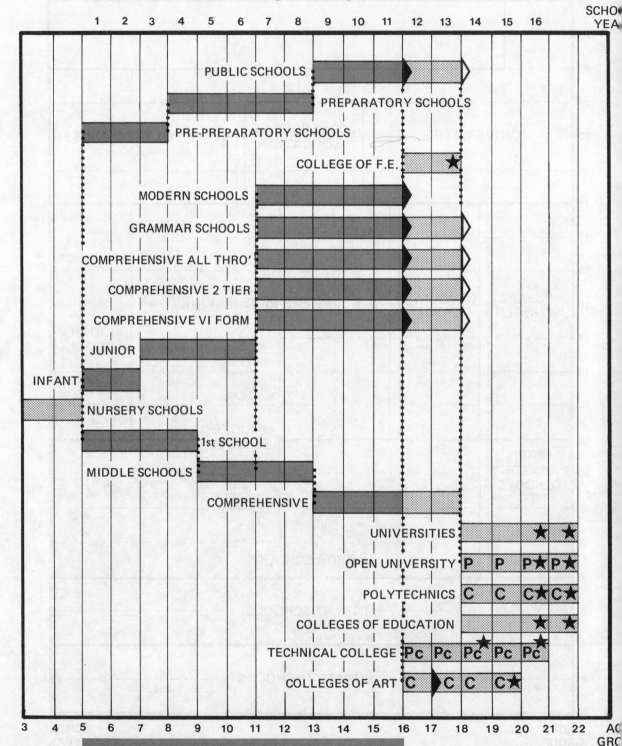

★ = Terminating examination not providing access to a higher stage.

◣ = Qualifying examination providing access to specialized education.

△ = Qualifying examination providing access to higher education.

P = Part-time classes.   C = Providing workshop practice.

SCHOOL YEAR

1 2 3 4 5 6 7 8 9 10 11 12 13 14 15 16

PUBLIC SCHOOLS

PREPARATORY SCHOOLS

PRE-PREPARATORY SCHOOLS

COLLEGE OF F.E.

MODERN SCHOOLS

GRAMMAR SCHOOLS

COMPREHENSIVE ALL THRO'

COMPREHENSIVE 2 TIER

COMPREHENSIVE VI FORM

JUNIOR

INFANT

NURSERY SCHOOLS

1st SCHOOL

MIDDLE SCHOOLS

COMPREHENSIVE

UNIVERSITIES   ★ ★

OPEN UNIVERSITY   P P P★P★

POLYTECHNICS   C C C★C★

COLLEGES OF EDUCATION   ★ ★

TECHNICAL COLLEGE Pc Pc Pc ★ Pc Pc★

COLLEGES OF ART   C ◣ C C C★

3 4 5 6 7 8 9 10 11 12 13 14 15 16 17 18 19 20 21 22

AGE GROUP

COMPULSORY EDUCATION

Glossary

Bilingual schools	Found in Wales only at both primary and secondary level, and characterized by the use of both English and Welsh as the media of instruction.
Committee of Inquiry	An *ad hoc* committee appointed by the government to investigate and make recommendations upon an area of particular concern. Members of such committees are usually drawn from professional bodies, universities, and local government, and from among people of relevant experience.
Comprehensive schools	Open to all children of secondary school age within a given neighbourhood or area and offering a wide range of subjects of both an academic and practical nature.
County schools	Provided and maintained by LEAs which are County Councils or County Borough Councils, but in practice schools administered by LEAs which are not County or County Borough authorities are also often referred to as 'County schools'.
CSE (Certificate of Secondary Education)	A subject examination normally taken at the age of 16 and intended for those pupils in the middle range of ability, marking being on a system of five grades, Grade 1 being equivalent to a pass at GCE O level.
Degree	The main higher education qualification granted by universities, polytechnics, and some colleges and institutes of higher education. Awarded at two levels, Ordinary and Honours, as a Bachelor degree after three or four years post-eighteen study. Awarded in Arts subjects as a Bachelor of Arts (BA), in Science subjects as a Bachelor of Science (BSc), in Education as a Bachelor of Education (BEd), in Law and Music as Bachelor of Law (LIB) and Bachelor of Music (BMus) respectively.
Dip HE (Diploma in Higher Education)	A recently developed scheme for post-eighteen higher education offering a broadly based course over two years which may be considered complete in itself or used as a basis for degree work.
Direct grant schools	Independent (i.e. private) schools partly financed directly by the Department of Education and Science and not through the LEAs. To qualify for this state aid the schools undertake to offer at least 25 per cent free places annually to pupils who have attended a public primary school for at least two years.
GCE (General Certificate of Education)	The main public examination set in a wide range of subjects at two main levels – Ordinary level (O level) and Advanced level (A level). Ordinary level is usually taken at the age of 16 and A level at 18 but there is no specific age requirement. A satisfactory performance at O and A level is usually a prerequisite to entering higher education or professional training.
Governors	Appointed from local councils to oversee the general running of each school in the maintained sector.
Grammar schools	Selective secondary schools catering for the academically able portion of the secondary school population and providing courses normally leading to GCE.
HMI (Her Majesty's Inspectorate)	Composed of senior civil servants in the Department of Education and Science who enjoy a considerable degree of professional independence and influence, and who regularly inspect schools and colleges and report to the Secretary of State on the education provided.
In-service courses	Short courses held for qualified serving teachers to instruct them in new educational developments or teaching methods.
LEAs (Local Education Authorities)	The bodies responsible for maintaining and running schools and colleges in each area of local government. An LEA is a subcommittee of the elected local authority (a few other persons with

knowledge of education may be co-opted). It decides on policy which is applied by professional administrators.

Maintained schools	Schools maintained by the State and therefore normally administered through the LEAs. Also used to refer to schools not owned by a public body but by a voluntary or religious body and yet financed mainly by the State.
Middle schools	Schools for children between the ages of 8 or 9 to 12 or 13 and combining some of the approaches of primary and secondary schools.
NFER (National Foundation for Educational Research)	National educational research organization which maintains a Register of Educational Research and produces a wide range of publications and psychological tests.
Nursery schools	Schools for children of 3 or 4 years old, i.e. prior to compulsory schooling and therefore operating on the basis of voluntary attendance.
PGCE (Post-graduate Certificate in Education)	The teaching qualification required for graduates other than those possessing a BEd and gained by means of a one-year course.
Playgroup	A voluntary group usually run by parents for children of pre-school age, i.e. under 5 and attended by the children for several hours a day.
Primary schools	Often known as an 'elementary' school, the first school which a child compulsorarily attends, and generally divided into an infants section – 5 to 7 years – and a junior section – 7 to 11 years.
PTA (Parent–Teacher Association)	An informal association found in many schools by which the teaching staff and the community are brought together. Often active in organizing extra-curricular events and in fund-raising.
'Public' schools	Not state-funded schools but private or independent schools for pupils aged 13 to 18, usually single sex, fee-charging, and in most cases residential. The criterion of the title 'public school' is whether the headmaster is a member of the Headmasters' Conference, the association of independent school headmasters.
Schools Council (for the curriculum and examinations)	An independent but official body set up by the Secretary of State in 1964 to develop and monitor new curricula and public examinations in all subjects in primary and secondary schools in England and Wales and sponsoring a large number of curriculum development projects.
Voluntary schools	Schools run by voluntary bodies, usually the Churches, who provide part or all of the building but who receive government aid for staffing and which are liable to inspection.

Bibliography

1. ASSOCIATION OF COMMONWEALTH UNIVERSITIES AND THE BRITISH COUNCIL. *Higher Education in the United Kingdom 1978–1980. A Handbook for Students from Overseas and their Advisers.* London: Longman Group.
2. COUNCIL OF EUROPE. COUNCIL FOR CULTURAL COOPERATION (1970). *Education in Europe Section II – General and Technical Education.* Strasbourg: Council of Europe.
3. COUNCIL OF EUROPE. DOCUMENTATION CENTRE FOR EDUCATION IN EUROPE (1975). *Problèmes de l'évaluation dans l'éducation préscolaire. Rapport d'une groupe de travail du comité pour la recherche en matière d'éducation.* Strasbourg: Council of Europe.
4. GREAT BRITAIN. CENTRAL OFFICE OF INFORMATION (1979). *Britain: Open University.* London: HMSO.
5. GREAT BRITAIN. CENTRAL OFFICE OF INFORMATION (1977). *Education in Britain.* London: HMSO.
6 GREAT BRITAIN. CENTRAL OFFICE OF INFORMATION (1972). *Educational Techniques in Britain.* London: HMSO.

7. GREAT BRITAIN. CENTRAL OFFICE OF INFORMATION (1974). *Educational Television and Radio in Britain.* London: HMSO.

8. GREAT BRITAIN. CENTRAL OFFICE OF INFORMATION (1971). *Teacher Training in Britain.* London: HMSO.

9. GREAT BRITAIN. CENTRAL OFFICE OF INFORMATION (1973). *Universities in Britain.* London: HMSO.

10. GREAT BRITAIN. DEPARTMENT OF EDUCATION AND SCIENCE. HM INSPECTORATE (1978). *Primary Education in England: A Survey by HM Inspectors of Schools.* London: HMSO.

11. GREAT BRITAIN. DEPARTMENT OF EDUCATION AND SCIENCE. HM INSPECTORATE (1979). *A Survey by HM Inspectorate of Schools.* London: HMSO.

12. GREAT BRITAIN. DEPARTMENT OF EDUCATION AND SCIENCE (1978). *The Educational System of England and Wales.* London: DES.

13. *Major Educational Trends in the United Kingdom 1976-1978.* Report to the 37th session of the International Conference on Education, Geneva, July 1979.

Scotland

Historical

Scotland has been an integral part of the United Kingdom since 1707, although the legislation which united the English and Scottish Parliaments provided, amongst other things, for the preservation of the distinctive Scottish legal and ecclesiastical systems. Scotland has also retained and developed a separate and distinctive educational system. The traditional importance of education was crystallized in the Education (Scotland) Act 1872, which introduced universal compulsory education for all children between the ages of 5 and 13; popularly-elected school boards in every parish and burgh as part of a uniform system of management of all public schools (that is, those financed by means of rates, a local property tax); and compulsory certificates of competency for headteachers. The 1872 Act also established the Scottish Education Department and marked the transfer from Church to State of the control of education.

The educational system in outline

Subsequent legislation has amended and extended the framework of the 1872 Act. Compulsory schooling begins at age 5 and ends at age 16; older and younger pupils may attend school voluntarily. Most children attend schools which are comprehensive, co-educational and provided free by local authorities. Independent schools charge economic fees and must be registered with the Scottish Education Department which lays down certain standards of accommodation and instruction. Twenty-two grant-aided schools are independently managed but have part of their fees subsidized; this assistance will be maintained pending the introduction of the Government's proposed assisted places scheme.

Although most Scottish schools are non-denominational, there are separate Roman Catholic schools within the public system; the Church approves teachers with regard to belief and character, and religious instruction is an integral part of the curriculum.

Post-school education is available at universities, central institutions (independent national or regional colleges of higher education), colleges of education and further education colleges or centres. The educational service also provides a wide range of social, recreational and cultural activities, youth centres and community centres.

Administration

Public sector education in Scotland is a partnership between central and local government. The Secretary of State for Scotland is a member of the UK Cabinet and is responsible to Parliament for central government policy on a wide range of issues, including the overall supervision and development of the education service through the Scottish Education Department. The Department controls the standard and cost of educational building; issues guidance on such matters as the curriculum and teaching methods; pays grant to the grant-aided secondary schools, colleges of education and central institutions; operates a students' allowance scheme; supports educational research through a number of agencies; and, together with the General Teaching Council, oversees teacher training and supply. It is also responsible for the oversight of informal education, including the youth and community service, and gives grants to a number of voluntary organizations. The Scottish universities, however, are financially assisted by the Department of Education and Science (which is otherwise responsible only for education in England) on the advice of the University Grants Committee.

The elected regional and islands councils have a statutory duty to ensure that there is an adequate and efficient provision of school and further education in their areas, and for this purpose are known as education authorities. They are responsible for the construction of buildings, the employment of teachers and other staff, and the provision of equipment and materials. Their responsibility for the curriculum taught in schools is normally delegated to individual headteachers. Their expenditure on education (which is much greater than on the other services provided by local authorities) is met from rates and from Rate Support Grant paid by the central government.

The Inspectorate

HM Inspectors of Schools are appointed by the Queen on the recommendation of the Secretary of State, and HM Inspectorate is a distinct unit within the Scottish Education Department. Inspectors have a statutory right to enter schools and other educational establishments in order to assess and report on the educational service provided.

HM Inspectors also have an important role as consultants and advisers. They provide professional advice to the Department on many matters involved in the formulation of national policy, and they act as liaison officers between the Department and education authorities. Their advice is also available to individual schools and other educational establishments, together with a wide range of educational organizations, on many of whose committees they sit as members or assessors. A number of Inspectors have national responsibility for particular subjects or aspects of education; the remainder are based in the territorial divisions, combining specialist and general duties.

School education

'School Education' is statutorily defined as progressive education appropriate to the requirements of pupils attending schools, with due regard to their age, ability and aptitude, and includes:

(a) activities, in nursery schools and classes, of a kind suitable for pupils who are under school age;

(b) special education; that is education by special methods appropriate to the requirements of pupils whose physical, intellectual, emotional or social development cannot be adequately promoted by ordinary methods of education;

(c) the teaching of Gaelic in Gaelic-speaking areas.

Pre-primary education

Pre-primary or nursery education is intended to give young children the opportunity to pursue natural interests appropriate to their age, and to develop their physical, intellectual, social and emotional capabilities. As at September 1977, 21 per cent of the 3–4 year old age group was receiving nursery education, mainly on a half-day basis. In recent years there has been a steady increase in the proportion of children attending nursery schools and classes, although expansion of provision has been affected both by the need for essential developments in the compulsory education sector, and more recently by the requirement placed on education authorities to limit public expenditure.

Primary education

Normally children enter a co-educational primary school at about the age of 5 and, after following a seven-year course, transfer to secondary school at about the age of 12. Schools vary in size according to the community they serve: a one-teacher rural school may serve a much bigger area than a larger city primary school. The staffing standards of primary schools are expressed as complements related to the size of school, and are designed to produce an average class size of 30 pupils. There has been a good deal of centralization of primary education in recent years, but it is rare for primary pupils to attend a school beyond daily travelling distance of their homes.

The primary curriculum is not centrally prescribed; within the overall policy of the education authority, headteachers are free to devise the type of education best suited to the needs of their pupils and their communities, and of the environment in which their particular school is situated. Education authorities actively encourage the development of curricula through in-service training, and the services of a system of primary advisers. Both education authorities and schools have available to them the advice of the Committee on Primary Education, and the primary education support service, of the Consultative Committee on the Curriculum.

Curriculum change of great significance has been taking place in primary schools over the past few years. Arithmetic, and the skills involved in the use and understanding of spoken and written English, remain the basic elements of the primary school course, but increased importance is attached to the practical application of these skills in real contexts. Arithmetic is regarded as one aspect of the many mathematical activities in which a pupil should be involved. In music, creative work is given an important place. The emphasis in art and craft activities has shifted from imitation to self-expression. The study of science provides opportunities for pupils to explore their environment systematically, through observation and experiment. Physical education includes the free use of movement as a means of expression and personal development. History and geography take their place along with science not so much as subjects in their own right but as aspects of environmental studies through which pupils can investigate and understand the past and the living world around them. Dramatic activities are increasingly recognized as playing an important part in a pupil's personal and social development.

These curriculum developments have been accompanied by changes in the organization and design of schools. Primary schools with rolls of over 210 pupils now have (according to size) at least one assistant headteacher, who may be given responsibility for the design, development and evaluation of the curriculum. An increasing number of schools are being built with varying degrees of open plan arrangements, which make it easier for the pupils to use a wide range of resources and encourage co-operative teaching.

Secondary education

The reorganization of secondary education along comprehensive lines is virtually complete, and most children attend co-educational schools which cater for pupils whose ages range from 12–18. For a variety of reasons, but principally because of remoteness, there are a few schools where secondary education is provided for only four years (or even less), but in such circumstances parents have the option of sending their child instead to the comprehensive school serving the area, rather than to the local school, although this would usually involve either a long daily journey or the child living away from home during the week at a school hostel.

During the first two years of secondary education, all pupils generally study a wide range of subjects on a common foundation course. On entering secondary education, they are normally organized into classes on a mixed ability basis, but most schools introduce some form of streaming, broadbanding or setting by the second year, at least in mathematics and modern languages.[1] Certain adjustments may be made to the course so that abler pupils may study, for example, additional subjects such as a second foreign language, and most schools employ special arrangements to provide for slow learners, usually either in separate classes or by withdrawing them for remedial education.

These first two years of secondary education have increasingly become an exploratory period during which the progress of each pupil is carefully observed. By giving pupils experience of a wide variety of subjects, they can find out where their particular interests, abilities and aptitudes lie. As pupils reveal their potentialities a guidance system, operated in conjunction with some form of assessment, assists them to choose at the beginning of the third year between four year general courses with a practical or vocational bias and more academic courses lasting four, five or six years which lead to the Scottish Certificate of Education (SCE) examinations, although most schools are now organized to enable elements of the two types of course to be combined in various ways to maintain a well-balanced curriculum, and only a relatively small proportion of pupils in the third and fourth years follow courses which do not include presentation for a SCE examination in at least one subject. At this stage, the number of subjects studied by each pupil may be reduced, but the range from which the subjects are drawn is widened by the addition of subjects not studied in the earlier years. During the last year of compulsory schooling, a number of pupils follow courses involving some attendance at further education colleges. These courses are jointly designed by school and college as a preparation for adult life, and provide an introduction to vocational skills while continuing their general education.

The appointment of teachers with special responsibility for pupil guidance and counselling in personal, curricular and vocational matters has enabled schools to develop their pastoral role. Guidance teachers work closely with officials of the careers service in providing advice and information.

Over the period 1962–63 to 1976–77, the proportion of 16 year old pupils staying on at education authority schools voluntarily beyond the statutory leaving age more than doubled, from 17.6 per cent to 37.9 per cent.

Curriculum development

The content of the curriculum is determined by individual education authorities and head-teachers. Education authorities assist their schools through advisory services which in recent years have been expanded to cover most aspects of the curriculum. Guidance may also be issued by the Secretary of State, who is in turn advised by the Consultative Committee on the Curriculum (CCC) and HM Inspectors of Schools. The Consultative Committee on the Curriculum, which is appointed by the Secretary of State, is not a statutory organization and has neither power over, nor responsibility for, the content or management of the curriculum, but it oversees a number of committees whose membership is drawn from a variety of backgrounds including schools, universities, colleges of education and further education, and education authorities, and a wide range of subject specializations.

To undertake the development work required by the CCC and its various committees, an integrated Scottish Curriculum Development Service has been established, consisting of four national curriculum development centres and the primary education support service. The publications of these committees, and the work of the curriculum development service, are readily available to education authorities and schools. In particular, the report of a committee set up under the chairmanship of Dr James Munn to consider the structure of the curriculum in the third and fourth years of secondary education has been the subject of wide-ranging consultation and study.

Examinations

National examinations are conducted by the Scottish Certificate of Education Examination Board. Candidates are normally presented for the SCE Ordinary grade in the fourth year, and for the broad-based Higher grade in the fifth and sixth year. Both Ordinary and Higher grade examinations may also be taken by external candidates. Passes at the appropriate level are the basic but not necessarily sufficient qualification for admission to any Scottish university and almost all English universities (see sections on universities on pp. 240 and 256), as well as to other centres of higher education. The Board's Certificate of Sixth Year Studies is open to pupils who have already passed the Higher grade examination in the one or two subjects concerned; the pupil has to demonstrate ability to pursue independent study, in most cases by completing a piece of research, as a test not only of intellectual ability but also of capacity for personal study.

After wide-ranging consultations on the recommendations of Dr J. Munn and the reports of two committees of inquiry set up under the chairmanships of Mr J. Dunning (the second of which considered assessment in the third and fourth years of secondary education), the Scottish Education Department announced a three year programme of development work to establish the requirements of a revised curriculum and assessment system based on awards at Foundation, General and Credit level in a national certificate.

Gaelic

Education authorities have a statutory duty to make adequate provision for the teaching of Gaelic in Gaelic-speaking areas; that is, the Western Isles (where 82 per cent of the population are Gaelic/English bi-linguals), and in certain districts in the Highland and Strathclyde regions, notably Skye and Lochalsh, Lochaber and Argyll and Bute. Even in the Western Isles, however, the number of children who speak only Gaelic when they first go to school is small.

Provision is made in schools in the Gaelic-speaking areas for pupils to study Gaelic throughout their primary course, and the use of Gaelic as a teaching and learning medium, alongside English, is also being developed in a number of primary schools. This is particularly the case in the Western Isles, where a policy of bi-lingual education is being adopted and where a Gaelic/English bi-lingual education project, involving a sample of 20 primary schools, is sponsored jointly by the Scottish Education Department and the education authority.

Gaelic is offered as a subject in the curriculum of 33 secondary schools. In the Western Isles, the general policy is for all secondary pupils to study Gaelic and French in their first year, and thereafter to choose one or the other. Elsewhere, secondary schools which offer Gaelic generally do so as an alternative to French from the first year onwards. Separate papers in Gaelic are set at both the Ordinary and Higher grades of the Scottish Certificate of Education Examination, one for native speakers of Gaelic and the other for those who have taken up the study of Gaelic as a second language at school.

Religious education

Education authority schools admit children regardless of religious denomination; parents have the right, however, if they so desire, to withdraw their children from any religious instruction and from any religious observance in school without prejudice to the children's secular instruction. Subject to this proviso, education authorities are free to provide in any school a form of religious observance and instruction which is acceptable to the parents, and they may not stop providing it without holding a local referendum. The Secretary of State has no power to inspect this instruction or to influence its character in any way. The Consultative Committee on the Curriculum has established the Central Committee on Religious Education to assume responsibility for curriculum development in religious education. In Roman Catholic schools religious instruction is given by Roman Catholic teachers and is inspected by a supervisor of religious instruction appointed by the education authority with the approval of the Roman Catholic Church.

Special education

Special arrangements are made for the education of children suffering from sensory, physical or mental handicap. Wherever possible, handicapped children attend ordinary schools, but for those whose degree of handicap is such that they would find it too difficult to cope in ordinary classes there are special schools and special classes associated with ordinary schools. Some 13,500 children receive such special education, of whom the majority are mentally handicapped. Children unable to receive suitable special education near their own home can be accommodated in residential special schools with the fees normally paid by the education authorities in whose area they live.

Special schools have more favourable staffing ratios than ordinary schools, and most of the teachers have additional specialist qualifications. Physiotherapy, speech therapy, medical supervision and nursing care are provided where appropriate.

School organization

Comprehensive education has encouraged a tendency to accommodate a larger number of pupils in a smaller number of schools; for example, whereas the number of pupils in education authority secondary schools rose from 272,000 in the 1959/60 session to 420,000 in 1977/78, the number of schools they attended was reduced from 757 to 433. The number of pupils in an average secondary school is likely to stabilize at about 1,000, although the decline in the birth rate in recent years will almost certainly lead to further reductions in the number of schools.

Over the past few years, schools have forged closer links with their communities. Representatives of parents, teaching staff and various community interests serve on school councils with the aim of promoting the general well-being of the school, its pupils and the community. Considerable efforts have been made to develop parental interest and co-operation and an increasing number of schools have formed parents' associations or parent–teacher associations to encourage and strengthen closer links between home and school. They organize meetings to discuss such topics as developments in the curriculum, recent innovations in teaching methods, or building matters affecting the school. There are also several national (that is, UK) associations such as the Confederation for the Advancement of State Education (CASE) which through their local associations seek to co-operate with education authorities and to foster closer relationships between schools and the community. A significant number of schools have become centres of community activities, and some schools have been built specifically to make it easier for the local residents to use them for out-of-school purposes.

Education authorities make arrangements for the provision of meals, milk and home-to-school transport. Where children live a long way from a suitable school, or where there are exceptional circumstances which require special arrangements to be made, education authorities have power, after consultation with the parents, to provide such children with board and lodging in a boarding school, in a school hostel or in private lodgings.

School Health Service

Health boards, in consultation with education authorities, arrange for the medical and dental inspection, supervision and treatment of pupils in order to foster their physical and emotional health so that they can profit to the full from their education. All children are medically examined during their first year in school and also a year or so before leaving age. Between these examinations, medical supervision depends on selective rather than routine examinations. Sight and hearing are tested periodically, and pupils referred by parents or teachers are examined and assessed. Health visitors and school nurses, assisted by nursing auxiliaries, provide additional links between the school, the home and the primary health care service. They supervise the general physical and mental health and hygiene of all pupils. Doctors and health visitors may also assist teachers with, or take part in, health education programmes.

Teachers

General Teaching Council for Scotland

All teachers employed in education authority and grant-aided schools must be registered with the General Teaching Council for Scotland. A majority of the members of the Council are teachers elected by the profession; other members are appointed by education authorities, the universities and other institutions of higher education, the churches and the Secretary of State. The Council is responsible for the registration of teachers and for matters of professional discipline, and is the Secretary of State's principal advisory body on teacher training and supply. It is also required to keep itself informed of the nature of instruction given in colleges of education. To be eligible for registration teachers must hold a Teaching Qualification awarded by a Scottish College of Education, or – in exceptional circumstances – an equivalent qualification approved by the Council. Registration is normally provisional for two years, after which, subject to a satisfactory report from the headteacher, the teacher is awarded final registration. The provisional registration period for further education teachers is normally one year.

Teacher qualifications and training

Primary school teachers must hold a teaching qualification in either primary or secondary education. The primary qualification can be obtained by graduates who successfully complete a one year course at a college of education, or by non-graduates who successfully complete a three year course at a college of education. Secondary school teachers are required to hold the Teaching Qualification (Secondary Education); they must be graduates or holders of an equivalent qualification and have completed a one year course at a college of education. An equivalent qualification may be an approved diploma in, for example, art, music, commerce or home economics.

There are ten colleges of education, all managed by governing bodies which include representatives of the education authorities, the universities, the churches and the teaching profession. Their expenditure is met in full by grants from the Scottish Education Department.

Most of the colleges of education, in conjunction with the universities or the Council for National Academic Awards, now offer four year Bachelor of Education degree courses leading to the award of a degree and the Teaching Qualification (Primary Education) or the Teaching Qualification (Secondary Education), depending upon the academic specialism studied. Professional teacher training is an integral part of the degree course, which is otherwise similar to that of the BA and BSc courses offered by the universities. This degree of Bachelor of Education may now be taken at honours level at two of the institutions; honours BEd students normally take five years to complete the degree and teaching qualification.

The other main courses provided in the colleges of education include:

- a combined pre-service and in-service course centralized at Jordanhill College of Education, Glasgow, which is only open to teachers who hold or have been offered an appointment in a further education centre. The course consists at present of ten weeks' full-time study at the College of Education, followed by two terms of supervised teaching employment in further education, and a further ten weeks' full-time study at the College, and leads to a Teaching Qualification (Further Education);
- specialized training courses for teachers who wish to gain additional qualifications as infant teachers, teachers in nursery schools or teachers of deaf or blind children, physically or mentally handicapped children, or children requiring remedial education. These courses are generally offered on a one-session or shorter (sandwich) basis combining college-based training with supervised teaching practice in selected schools.

In 1977/78, almost 7,000 students were taking initial training courses in colleges of education; of those successfully completing training, 1,305 were graduates or holders of an equivalent qualification.

The University of Stirling also makes provision for teacher training with a course leading concurrently to a degree and to a teaching qualification for secondary work. Additional opportunities for post-graduate study in colleges of education are available in three fields:

- Educational Technology;
- a special qualification course providing for the needs of the upper primary school;
- a course for a Diploma in Advanced Educational Studies.

In-service training

The main agencies for providing further training for teachers are the education authorities and the colleges of education, though there are contributions from other institutions such as the universities (including the Open University) and the central institutions. These courses are administered through the National Committee for the In-Service Training of Teachers, a body representative of all appropriate educational interests. Courses are held during the school year as well as in the vacations, and include full-time courses which require teachers to be released during the school term and a variety of shorter courses. There is a range of high level national courses, mostly concerned with the implications of current curricular, managerial and other educational developments for particular subjects and for the educational system generally.

Further and higher education

School leaving

Young people aged 16 and over are not obliged to attend school. Those who then leave school and discontinue their formal education may take advantage of the careers service provided by education authorities, which gives information, guidance and assistance in obtaining occupational training and employment to anyone (irrespective of age) attending educational institutions other than universities, central institutions and colleges of education. Other school-leavers may go into some form of further education, which includes both part-time and full-time courses at advanced and non-advanced levels. However, the term 'higher education' is generally used to denote advanced further education; that is, courses provided at universities, central institutions etc. for those who have attained a standard equivalent to the Higher Grade of the Scottish Certificate of Education in a group of subjects. A wide variety of further education courses is available in vocational and non-vocational subjects. In the 1977–78 session there were some 127,500 students on non-advanced vocational further education courses at further education colleges and central institutions, and some 32,000 students on advanced courses.

Further education

There are 55 further education day colleges, which are maintained by education authorities; courses in vocational and academic subjects range from craft to professions and from SCE Ordinary grade to degrees awarded by the Council for National Academic Awards. There is also provision for cultural and leisure activities. The colleges are managed by councils which are representative of industry, commerce, education authorities and college staff and may also include students on courses at the college. Most of the larger colleges have established specific links between their major departments and the industrial and commercial interests they serve.

To meet the needs of industry, there is a comprehensive range of courses at technologist, technician, craft and operative levels leading to the award of national certificates and diplomas and to certificates of the City and Guilds of London Institute. National certificates and diplomas are being replaced by those of the Scottish Technical Education Council (SCOTEC) which is responsible for organizing, developing and reviewing courses at technician level in the technical sector of employment. Colleges also provide special courses to meet the needs of local industry.

In the business sector, courses are provided leading to diplomas and certificates awarded by the Scottish Business Education Council (SCOTBEC) and professional institutes and associations. The range of courses offered extends from basic office skills to advanced level accountancy, banking, management, etc.

Further education courses include both theoretical and practical work. Participation may be on a full-time basis; by release from employment for one full day a week or equivalent periods lasting for a few weeks at a time; for part of a day or in the evenings only. Further education establishments provide a very flexible system of courses which enable anyone to acquire whatever standard of qualification his or her capabilities and available time allow. There are no age limits, and basic qualifications can be acquired as a preliminary to more advanced courses.

The Training Services Division of the Manpower Services Commission (MSC) is responsible for the co-ordination of industrial training as a whole. Close co-operation has developed between the MSC and the education service in relation to the Training Opportunities Scheme (TOPS) and the MSC's special programmes to counter unemployment: the Special Temporary Employment Programme (STEP), which is for those over 19, and the Youth Opportunities Programme (YOP) for 16–19 year olds. Specific provision for an educational or training component is a feature of many YOP initiatives.

Higher education

Central institutions

Most of the full-time vocationally-orientated courses of education of degree standard outside the universities and colleges of education are provided in 14 colleges of higher education known as 'central institutions'.

Their courses lead to the degrees of nearby universities or of the Council for National Academic Awards, to diplomas or certificates which are equivalent to university degrees, and to professional and other qualifications. Participation in courses may be on a full-time or part-time basis.

Eleven of the central institutions are financed by the Scottish Education Department. The three agricultural colleges are financed by the Department of Agriculture and Fisheries for Scotland and, in addition to providing agricultural education, mainly at diploma level, they maintain comprehensive advisory services, backed by experimental and developmental work, to commercial agriculture and horticulture.

All of the central institutions, which have a large measure of autonomy, are managed by independent boards of governors which include representatives of appropriate educational, professional, industrial and other organizations, college staff and students.

Universities

All the universities in the United Kingdom are financed, and operate, on a national basis, so that suitably qualified students from any part of the country may seek admission to any university. There are eight universities in Scotland, a large number in proportion to the country's population, and Scotland has a long tradition of university education.

In 1977–78, there were more than 42,000 students enrolled for full-time courses in Scottish universities; 37,000 of these were undergraduates, and 5,000 full-time post-graduates. About 10,000 of these students were normally resident outside Scotland.

The Secretary of State for Education and Science (who is otherwise concerned only with education in England) is responsible for financial assistance to the universities, on the advice of the University Grants Committee. Universities are, however, autonomous bodies enjoying complete academic freedom with the power to admit students, appoint academic staff, make decisions on specific courses and the subject matter of such courses, and to award degrees.

Thus, although the holders of a Scottish or General Certificate of Education in five subjects, with a minimum of either three passes at the Higher grade or two passes at the GCE Advanced level are the basic qualifications for admission, each university is free to select students in accordance with its resources of staff and accommodation, and to set its own academic standards. Applications for admission to first degree courses are submitted to and processed by the Universities Central Council on Admissions, except that UK students who choose to apply only to one or more of the universities of Glasgow, Aberdeen and Strathclyde apply direct to those universities. Mature students and all applicants for post-graduate courses apply direct to the universities concerned.

The full-time first degree course is generally four years and an honours degree and three years for the broad-based ordinary degree which is a particular feature of the Scottish system; the degree courses in some professional subjects, however, such as medicine, dentistry and veterinary medicine, take five or six years' study. More than one quarter of the undergraduates read arts subjects, less than one quarter pure science, about one fifth social studies, about one eighth medicine and dentistry, and about one sixth applied science.

The Open University provides part-time degree level courses, which are open to adults throughout the United Kingdom, by means of a combination of television, radio, correspondence, tutorials, short residential courses, and local audio-visual centres. No formal academic qualifications are required for entry. In 1977, more than 500 of the Open University's graduates were from Scotland.

Financial support for pupils and students

Although in general education authorities provide school education without charge to pupils or their parents, they have discretionary powers to grant bursaries to meet part at least of the living expenses of pupils and students ordinarily resident in their areas. The bursaries scheme includes grants for pupils who remain at school beyond the age of compulsory attendance (Higher School Bursaries); for students attending part-time courses of further education; and for students attending full-time courses of non-advanced further education. The rates and scales of Higher School Bursaries and full-time Further Education Bursaries are prescribed in statutory regulations made by the Secretary of State.

The students' allowance scheme provides financial assistance for students ordinarily resident in Scotland who are attending for the first time a first degree or comparable course of further education or teacher training, and is administered centrally by the Scottish Education Department. The maximum grant consists of tuition fees plus an allowance for maintenance, travel and the purchase of items required for the course; it is subject to reduction by a contribution calculated on the financial circumstances of the student's parents or spouse. The minimum grant consists of tuition fees plus a fixed cash allowance.

Post-graduate students' allowances are granted by the Department, subject to certain conditions, for a wide range of short courses of a professional or vocational nature, intended to bring the student to the level of qualification for admission to a particular career. Under the Scottish Studentship Scheme, a limited number of studentships are given each year for advanced post-graduate study in the Humanities; these studentships are awarded on the basis of recommendations made by a selection committee comprising representatives of the Scottish universities. Other post-graduate students may receive awards from the research councils.

Community education, recreation and the arts

Adult education

Education authorities, either by their own efforts or in association with the Workers' Educational Association or the extra-mural departments of universities, provide a wide range of leisure-time courses in academic and non-academic subjects for people of all ages and interests. Most of the courses are held in the evenings in schools, colleges, community centres etc., and in 1977 attracted 165,000 students.

Youth and community service

The youth and community service is a partnership of voluntary organizations, education and other local authorities and central government in promoting social, cultural and recreational activities. Education authorities provide youth and community centres, often attached to schools, for the leisure time needs of young people and adults, and they assist local youth and adult organizations. Additional clubs and centres are provided by other local authorities and by national voluntary organizations, many of which receive financial assistance from central and local government. Courses of professional training are provided at four of the colleges of education.

Most education authorities have combined adult education with the youth and community service into a community education service, whose national development is overseen by the Scottish Council for Community Education.

The arts, libraries, museums and galleries

Education and other local authorities not only provide cultural activities and entertainment of various kinds but, together with the central government, provide financial assistance to independent cultural organizations. Local authorities provide a public library service, many provide museums and some provide art galleries, arts centres and theatres. The Royal Scottish Museum, the National Galleries of Scotland, the National Museum of Antiquities of Scotland and the National Library of Scotland are maintained by the Scottish Education Department. The Scottish Arts Council (which receives grant from the Arts Council of Great Britain) is responsible for central government support for the arts in Scotland; it assists a wide range of professional musical, dramatic and artistic activities, including not only major organizations such as Scottish Opera, Scottish Ballet, the Scottish National Orchestra, the Scottish Chamber Orchestra, the Scottish Baroque Ensemble and the Edinburgh Festival, but also many smaller organizations and individuals.

Sport and recreation

A wide range of recreational facilities are provided by regional and islands councils through the youth and community service, but most public recreational facilities – including swimming pools, sports centres and playing fields – are provided by district councils, sometimes in co-operation with education authorities and independent, voluntary organizations. Many local authorities have set up co-ordinating departments of leisure and recreation.

The Scottish Sports Council is charged with promoting the general development of sport in Scotland and receives an appropriate annual grant from the Scottish Education Department. The Council runs three national sports centres, advises central and local government on sports matters, and makes grants to national governing bodies of sports, to independent local sports organizations, and to local authorities for special facilities and for projects in areas of multiple deprivation. Local organizations provide a great variety of specialist sports facilities for their members.

Note

1. Streaming: division into groups for teaching across the whole curriculum according to both age and academic ability. Setting: grouping for subjects on the basis of ability in those subjects. Broadbanding: division of a particular age group into two or more broad bands on the basis of general ability and within each band grouping for particular subjects either on a mixed ability basis or by variable setting.

Bibliography

1. DUNNING REPORT. GREAT BRITAIN. SCOTTISH EDUCATION DEPARTMENT (1977). *Assessment for all: Report of the Committee to Review Assessment in the Third and Fourth Years of Secondary Education in Scotland.* Edinburgh: HMSO.
2. GREAT BRITAIN. DEPARTMENT OF EMPLOYMENT (1979). *A Better Start in Working Life: A Consultative Paper on Vocational Preparation.* London: DES.
3. GREAT BRITAIN. SCOTTISH EDUCATION DEPARTMENT (1976). *Circular No. 965: Report of the 1978 Seminar on Educational Disadvantage.* Edinburgh: SED.
4. GREAT BRITAIN. SCOTTISH EDUCATION DEPARTMENT (1979). *Curriculum and Assessment in the Third and Fourth Years of Secondary Education in Scotland: A Feasibility Study.* Edinburgh: HMSO.
5. GREAT BRITAIN. SCOTTISH EDUCATION DEPARTMENT (1979). *Curriculum and Assessment in the Third and Fourth Years of Secondary Education in Scotland: Proposals for Action.* Edinburgh: SED.
6. GREAT BRITAIN. SCOTTISH EDUCATION DEPARTMENT (1978). *Education and the Youth Opportunities Programme in Scotland.* Edinburgh: SED.
7. GREAT BRITAIN. SCOTTISH EDUCATION DEPARTMENT (1977). *The Education System of Scotland.* New Edition. Edinburgh: HMSO.
8. GREAT BRITAIN. SCOTTISH EDUCATION DEPARTMENT (1980). *The Munn and Dunning Reports: The Government's Development Programme.* Edinburgh: SED.
9. GREAT BRITAIN. SCOTTISH INFORMATION OFFICE (1978). *Consultative Committee on the Curriculum.* Edinburgh: SIO (Factsheet RF21).
10. GREAT BRITAIN. SCOTTISH INFORMATION OFFICE (1979). *Scottish Education.* Edinburgh: SIO (Factsheet RF15).
11. MUNN REPORT. GREAT BRITAIN. SCOTTISH EDUCATION DEPARTMENT CONSULTATIVE COMMITTEE ON THE CURRICULUM (1977). *The Structure of the Curriculum in the Third and Fourth Years of the Scottish Secondary School.* Edinburgh: HMSO.
12. PACK REPORT. GREAT BRITAIN. SCOTTISH EDUCATION DEPARTMENT (1977). *Truancy and Indiscipline in Schools in Scotland: the Pack Report.* Edinburgh: HMSO.
13. WARNOCK REPORT. GREAT BRITAIN. PARLIAMENT. HOUSE OF COMMONS (1978). *Special Educational Needs: Report of the Committee of Enquiry into the Education of Handicapped Children and Young People.* London: HMSO.

Northern Ireland

Historical background and summary of the present system

The Parliament of Northern Ireland was established by the Government of Ireland Act 1920. Development of educational policy in Northern Ireland in the 1920s was centred on establishing a co-ordinated regional educational system under a single, unified Ministry of Education. Policy was also influenced by current educational trends in England, involving rate aid[1] and introducing at least partial local control of education. Since 1921, the most appropriate comparison for Northern Ireland's educational development has been with that of England and Wales, and the two systems have much in common although naturally incorporating distinctive features geared to local circumstances.

Three major themes run through the history of education provision in Northern Ireland. These are:

(a) The balance between voluntary and public provision, including the role of the Churches in school management and the degree of support available from public funds for voluntary schools.

(b) The provision for religious education in both voluntary and publicly owned schools.

(c) The post-war expansion of the education service.

The education system as it exists today reflects the solutions which have been developed over the years to the problems thrown up by these three main issues. The arrangements are generally regarded as commanding wide support in the Northern Ireland community and as satisfying the legitimate wishes of parents, Churches and the State.

The system therefore recognizes the right of parents to have their children educated in a school with a distinctive religious ethos if they so wish; provides for both voluntary schools which are partly financed from public funds and controlled schools which are wholly publicly financed; and is aimed at giving children and students efficient education suitable to their ages, abilities and aptitudes.

Controlled schools are owned and managed by Education and Library Boards. All the capital and recurrent expenditure of these schools is met from grants paid to the Boards by the Department of Education for Northern Ireland. Voluntary schools can receive substantial grants towards capital expenditure (up to 85 per cent, depending on the degree of public representation on their governing bodies) and in addition almost all their recurrent expenditure is met directly or indirectly from public funds (somewhat less where there is no representation of public authorities on their governing bodies). Most, but by no means all, voluntary schools are under Roman Catholic management.

Both controlled and voluntary schools operate under common regulations and provide education which in both scope and quality is broadly comparable. The Inspectorate of the Department of Education works closely with all schools on educational matters such as curriculum development and in-service training of teachers.

It is a statutory requirement that religious instruction be given in all controlled and voluntary schools (except nursery and special schools) in Northern Ireland, and that the school day should include collective worship (this may require more than one assembly depending on the size of the school and the accommodation available).

In controlled schools the religious instruction required by law must be undenominational, i.e. based on the Holy Scriptures according to some authoritative version or versions. The collective worship also must not be distinctive of any particular religious denomination. Denominational instruction may also be given (see below). In voluntary schools both the religious instruction and the collective worship are under the control of the managers of the school and are not required to be undenominational.

Religious instruction and collective worship in both controlled and voluntary schools must be arranged so that the school is open to pupils of all religious denominations for instruction other than religious instruction and that no pupil is excluded either directly or indirectly from the other advantages which the school affords. Pupils may be excused from attendance at religious instruction or collective worship if parents so request.

Ministers of religion or other suitable persons to whom the parents do not object, must be granted reasonable access to pupils in controlled and certain voluntary schools other than nursery and special schools for the purpose of giving religious instruction, which may be denominational, or of inspecting any religious instruction given in the school. This does not apply, unless the managers consent, to voluntary schools which were already in operation before the statutory requirement was first introduced. In cases where such access has not been granted any pupil who has been excused attendance at religious instruction in the school may be removed from the school for reasonable periods to enable him to receive religious instruction of which his parents approve.

Thus in law every school in Northern Ireland is open to pupils of any religious denomination and there are in fact a number of schools which are attended by pupils of different denominations. No statistics are collected of the enrolments of pupils in schools by religious denomination so it is not possible to quantify the extent to which such integration exists. Government policy is to encourage integrated education wherever there is a local wish for it but there is no question of the Government's attempting to force integration on anyone who does not want it. The Education (NI) Act 1978 had as its objective facilitation of the establishment of schools likely to be attended by pupils of different religious affiliations or cultural traditions. These schools would be known as controlled integrated schools and their management arrangements would reflect their integrated status. There are no controlled integrated schools in operation at the present time.

Administration

Northern Ireland has a three-tier arrangement of educational administration. The tiers are the *schools and other institutions*, with their management Committees and Principals, responsible for the day-to-day operation; the five *Educational and Library Boards*, responsible for the administration of the service in their respective geographic areas; and the *Department of Education*, with overall responsibility to the Government.

As in England and Wales organization of the schools and other institutions is in three stages – primary (including nursery) education, secondary education and further education; and the parents or legal guardians of children of compulsory school age (from 5 to 16 years) must ensure that their children receive efficient full-time education suitable to their ages, abilities and aptitudes, either by regular attendance at school or otherwise.

Public education in Northern Ireland, other than university education, is administered centrally by the Department of Education and locally by the Education and Library Boards which are broadly equivalent to local education authorities in England and Wales. The Boards are required to ensure that there are sufficient schools of all kinds to meet the needs of their areas. They provide primary and secondary schools, special schools for handicapped pupils requiring special educational treatment and institutions for further education. The Boards also make contributions towards the cost of maintaining voluntary schools; award university and other scholarships; provide milk and meals; free books and transport for pupils; enforce school attendance; regulate the employment of children and young people; assist in educational research and secure the provision of recreational and youth service facilities. The Boards, which are financed entirely from central funds, include in their membership Councillors nominated by the District Councils, persons representing the interest of the transferers of the schools and of the maintained school authorities, teachers and other persons appointed by reason of their interest in or knowledge of the services for which the Boards are responsible.

The Department of Education

The Department's responsibilities cover the whole range of education from nursery education through to higher and continuing education; sport and recreation; youth services; arts and culture (including libraries); and community relations and community development. It is responsible generally for policy, financial control, legislation, standards and programmes and priorities. The Department is headed by a Minister of State who is himself responsible through the Secretary of State for Northern Ireland to Parliament.

The Inspectorate

The Department is advised on the educational, as distinct from the administrative, aspects of its work by the Inspectorate. Inspectors provide the Department with information on the operation and efficiency of schools and institutions of further education and are closely involved in implementing in schools and colleges and in the youth service programmes accepted for the other divisions of the Department. They also provide a professional advisory service for other government departments. They play an active role in curriculum development, in the in-service training of teachers and in the development of induction training for newly qualified teachers. They maintain close links with the Education and Library Boards and with maintained and voluntary school authorities. They are also involved with colleges of education and with the Northern Ireland Schools Examinations Council and its Examination Boards. They represent the Department on a wide variety of national and other committees.

Advisory bodies

The Department is advised by various bodies upon matters connected with educational policy and practice among which are the Northern Ireland Schools Curriculum Committee, the Council for Continuing Education, the Northern Ireland Committee for Educational Technology and the Advisory Committee on the Supply and Training of Teachers.

The education budget

Public expenditure on education, libraries and allied services represents the second largest element in the budget for Northern Ireland and is provisionally estimated at some £327m in 1978/79 (£332m including Museums and Arts). Of this total about 85 per cent is for recurrent expenditure and 15 per cent for capital expenditure. Actual figures for 1976/77 and 1977/78 are given in Table 1.

The two main items of recurrent expenditure by the Department of Education are teachers' salary costs and grants to the five Education and Library Boards. The Department pays the salaries and employers' National Insturance and Superannuation contributions of most teachers in Northern Ireland. The Education and Library Boards receive grant at the rate of 100 per cent on approved expenditure in respect of their functions under the Education and Libraries (Northern Ireland) Order 1972. Facilities for sport, recreation, community and other services provided by the District Councils are grant-aided by the Department at the rate of 75 per cent on the expenditure involved.

Schools and other educational institutions

Schools in Northern Ireland fall into two main categories:

(a) Controlled Schools are under the direct management of the Education and Library Boards who make provision for certain functions to be carried out by the School Management Committee of the Schools;

	1976/77	*1977/78*
Primary (including nursery)	60.8	68.9
Secondary education	77.2	87.0
Further education	26.2	30.9
Universities	27.6	29.6
Teacher training	7.8	8.1
Library services	6.9	8.8
Youth services	4.3	6.2
Sport and community services	6.8	7.7
Other	38.1	42.0
(Museums and Arts)	(2.8)	(3.7)
Total	255.7	289.2
	(258.5)	(292.9)

Table 1: Summary of public expenditure on education and related services £m

(b) Voluntary Schools are under the management of the Governing Bodies, Maintained School Committees or Managers approved by the Department. A Maintained School Committee is comprised of at least six persons of whom one-third is appointed by the Education and Library Board for the area and two-thirds by the Trustees who provide the school.

Primary including nursery education

All primary schools provide for children up to the age of 11–12 and education is free. A small proportion of pupils of primary school age attend preparatory departments of grammar schools which charge fees.

There are a number of nursery schools which cater for children between the ages of 2 and 5 years and nursery classes are operated in some primary schools.[2]

Secondary education

Secondary education normally begins at the age of 11–12 when transfer to a secondary (grammar) school or secondary (intermediate) school takes place. The system is not a rigid one however and provides for subsequent transfer between secondary schools of different types. (The transfer procedure is now under review.) Non-selective (comprehensive) schools operate in some areas.

Secondary (intermediate) schools

As the minimum school leaving age is now 16 the great majority of children have at least five years of secondary education. During the first three years in secondary school pupils generally follow basic courses containing common core subjects of both a practical and a general nature; in the fourth and fifth years they have the opportunity of preparing for Certificate of Secondary Education or General Certificate of Education or other examinations or of participating in the outward-looking courses which the schools have devised for those who do not wish to take external examinations. Pupils over 15 years may spend their last year of compulsory schooling in an institution of further education.

Secondary (grammar) schools

These schools provide an academic type of secondary education. Tuition fees are payable in all grammar schools but the great majority of pupils in secondary departments are in receipt of non-fee-paying places. These schools provide seven year courses. Pupils normally take the

Ordinary-level examinations of the Northern Ireland General Certificate of Education at the end of the fifth year and the Advanced-level examinations at the end of the seventh year.

Special education treatment
Education and Library Boards are required to determine the handicapped children in their areas who require special educational treatment and to make suitable arrangements for its provision free of charge. Some handicapped children may be able to attend ordinary schools. Those seriously handicapped may be sent to special schools which cater for primary or secondary levels; others may be taught in special units attached to ordinary schools or home tuition may be arranged when a pupil is unable to attend school. Where suitable facilities are not available in Northern Ireland pupils may be placed in boarding schools elsewhere.

Independent schools
There are only six wholly independent schools in Northern Ireland. None of these schools receives financial assistance from public funds and all charge fees.

Examinations
The conduct of the General Certificate of Education and Certificate of Secondary Education examinations is the responsibility of the Northern Ireland Schools Examinations Council.

The Northern Ireland GCE Examinations are conducted at two levels – Ordinary and Advanced – which correspond in standard with the Ordinary and Advanced levels of the examinations of GCE examining bodies in England and Wales.

Technical and vocational education
Northern Ireland's institutions of further education provide technical and commercial education for full-time and part-time students as well as courses in leisure and creative pursuits. Students may be admitted from the age of 15. Some apprentices are given day release facilities by their employers to attend courses on one day each week. Courses may also be provided for the training or retraining of unemployed adults. The wide variety of courses available in institutions of further education includes pre-apprenticeship and pre-vocational full-time courses with a bias towards practical preparation for employment, full-time and part-time commercial and secretarial courses leading mainly to the award of Royal Society of Arts certificates, part-time craft and technician courses leading to the award of certificates of the City and Guilds of London Institute, full-time and part-time courses leading to the award of the General Certificate of Education at Ordinary and

TYPE OF SCHOOL	NUMBER	PUPILS	FULL-TIME TEACHERS	PUPILS PER FULL-TIME TEACHER
Nursery	61	3,260	110	24.9
Primary (including preparatory departments of grammar schools)	1,069	205,720	8,632	23.8
Secondary (grammar)	78	52,728	3,192	16.5
Secondary (intermediate)†	183	105,873	6,968	15.2
Special	33	2,467	290	8.5
Totals	1,424	370,048	19,192	19.3

† Excludes pupils completing their compulsory school education in establishments of further education.

Table 2: Schools, pupils and teachers at grant-aided schools in Northern Ireland – January 1979.

| | NUMBER OF STUDENTS | |
	Full-time	Part-time
Institutions of further education (27)	11,442	29,595
Queen's University, Belfast	5,816	930
New University of Ulster	1,693	347
Ulster Polytechnic	3,939	2,936
Colleges of Education (3)	1,704	–

Table 3: Numbers in further and higher education 1978/79

Advanced level and full-time and part-time courses leading to the award of Ordinary National Certificates and Diplomas in many subjects.[3] A wide range of part-time hobby and recreational classes is provided in outcentres as well as in the main institutions.

Higher education

Universities

There are two universities in Northern Ireland, the Queen's University of Belfast founded in 1908 and the New University of Ulster which received its charter in 1970. Queen's University offers courses leading to both primary and post-graduate degrees in the major branches of languages, philosophy, physical and biological sciences, applied science, law, economics, medicine, dentistry, agriculture and theology. The degree of Doctor of Philosophy is open to graduates (normally honours) of other universities after individual full-time study and research lasting at least two years. The New University of Ulster, situated at Coleraine in the north-west of the Province, includes four schools, Biological and Environmental Studies, Physical Sciences, Social Sciences and Humanities and an Education Centre which has the status of a school. An Institute of Continuing Education has been established in Londonderry as an integral part of the New University and has four divisions, Public Service, Community Studies, Liberal and Contemporary Studies and Education. The Universities are autonomous bodies grant-aided by the Department of Education which is advised on all university matters by the University Grants Committee.

The Ulster Polytechnic

In 1971 the need for vocational higher education was recognized with the amalgamation of nearly all advanced further education courses in the Ulster College, renamed the Ulster Polytechnic in 1978. The Polytechnic comprises six faculties, Arts, Business Administration, Education, Science, Social and Health Sciences and Technology. Courses are provided in specialist teacher training[4] as well as those leading to professional and degree qualifications, the Higher National Diploma and the Higher National Certificate.[5]

Teacher training

Teacher training is provided in three general colleges of education: Stranmillis College, a non-denominational college for men and women, controlled by a Governing Body on behalf of the Department of Education; and two colleges under Roman Catholic management, St Mary's College of Education for Women and St Joseph's College of Education for Men.[6]

Teacher training is also conducted at Queen's University and at the New University of Ulster and specialist training facilities are available at the Ulster Polytechnic and Londonderry College of Technology.

Miscellaneous information
Teacher/pupil ratios in Northern Ireland secondary schools = 15.6 (January 1979).
Teacher/pupil ratios in Northern Ireland primary schools = 23.8 (January 1979).
Scale of grants in aid to voluntary schools: (in general terms):
Voluntary maintained (4 and 2 committee) = 85% on capital expenditure
                                        = 100% maintenance, text books etc.

Purely voluntary = 65% capital expenditure
                 = 65% on equipment
                 = 65% on maintenance etc.

Bibliography

1. COUNCIL OF EUROPE. COUNCIL FOR CULTURAL CO-OPERATION (1970). *Education in Europe Section II − General and Technical Education.* Strasbourg: Council of Europe.
2. *Development of Education in the United Kingdom 1973-1975.* Report to the 35th Session of the International Conference on Education, Geneva, September 1975.
3. GREAT BRITAIN. CENTRAL OFFICE OF INFORMATION (1972). *Educational Techniques in Britain.* London: HMSO.
4. GREAT BRITAIN. CENTRAL OFFICE OF INFORMATION (1974). *Educational Television and Radio in Britain.* London: HMSO.
5. GREAT BRITAIN. CENTRAL OFFICE OF INFORMATION (1971). *Teacher Training in Britain.* London: HMSO.
6. GREAT BRITAIN. CENTRAL OFFICE OF INFORMATION (1973). *Universities in Britain.* London: HMSO.
7. GREAT BRITAIN. CENTRAL OFFICE OF INFORMATION REFERENCE DIVISION (1974). *Education in Britain.* Sixth Edition. London: HMSO.
8. GREAT BRITAIN. DEPARTMENT OF EDUCATION OF NORTHERN IRELAND. *Annual Report.*
9. GREAT BRITAIN. DEPARTMENT OF EDUCATION OF NORTHERN IRELAND. *Educational Statistics* No. 1 October 1965 (published twice annually) Belfast: HMSO.

Notes

1. Supplementary grants from local government funds to local authority income from rates (i.e. local taxes on houses and land).
2. *At January 1979*

Nursery Schools

Double Unit (50 places)	*Single Unit (25 places)*
49	12
(40 Controlled − 9 Voluntary)	*(11 Controlled − 1 Voluntary)*

Places	2,450	300
Total places	2,750	

Nursery Classes (at Primary Schools)

Double Unit (50 places)	*Single Unit (25 places)*
25	19
(17 Controlled − 8 Voluntary)	*(16 Controlled − 3 Voluntary)*

Places	1,250	475
Total places	1,725	

Total places (Nursery Schools and Classes) = 4,450

At January 1979

A. *3 Year Olds in Nursery Schools and Classes*

Nursery Schools 2,009
Nursery Classes   1,026
　　　　　　　　　　3,035 = 12.3% of total 3-year-old population (24,700)

B. *4 Year Olds in Nursery Schools and Classes*

Nursery Schools 1,188
Nursery Classes   715
　　　　　　　　　　1,903 = 7.5% of total 4-year-old population (25,300)

C. *4 Year Olds In Primary Schools*

　　　　　　　17,896 = 70.7% of total 4-year-old population

At November 1979

Nursery Schools	*Nursery Classes (at Primary Schools)*
67	51
(55 Double Units − 12 Single Units)	(27 Double Units − 24 Single Units)
(Vol = 9 Double Units + 1 Single Unit)	(Vol = 8 Double Units + 3 Single Units)
Places = 3,050	Places = 1,950

Total Places = 5,000

The children are in the charge of specially trained teachers (one nursery teacher and one nursery assistant for each 25 children). There are no nursery school fees. Play groups are separately organized and come within the scope of the Department of Health and Social Services.

3. Numbers of day release students:

　　　　　　　15 year olds =   13
　　　　　　　16 year olds = 1,481
　　　　　　　17 year olds = 2,579
　　　　　　　18 year olds = 2,374
　　　　　　　19 year olds = 1,696
　　　　　　　20 year olds = 1,054

Total for all participants in day release schemes = 13,347
Those participating in full-time pre-apprenticeship courses = 1,102

Numbers of students (16–18) following technical and vocational education:

Secondary schools = 16 year olds = 6,935
　　　　　　　　　 17 year olds = 7,107
　　　　　　　　　 18 year olds = 3,020
　　　　　　　　　 19 year olds =   275

1978/79

FE colleges　　　 16 year olds = 2,389
.　　　　　　　　 17 year olds = 2,631
　　　　　　　　　 18 year olds = 1,254
　　　　　　　　　 19 year olds =   526

Ulster Polytechnic 1978/79

16 year olds =   3
17 year olds =   19
18 year olds =   426
19 year olds =   837

4. Specialist teacher training offered by the Ulster Polytechnic:

> physical education
> home economics
> art
> music
> craft design and technology

5. Present enrolment at the Ulster Polytechnic = 3,928 full-time
                                                 3,500 part-time

                                                 7,428

                                                 (or 5,490 full-time equivalent)

Staff/student ratio in Ulster Polytechnic = 10 : 1
For details on admission of students from other countries see Department of Education and Science booklet 14/78, *Admission of Overseas Students to Further Education and Higher Education.*

6.

Colleges of Education

Staff/student ratios: Stranmillis = 12.15/1
St Mary's = 9.4/1
St Joseph's = 10.2/1

Universities: The Queen's University of Belfast = 7.22/1
The New University of Ulster = 6.94/1

Duration of in-service courses varies from 2 hours to one year (for MA, MSc, DASE etc.). Also part-time courses held over 3/4 years.

| TYPE OF COURSE | TYPE OF TEACHER | | | | TOTALS |
	Primary	Secondary	Grammar	Further Education	
Part-time courses (1–3 yrs) All types of award	305	403	159	119	986
Open University courses (1978) Degree courses Associate student courses	110 30	145 15	11 5	30 2	296 52
1 year full-time courses All types of General Award	62	33	16	9	120
1 year full-time course at Public Record Office for Northern Ireland	1	1	1	–	3
1 term full-time course at Ulster Folk and Transport Museum	1	1	–	–	2
1 term full-time course in careers education	2	41	8	3	54
1 term full-time course in nursery education	18	–	–	–	18
4 weeks – 1 term full-time courses general topics	Estimate 44	26	–	–	70 approx.
Short courses	Detailed figures are not available, but attendance at short courses is encouraged and is very common				

Numbers of teachers to whom financial assistance has been offered 1.9.78–31.8.79

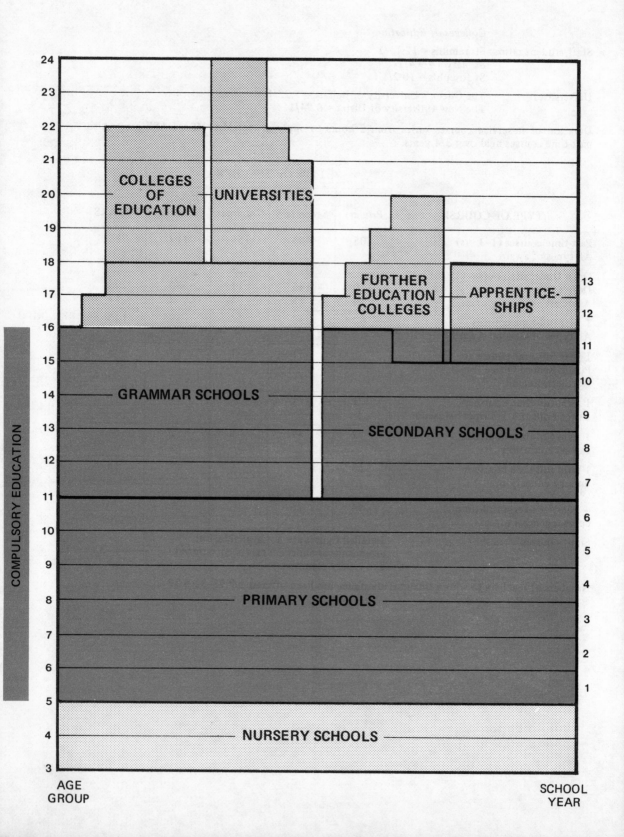

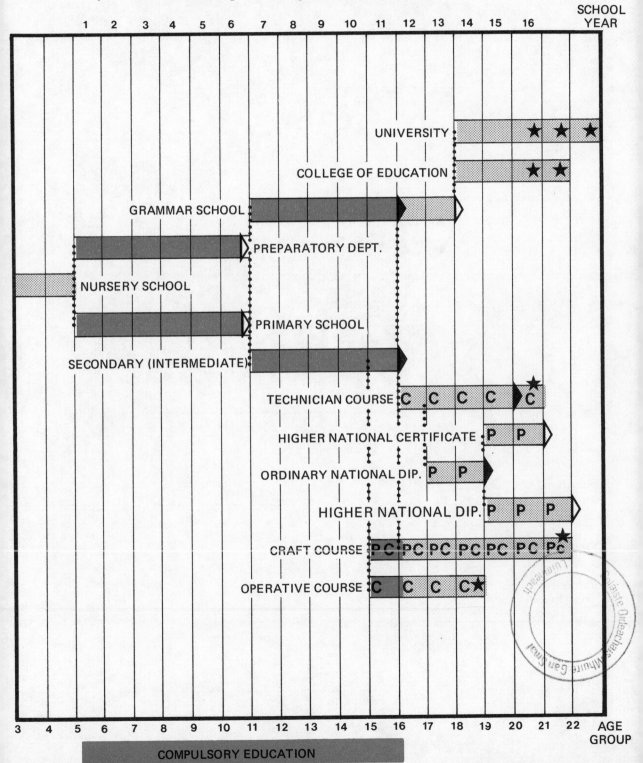

★ = Terminating examination not providing access to a higher stage.

▲ = Qualifying examination providing access to specialized education.

△ = Qualifying examination providing access to higher education.

P = Part-time classes. **C** = Providing workshop practice.

SCHOOL YEAR

1 2 3 4 5 6 7 8 9 10 11 12 13 14 15 16

UNIVERSITY ★ ★ ★

COLLEGE OF EDUCATION ★ ★

GRAMMAR SCHOOL

PREPARATORY DEPT.

NURSERY SCHOOL

PRIMARY SCHOOL

SECONDARY (INTERMEDIATE)

TECHNICIAN COURSE C C C C C ★

HIGHER NATIONAL CERTIFICATE P P

ORDINARY NATIONAL DIP. P P

HIGHER NATIONAL DIP. P P P

CRAFT COURSE PC PC PC PC PC PC Pc ★

OPERATIVE COURSE C C C C★

3 4 5 6 7 8 9 10 11 12 13 14 15 16 17 18 19 20 21 22   AGE GROUP

COMPULSORY EDUCATION